How to Manage Your Network Using SNMP

The Networking Management Practicum

Marshall T. Rose

Keith McCloghrie

P T R Prentice Hall
Englewood Cliffs, New Jersey 07632

Library of Congress Cataloging-in-Publication Data

Editorial/production supervision: *Harriet Tellem*
Cover design: *Anthony Gemmellaro*
Cover art: *Whitman Studio, Inc.*
Manufacturing manager: *Alexis Heydt*
Acquisitions editor: *Mary Franz*
Editorial assistant: *Noreen Regina*

 ©1995 by P T R Prentice Hall
Prentice-Hall, Inc.
A Paramount Communications Company
Englewood Cliffs, New Jersey 07632

The publisher offers discounts on this book in bulk quantities. For more information contact:

Corporate Sales Department, P T R Prentice Hall,
113 Sylvan Avenue, Englewood Cliffs, New Jersey 07632
Phone: 201-592-2863; FAX: 201-592-2249

 Text printed on recycled paper.

Printed in the United States of America
10 9 8 7 6 5 4 3 2 1

ISBN 0-13-141517-4

Prentice-Hall International (UK) Limited, *London*
Prentice-Hall of Australia Pty. Limited, *Sydney*
Prentice-Hall Canada Inc., *Toronto*
Prentice-Hall Hispanoamericana, S.A., *Mexico*
Prentice-Hall of India Private Limited, *New Delhi*
Prentice-Hall of Japan, Inc., *Tokyo*
Simon & Schuster Asia Pte. Ltd., *Singapore*
Editora Prentice-Hall do Brasil, Ltda., *Rio de Janeiro*

to KLM
(kzm)

to my friend the Phoenix
(mtr)

Contents

List of Tables

List of Figures

Foreword

I am very pleased to say a good word about *The Networking Management Practicum*. Marshall T. Rose and Keith McCloghrie are leading experts in the field and are two of the most productive and sensible people I have had the pleasure to work with. Marshall and Keith have been key contributers to the depth and breadth of the SNMP Network Management Framework which has become hugely successful in the marketplace and is being used pervasively and continuously.

In this realistic and thought-provoking work, they have compiled explanations of network technologies in use today, the SNMP standards and tools that manage those technologies, and strategies and hints for how to solve real problems with these tools. The numerous examples make concrete the general strategies that are presented.

This book is an important contribution because it ties together the underlying network technology, management standards, and management tools in a way that is very useful to a network manager — answering the *how's* and *why's* that are not apparent when dealing individually with these three areas.

Finally, *The Networking Management Practicum* is unique in that it presents examples of tools written with *Tcl* and the *Tk* toolkit so that the reader can see how a network management application works while looking at a picture of that application in action. This also provides a convenient mechanism for readers to experiment with their own applications. The lessons learned from using this toolkit will be a catalyst which is needed to move the industry forward.

Steven L. Waldbusser

Preface

Tim O'Reilly has noted that there are typically two kinds of books dealing with computing: *guilt* books and *panic* books. A guilt book discusses technology, whilst a panic book discusses technical solutions. When someone feels they have a general need for knowledge about a given technology, they purchase a guilt book ("gee, I really ought to learn about SMTP sometime"); in contrast, when someone knows they are unable to perform their job without knowledge about a specific software implementation, they purchase a panic book ("yikes! *sendmail* is hosed"). Examples of a guilt book might be something like *The Internet Message*, which discusses Internet e-mail services and protocols, and coincidentally was written by one of the authors of this book. If you need to understand the architectural and engineering principles of Internet messaging, then that's the book for you.[1] But, if you need to understand how to configure and maintain the Internet messaging software on your system, that book isn't nearly so useful. In fact, the only real use you'll get out of the book is being able to identify when your Internet messaging software isn't conforming to the standards, and in that case, that book may help you in "educating" whoever supplied you with your Internet messaging software. But, that won't be of much help on a day-to-day basis; instead, you need a panic book. In fact, the second time your Internet messaging software unexpectedly breaks, you will march to the nearest payphone, dial the publisher of the appropriate panic book, and order the book for next-day delivery.[2]

---

[1] This is, of course, a shameless product placement by the author of *The Internet Message*.

[2] You will call from a payphone because the first time the software broke, you couldn't call the publisher because of all the users calling your office.

This book, *The Networking Management Practicum*, is neither a guilt book nor a panic book — it is a *preparedness* book. It is written for network administrators who want to manage their network using SNMP, the Simple Network Management Protocol, the standard for open, interoperable network management. However, unlike a guilt book, this book doesn't spend a lot of time on the architectural and engineering principles of SNMP; and, unlike a panic book, this book doesn't spend a lot of time on a particular software implementation. Instead, this book was written as an application of the *7p principle*:

> *"Proper preparation prevents persistent peccability and palpable panic."*

So, the authors expect you to familiarize yourself with this book before you need it, to be prepared; but, the authors also expect you to use this book when day-to-day problems arise.

How do the authors hope to achieve this? Well, for several networking technologies, this book tries to integrate an understanding of both the underlying concepts and the management infrastructure. So, each of the primary chapters has three parts:

- a tutorial on a technology (e.g., wide-area networking);

- a discussion of the management instrumentation available (in, e.g., wide-area networks); and,

- some application fragments which show how problems (in, e.g., wide-area networking) can be solved by monitoring and controlling the instrumentation.

So, the application fragments serve as the means of integration. That's the theory behind *The Networking Management Practicum*.

In terms of practice, there are two important issues the authors considered when writing *The Networking Management Practicum*: coverage and code.

First, the authors can't possibly cover every networking technology in a single book. They have neither the time nor (honestly) the expertise. On page 32, the list of technologies discussed (and not discussed) is presented. Hopefully you will find this set of technologies to be useful. As you might expect, future editions of *The Network-*

ing Management Practicum will include additional technologies (and additional authors will probably be added as well).

Second, if *The Networking Management Practicum* is going to contain application fragments, then the fragments should come from real applications. There are several management platforms on the market today. However, the authors didn't feel that any of them was suitable for the task at hand — because different organizations (and their networks) are managed differently, it is difficult for a commercial vendor to produce a package with universal utility. So, whilst this book briefly surveys existing platforms (in Section 1.2 starting on page 25), the authors decided to develop their own toolkit for writing SNMP-based applications. As of this writing, the code runs, but is not widely-deployed. So initially, the software isn't included with this book. Instead, the software is being made available on the Internet, to see if people find it useful. If this is the case, the software will be included in future editions of *The Networking Management Practicum.*

It turns out that the two issues discussed above are related. In fact, the best-case scenario goes something like this: people use the software, find it useful, and contribute enhancements; further, some of these people are expert practitioners with other networking technologies, and they are interested in becoming co-authors of future editions. So, future editions of *The Networking Management Practicum* would contain not only more applications, but also wholly new topics. Who knows, there might even be an on-line edition of this book someday! Even so, the authors view *The Networking Management Practicum* as something of an experiment — to see if there is a place in the market for something besides guilt and panic books.

Finally, if you already have a management platform, you might wonder how the software we describe will interact with your existing platform. For the first edition, we intend our software to be complementary — it won't interact with, and therefore shouldn't interfere with, the management platform you use today. However, depending on how well our experiment goes, subsequent versions of the software might actually share information with various platforms.

Acknowledgements

Marshall has only one acknowledgement, and that's to thank Keith McCloghrie for co-writing this book. In fact, Marshall will let you in on a little secret: the only reason that his name is listed first is for (gasp) marketing purposes. Marshall wants you to know that Keith did about 60% of the work, and he wanted Keith's name to go first, but Keith thought that the book would "have greater visibility" (a euphemism for "sell better"), if Marshall's name went first.

Keith has several acknowledgements: to Marshall for the privilege of working with him, both on this project and on others over the years; to Hughes LAN Systems, particularly to Tim Zimmer, and Cisco Systems for permission to use their facilities in preparing several of the chapters; to Sridhar Acharya for help in obtaining some of the window displays for inclusion; and to Claude Cartee for advice on Source Routing bridges.

Tcl and the *Tk* toolkit were developed by John K. Ousterhout. Certainly we could not have written this book without this excellent platform. In addition, we also make use of the *BLT* library, an extension to the *Tk* toolkit, written by George Howlett. The notion of using *Tcl* and SNMP has a long history, originally having been discussed in 1992, and at least three different APIs for SNMP were developed by the end of that year. In April of 1993, an informal group met to develop a common *Tcl*-based API for SNMP. In addition to the two authors, the group consisted of Barry Bruins, Jeffrey D. Case, Poul-Henning Kamp, Jon Saperia, Glenn Trewitt, and Steven L. Waldbusser. Although this group wasn't able to achieve cohesion and was subsequently disbanded, Poul-Henning and Glenn later developed the *tclsnmp2* package. (We've included an announcement on page 504). The toolkit discussed in *The Networking Management Practicum* has benefited from all of this previous work.

Cisco Systems, Inc. and SNMP Research, Inc. generously provided us with agents to aid in the development of our software. All testing, of course, was done over the Internet.

Finally, both authors would like to acknowledge the reviewers of *The Networking Management Practicum* who have provided many useful comments: Frederick J. Baker, Jeffrey D. Case, Frank J. Kastenholz, Deirdre C. Kostick, Ian McCloghrie, Evan McGinnis, Donna McMaster, David T. Perkins, Samuel M. Roberts, Vikram Saksena, Robert W. Snyder, Robert L. Stewart, Kaj Tesink, Steven L. Waldbusser, and, James W. Watt. In addition, Ole J. Jacobsen, editor and publisher of *ConneXions—The Interoperability Report*, was kind enough to perform the copy-editing on *The Networking Management Practicum*. His efforts brought this work to print in time for the NetWorld®+INTEROP® conference and trade show of September 1994.

/kzm
San Jose, California

/mtr
Mountain View, California

Part I

The Basics of Management

Chapter 1

Introduction

Welcome to *The Networking Management Practicum*. This book was written to help you use the *Simple Network Management Protocol* (SNMP) to manage your network. SNMP is the standard for open, interoperable network management, and is found on just about any kind of device that attaches to a network. However, this book isn't about SNMP — instead, it is intended to help you understand how to *use* SNMP to manage your network.

But, before we can talk about using SNMP to manage networks, we have to spend some time discussing what SNMP is and how it works. So, in this chapter, we'll look at the fundamentals of SNMP, along with the capabilities of the current generation of SNMP-based management software. Finally, we'll conclude with a "roadmap" explaining the layout of the remainder of *The Networking Management Practicum*.

1.1   Fundamentals of SNMP

The *Internet-standard Management Framework* is based on a collection of documents that define:

- management *information*, which describes the information available in a managed node that may be monitored or controlled by a management station; and,

- a management *protocol*, used to exchange management information between a managed node and a management station.

The protocol, of course, is SNMP, whilst the rules for defining management information are termed the *Structure of Management Information* (SMI), and the collection of management information is termed the *Management Information Base* (MIB).

There are actually two versions of this framework: the original framework, which consists of four documents ([1] through [4]), each a full Internet-standard; and, the successor framework, which consists of 12 documents ([5] through [16]), each having just entered onto the Internet's standards-track. In time, the documents comprising the successor framework likely will become a full Internet-standard. At that time, the original framework will be declared historic, and the Internet community will have but a single framework.

For our purposes, the choice of version is largely irrelevant: the newer framework was carefully engineered to maximize coexistence with the original framework. So, the term "management framework" can be used to refer to either the original or newer framework. However, in those cases where it makes a difference, the terms "SNMPv1 framework" and "SNMPv2 framework" will be used accordingly.

For a full treatment of the management framework, the reader should consult *The Simple Book* [17].[1]

Given with the nature of *The Networking Management Practicum*, only the basics of SNMP are discussed here. Further, readers well-versed in SNMP might not like the remainder of this chapter — the authors have taken considerable liberties to maximize the accessibility

---

[1] This really isn't a product placement by the author of *The Simple Book*. However, as long as you're ordering a copy, why not order a copy of *The Internet Message* [18]? (That's a product placement.)

of this material for the reader who knows nothing about SNMP and wants only the minimal amount of information necessary to use it.

With that in mind, let's begin by looking at the underlying model of the management framework and then consider the management protocol and information in greater detail.

1.1.1 The Model

The management framework views a network management system as containing four components:

- one or more *managed nodes*, each containing an *agent*;
- at least one *network management station* (NMS), on which one or more network management applications (which are often imprecisely termed *managers*) reside;
- a network management *protocol*, which is used by the station and the agents to exchange management information; and,
- management information.

Note that the terms "client" and "server" do not appear in the management framework's lexicon.

A managed node usually falls into one of two categories:

- a physical system, such as a host, router, or media device; or,
- a logical system, such as a network service or an application.

The commonality between these categories is that all devices have some sort of network capability. As can be seen, the potential diversity of managed nodes is quite high, spanning the spectrum from mainframes to modems.

Given that network management must be *ubiquitous* if it is to be truly useful:

> *The impact of adding network management to managed nodes must be minimal, reflecting a lowest common denominator.*

This *Fundamental Axiom* is mandated by the wide differences between managed nodes, and is argued quite eloquently in [19]. Given the focus of the Fundamental Axiom, what commonalities between managed nodes can we exploit?

Any managed node can be conceptualized as containing three components:

```
+----------------------------+---+---+---+---+
|                            | m | i |   |   |
|                            | a | n |   |   |
|                            | n | s |   |   |
|                            | a | t | m | p |
|                            | g | r | a | r |
|                            | e | u | n | o |
|                            | m | m | a | t |
|          "useful stuff"    | e | e | g | o |
|                            | n | n | e | c |
|                            | t | t | m | o |
|                            |   | a | e | l |
|                            |   | t | n |   |
|                            |   | i | t |   |
|                            |   | o |   |   |
|                            |   | n |   |   |
+----------------------------+---+---+---+---+
              |
           network
```

These are:

- *"useful stuff"*, which performs the functions desired by the user;

- a *management protocol*, which permits the (remote) monitoring and control of the managed node; and,

- *management instrumentation*, which interacts with the implementation of the managed node in order to achieve monitoring and control.

The interaction between these components is straightforward: the instrumentation acts as "glue" between the useful processes and the management protocol. This is usually achieved by an internal communications mechanism in which the data structures in the useful processes may be accessed and manipulated at the request of the management protocol.

In contrast, an NMS refers to a host system which is running:

- the network management protocol; and,

- one or more network management applications.

If the network management protocol is viewed as providing the mechanism for management, then it is the network management applications that determine the policy used for management. Note that since the Fundamental Axiom states that adding "network management" should have a minimal impact on the managed nodes, the resulting design favors reducing the load on managed nodes at the expense of an increased burden on the management stations. However, since there are many more managed nodes than management stations in an internet, scalability also favors such a design — it is better to require significant functionality from a small percentage of devices, rather than from the vast majority.

The distinction between managed nodes and management stations is usually clear-cut. However, suppose that the managed node is itself a management station? It is important to appreciate that the agent-manager model can directly support this by viewing the software in each management station as taking on two distinct roles: a *manager role* and an *agent role*. That is, the agent-manager model is also a peer-to-peer model, in that each node can query other nodes including each other. With this in mind, one can construct hierarchical relationships between management stations. For example, one could imagine constructing a management system in which each LAN segment had a management application which kept track of the state of the devices on that segment. These management applications might report to applications running on "regional" management stations, which, in turn, might report to applications running on enterprise-wide management stations. In this example, the software in each management station takes on both a manager role when monitoring and controlling devices which are subordinate in the hierarchy, and an agent role when reporting information and acting upon the commands given from a superior in the hierarchy. Because dual-role entities are based on a peer-to-peer architecture, one can implement a hierarchical relationship or some other kind of relationship, between entities as a "simple" matter of configuration.

Earlier, we noted that the framework was divided into two parts: management information and the management protocol. Let's now look at each of these in turn.

1.1.2   SMI/MIB

The SMI defines a language which is used to define *object types*.

An object type is an abstract definition of a managed object. When implemented in a managed node, one or more *instances* of the object are present, and these are termed *variables*. Each managed object consists of several properties, as shown in Table 1.1. Of these, a few require further elaboration.

The descriptor and value properties

Consider this simple example, which shows the definition of a managed object:

```
snmpStatsPackets OBJECT-TYPE
    SYNTAX      Counter32
    MAX-ACCESS  read-only
    STATUS      current
    DESCRIPTION
            "The total number of packets received by the
             SNMPv2 entity from the transport service."
    REFERENCE
            "Derived from RFC1213-MIB.snmpInPkts."
    ::= { snmpStats 1 }
```

For all but the `descriptor` and `value` properties, the name of the property appears before its value (e.g., "SYNTAX Counter32").

The descriptor is the word appearing to the left of "OBJECT-TYPE", and gives the human-readable name for the managed object. A collection of related managed objects is defined in a document termed a MIB module. Descriptors are used only by people; when machines

property	meaning
SYNTAX	the data type (e.g., integer, string, or pointer)
UNITS[†]	the units associated with the data type (e.g., seconds)
MAX-ACCESS[*]	an indication of maximum access level possible (e.g., read-only or read-write)
STATUS	the currency of the definition (e.g., current or obsolete)
DESCRIPTION	the textual definition of the object's semantics
REFERENCE[†]	a textual citation to a related object
INDEX[†], AUGMENTS[‡]	instructions on identifying instances
DEFVAL[†]	advice on instance creation
descriptor	the human-readable name
value	the machine-processible name

†   Optional property
‡   In the original framework, this optional property is not present
⋆   In the original framework, this property is called ACCESS

Table 1.1: Properties of Managed Objects

communicate they need a different means of identifying an object, the `value` property. Although written like a string, the `value` is actually a sequence of integers termed an `OBJECT IDENTIFIER`, where each integer is termed a *sub-identifier*. The details as to how a string (e.g., "`{ snmpStats 1 }`") turns into a sequence of integers (e.g., "`1.3.6.1.6.3.1.1.1.1`") are unimportant. For now, just think of this integer sequence as a serial number: each time a managed object is defined, it is assigned a unique serial number. Although people who define managed objects need to know the rules for picking a serial number, the people who use managed objects may remain blissfully uninformed!

Note that every managed object defined in a MIB module must be unique, so each has a unique `descriptor` and a unique `value`. It turns out that an object's `descriptor` property need be unique only within a MIB module, since humans "know" which module they're reading or discussing. For machines, an object's `value` property must uniquely identify the object, regardless of where it is defined.

The SYNTAX property

The `SYNTAX` property defines the managed object's data type. The management framework requires that each object instance be a simple data type, such as an integer, string, or pointer (the basic units of computing). Complex data types are modeled as tables of these simpler data types. As such, the SMI defines the syntaxes shown in Table 1.2. Of these, a few require further elaboration.

SYNTAX	range	meaning
Integer32*	-2B..2B	signed integer
Counter32*	0..4B	monotonically increases, then wraps back to zero
Counter64‡	0..18Q	monotonically increases, then wraps back to zero
Gauge32*	0..4B	maximum reporting value
UInteger32‡	0..4B	unsigned integer
TimeTicks	0..4B	hundredths of a second since an epoch
OCTET STRING		string of 8–bit values
BIT STRING‡		string of bits
OBJECT IDENTIFIER†		object pointer
IpAddress		IP address
NsapAddress‡		OSI network address
Opaque		unused

† No more than 128 sub-identifiers may be present,
and each sub-identifier is in the range 0..4B

‡ In the original framework, this syntax is not present

⋆ In the original framework, the trailing 32 was omitted,
i.e., INTEGER, Counter, and Gauge

-2B: -2^{31} (-2,147,483,648)
2B: $2^{31} - 1$ (2,147,483,647)
4B: $2^{32} - 1$ (4,294,967,295)
18Q: $2^{64} - 1$ (18,446,744,073,709,551,615)

Table 1.2: The SYNTAX Property

The BIT STRING syntax is used when an object type models a collection of enumerated bits. The SNMPv1 framework uses an integer sum instead. Consider a fragment of an object type definition using the original framework:

```
sysServices OBJECT-TYPE
    SYNTAX     INTEGER (0..127)
    ...
    DESCRIPTION
            "... The value is a sum.  This sum initially
            takes the value zero.  Then, for each layer,
            L, in the range 1 through 7 that this node
            performs transactions for, 2 raised to
            (L - 1) is added to the sum. ..."
    ...
```

In this example, if layers 4 and 7 were active, the value would be 72 ($2^{4-1} + 2^{7-1}$). In contrast, using the BIT STRING syntax, the SYNTAX property might look like:

```
    SYNTAX     BIT STRING {
               physical(0), datalink(1), network(2),
               transport(3), session(4),
               presentation(5), application(6)
               }
    ...
```

and the SMI automatically defines the rules for how different bit combinations are exchanged between machines.

The counter syntaxes (Counter32 and Counter64) are used when an object type models a value which monotonically increases until it reaches a maximum value, and then wraps back to zero. In order to "make sense" of an object having this syntax, its value must be sampled at least twice — only the delta between two values has any meaning. Of course, if the object isn't sampled often enough, a discontinuity will result. As such, the Counter64 syntax may be used (in a standard MIB) only if a 32–bit quantity would wrap in less than one hour.

Finally, the Gauge32 syntax differs from Integer32 in that it models a value that can increase or decrease, and can exceed a fixed maximum level. As long as the actual value is below (or equal to

SYNTAX	refines	meaning
DisplayString	string	an ASCII string (up to 255 characters)
PhysAddress	string	a media address (no fixed length)
MacAddress	string	IEEE 802 address (6 octets long)
TruthValue	integer	1 for true, 2 for false
TestAndIncr	integer	a spin-lock
AutonomousType	pointer	an object name (MIB module)
InstancePointer	pointer	a variable name (object instance)
TimeStamp	integer	when an event occurred
TimeInterval	integer	the delta between two events
DateAndTime	string	a date-time specification

Table 1.3: Commonly-used Textual Conventions

the maximum), an accurate value is reported; but, if the actual value exceeds the fixed maximum, then the fixed maximum value is reported. Of course, if the actual value once again drops to (or below) the maximum, then an accurate value is reported.

When defining a managed object, it may be more natural to use a "refinement" of one of these data types. For example, it may be useful to indicate that a string-valued data type has a maximum length, or that an integer-valued data type is really one of a small list of enumerations. If a refinement is commonly used, then it is usually defined in a special way and termed a *textual convention*. For example,

```
DisplayString TEXTUAL-CONVENTION
    DESCRIPTION
        "... NVT ASCII character set ..."
    SYNTAX OCTET STRING (SIZE (0..255))
```

defines DisplayString which refines a string-valued data type of up to 255 ASCII characters. Table 1.3 shows several commonly-used textual conventions. The SYNTAX property can specify a textual convention instead of one of the basic data types. For example:

```
sysDescr OBJECT-TYPE
    SYNTAX      DisplayString
    ...
```

The INDEX and AUGMENTS properties

As noted earlier, an object type is really a "template" for a variable —
if a managed node implements a particular object type, then it has
zero, one, or more instances of that object. These instances are termed
variables.

For a given object type, the `descriptor` and `value` properties contain its human-readable and machine-processible names, respectively.
So, how are variables named? The answer is simple; you start with the
name for the object type and then you append an *instance identifier*,
which is simply a sequence of integers which uniquely distinguishes
one instance of the object from all other instances in the managed
node.

For those cases where there can be at most one instance of an
object type, the sequence ".0" is added. Consider an earlier example:

```
snmpStatsPackets OBJECT-TYPE

    ...
    ::= { snmpStats 1 }    -- i.e., 1.3.6.1.6.3.1.1.1.1
```

To identify the only instance of this object, a human would use

```
snmpStatsPackets.0
```

whilst a computer would use

```
1.3.6.1.6.3.1.1.1.0
```

But, what about the cases where there can be more than one instance?
Well, to begin with, these are always objects belonging in tables.
Think of these objects as the columns in the table. To identify a
particular cell in the table, we need a way to uniquely identify a row
in the table. Then, by appending the row identity onto the name
of the column, we have uniquely identified the cell — which is the
desired instance of that object!

To accomplish this, each table has a "row template" which contains information indicating how a row can be uniquely identified.
This row template is simply a special kind of object type, and what
makes it special is that it has either an `INDEX` property or an `AUGMENTS`
property, which contains this information.

If the row object has an `INDEX` property, then the property identifies one or more objects which, taken together, will uniquely identify

a row. For example, suppose we have a table where one of the columns is a unique number, contiguously assigned, for each row — a "row number" expressed as an integer. The INDEX property of the row object would simply identify that columnar object. To uniquely identify an instance of any object in the table, start with the columnar object's name and append the value of the "row number" object. Here's a concrete example: consider a table contains information about network attachments on a managed node. This table has several columns, one of which is ifIndex, the value of which is unique for each row in the interfaces table. A second column is ifDescr, which contains a description of the interface. The row template for the interfaces table looks something like this:

```
ifEntry OBJECT-TYPE
    ...
    INDEX       { ifIndex }
    ...
```

Putting this all together, suppose we wanted to identify the ifDescr variable in the third row of the interfaces table. The answer (for humans) would be ifDescr.3.

There are two ways in which this could be more complicated: first, suppose that the INDEX property identifies an object whose data type isn't an integer; and, second, suppose more than one object is required to uniquely identify the row.

If the data type isn't an integer, then the rules for constructing the instance identifier are:

fixed-length strings: n sub-identifiers, where n is the length of the string (the value of each octet of the string is encoded in a separate sub-identifier);

variable-length strings: $n + 1$ sub-identifiers, where n is the length of the string (the first sub-identifier is n itself; following this, the value of each octet of the string is encoded in a separate sub-identifier); and,

pointers: $n + 1$ sub-identifiers, where n is the number of sub-identifiers in the value (the sub-identifier octet is n itself; following this, each sub-identifier in the value is copied).

For example:

```
printQEntry OBJECT-TYPE
    ...
    INDEX        { printQName }
    ...


printQName OBJECT-TYPE
    SYNTAX       DisplayString
    ...


printQEntries OBJECT-TYPE
    SYNTAX       Gauge32
```

Suppose we wanted to identify the **printQEntries** variable in the row of the print queue table corresponding to the queue called "**barney**". The answer would be

```
printQEntries.6.98.97.114.110.101.121
```

Why? Since the value of the INDEX property for **printQEntry** contains one string-valued object (**printQName**, a variable-length string), the instance-identifier is $n + 1$ sub-identifiers long: the first sub-identifier is the length of the string (**6**), and the remaining sub-identifiers each correspond to one character from the string (ASCII **b** is decimal 98, **a** is 97, and so on). Fine, so what if more than one object is required to uniquely identify the row? In this case, the INDEX property specifies the multiple objects and their values are appended, in order, to the columnar object's name. For example:

```
printJEntry OBJECT-TYPE
    ...
    INDEX        { printQName, printJRank }
    ...


printJRank OBJECT-TYPE
    SYNTAX       INTEGER (0..2147483647)
    ...


printJName OBJECT-TYPE
    SYNTAX       DisplayString
    ...
```

Suppose we wanted to identify the `printJName` variable in the row of the print job table corresponding to the job number 3 in the queue called "`barney`". The answer would be to append both the values

    6.98.97.114.110.101.121

and 3 to `printJName`, i.e.,

    printJName.6.98.97.114.110.101.121.3

You may have noticed that the leading 6 is redundant in both of these examples. In some cases, the MIB designer can get away without requiring it. In that case, the `IMPLIED` keyword appears before the corresponding object, e.g.,

```
printQEntry OBJECT-TYPE
    . . .
    INDEX      { IMPLIED printQName }
    . . .


printJEntry OBJECT-TYPE
    . . .
    INDEX      { IMPLIED printQName, printJRank }
    . . .
```

and the answers to our two examples would become:

    printQEntries.98.97.114.110.101.121
    printJName.98.97.114.110.101.121.3

For our purposes, we don't need to know when `IMPLIED` can be used — we need only be concerned with what it does.

Finally, if the row object has an **AUGMENTS** property, then it specifies the row object of another table, to indicate that the same rules are used for both tables, e.g.,

```
newifEntry OBJECT-TYPE
    ...
    AUGMENTS { ifEntry }
    ...
```

Congratulations! Instance identification is the hardest thing to understand about the management framework. We're done with management information and ready to discuss the management protocol.

1.1.3   SNMP

The Simple Network Management Protocol (SNMP) is a request-response protocol, e.g.,

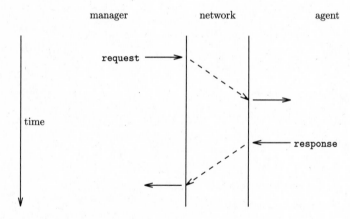

Each request consists of:

operation: one of **get**, **get-next**, **get-bulk**, or **set**;

request-id: an integer-value used by a management application to distinguish among outstanding requests; and,

variable-bindings: a list of variables, each containing a name and value.

The **get** operation retrieves the values associated with each variable contained in the request, whilst the **set** operation modifies each variable to have the associated value contained in the request. The `get-next` and `get-bulk`[2] operations also retrieve the values of variables but differ from the `get` operation in that they traverse the variables in the managed node (we'll explain this in more detail later).

Each request is processed in the context of a MIB *view*: the collection of variables that the management application is allowed to access. (This is usually a subset of the variables contained within the agent.) A response is then sent back to the management application. In addition to the original `request-id`, each response contains:

error-status: if non-zero, this indicates an error occurred when processing the request, and that the `variable-bindings` field should be ignored.

error-index: if non-zero, this indicates which variable in the request was in error.

variable-bindings: a list of name-value pairs (variables), updated for successful `get`, `get-next`, and `get-bulk` operations.

So, the typical successful interaction goes something like this:

1. The management application issues a request with:

   - a unique `request-id`;
   - a zero-valued `error-status`/`error-index`; and,
   - zero or more variable bindings.

2. The agent issues a response with:

   - the same `request-id`;
   - a zero-valued `error-status`; and,
   - (possibly updated) variable bindings.

While processing a request, the agent might encounter an error, indicating that the operation cannot be processed. There are several kinds of errors and, unlike exceptions (explained momentarily), they occur on a per-operation basis. If an error occurs, the response has a non-zero `error-status` field. (The value of `error-index` is

---

[2]The `get-bulk` operation is not available in the SNMPv1 framework.

condition	operation	error codes
permanent	any	tooBig
	set	noCreation
	set	notWritable
logic error	set	wrongType
	set	wrongLength
	set	wrongEncoding
	set	wrongValue
transient	any	genErr
	set	inconsistentName
	set	inconsistentValue
	set	resourceUnavailable
	set	commitFailed
	set	undoFailed

Table 1.4: SNMP Error Codes

usually also non-zero.) The SNMP error codes are shown in Table 1.4. The actual meanings of these error codes will be discussed later, in Section 3.1.3 starting on page 94. For now, the important thing to grasp is that some error conditions are permanent, others are transient, and still others refer to logic errors in either the agent or the management application.

Finally, it's possible that a request is sent but a response is never received. There are several possible reasons:

- the network dropped the request;

- the agent isn't running;

- the agent didn't generate a response to the request;

- the network dropped the response; or,

- the management application's timeout was too short.

Retrieval Operations

The `get` operation is straightforward — for each variable in the request:

- if the agent doesn't implement the object type associated with the variable, a special value — the `noSuchObject` exceptional value — is put in the response; otherwise,

- if the specified instance doesn't exist, or if it is outside the MIB view for this operation, the `noSuchInstance` exceptional value is put in the response; otherwise,

- the value associated with the instance is put in the response.

In the SNMPv1 framework, exceptions are not present, so the logic is even simpler — for each variable in the request:

- if the agent doesn't implement the object type associated with the variable, or if the instance specified doesn't exist, or if it is outside the MIB view for this operation, then a `noSuchName` error code is returned (we'll discuss this later on page 95); otherwise,

- the value associated with the instance is put in the response.

Of course, if an error code is generated, then no useful information is returned for any of the variables in the response. (This proved to be an inefficiency in SNMPv1, hence the introduction of exceptions in SNMPv2.)

The `get-next` operation is a little more tricky — for each variable in the request, the first named instance that follows the variable is retrieved from the MIB view for this operation:

- if there is no next instance in the MIB view for this variable, the `endOfMibView` exceptional value is put in the response; otherwise,

- the name in the variable-binding is updated to identify the next instance in the MIB view for this variable, and the value associated with the next instance is put in the response.

How does the agent know the order of the variables it contains? Since the variables are named using sequences of integers, `OBJECT IDENT IFIER`s, it simply compares the sequences, element by element, and the variables are ordered according to the first elements that differ. For example, `ifDescr.1` and `ifDescr.2` are equal in all but the last element:

```
1.3.6.1.2.1.2.2.1.2.1
1.3.6.1.2.1.2.2.1.2.2
```

(so `ifDescr.1` < `ifDescr.2`). Of course, in the SNMPv1 framework, exceptions are not present, so the logic is slightly different — for each variable in the request:

- if there is no next instance in the MIB view for this variable, then a `noSuchName` error code is returned; otherwise,

- the variable name is updated to identify the next instance in the MIB view for this variable, and the value associated with the next instance is put in the response.

Of course, if an error code is generated, then no useful information is returned for any of the variables in the response.

Finally, the `get-bulk` operation is like a `get-next` operation that executes repeatedly at the agent. There are actually two additional parameters to the `get-bulk` operation:

non-repeaters: the number of variables which should be retrieved at most once; and,

max-repetitions: the maximum number of times that other variables should be retrieved;

When an agent performs the `get-bulk` operation, it first calculates the size of the largest response it could send back to the management application. It then cycles through the first **non-repeaters** variables in the request, using the `get-next` operator on each, appending the new instance and value to the response, and decreasing the amount of free space accordingly. If there isn't enough room, the response is sent before it would overflow. Then, for up to `max-repetition` times, the agent cycles through any repeating variables in the request (all the variables after the first **non-repeater** variables). For each repetition, the `get-next` operator is used on the results of the previous repetition; the new instance and value are appended to the response, and the amount of free space is decreased accordingly. Ultimately, either the free space is exhausted or the maximum number of repetitions is performed. It is important to appreciate that the agent may terminate a repetition at any time — before the first variable, after the last variable, or anywhere in between. The agent may also terminate the operation when a repetition exhausts the MIB view. Regardless, the management application must deal with the result.

Finally, note that for both the `get-next` and the `get-bulk` operation, the variables listed in the request don't have to identify actual variables in the agent — the request contains arbitrary pointers, and it is up to the agent to find the first variable which occurs after the pointer contained in the request. This makes it very easy to scan entire tables using either operator: simply start with the name of the columnar objects, and either operation will start by returning the first instance in the table, e.g.,

```
get-next (ifDescr) -> ifDescr.1

get-bulk [non-repeaters = 0, max-repetitions = 2]
    (ifDescr) -> (ifDescr.1, ifDescr.2)
```

Note that although both of these operations return variables which are "greater" than their operands, there is no guarantee as to "how much greater" the variables will be. As such, all management applications should carefully examine the results of these operations to ensure that the desired information is returned.

Modification Operations

The `set` operation is conceptually quite simple — for each variable in the request, the agent updates its copy of the variable. However, the `set` operation succeeds if, and only if, all variables are updated ("all or nothing"). Further, if the operation succeeds, this implies that the variables were updated "as if simultaneously". Of course, in practice it may be difficult to implement these semantics.

Notification Operations

At the beginning of this section, SNMP was termed a request-response protocol. In fact, there is one kind of unsolicited interaction taken by an agent — when an agent detects an extraordinary condition, an `snmpV2-trap` operation is generated, and may be sent to one or more management applications:

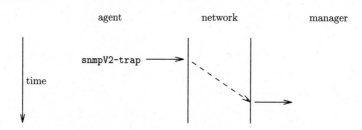

The `snmpV2-trap` operation contains a `request-id` and several `variable-bindings`. The first variable binding contains a timestamp indicating when the trap was generated, and the second variable binding identifies the trap. The remaining variable bindings contain additional information about the trap.

Note that in the SNMPv1 framework, there is a similar `trap` operation which carried the same information, but in a different format. For our purposes, the format is irrelevant — both the original and the successor frameworks view unsolicited notifications in the same way.

Well, it took a little over 20 pages, but hopefully this is all the SNMP you'll ever have to know. The authors hope that 20 pages isn't too much, but frankly, we had a dilemma: you can't build management applications or manage a network without knowing something about SNMP. The authors hope they explained the right things!

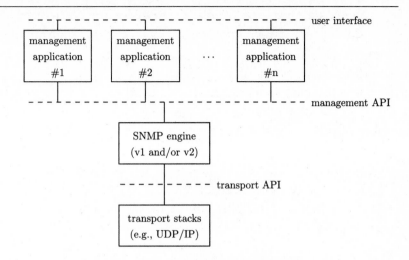

Figure 1.1: Initial Model of a Network Management Station

1.2 Network Management Stations

A *network management station* (NMS) is a computer system, typically a workstation, which executes network management applications. It has one or more users who interact with the network management applications through the user-interface provided by the applications. The user-interface is provided at the workstation's console(s).

Applications can also execute on lower-level devices, such as LAN-monitoring probes, hub management cards, and other general proxy agents. These are not considered here. Similarly, the operation of an NMS, when acting as a lower-level (or peer) manager to other network management stations, is not considered here.

There is no requirement that the internal software structure of an NMS be implemented in any specific manner. The only requirement is that its external interfaces conform to the framework described earlier in Section 1.1. Nevertheless, it is useful to have a model of how the various parts of an NMS fit together. Figure 1.1 shows our initial model.

Management of network equipment necessarily requires tracking a number of other data items besides the MIB information accessible via SNMP. Examples include installation records, inventory serial numbers, maintenance contracts, maintenance schedules/records, the current status of problem resolution, etc. It is often useful to have some of this information on-line, so that it can be correlated to the SNMP management of the network. Typically, this is accomplished by storing the information in a database and having a front-end application that provides a friendly user-interface into the data. Such applications are beyond the scope of this book, but some of them are appropriate for integration with the applications that do make use of SNMP. This level of integration does exist today for some applications. A particular example is a trouble-ticket application, for which a new trouble-ticket might be opened on the receipt of certain types of SNMP notifications.

1.2.1 Operating Systems

There is a variety of operating systems for use on workstations, for example, MS-DOS, Microsoft Windows, UNIX®, OS/2, and Windows/NT. These vary in their strengths and weaknesses for use in an NMS.

An MS-DOS or Microsoft Windows workstation is generally considered to be more "user-friendly" than other more featureful operating systems, even if only because it is generally perceived to be simpler to install and maintain. It is generally operated only from a single user-interface, and can handle at most a few concurrent applications. MS-DOS and Microsoft Windows tend to run on less expensive hardware and, thus, their software, including NMS software, tends to be less expensive as well. In keeping with the inexpensive hardware, the typical workstation has a relatively small display screen. These characteristics tend to make MS-DOS and Microsoft Windows workstations suitable for users who manage small, simple networks.

UNIX® is probably the most popular operating system for an NMS. In comparison with MS-DOS or Microsoft Windows, UNIX® provides more facilities for background or scheduled processes, and is more robust when running multiple concurrent applications. UNIX® generally executes on more expensive workstations, and consequently, network management software for UNIX® is generally more expensive. One UNIX® workstation can support multiple users each with a relatively large workstation screen, either a local console or a remote (e.g., X Window System) terminal. Due to these characteristics, a UNIX® workstation is suitable for users who have greater network management needs and/or are managing larger/more complex networks.

OS/2 has characteristics similar to UNIX®. There are a few NMSs running on OS/2, but, as of this writing, their number seems to be declining rather than increasing.

Windows/NT also has characteristics similar to UNIX® and OS/2, but with its genesis in Microsoft Windows, it is again perceived to be more "user-friendly". Although initial versions of Windows/NT were less than robust, there will likely be increasing NMS usage of Windows/NT in the future.

1.2.2   Network Management Station Evolution

The first SNMP-based NMS software packages were fairly basic packages intended for incorporation into third-party products. They consisted of an "SNMP stack" with an application programmer's interface (API), plus a few basic applications. The applications were invoked from a command line to issue individual requests, and could be included in user-generated shell scripts to collect data and produce reports. Usually, there was also a process which received and printed `trap`s.

The first widely-used commercial SNMP-based NMS products introduced window-based graphical user interfaces, principally: a network map, a MIB browser, and a `trap` browser. The map represented managed nodes as icons within a window, and most products supported a single map with just enough graphics in the icons to display alarm and/or reachability status using color. The MIB browser allowed the user to select, via a point-and-click interface, the variables to be retrieved, with the output displayed in a scrollable window. Typically, there were no, or very limited, capabilities for the `set` operation. The `trap` browser provided a user interface to received `trap`s stored in a log file, allowing the user to scroll through and acknowledge them.

Over time, most commercial NMS products have evolved into one of two types:

- an NMS platform, providing a basic set of capabilities for use by other applications running on top of it; or,

- a set of applications to run on one or other of the platforms.

Most NMS platforms are the products of large manufacturers of workstations. Their basic capabilities include the SNMP stack with an API, multiple maps linked together as a hierarchy through "submap" icons, and a MIB compiler. Particular applications can be associated with icons within a map, allowing the application to be invoked by clicking on the icon. However, few of them provide the means for the sharing of data (e.g., at least the output of a MIB compiler) between applications, and they provide limited or no use of a commercial-quality *database management system* (DBMS) needed for handling large amounts of collected data.

Many of the applications that run on the platforms are from

device manufacturers, and are generally specific to a particular type of device. In most cases, the application provides its own window-based user-interface when invoked from an icon in the platform's map. In some cases, the application provides its own submap specific to a group of devices of a particular type (e.g., a representation of which cards are in which slots of a hub chassis).

A feature of network maps on which vendors have expended a lot of effort is automated map-drawing. The results tend to be useful, but limited. The discovery of devices and their network topology is generally supported only on a protocol-specific basis, and the topology data is not made available to other applications. Some placement of map icons representing discovered devices and links is performed, but except in special cases (e.g., cards in a hub chassis), such auto-placement generally needs user editing in order to represent geographic or organizational relationships.

Other vendors have incorporated the use of "artificial intelligence" and *rule-based methods* into NMS products. Such techniques can be useful in specific environments, but their use has, to date, been largely unsuccessful in commercial products since the rules are dependent on individual networks, and the definition of rules is too difficult a task for the majority of network administrators.

1.2.3   Current Status

As of this writing, there are about five widely-used NMS platforms. Most of these are based on UNIX®, but some are MS-DOS or Microsoft Windows platforms. Unfortunately, each has a different API, few support the SNMPv2 framework, and there are still areas in which their capabilities are limited.

One of the areas where improved capabilities are needed is the provision of data-handling facilities. At present, platforms generally provide little or no capabilities for the handling of data beyond that provided by the workstation's operating system. As a result, each application must store and retrieve its own data in its own application-specific format, and there is no sharing of data between multiple applications. With large amounts of data, a common data storage facility potentially based on a commercial-quality DBMS is appropri-

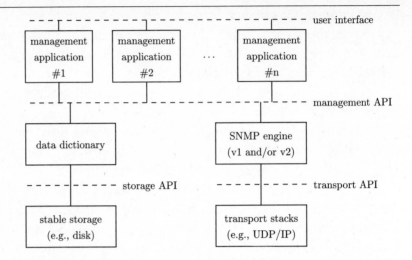

Figure 1.2: **A New Model for a Network Management Station**

ate. Further, a common format should be defined for particular types of data. This would allow additional capabilities to be added to the management API for any application to store, retrieve, or interrogate particular types of data. With this in place, data stored by one application could be retrieved or interrogated by other applications.

For example, with a defined format for the *management data dictionary* information, the platform's MIB compiler could process MIB modules to create the management data dictionary in the database. Then, through enhancements to the management API, every application could be provided with access to the information on managed objects and how particular agents implement them. Figure 1.2 shows a new model which incorporates this notion.

Other data types for which defined formats and management API capabilities would be useful are:

network topology data: which can be used not only for drawing maps, but also by other applications for such purposes as narrowing down the causes of network outages; and,

historic data: which can be retrieved by one or more applications, condensed over time by another application, and referenced by other applications that look for anomalies or perform trend analyses.

Current applications are available from a variety of sources and have a wide range of applicability. Some are available from the vendor of the platform; most are device-specific and available from the device vendor; and some are available for multiple platforms. Very few MIB modules have had device-independent applications written specifically for them. This is both surprising and a bit disappointing since there is a surfeit of standard MIB modules providing a vast array of lower-level management information, and many of these modules are implemented by many devices. There are also a few device-independent/MIB-independent applications which go beyond the ubiquitous MIB browser, in that they do more with retrieved data than just display it. Even fewer applications go beyond managing each device individually, by operating on multiple devices at the same time, and thereby managing the network as a whole. This requires an understanding of the relationship between the devices in the network. At present, users have to provide the majority of this understanding.

Part II: Managing Wires		
chapter	**technology**	**topics**
4	interfaces	network attachments
		address translation
		IP, ICMP
5	LAN devices	802 bridges
		Ethernet repeaters
	LAN interfaces	Ethernet
		Token Ring
6	WAN interfaces	DS1/E1, DS3/E3
Part III: Managing Hosts and Network Services		
chapter	**technology**	**topics**
7	hosts	host components
8	network services	TCP, UDP
		networked applications
9	SNMP agents	agent performance

Table 1.5: Roadmap

1.3   Roadmap

The Networking Management Practicum is divided into three parts. The first part is all introductory. It consists of this chapter, along with Chapters 2 and 3. The next chapter, Chapter 2, discusses an API for management applications, whilst Chapter 3 discusses strategies for communicating with managed devices.

The chapters in Parts II and III all discuss a particular kind of network management. The layout of each chapter is the same: a minimalist tutorial on a networking technology is presented; a discussion of the managed objects defined for the technology follows; and, the chapter concludes with some application fragments showing how problems can be solved by using SNMP. Table 1.5 summarizes the technologies covered in *The Networking Management Practicum*.

The good news is that the managed objects for all these technologies are standardized in the Internet community. However, there are a lot of topics that we don't cover, such as management of:

- additional local and wide-area networking technologies;

- routing and virtual networks;

- character-oriented devices;

- other applications, such as electronic mail;

- SNMP agent configuration;

- mid-level management entities;

- other protocol suites, such as AppleTalk®, DECnet, or SNA; and,

- non-traditional devices, such as uninterruptable power supplies.

All these technologies have managed objects either on the Internet's standards-track or (as of this printing) about to enter the standards-track. However, we decided not to cover them in this edition, either due to space limitations or because the corresponding MIB modules are rather new and we couldn't find an agent suitable for use as of this writing. As noted in the preface, we hope that future editions of *The Networking Management Practicum* will contain information on how to manage these and other technologies.

So, how should you proceed? You have two choices: If you want to write new management applications, start with Chapters 2 and 3, as these provide the framework for all the other chapters. After that, read the chapters in which you're interested.

Otherwise, if your interest is primarily in reading about how to manage a particular technology, just skip to that chapter and start reading. You shouldn't have any problems with the first two sections of each chapter; however, the third section of each chapter builds on materials presented in Chapters 2 and 3, so you may find that section a little difficult. Don't worry though, you should be able to get the gist of each example, even if a few of the details elude you. In any event, on your second reading of *The Networking Management Practicum*, you can always get more background by reading Chapters 2 and 3.

Regardless of your choice, the authors hope that you will ultimately become a producer of management applications — even if your original interest is simply to familiarize yourself with what's available to manage "something".

1.3.1   We Need Your Help

The authors feel that the first edition of *The Networking Management Practicum*, and the software which accompanies it, provides a good foundation for developing management applications. However, the authors' expertise is limited in many areas of networking — further, neither of them is currently responsible for managing production systems. That's where you, the reader, come in!

If you are excited by the possibilities provided by *The Networking Management Practicum*, then there are two mailing lists you might wish to join. Send a message to:

        snmptcl-users-request@cisco.com

to join the **snmptcl-users** list which discusses how to use the accompanying software. Further, if you're interested in actually developing additional software, send a message to:

        snmptcl-workers-request@cisco.com

to join the **snmptcl-workers** list.

The authors are particularly interested in hearing from people who use or extend the software for production use. In particular, if you actually do code something up, think about contributing a new chapter or section to *The Networking Management Practicum*. Although the current authors will remain involved for subsequent editions, we're looking to additional members of the community to help fill in the gaps!

Chapter 2

An API for Management Applications

Since the introduction of SNMP in mid-1988, a plethora of different *application programmer's interfaces* (APIs) have been developed for use. Each of these seeks to (somehow) make it easier for the writers of SNMP-based management applications. Collectively, the authors have been involved in the design, specification, and implementation of no fewer than six APIs! Nevertheless, when we began writing *The Networking Management Practicum*, because of our experiences with existing APIs, we decided to develop a new API.

There were five features we decided were needed:

- the API must be based on an *embedded* language — a language that is designed to coexist as a computational extension to a larger application, because we want developers to easily integrate the API into their applications;

- the API must be based on an *extensible* language, because we want developers to easily add new functionality to the API, based on their requirements;

- the API must be based on an *existing* and *widely-used* language, because we don't want to reinvent the wheel and we want to leverage the knowledge of a community of application writers;

- the API must be based on an *easily-learned* language, because we want to attract application writers who aren't presently familiar with the language; and,

- the API must be be based on a language that has a high-level graphical toolkit, because we are tired of spending more time writing windowing code than network management code when we write a management application.

We know of no existing API which meets all of these criteria. Thus, our choice was to use the *Tool Command Language* (*Tcl*) designed and implemented by John K. Ousterhout, and thereby have our API meet all the criteria. In addition, *Tcl* (pronounced "tickle") has a high-quality, multi-platform, openly-available implementation. The primary disadvantage of our choice is that the graphical toolkit, *Tk* (pronounced "tee-kay"), is implemented only over the X Window System. Although this is the windowing platform of choice for UNIX® systems, other systems have made other choices. However, as the *Tk* toolkit has only loose ties to the X Window System, *Tk* could be implemented on top of other windowing systems. Finally, because *Tcl* is an evolving language, it is important to choose a baseline version. For our purposes, the baseline is *Tcl* 7.3 and *Tk* 3.6.

If you're already familiar with *Tcl/Tk*, then you should skip ahead to Section 2.2 starting on page 68. Otherwise, the next section will introduce you to just enough *Tcl* so that you can *read* the application fragments contained in *The Networking Management Practicum*. If you are interested in *writing* applications using *Tcl*, then you should consult [20]. The authors **strongly** recommend it.

2.1 Fundamentals of Tcl and Tk

Tcl is a scripting language, consisting of an interpreter and a core set of command procedures. The interpreter evaluates programs, termed scripts, written in the *Tcl* language, calling the procedures as appropriate. There are two ways to extend the *Tcl* language:

- a script may define new command procedures, which build upon existing procedures; and,

- a programmer may write new command procedures in the *C* programming language and export these to the interpreter.

The first approach is by far the most common since it allows for rapid prototyping and development, whilst the second approach is used to provide functionality that is outside the scope of the core set of command procedures. For example, the *Tcl* core provides low-level access to local files, so an application might wish to provide higher-level file operators, and would likely do so by defining a new command procedure in a *Tcl* script. In contrast, the *Tcl* core doesn't provide any access to remote files, so an application writer would probably write some new *C* procedures and then tell the interpreter about them. These newly-exported command procedures can be used by a *Tcl* script, either directly, or when defining new command procedures.

The interpreter provides a unified environment to the application — it is actually a command-evaluator and data-structure. Thus, an application may have multiple interpreters, each with a different collection of commands and variables.

Let's look at the syntax and control aspects of *Tcl*.

2.1.1 Syntax

The syntax of *Tcl* is straightforward:

- commands are separated either by end-of-line or a semicolon (";");

- each command consists of a command procedure followed by zero or more arguments, all separated by spaces or tabs;

- double-quotes ("""") or curly-braces ("{" and "}") are used to delimit an argument which contains spaces or tabs; and,

- comments start with the sharp character ("#") after a command terminator (end-of-line or semicolon) and continue until end-of-line.

For example:

```
puts stdout "Hello world!" ; exit
```

contains two commands. The first command consists of the command procedure "`puts`" and two arguments, "`stdout`" and "`Hello world!`", whilst the second command consists of the command procedure "`exit`" and no arguments.

There are three types of characters which are special to *Tcl*:

- brackets ("[" and "]"), which indicate command-substitution;

- dollar-sign ("$"), which indicates variable-substitution; and,

- backslash ("\"), which indicates that the next character is interpreted literally (e.g., "\"" which means treat this as a simple character, not as an argument delimiter), or specially (e.g., "\n" which means treat this as the newline character), just as in the *C* programming language.

Let's look at each of these in turn.

Suppose we want to take the return value of one command and use it as an argument to another command. One way of doing this is to assign the return value of the first command to a variable, and then to use it as an argument to the second command. However, the easier way is to use command-substitution, e.g.,

```
puts stdout [dial popcorn]
```

which invokes a command consisting of the command procedure "`puts`" and two arguments, "`stdout`" and "`[dial popcorn]`". The interpreter first evaluates the command

```
dial popcorn
```

and then supplies its return value as the second argument to the "`puts`" command procedure. This example points out an **important** syntax rule: the brackets are used to form a single argument to "puts"; no matter what kind of result is returned by "dial popcorn", it is passed as a single argument to the "puts" procedure.

Suppose we decide to use variable-substitution instead, e.g.,

```
set timenow [dial popcorn]
puts stdout $timenow
```

which consists of two commands. The first invokes the set command procedure, which assigns the value returned by "[dial popcorn]" to the variable "timenow". The second invokes the puts command procedure, which uses the value of "timenow" as its second argument. Some readers may be a bit surprised that variable-assignment is done using a command procedure ("set") rather than an assignment operator ("="), e.g.,

```
timenow = [dial popcorn]; # wrong!
```

Don't worry; you'll be typing "set" instead of "=" in no time!

It is important to appreciate that *Tcl*'s syntax isn't tricky: for each line, the interpreter breaks the line into commands and then breaks the commands into words. Then, for each command, the words are evaluated (command-substitution and variable-substitution are performed), and finally the command procedure is invoked. For example, consider this combination:

```
puts stdout "Hello $user, the time is [dial popcorn]."
```

which invokes the "puts" command procedure with two arguments. The second argument contains spaces (that's why it's surrounded by quotation marks), variable-substitution (i.e., "$user"), and command-substitution (i.e., "[dial popcorn]").

Having noted this, there is one exception: if a line ends with the backslash character ("\"), this indicates that the command is continued on the next line, e.g.,

```
puts stdout \
     "Hello $user, the time is [dial popcorn]."
```

which works just like the preceding example.

Finally, let's go back to the first example:

```
puts stdout "Hello world!" ; exit
```

This could have been written as

```
puts stdout {Hello world!} ; exit
```

What's the difference? Well, when curly-braces, rather than double-quotes, are used to delimit an argument, neither command-substitution nor variable-substitution is performed.[1] So,

```
puts stdout "Hello $user, the time is [dial popcorn]."
```

and

```
puts stdout {Hello $user, the time is [dial popcorn].}
```

are entirely different. Further, when curly-braces are used as delimiters, not only can the argument span multiple lines, but the curly-braces nest. For example, in

```
if {$i > 0} {
    set i 1
} else {
    set i 0
}
```

there are four arguments: the first is "`{$i > 0 }`", the second is

```
{
    set i 1
}
```

the third is "`else`", and the fourth is

```
{
    set i 0
}
```

Later, on page 54, this will turn out to be a very important facility.

To complete our tour of *Tcl*'s syntax, we now examine data values and variables.

---

[1]Actually, substitution may be deferred — this is discussed later, on page 54.

Data Values

In *Tcl*, all arguments are simply textual strings. The interpretation of the string depends on the command procedure. In general, there are five intepretations:

number-valued: the argument is an integer or floating point number;

string-valued: the argument is text;

list-valued: the argument is a list of zero or more elements;

keyword-valued: the argument is a keyword; or,

variable-valued: the argument is the name of a variable.

There are a number of command procedures in the *Tcl* core which manipulate these values. Each is now examined in turn.

Numbers are either integer or floating point, expressed using the usual syntax:

number	syntax
decimal integer	ddd
octal integer	$0ooo$
hexadecimal integer	$0xxxx$
floating point	$ddd.ddde{+}dd$
	$ddd.ddde{-}dd$
	$ddd.ddd$
	$ddd.$
	$dddedd$

(Of course, a minus sign can be used in front of decimal or floating point numbers.)

Command procedures that expect numeric arguments expect a single number, e.g., "1" or "3.14", not an expression, e.g., "1+2". So *Tcl* provides the "expr" command procedure which evaluates expressions, e.g.,

```
expr 1+2
```

Tcl provides the usual arithmetic, logical, bit-wise, and relational operators, in addition to the usual math functions that you'd find in a *C* library. The only difference is that the relational operators are also used on string-values, using the expected rules for comparison. The syntax of the "expr" command procedure is shown in Table 2.1.

Since this is our first table to summarize a *Tcl* command procedure, a bit of explanation is in order:

- items such as "arg" refer to a single word which must be present;
- items such as "?arg?" refer to a single word which may be present; and,
- items such as "?arg... ?" refer to zero or more words which may be present.

Of course, all arguments and return values are strings, but sometimes they are required to be in a certain format, such as **number** or **list**.

procedure	arguments	returns
expr	arg ?arg ... ?	`value`
	concatenate **args**, evaluate the expression, and return the result (usually **number**)	

expr operators in decreasing order of precedence		
symbol	**operation**	**operands**
~	arithmetic negation (unary)	`number`
!	logical negation (unary)	`number`
~	bitwise negation (unary)	`integer`
*	multiplication	`number`
/	division	`number`
%	remainder	`integer`
+	addition	`number`
~	subtraction	`number`
<<	left-shift	`integer`
>>	right-shift	`integer`
<	less than	`value`
>	greater than	`value`
<=	less than/equal to	`value`
>=	greater than/equal to	`value`
==	equality	`value`
!=	inequality	`value`
&	bitwise and	`integer`
^	bitwise xor	`integer`
|	bitwise or	`integer`
&&	logical and	`number`
||	logical or	`number`
x?y:z	if-then-else	x: `number` y,z: `value`

Table 2.1: Command Procedures dealing with Integers

Strings are the primary (perhaps *only*) data-structure in *Tcl*. The *Tcl* core provides many command procedures that manipulate string-values. The syntax of these commands is summarized in Table 2.2 which starts on page 45.

These command procedures provide functionality for:

comparison: Two strings can be lexicographically compared using "`string compare`".

extraction: A copy of a single character can be extracted with "`string index`", whilst a copy of an entire substring can be extracted with "`string range`". Characters are identified by an integer-value index (starting at zero).

conversion: "`string tolower`" and "`string toupper`" create a new string with all characters converted to lower- or upper-case (respectively), whilst "`string trim`", "`string trimleft`", and "`string trimright`" create a new string with whitespace (or other unwanted characters) stripped off the edges, the beginning, or the end, respectively.

conversion to other values: *Tcl* supports the %-escape notation used in many *C* libraries by providing the "`format`" and "`scan`" procedures, e.g.,

```
scan $input "%d %s" i name
```

which scans the variable "`input`" and extracts an integer into the variable "`i`" and puts a string into the variable "`name`", and

```
format "%03d %s" $i $name
```

which creates a string that starts with the value of the variable "`i`" formatted in three characters with leading zeroes, followed by a space and then the value of the variable "`name`".

searching: substring searching is performed by "`string first`" and "`string last`", whilst "`string match`" performs *C-shell* glob-matching, and "`regexp`" and "`regsub`" perform regular-expression matching. (These last two command

procedure	arguments	returns
format	`fmt ?value ... ?`	`string`
	for each %-escape in `fmt`, substitute the corresponding `value`, return the result	
scan	`string fmt var ?var ... ?`	`number`
	for each %-escape in `fmt`, extract a value from `string` and update the corresponding `var`, return the number of `vars` updated	
string compare	`string1 string2`	`number`
	if `string1` is lexicographically less than `string2`, return `-1`; if the two `strings` are equal, return 0; otherwise, return 1	
string first	`string1 string2`	`number`
	if `string1` occurs in `string2`, return the `index` in `string2` of the first such occurrence; otherwise, return `-1`	
string index	`string index`	`string`
	if there is a character residing at `index` in `string`, return a string containing a copy of it; otherwise, return the empty string	
string last	`string1 string2`	`number`
	if `string1` occurs in `string2`, return the `index` in `string2` of the last such occurrence; otherwise, return `-1`	
string length	`string`	`number`
	return the length of `string`	
string match	`pattern string`	`number`
	if `string` matches `pattern` using glob-matching, return 1; otherwise, return 0	
string range	`string first last`	`string`
	return a string formed by copying the characters residing between `first` and `last` in `string`	
string tolower	`string`	`string`
	return a string formed by copying `string` and making any upper-case letters into their lower-case equivalents	
string toupper	`string`	`string`
	return a string formed by copying `string` and making any lower-case letters into their upper-case equivalents	

Table 2.2: Command Procedures dealing with Strings

procedure	arguments	returns
string trim	**string ?trim?**	**string**
	return a string formed by copying **string** except for any occurrences of any character in **trim** found at the beginning and end; **trim** defaults to all white-space characters	
string trimleft	**string ?trim?**	**string**
	return a string formed by copying **string** except for any occurrences of any character in **trim** found at the beginning; **trim** defaults to all white-space characters	
string trimright	**string ?trim?**	**string**
	return a string formed by copying **string** except for any occurrences of any character in **trim** found at the end; **trim** defaults to all white-space characters	

Table 2.2: Command Procedures dealing with Strings (cont.)

procedures aren't germane to the *The Networking Management Practicum* and aren't shown in Table 2.2.)

A list is a way of grouping strings together. The *Tcl* core provides many command procedures which manipulate list-values. The syntax of these commands is summarized in Table 2.3.

procedure	arguments	returns
concat	`list ?list ... ?`	`list`
	return a list formed by copying each element of each **arg**	
join	`list ?separator?`	`string`
	return a string formed by concatenating each element in `list` using **separator**	
lindex	`list index`	`value`
	return the element specified by `index` from `list`	
linsert	`list index arg ?arg ... ?`	`list`
	return a new list formed by copying each **arg** as a new element inserted before the element of `list` specified by `index`	
list	`arg ?arg ... ?`	`list`
	return a new list formed by copying each **arg**	
llength	`list`	`number`
	return the number of elements in `list`	
lrange	`list first last`	`list`
	return a list formed by copying the elements of `list` specified by **first** and **last**	
lreplace	`list first last ?arg ... ?`	`list`
	return a list formed by replacing the elements of `list` specified by **first** and **last** by **args**	
lsearch	`?match? list pattern`	`number`
	if an element in `list` matches **pattern**, return the index of the first such occurrence; otherwise, return −1; if present, **match** is one of "**-exact**", "**-glob**", or "**-regexp**", for exact-matching, *C-shell* glob-matching (the default), or UNIX® regular-expression matching, respectively	
lsort	`?type? ?-command command? ?ordering? list`	`list`
	return a list formed by sorting `list` using the specified **ordering** treating each element as the specified **type**; **type** is one of "**-ascii**", "**-integer**", or "**-real**", and **ordering** is one of "**-increasing**" or "**decreasing**"	
split	`string ?separators?`	`list`
	return a list formed by adding a new element whenever a character in **separators** is found in **string**; if no **separators** are specified, split **string** at each character	

Table 2.3: Command Procedures dealing with Lists

These command procedures provide functionality for:

creation: A list is created by "`list`". Once created, lists are combined into a new list with "`concat`", whilst "`lreplace`" is used to create a new list by replacing a range of elements in an existing list, and "`linsert`" is used to create a new list by inserting a range of elements in an existing list.

access: The number of elements in a list is determined by using "`llength`", whilst a copy of a particular element is returned by "`lindex`", and a range of elements (a new sub-list) is returned by "`lrange`".

searching and sorting: Elements in a list are identified by an integer-value index (starting at zero), so "`lsearch`" is used to find the first element in a list that matches a string, and "`lsort`" is used to create a new list that represents a collation of a list.

string-conversion: Finally, "`join`" is used to take a list and return a string-equivalent, whilst "`split`" performs the inverse operation.

Some examples will make this clear. The commands

```
set    x  [split 1.3.6.1.2.1.2.2.1.2.1 .]
set    y  [lindex [expr [llength $x]-1]
```

set "x" to a list containing 11 elements, and then set "y" to the last element (we had to subtract one from the return value of "`llength`" because elements are numbered starting at zero, not one). Instead, if we wanted to create a list which was missing just the last element of "x", then

```
lrange $x 0 [expr [llength $x]-1]
```

would do the trick. Finally, the command

```
set    z  [join [lreplace $x end end 0] .]
```

makes a copy of the list in "x", replacing the last element with "0" and then joins the elements together using the period as a separator to form a new string to assign to "z", i.e.,

```
1.3.6.1.2.1.2.2.1.2.0
```

(The "`lreplace`" command procedure recognizes "`end`" as a keyword referring to the last element in a list.)

Variables

In *Tcl*, there are two kinds of variables, *scalars* and *associative arrays*, e.g.,

```
set a      "a string"
set x($a) "another string"
```

The first command sets the value of the variable "`a`" to "`a string`"; the second sets the value of the element in the array "`x`" indexed by "`a string`" to "`another string`". Array variables can have multiple indexes; simply separate them by commas, e.g.,

```
set y($a,2) "a third string"
```

The only tricky part about arrays is indicating whether you are referring to:

- the entire array (e.g., "`x`");

- an element in the array (e.g., "`x($a)`"); or,

- the value of an element in the array (e.g., "`$x($a)`").

Also, to avoid ambiguity with the "`expr`" command procedure, you will want to name variables starting with an alphabetic character, followed by any number of alphanumeric characters or underscores ("`_`").

The *Tcl* core provides many command procedures that manipulate variables. The syntax of these commands is summarized in Table 2.4 on the next page.

procedure	arguments	returns
append	`var arg ?arg ... ?`	`value`
	append **args** to **var**, return the new value	
array names	`array-var`	`list`
	return a list containing an element for each **element** in **array-var**	
array size	`array-var`	`integer`
	return the number of elements in **array-var**	
array startsearch	`array-var`	`handle`
	return a search-handle used as an argument for the next four command procedures	
array nextelement	`array-var handle`	`element`
	return the next element for the specified **array-var** and **handle**	
array donesearch	`array-var handle`	the empty string
	delete relationship between **array-var** and **handle**	
array anymore	`array-var handle`	`integer`
	return 1 if any elements in the array have not yet been returned by **array nextelement** for **array-var** and **handle**	
incr	`var ?integer?`	`integer`
	adds **integer** (default 1) to **var**, return the new value	
lappend	`var arg ?arg ... ?`	`value`
	appends each **arg** to **var** as a new element, return the new value	
set	`var ?arg?`	`value`
	set **var** to **arg** (if any), return the new value	
unset	`var ?var ... ?`	the empty string
	delete any knowledge of each **var**	

Table 2.4: Command Procedures dealing with Variables

These command procedures provide functionality for:

creation: A variable is created (or updated) by "set", which assigns a value; "append", which appends to an existing value (if any); and, "lappend", which treats the value (if any) of the variable as a list, and appends new elements to the variable.

interrogation: Variable-substitution is the easiest way to retrieve the value of variable, but "set" without a value may also be used, e.g.,

```
puts stdout $a
```

and

```
puts stdout [set a]
```

do the same thing.

modification: A variable holding an integer value can be modified by "incr", which simply adds any integer (positive or negative) to the variable, and returns the new value.

deletion: A variable, an array element, or an entire array can be deleted by using "unset", e.g., given

```
set a        "a string"
set x($a)    "another string"
```

then

```
unset a
```

deletes the variable "a", whilst

```
unset x("a string")
```

deletes just that one element of the array "x", but

```
unset x
```

deletes all elements of the array "x".

array-handling: Finally, the "array" command procedure is used to return information about the elements of an array.

The array-handling command procedure needs a bit more explanation. Earlier we noted that some command procedures interpret their arguments as keywords. The "`array`" command procedure is our first example of this, e.g., "`array size x`" returns the number of elements in the array "`x`". There are two ways in which to examine each element of an array. Both ways require using a *Tcl* looping-construct. The first way makes use of the "`array names`" command procedure which returns a list containing the name of each element, e.g.,

```
foreach element [array names x] {
#   handle x($element) here...
}
```

where the foreach-loop is evaluated once for each element in the array "`x`". The second way makes use of the "`array startsearch`" command procedure, e.g.,

```
set   id [array startsearch x]
while {[array anymore x $id]} {
    set element [array nextelement x $id]
#   handle x($element) here...
}
array donesearch x $id
```

which uses "`array startsearch`" to assign a search-handle to the variable "`id`". Then, "`array anymore`" is evaluated prior to each iteration of the while-loop. If a non-zero value is returned, then "`array nextelement`" is used to determine the name of another element in the array. Finally, "`array donesearch`" is used to destroy the search-handle. The second approach is somewhat more efficient in that less data is passed between the *Tcl* interpreter and script. Further, by using a search-handle, multiple searches through an array can be made at the same time.

2.1.2   Control

Tcl has the usual looping, branching, and procedural constructs found
in most "structured" programming languages. However, *Tcl* differs
from programming languages in its scoping rules: procedures definitions do not nest, and variables are either universally global or local
to an invocation of a procedure.

Since our last example introduced two looping-constructs, let's
start with them.

Looping-Constructs

The *Tcl* core provides three looping-constructs. The syntax of these
command procedures is summarized in Table 2.5.

The looping-constructs are:

`foreach:` for each element in an array, repeatedly evaluate an
iteration script, e.g.,

```
foreach element [array names x] {
#    handle x($element) here...
}
```

`for:`   evaluate an initialization script, and then evaluate an
expression; if the expression is non-zero, then evaluate an
iteration script followed by a re-initialization script, and
test the expression again; continue iterating until the expression is zero, e.g.,

```
for {set elements [array names x]} \
    {[llength $elements] > 0} \
    {set elements [lreplace $elements 1 end]} {
    set element [lindex $elements 0]
#    handle x($element) here...
}
```

which is a very clumsy version of the preceding example.

`while:` evaluate an expression; if the expression is non-zero, then
evaluate an iteration script, followed by another test of the
expression, etc., e.g.,

```
set elements [array names x]
while {[llength $elements] > 0} {
    set element [lindex $elements 0]
#    handle x($element) here...
    set elements [lreplace $elements 1 end]
}
```

which is an even clumsier version.

With each of these looping-constructs, note that it is critical that each
argument which contains a script be delimited by curly-braces — this

procedure	arguments	returns
break	none	special
	terminate innermost looping-construct	
continue	none	special
	begin new iteration of innermost looping-construct	
for	`init testexpr reinit body`	the empty string
	evaluate `init` once, if `testexpr` is non-zero, evaluate `body` and `reinit`, and then iterate until `testexpr` is zero	
foreach	`var list body`	the empty string
	for each element in `list`, set `var` to the element's value and evaluate `body`	
while	`testexpr body`	the empty string
	if `testexpr` is non-zero, evaluate `body`, and then iterate until `testexpr` is zero	

Table 2.5: **Command Procedures dealing with Looping**

postpones command-substitution and variable-substitution until it is performed at the appropriate time by "`for`", "`foreach`", or "`while`".

As you might expect, the "`break`" command procedure is used to prematurely terminate a looping-construct by jumping to the first statement which follows; whilst the "`continue`" command procedure is used to prematurely terminate an iteration by jumping back to the expression test.

Branching-Constructs

The *Tcl* core provides two branching-constructs. The syntax of these command procedures is summarized in Table 2.6.

The branching-constructs are:

if: evaluate an expression; if the expression is non-zero, then evaluate a script; otherwise, evaluate another expression, if the expression is non-zero, then evaluate a script; and so on; if no more expression/script pairs remain, then evaluate a default script, e.g.,

```
if {$i > 0} {
# evaluate if i is greater than zero
} elseif {$i < 0} {
# evaluate if i is less than zero
} else {
# evaluate if i is equal to zero
}
```

switch: compare a string to a list of patterns, evaluate the body script associated with the first pattern that matches the string; if no patterns match, evaluate a default script, e.g.,

```
switch $i {
    0 {
# evaluate if i is equal to zero
    }

    barney
    -
    fred {
# evaluate if i is the string "barney" or "fred"
    }

    default {
# evaluate otherwise
    }
}
```

procedure	arguments	returns

if	`testexpr then body \`
	    `?elseif testexpr then body ... ? \`
	    `?else body?`
		value

	evaluate expressions until one is non-zero, evaluate the corresponding body, and return its value	

switch	`?match? string {`
	    `pattern body`
	    `?pattern body ...?`
	`}`
		value

	find the first `pattern` that matches `string`, evaluate the corresponding body, and return its value; where `match` is one of "`-exact`", "`-glob`", or "`-regexp`", for exact-matching (the default), *C-shell* glob-matching, or UNIX® regular-expression matching, respectively; if the corresponding body is "`-`", then the following body is evaluated	
switch	`?match? string pattern body ?pattern body ...?`	value
	identical to previous command, except that command- and variable-substitution are performed on all `patterns` prior to any comparison	

Table 2.6: Command Procedures dealing with Branching

As with the looping-constructs, it is critical that each argument which contains a script be delimited by curly-braces.

procedure	arguments	returns
catch	`body ?var?`	`integer`
	evaluate `body`, assign return value to `var` on normal or error returns, return `integer` corresponding to return code: 0 for a normal return, 1 for an error return, 2 for a return outside of a procedure, 3 for break, or 4 for continue	
error	`value`	special
	error return from procedure with `value`	
global	`var ?var ... ?`	the empty string
	declares each `var` to be global	
proc	`name list body`	the empty string
	defines `name` to be a command procedure having the specified argument `list` and `body`	
rename	`oldname newname`	the empty string
	change the name of the command procedure `oldname` to `newname`	
return	`?value?`	special
	normal return from procedure with `value`	
uplevel	`?level? arg ?arg ... ?`	value
	concatenate `args`, perform command-substitution and variable-substitution, evaluate the result in the execution context `level`, and return the `value`	
upvar	`?level? gvar lvar ?gvar lvar ... ?`	the empty string
	make the local variable `lvar` refer to the variable `gvar` in the execution context `level`	

Table 2.7: Command Procedures dealing with Procedures

Procedures

The *Tcl* core provides a general procedural interface. The syntax of the associated command procedures is summarized in Table 2.7.

The "**proc**" command procedure is used to define a new command procedure, and takes three arguments:

- the name of the new command procedure;

- a list containing the arguments to the procedure; and,

- a *Tcl* script containing the body of the procedure.

For example,

```
proc newproc {arg1 arg2} {
#    body of procedure
}
```

defines "`newproc`" as a command procedure taking two arguments. If we wanted to change the name of the command procedure, *Tcl* provides a "`rename`" command procedure. This is useful for providing a "wrapper" around an existing procedure, e.g.,

```
rename exit exitaux
proc exit {status {0}} {
# perform application-specific clean-up here...

# then call the real exit command procedure
    exitaux $status
}
```

Normally, each argument specified in the definition must be supplied by the caller. However, there are two exceptions:

- a default may be specified for each argument, e.g.,

  ```
  proc newproc {arg1 {arg2 def2}} { ... }
  ```

  specifies a default (the string "`def2`") for the second argument.

- if the last argument is named "`args`", then it "absorbs" any remaining arguments for the command, e.g., given

  ```
  proc newproc {arg1 args} { ... }
  ```

then

```
newproc abc def ghi
```

would assign "`abc`" to the parameter "`arg1`", and a list containing the strings "`def`" and "`ghi`" to the parameter "`args`".

A command procedure returns not only a data value, but also a *return code*. In addition to a "normal return", three other return codes are possible:

error: which indicates that an error occurred during processing;

break: which indicates that the "`break`" command procedure was evaluated; and,

continue: which indicates that the "`continue`" command procedure was evaluated;

We've already seen the definitions of the "`break`" and "`continue`" command procedures, so it shouldn't be surprising to find there are also "`return`" and "`error`" command procedures, each doing what you'd expect.

All four of these return codes cause the execution stack to unwind until they are *caught*. As you might expect, normal returns always unwind the stack by one, and the "`break`" and "`continue`" return codes are caught by the looping-constructs.[2] However, the "`error`" return code is normally caught by the top-level interpreter, which results in an error message being printed.[3] However, there is a "`catch`" command procedure which may be used to continue processing when any of these return codes is used.

Finally, when a procedure is invoked, it begins its execution with its parameters as its only local variables; further, global variables are inaccessible. Whenever a variable is created during evaluation of the procedure, it is created as a local variable. The "`global`" command may be used to change this default by specifying which global variables are accessible during the procedure's evaluation. *Tcl* uses a call-by-value model of parameter-passing. However, two command procedures, "`upvar`" and "`uplevel`", are used to implement call-by-reference parameters, e.g.,

```
upvar #0 global local
```

---

[2]Observe that "`break`" and "`continue`" are just like any other command procedure — they simply have a different return code than most others!

[3]Return processing is actually more complicated than this: *Tcl* allows user-defined return codes; further, there are two global variables, "`errorCode`" and "`errorInfo`", which contain stack-trace and other information.

procedure	arguments	returns
eval	arg ?arg ... ?	value
	concatenate **args**, perform command-substitution and variable-substitution, evaluate the result, and return the value	
source	file	value
	evaluate the contents of **file**, return the value of the last statement evaluated	

Table 2.8: Miscellaneous Command Procedures

says that the "**local**" variable refers to the "**global**" variable when the procedure is evaluated. Similarly, "**uplevel**" arranges for its arguments to be evaluated in a different execution context (e.g., the global environment).

2.1.3   Other Command Procedures

There are two other command procedures in the *Tcl* core which warrant discussion:

eval: invokes the *Tcl* interpreter on its arguments; and,

source: invokes the *Tcl* interpreter on the contents of a file.

The syntax of these command procedures is summarized in Table 2.8.

Earlier, on page 39, we saw how *Tcl*'s syntax wasn't tricky: a word occurring in a command might evaluate into a number, string, or list, but it is always passed to the command procedure as a single argument. The "**eval**" command procedure can be used if you want to force a word containing a list to be passed as several arguments. For example, in:

```
set x [list a b c] ; myproc $x
```

a single argument is passed to "**myproc**", but in:

```
set x [list a b c] ; eval myproc $x
```

three arguments are given to "`myproc`". Why? Because "`eval`"
gets two arguments: "`myproc`" and a list containing three strings,
so "`eval`" invokes the *Tcl* interpreter to evaluate:

```
myproc a b c
```

Finally, the *Tcl* core has a few other sets of command procedures, but these aren't really germane to *The Networking Management Practicum*, so we'll mention them just in passing:

interpreter management: *Tcl* contains an "`info`" command
procedure that allows a script to query the state of the interpreter; for example, you can find out about the command
procedures and variables currently defined;

history mechanism: *Tcl* contains a "`history`" command procedure that allows an interactive user to review commands
already typed, and re-use them for subsequent typing;

tracing mechanism: *Tcl* contains a facility that allows you to
trace variables as they are accessed;

library handling: *Tcl* contains a facility that allows a command
procedure to be automatically loaded from a library when
the procedure is invoked for the first time; and,

file and process handling: if *Tcl* is running under UNIX®,
there are several command procedures that permit reading
and writing of files and creating subprocesses.

2.1.4 The Tk Toolkit

Tk is the *graphical user interface* toolkit for *Tcl*. Unlike *Tcl*, which is primarily procedural, *Tk* is *event-driven*:

- a program executes some initialization code (sometimes written entirely in *Tcl*);

- this code puts one or more "top-level" windows up on the screen (each of these is termed an *application*); then,

- the program enters an event-loop:

  - whenever the user interacts with one of the windows (e.g., clicks with the mouse),

  - a *Tcl* script is evaluated which performs an action (e.g., performs a computation and displays the result).

Anyone who has programmed a windowing system is already familiar with event-driven programming. What makes *Tk* special is that the programmer uses *Tcl* instead of the usual compiled language such as *C*. As with any programming effort using *Tcl*, this tends to vastly reduce the time to implement (and more importantly, debug) an application.

The *Tk* toolkit contains three sets of functions:

window management: There are several command procedures to create and manipulate many kinds of windows, e.g., windows that:

- contain static text or images, such as single-line *labels*, or multi-line *messages*;

- evaluate a *Tcl* script when you click on them, such as *command-buttons*, or *menu-buttons*;

- allow you to select from among several alternatives, such as *check-buttons* (which allow zero or more to be selected), *radio-buttons* (which allow exactly one to be selected), *listboxes* (which allow a range to be selected), or *sliders* (which allow one point in a continous range to be selected);

- allow you to enter and edit text, such as *entries* (which deal with a single line), or *text* (which are multi-line, and allow for multiple fonts, colors, and imaging options); or,

- allow you to combine arbitrary objects, such as lines (straight or smoothed), rectangles, ovals, arcs, polygons, etc., on a single *canvas*.

These command procedures allow many customization options for choice of color, depth, font, background, keystroke and mouse bindings, and so on.

geometry: There are command procedures for geometry management which implement different policies for arranging windows; in addition, *scrollbars* may be used on multi-line windows.

inter-process communication: There are a few command procedures to interact with the user's window manager, to schedule events after a delay (e.g., to change a bitmap to indicate activity), and to communicate with any other *Tk* applications that the user might be running.

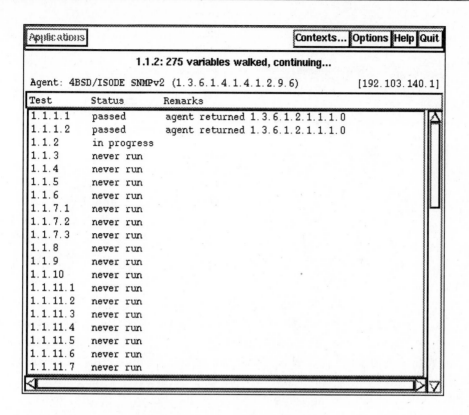

Figure 2.1: A Top-level Window

Although these procedures are all implemented in the *C* programming language, they are accessed through *Tcl*.

Let's look at a few examples to get a feel for what a *Tk*-based application might look like. Figure 2.1 shows the top-level window for an application. The top row of the window contains five command-buttons, one of which ("**Applications**") is disabled. Below, there are two label windows, each displaying some static text ("**Agent: ...**" and "**Test ...**"). The main area is taken up by a listbox, containing several entries. Scrollbars are used to change the portion of the listbox which is visible.

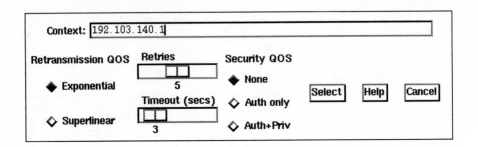

Figure 2.2: A Window to Select a Management Context

If the user double-clicks on the "Contexts..." button, then the window shown in Figure 2.2 appears. Although it looks like the window starts with a label ("Context:"), the label is actually a menu-button. When the user moves the mouse over the menu-button, it is highlighted, and if the user then click-holds the mouse, then a menu of possible choices appears. Alternately, the user might choose to enter or edit text. Below, there are four input areas. The one on the left hand side contains two check-buttons ("Exponential" and "Superlinear") to select the retransmission quality-of-service. To its right, there are two sliders to determine the number of retries and timeout duration. Next are three check-buttons to select the security quality-of-service. Finally, there are three command-buttons ("Select", "Help", and "Cancel"). As you might expect, clicking on "Superlinear" would cause its diamond-tick to darken, and the diamond-tick for "Exponential" to lighten. Similarly, click-holding the mouse on the "Retries" and then moving it would result in the corresponding value being changed. Finally, clicking on the "Select" button causes the information to be used, whilst clicking on "Cancel" aborts the operation, and clicking on "Help" brings up a new window containing instructions.

Instead, if the user double-clicks on the "Options" button (in Figure 2.1), then the window shown in Figure 2.3 appears. It displays a label and three check-buttons. Below the check-buttons are two command-buttons, having the expected semantics.

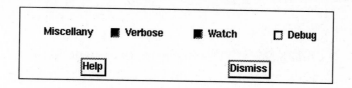

Figure 2.3: A Window to Select Options

2.1.5   Other Libraries

There are a lot of people writing applications in *Tcl* these days, and many of them share their code with the Internet community. One package which we'll make use of in *The Networking Management Practicum* is the *BLT* library. This is an extension to the *Tk* toolkit that adds several powerful windows, such as hypertext, plotting, barchart, along with a new geometry manager, and interprocess communication via a *drag-and-drop* protocol.

This, of course now brings us to introduce a new library, one that makes SNMP available to the *Tcl/Tk* user. With that in place, the environment for a management application looks like this:

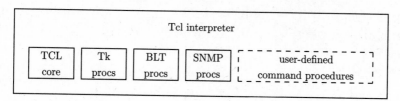

So, let's look at the final piece of the puzzle.

2.2   A Tcl-based API for SNMP

Our API for SNMP consists of two parts:

- *protocol operations*, allowing a management application to exchange management information with an agent; and,

- *management information knowledge*, allowing a management application to access "meta-information" about management information.

Let's look at each in turn.

2.2.1   Protocol Operations

In keeping with the event-driven nature of *Tk*, protocol operations are entirely asynchronous:

- the application calls a command procedure to initiate an operation; and,

- at some time later, when the response to the operation is received, a command procedure supplied by the management application is evaluated.

Because the protocol engine never blocks, it may support multiple management applications simultaneously.[4]

---

[4]This is analagous to the way *Tk* works: when a window is created, command procedures are registered to deal with events such as user-input; some time later, an event triggers the evaluation of one or more of the commands.

Management Contexts

Before any protocol operation can take place, the management application must identify the agent with which it wants to communicate. Actually, the management application must do more: it must identify which collection of management information held by the agent it wishes to access! There are two reasons for this:

- Although one might imagine an agent making all of its management information available, it may wish to make different subsets of its information available to different management applications. Each subset, whether it encompasses all the management information held by the agent, or only a small part, is termed a *MIB view*. So, one could imagine an agent configured to support multiple MIB views, perhaps one for general interrogation, another for a network operator, and a third for the network administrator. Of course, these MIB views would probably have several objects in common, so the MIB views held by an agent needn't be disjoint.

- Although one might think of an agent as allowing access to only local management information, it may be able to provide access to management information held on other network devices, e.g., on a device that doesn't support SNMP. This is called a *proxy relationship*, whereby an agent acts as a management proxy for some other device.

For now, understand that it is not enough to identify the agent. A management application must also identify what collection of management information held by the agent it wishes to access.

A collection of management information is termed a *management context*, regardless of whether it is held locally or remotely, and regardless of whether it encompasses all of the management information on a device, or just a subset. The key idea is that an SNMP operation is evaluated with respect to a single management context — a single operation can't span more than one context.

So, how does a management application know which management context to use? The answer is: it doesn't; the user knows! The API has access to a database, configured by the network administrator,

procedure	arguments	returns
newsnmp	`ctxproc string ?options?`	`ctxproc`
	find the management context associated with `string`, create a new context procedure, `ctxproc`, which is used to talk to the corresponding agent	

`newsnmp` options			
option	value	meaning	default
rtrqos	`string`	retransmission quality-of-service, one of: `exponential`, `superlinear`	`exponential`
retries	`integer`	number of retries for retrieval operations	5
timeout	`integer`	number of seconds before initial retry, `rtrqos` determines timeout for additional retries	10
secqos	`string`	security quality-of-service, one of: `none`, `auth`, `authpriv`	`none`
maxrept	`integer`	max-repetitions field for `get-bulk` operations	1
nonrptr	`integer`	non-repeaters field for `get-bulk` operations	0

Table 2.9: The `newsnmp` Command Procedure

which contains information about the relevant management contexts. This information includes a unique string, termed a *textual handle*. So, the first command procedure the API provides, "`newsnmp`", takes a string and creates a new command procedure that can be used to access information held in the management context. This new command procedure is termed a *context procedure*. The syntax of this procedure is shown in Figure 2.9.

Only two parameters are required: the name of the context procedure, and a string identifying the desired management context, e.g.,

```
newsnmp agent "router.xyz.com-public"
```

says to create a context procedure "`agent`" which will be used to access the management information held in a management context known as "`router.xyz.com-public`".

The API doesn't require that the network administrator provide complete configuration information for every agent to which the man-

agement application talks. If the string supplied by the management
application doesn't correspond to something already configured, the
API has two alternatives:

- if the string supplied could refer to one or more textual handles,
  the API will treat the string as identifying a *wildcard* context —
  it simply uses whichever context is appropriate when performing
  a protocol operation. For example, if the network administrator
  has configured two contexts, e.g.,

      router.xyz.com-public

  and

      router.xyz.com-all

  then if the management application specifies simply

      router.xyz.com

  the API treats this as identifying a wildcard context.

- if the string supplied identifies the address of a managed node
  (i.e., contains an IP-address or domain-name), the API will
  generate transient information for an appropriate context. For
  example, if the management application specifies

      192.103.140.1

  the API adds a transient context and associated information to
  its configuration.

The key thing to understand is that the management application
doesn't have to know about the information configured by the network
administrator. And, if the network administrator doesn't supply any
information, the API can usually derive the appropriate configuration
based on input from the user.

The remaining parameters are options which are used to provide defaults for subsequent protocol operations. The options fall into three categories:

retransmission strategy: On retrieval operations (either `get`, `get-next`, or `get-bulk`), it is safe for the protocol engine to retry a request if a response is not received within a "reasonable" amount of time. Earlier, on page 20, several possibilities were listed as to why a response might not be received in a timely fashion. So, the API provides a mechanism by which the management application can specify an automatic retransmission policy, either *exponential* or *superlinear*. As shown in Figure 2.4, these differ in the formula used to determine the amount of time to wait before the next retransmission. The exponential policy simply doubles the amount of time, whilst the superlinear policy increases it less aggressively.

Note that for modification requests (`set`), it is not always safe to automatically retry the request — it's possible that the request got through, but the response was lost. In this case, automatic retransmission could have unexpected (and unwanted!) consequences.

security requirements: The SNMPv2 framework allows both authentication and privacy. So, the API allows the management application to indicate its own minimum level of security, and when performing protocol operations, security options are used which satisfy both administrator and application (i.e., the greater of the two requirements is always used).

get-bulk operation: Earlier, on page 22, it was noted that the `get-bulk` operator has two parameters which control its behavior. The defaults for these two parameters can be set when the context procedure is created.

Note that with the exception of setting defaults for future use of the `get-bulk` operation, the management application doesn't need to know which version of SNMP is being used. In fact, this will be a con-

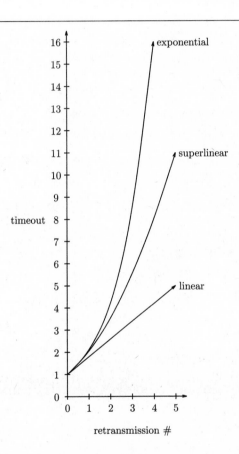

Figure 2.4: Exponential and Superlinear Retransmission Policies

sistent theme throughout the API: the management application states its requirements and, then, based on the configuration established by the network administrator, the protocol engine will simply "do the right thing". For example, if the `get-bulk` operation is requested, but the management context can be reached only with SNMPv1, the protocol engine applies the convergence rules defined in the SNMPv2 standard, and transparently converts it to a `get-next` operation.

Once a context has been identified and bound to a context procedure, there are several commands available:

operation: to invoke a protocol operation (e.g., `get`);

wait: to wait for a particular invocation to complete, or to wait for all outstanding invocations to complete;

register: to register a command procedure to be evaluated when an unsolicited message is received;

config: to examine or change the configuration of the context procedure; or,

destroy: to discard any invocations in progress, and then delete the context procedure from the interpreter.

The syntax of these commands is shown in Table 2.10. Let's look at each in turn.

Operations and Waiting

To invoke a protocol operation, specify the name of the operation after the context procedure, followed by the name of a *Tcl* command procedure to be called when a response is received, and the variable-bindings for the operation, e.g.,

```
newsnmp device "router.xyz.com-public"
device get myproc 1.3.6.1.2.1.1.5.0
```

The return value is an *invocation-identifier*, which is a unique value for this invocation that can be used to distinguish this request from other invocations that might also be in progress, regardless of the invoking context procedure.

procedure	arguments	returns
ctxproc operation	`callback vBinds ?options?`	`integer`
	invoke the specified `operation` on the `vBinds` found in the context associated with `ctxproc`, when a response is received, evaluate the `callback` command, return an `integer` which is used to identify the invocation	
ctxproc wait	`?integer?`	the empty string
	wait for the `callback` command associated with the invocation specified by `integer` to be evaluated; if `integer` isn't present, wait for the `callback` commands associated with all outstanding invocations to be evaluated	
ctxproc register	`?-add? ?-remove? notify callback`	the empty string
	on `-add` (the default), add `callback` to the list of commands to be evaluated when an unsolicited message is received; on `-remove`, remove `callback` from the list; `notify` is either `trap` or `inform`	
ctxproc config		`list`
	return a list containing the current configuration options associated with `ctxproc`; each element is a list containing an option and a value	
ctxproc config	`option ?value?`	`value`
	return the present value of the specified configuration `option`; if `value` is specified, make this the new value	
ctxproc destroy		the empty string
	discard any invocations in progress (evaluating each `callback`) and delete the context procedure	

Table 2.10: Using a Context Procedure created by `newsnmp`

operation	parameter
keyword	specifies
get	`get`
next	`get-next`
bulk	`get-bulk`
set	`set`
inform	`inform`

vBinds **parameter**		
syntax	**type of value**	**example**
Integer32	`integer`	`42`
BitString	`string`	`101010`
OctetString	`string`	`0x01:fe:23:dc:45:ba:67:98`
DisplayString	`string`	`{4BSD/ISODE SNMPv2}`
ObjectID	`string`	`1.3.6.1.6.3.1.1.1.1`
IpAddress NetworkAddress	`string`	`192.103.140.1`
Counter32 Gauge32 TimeTicks Counter64 UInteger32	`number`	`42.0`
Opaque	the empty string	
NsapAddress	`string`	`0x47:00:05:80:ff:ff:00:00`

Table 2.11: Parameters when invoking SNMP operations

Table 2.11 shows the parameters used when invoking an SNMP operation. In addition, any of the options specified in Table 2.9 back on page 70 can be specified, to override the default established when "`newsnmp`" is used to create the context procedure.

However, the `vBinds` parameter requires a bit more explanation. This parameter is a list. Each element in the list is either:

- an `OBJECT IDENTIFIER` (this was introduced earlier, starting on page 10); or,

- a list containing an `OBJECT IDENTIFIER`, a syntax, and a value.

Returning to the preceding example,

```
device get myproc 1.3.6.1.2.1.1.5.0
```

specifies a **vBinds** parameter containing one element, which is an
OBJECT IDENTIFIER. The same is true for:

```
device get myproc { 1.3.6.1.2.1.1.5.0 }
```

and for:

```
device get myproc { { 1.3.6.1.2.1.1.5.0 } }
```

In fact, for retrieval requests (**get**, **get-next**, and **get-bulk**), you
need to specify only the **OBJECT IDENTIFIER**s, the API will fill-in the
rest. But, for modification requests (**set**), you have to specify the
syntax and value as well, e.g.,

```
device set myproc \
  { 1.3.6.1.2.1.1.5.0
    DisplayString "dbc.mtview.ca.us" }
```

or,

```
device set myproc \
  { { 1.3.6.1.2.1.1.5.0
      DisplayString "dbc.mtview.ca.us" }
    { 1.3.6.1.2.1.1.6.0
      DisplayString "upstairs library" } }
```

Don't panic: you won't have to type-in the actual **OBJECT IDENT-
IFIER**; later, on page 84, we'll introduce a command procedure that
takes a descriptor, such as "**sysName**" and turns it into an **OBJECT
IDENTIFIER**.

Finally, the "**-timeout**" option (shown back in Figure 2.9 on
page 70) is used only in two situations: either the protocol engine has
never talked to the agent before, or a **set** operation is being invoked.
Otherwise, the protocol engine dynamically determines the initial
timeout value, using a smoothed formula based on past round-trip
delays. As you might expect, if no "**-timeout**" option is specified
for a **set** operation, the protocol engine selects a value longer than
it would for a retrieval operation — as there will be no automatic
retransmissions!

Callbacks

Table 2.12 shows how a callback procedure is evaluated when an invocation completes.

The first two parameters are simple enough: the context procedure used to invoke the operation, and the corresponding invocation-identifier. The remaining three parameters correspond to error-status, error-index, and variable-bindings, which were introduced earlier on page 19. The `eStatus` parameter takes any SNMP error-status code, plus three others:

timeout: which indicates that a response was not received in a timely fashion;

failed: which indicates an internal error of some sort; and,

destroy: which indicates that the associated context procedure was destroyed.

If the `eStatus` parameter is one of these three values, then the `eIndex` parameter always has the value 0, and the `vBinds` parameter is the empty list. Otherwise, these two parameters are taken from the SN-MP response. Each element in the `vBinds` parameter always contains an `OBJECT IDENTIFIER`, syntax, and value. However, in addition to the syntaxes shown in Table 2.11 back on page 76, the two new syntaxes shown in Table 2.12 may also be present:

exception: which indicates that an SNMPv2 exceptional value is present in the response (these were discussed back in Section 1.1.3 starting on page 21); and,

error: which indicates an internal error of some sort.

procedure	arguments	returns
callback	`ctxproc integer eStatus eIndex vBinds`	ignored
	indicates that the invocation identified by `integer` is completed, having the specified error-status (`eStatus`), error-index (`eIndex`), and variable-bindings (`vBinds`)	

eStatus parameter	
category	**keyword**
SNMP error	`noError`
	`tooBig`
	`noSuchName`
	`badValue`
	`genErr`
	`noAccess`
	`wrongType`
	`wrongLength`
	`wrongEncoding`
	`wrongValue`
	`noCreation`
	`inconsistentValue`
	`resourceUnavailable`
	`commitFailed`
	`undoFailed`
	`authorizationError`
	`notWritable`
	`inconsistentName`
invocation timed-out	`timeout`
internal error	`failed`
ctxproc destroy	`destroyed`

vBinds parameter	
syntax	**value**
exception	`noSuchObject`
	`noSuchInstance`
	`endOfMibView`
error	any `eStatus` value above
unknown	any implementation-specific diagnostic

Table 2.12: Evaluating an SNMP Callback Procedure

More on Invocations and Callbacks

When an operation is invoked by a context procedure, the API makes two guarantees:

- if the context procedure makes a normal return, the request has left the protocol engine and is either queued for transmission or being transmitted; and,

- the callback procedure will not be evaluated until some time after the calling procedure returns control to the event-handler (usually after the procedure returns).

These two properties are very important, because:

- if some error is detected when invoking the operation (e.g., the management context is not allowed to perform the invocation), then the context procedure makes an immediate error return;

- the management application can use the return value from the context procedure as a key into an array, where it can store information for the callback procedure — this is critical if several invocations are active simultaneously.

For example,

```
global snmptcl_info

set     iHandle [device get myproc 1.3.6.1.2.1.1.5.0]
# assuming an error didn't occur...
set     snmptcl_info($iHandle) "whatever you want"
```

does the trick quite handily.

Of course, the management application might want to block until the callback procedure is evaluated. This is accomplished by calling the context procedure with the "`wait`" option, e.g.,

```
global snmptcl_info

set     iHandle [device get myproc 1.3.6.1.2.1.1.5.0]
set     snmptcl_info($iHandle) "whatever you want"
device wait     $iHandle
```

In fact, if you didn't have to pass any data, this could be simplified to just

```
device wait [device get myproc 1.3.6.1.2.1.1.5.0]
```

Note that using the "**wait**" option doesn't block the protocol engine, or your application — it merely suspends processing of the script which made the call. This means that *Tk* will remain responsive to windowing events, that any other outstanding invocations will be processed, and so on.

Finally, although it is tempting to think of the invocation-identifier as an SNMP request-id, it is merely a unique identifier. The protocol engine will use a different request-id for each (re)transmission of a request, in order to accurately calculate the round-trip delay between the management application and the agent. Of course, the protocol engine keeps track of all outstanding (re)transmissions, so that when any response for an invocation is received, the callback procedure can be immediately invoked (and any subsequent responses ignored).

Registering for Unsolicited Messages

If the management application expects to receive traps or to take part in manager-to-manager interactions, it will need to register one or more callback procedures. This is accomplished by calling the context procedure with the "**register**" option. (The syntax for this was shown earlier in Table 2.10 back on page 75.) When a **trap** or **inform** is received, any callback procedures which are currently registered are evaluated using the same syntax as shown in Table 2.12 on page 79. There are two things to note:

- for **trap**s, it doesn't matter if the trap format used is from SNMPv1 or SNMPv2 — the protocol engine applies the convergence rules defined in the SNMPv2 standard, and always presents the trap to the management application as if it were an **snmpV2-trap**; and,

- for **inform**s, if at least one callback procedure is evaluated, then the protocol engine will automatically generate the SNMPv2 response.

option	writable	value
active		0 or 1 context is able to generate traffic
identity		OBJECT IDENTIFIER globally-unique identity of context
maxrept	√	see Table 2.9
name		string textual handle for context
nonrptr	√	see Table 2.9
resources	√	list object resources present in context
retries	√	see Table 2.9
rtrqos	√	see Table 2.9
secqos	√	see Table 2.9
timeout	√	see Table 2.9

Table 2.13: **Configuring a Context Procedure**

Configuration

There are a number of configuration options associated with a context procedure. These are shown in Table 2.13.

Although most of these were explained earlier in Table 2.9, a few require further exposition:

active: indicates whether the context procedure can be used to generate traffic (it's hard to imagine this ever not being the case, but it's left as a hook for the API);

identity: the administratively-assigned name for the management context associated with the context procedure (note this is the empty string for wildcard contexts);

name: the textual handle of the management context associated with the context procedure;

resources: a list of OBJECT IDENTIFIERs giving a coarse indication of the management information held in the management context (this is explained later in Section 3.1.4 starting on page 98).

There are three ways to invoke the "`config`" option:

- without any additional arguments, a list is returned, where each element contains an option name and associated value;

- with one additional argument, the current value of that option name is returned; or,

- with two additional arguments, the current value is returned, but the option is updated to have the specified value.

Destruction

Finally, to destroy a context procedure, use the "**destroy**" option, e.g.,

```
device destroy
```

This will cause any outstanding invocations to be terminated, and the corresponding callback procedure will be evaluated with an **eStatus** parameter of "**destroyed**".

Congratulations! You've just gotten through the hardest part of the API, understanding how context procedures work. Only one more command procedure to go, and it's easy in comparsion.

2.2.2   Management Information Knowledge

A management application needs to determine information about the management information which it communicates with the agent. The command procedure "`snmpinfo mibprop`" is used for this purpose. The syntax of this command procedure is shown in Table 2.14.

In order to understand how this command procedure works, let's recall (and expand) an earlier example:

```
printJEntry OBJECT-TYPE
    ...
    INDEX       { IMPLIED printQName, printJRank }
    ::= { printJTable 1}   -- i.e., 1.3.6.1.4.1.4.6.2.1

printJRank OBJECT-TYPE
    SYNTAX      INTEGER (0..2147483647)
    ...
    ::= { printJEntry 1 }  -- i.e., 1.3.6.1.4.1.4.6.2.1.1

printJName OBJECT-TYPE
    SYNTAX      DisplayString (SIZE (1..255))
    MAX-ACCESS  read-only
    STATUS      current
    ...
    ::= { printJEntry 2 }  -- i.e., 1.3.6.1.4.1.4.6.2.1.2

printJAction OBJECT-TYPE
    SYNTAX      INTEGER {
                    other(1), -- returned when retrieved
                    topq(2),
                    remove(3)
                }
    ...
    ::= { printJEntry 6 }  -- i.e., 1.3.6.1.4.1.4.6.2.1.6
```

This shows the skeletal outline of a table whose "row template" is called "`printJEntry`". Recall from page 14, a row template indicates how a row can be uniquely identified, usually by containing an "**INDEX**" property.

procedure	arguments	returns
snmpinfo mibprop	object property	string
	return the value of the **property** associated with the definition of object	
snmpinfo mibprop	object descriptor	string
	return the value of descriptor associated with the definition of object	
snmpinfo mibprop	object enums	list
	return a list containing the enumerations associated with the subtype associated with the **SYNTAX** property of object; each enumeration is a list containing an integer value and the associated **string**	
snmpinfo mibprop	object full	list
	return a list containing the descriptor, type, value, instance-identifier, and instance-fields associated with (the definition) of object	
snmpinfo mibprop	object range	list
	return a list containing the lower-and upper-bounds of the value of the **INTEGER** subtype associated with the **SYNTAX** property of object	
snmpinfo mibprop	object size	list
	return a list containing the lower- and upper-bounds of the value of the **SIZE** subtype associated with the **SYNTAX** property of object	
snmpinfo mibprop	object type	string
	return the name of the macro used to define object	
snmpinfo mibprop	object value	string
	return the **OBJECT IDENTIFIER** value of the definition of object	

Table 2.14: The `snmpinfo mibprop` Command Procedure

In order to print the value of the "MAX-ACCESS" property for
"printJName", either

```
puts stdout [snmpinfo mibprop printJName MAX-ACCESS]
```

or

```
puts stdout \
        [snmpinfo mibprop 1.3.6.1.4.1.4.6.2.1.2 MAX-ACCESS]
```

would suffice. This illustrates an important point about "snmpinfo
mibprop" — it accepts either descriptors or OBJECT IDENTIFIERs
which correspond to an object definition.

When using this command procedure to retrieve a property, the
property value is normally returned as a string. However, there are
two exceptions:

- for the "SYNTAX" property, only the basic syntax is returned (i.e.,
  one of the syntaxes shown in the second table on page 76) —
  textual conventions and range restrictions will be removed; for
  example, as returned by "snmpinfo mibprop" the value of the
  "SYNTAX" property for "printJRank" and "printJAction" is
  Integer32; and,

- for the "INDEX" property, a list is returned — each element containing the name of an object (possibly preceded by "IMPLIED");
  for example, according to "snmpinfo mibprop" the value of the
  "INDEX" property for "printJEntry" is a list containing:

  ```
  { IMPLIED printQName } printJRank
  ```

  which is actually useful, as the property is already parsed for
  the management application.

The first exception is not really a restriction, because "snmpinfo
mibprop" can return additional information about the "SYNTAX" property of an object. For example,

```
snmpinfo mibprop printJAction enums
```

returns an (unordered) list containing three elements:

```
{1 other} {2 topq} {3 remove}
```

(The "**enums**" option returns information for objects having a "SYNTAX" property of `Integer32` or `BIT STRING`.) Similarly,

> `snmpinfo mibprop printJRank range`

returns a list containing:

> `0 2147483647`

(The "**range**" option returns information for objects having a "SYNTAX" property of `Integer32`.) Finally,

> `snmpinfo mibprop printJName size`

returns a list containing:

> `1 255`

(The "`size`" option returns information for objects having a "SYNTAX" property of `OCTET STRING` or `DisplayString`.)

Next, suppose we had an `OBJECT IDENTIFIER` and wanted to get the corresponding descriptor, using

> `snmpinfo mibprop 1.3.6.1.4.1.4.6.2.1.2 descriptor`

would return "`printJName`". Similarly,

> `snmpinfo mibprop printJName descriptor`

would return "`1.3.6.1.4.1.4.6.2.1.2`".

However, the most useful option is "`full`" which is used to return information about a variable (an *instance* of an object). Suppose an agent told a management application about a variable called

> `1.3.6.1.4.1.4.6.2.1.2.98.97.114.110.101.121.3`

(Remember, machines use `OBJECT IDENTIFIER`s; humans use descriptors.) Recall that a variable name consists of two parts: the `OBJECT IDENTIFIER` of the defining object, and an *instance-identifier* used to distinguish the variable from other instances of the same object.

So, it would be useful if the management application could determine information about the object associated with the variable,
i.e.,

- the descriptor associated with this variable;

- the macro (e.g., "OBJECT-TYPE") used to define the object; and,

- the OBJECT IDENTIFIER associated with the object.

It would also be useful if the management application could determine
information about the instance-identifier associated with the variable.
Using the "full" option:

```
snmpinfo mibprop \
    1.3.6.1.4.1.4.6.2.1.2.98.97.114.110.101.121.3 full
```

would return a list containing:

```
printJName OBJECT-TYPE 1.3.6.1.4.1.4.6.2.1.2 \
    98.97.114.110.101.121.3 {barney 3}
```

The first three items contain information about the object definition — the descriptor, macro, and value. The last two items contain
information about the instance-identifier:

- the instance-identifier; and,

- a list containing the "instance-fields".

This second item is actually rather clever — the instance-identifier
has been analyzed according to the "INDEX" property of the row
template and then reconstituted using the "SYNTAX" property of the
objects which uniquely identify the row. For this example, the relevant
"INDEX" property is:

```
INDEX { IMPLIED printQName, printJRank }
```

and "snmpinfo mibprop" says that for the variable

```
1.3.6.1.4.1.4.6.2.1.2.98.97.114.110.101.121.3
```

the corresponding value of "printJName" is "barney" and the corresponding value of "printJRank is "3".

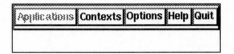

Figure 2.5: The Default Program

2.3 The Default Program

So, now that we've discussed the API, let's briefly look at the default program supplied with the API. Figure 2.5 shows its top-level window. As the user selects applications to run, they add themselves to the "`Applications`" menu-button, and perhaps add other windows below. (Recall Figure 2.1 on page 65.)

If the user click-holds on the "`Contexts`" button, then the

menu appears, and if the user click-releases over "`Select...`", then the window shown in Figure 2.2 on page 66 appears. Similarly, if the user double-clicks on the "`Options`" button, then the window shown in Figure 2.3 on page 67 appears. Finally, if the user double-clicks on the "`Help`" button, then the window shown in Figure 2.6 on the next page appears.

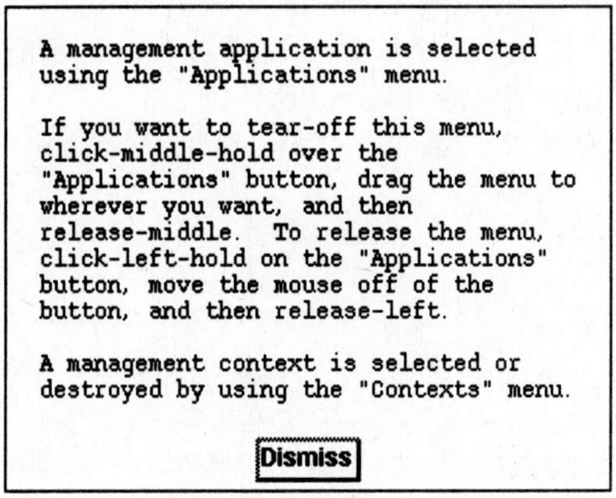

```
A management application is selected
using the "Applications" menu.

If you want to tear-off this menu,
click-middle-hold over the
"Applications" button, drag the menu to
wherever you want, and then
release-middle.  To release the menu,
click-left-hold on the "Applications"
button, move the mouse off of the
button, and then release-left.

A management context is selected or
destroyed by using the "Contexts" menu.

              Dismiss
```

Figure 2.6: The Help Window

Chapter 3

Agent Communications

In this chapter, we consider the strategies used when communicating with an agent.

SNMP is based on a model of *trap-directed polling*. Most management applications simply initiate requests to an agent, and act upon the responses. If an extraordinary event occurs, the agent sends a single, simple trap to the management application, which is then responsible for further interactions with the agent in order to determine the nature and extent of the problem. Of course, since traps are unreliable, a management application must also use low frequency polling — receipt of a trap is merely a trigger to restart the polling cycle.

In this final chapter of Part I, we start using the format employed by all the chapters in Parts II and III: we'll begin by discussing the technology involved, follow this with a look at the corresponding managed objects, and then conclude with some application fragments.

3.1   Concepts

As might be expected, management applications differ widely in their level of sophistication.

The simplest are termed *browsers*. A browsing application is one which:

- polls an agent to retrieve some values;

- performs some modest processing on the response; and,

- then displays the resulting information to the user.

The key to understanding the limitations of a browsing application is to understand the kind of processing which occurs in the second step. Basically, a browsing application doesn't have any semantic knowledge of the objects — it can understand every property **except** the `DESCRIPTION` property — so the enhancement occurring in the second step is minimal. More sophisticated management applications "understand" the objects, and so the enhancement occurring in the second step can be significant.

In this chapter, we'll focus primarily on what it takes to build a browser — not because the authors think browsers are good management applications (quite the reverse), but because the strategies used to realize a browser are also used when building superior management applications.

In order to understand how to communicate with an agent, we need to look at four concepts:

- *timestamps*, which a management application uses to determine when the agent observed something;

- *counters*, which a management application uses to calculate rates;

- *error codes*, which a management station analyzes when an operation fails; and,

- *agent capabilities*, which a management application uses to customize its interactions with an agent.

Each is now examined in turn.

3.1.1 Timestamps

An agent knows whenever the device's management subsystem is started. However, this notion of time isn't absolute for two reasons:

- the managed device might not have a clock which keeps track of time when the device is turned off; or,

- the managed device and the management station may not have their notions of absolute time synchronized (which is difficult in a network environment).

So, instead the agent keeps track only of how long it's been since the management subsystem last restarted. The unit of measurement is `TimeTicks`, which is in hundredths of a second, kept in 32–bits of precision. Thus, this value wraps roughly every 1 year, 4 months, and 10 days.

The agent's notion of its restart time is very important, and is sometime referred to as the agent's *epoch*. Whenever instrumentation keeps track of when something happened, a `TimeStamp` object is used — an object whose value is defined as the value of the agent's epoch when the event occurs. So, a `TimeStamp` object is just a snapshot of a `TimeTicks` value.

Whenever instrumentation keeps track of the difference in time between two events, a `TimeInterval` object is used. The unit of measurement continues to be hundredths of a second, but kept in 31–bits of precision.

3.1.2   Counters

In the authors' experience, counters are easily the most misunderstood data type in SNMP. Recall that a counter models a value which increases only until it reaches a maximum value, and then wraps back to zero. So, the only way to make sense of a counter object is to observe the difference between two consecutive samples.

Unfortunately, this isn't as easy as it sounds for two reasons:

- if the management application polls infrequently, a counter may wrap more than once in between two samplings; or,

- the management subsystem of the device may restart, and counters may be reset back to zero.

In both cases, information is lost and a *sampling discontinuity* is said to have occurred.

The solution to the first problem is for the management application to be configured to poll at the appropriate rate. Unfortunately, this polling interval depends on the counter being sampled. Having said that, recall that a 64–bit counter may be used only when a 32–bit quantity would wrap in less than one hour. In the absence of object-specific or user-supplied information, one hour appears to be a reasonable upper-bound.

The solution to the second problem is to always check if the management subsystem has been restarted whenever polling occurs. If so, then information may have been lost.

3.1.3   Error Codes

Earlier, on page 19, it was noted that each SNMP response contains an `error-status` field. If the value of this field is non-zero, then this indicates that the operation was not performed and that the variable bindings contained in the response are meaningless.

Table 1.4 back on page 20 listed the SNMP error codes, which are actually the error codes used in the SNMPv2 framework. So, now is as good a time as any to understand the relation between the error codes used in the two frameworks. Table 3.1 summarizes this relationship.

condition	SNMPv1	SNMPv2
permanent (any)	`tooBig`	`tooBig`
permanent (retrieval)	`noSuchName`	`noSuchObject` `noSuchInstance` `endOfMibView`
permanent (modification)	`noSuchName`	`noAccess` `noCreation` `notWritable` `inconsistentName`
logic error (modification)	`badValue`	`wrongType` `wrongLength` `wrongEncoding` `wrongValue`
transient (any)	`genErr`	`genErr`
transient (modification)	`genErr`	`resourceUnavailable` `commitFailed` `undoFailed`
transient (modification)	`badValue`	`inconsistentValue`

Table 3.1: Relation between SNMPv1/v2 Error Codes

There are two error codes which are the same:

tooBig: indicates that the response to this request would be too large to send back in a single packet; and,

genErr: a catch-all error, which shouldn't be returned unless no other recourse is available.

Otherwise, the two frameworks use different error codes. In the case of the SNMPv1 framework, the other two error codes are:

noSuchName: which indicates that a request contains a variable which isn't accessible; and,

badValue: which indicates that a `set` contains a variable/value pairing which the agent doesn't like.

Both of these are somewhat ambiguous.

On a retrieval operation (`get` or `get-next`), a `noSuchName` could be returned if:

- the agent doesn't implement the object associated with the variable; or,

- the agent implements the object, but the variable (instance of the object) doesn't exist; or,

- the agent implements the object, and the variable (instance of the object) exists, but the variable is outside the MIB view for the request.

In fact, these three correspond exactly to the three exceptional responses discussed earlier starting on page 21.

In the case of a modification operation (`set`), four different failures could result in a `noSuchName` being returned, so SNMPv2 introduced an error code for each:

noAccess: the variable is outside the MIB view for this operation;

noCreation: the variable doesn't exist, and the agent isn't able to create instances of the corresponding object type;

notWritable: the variable does exist, but the agent isn't able to modify instances of the corresponding object type; and,

inconsistentName: the variable doesn't exist, and can't be created because the instance named is inconsistent with the values of other managed objects in the agent.

In the case of `badValue`, the error code refers to either a logic error or a transient condition. Accordingly, SNMPv2 introduced several new error codes:

wrong...: which indicates that a `set` contains a value which is syntactically inconsistent with the object's definition in the MIB module; and,

inconsistentValue: which indicates that a `set` contains a value which is semantically inconsistent with the values of other variables in the agent.

In the case of this latter error code, the situation is transient, and the management application might wish to retry the request (perhaps with a different value) sometime later.

Finally, SNMPv2 added three new error codes which, in SNMPv1, were reported as `genErr`:

resourceUnavailable: which indicates that a required resource cannot be reserved to perform the `set`;

commitFailed: which indicates that an internal error prevents the agent from performing the `set`, but that the agent is in its previous state; and,

undoFailed: which indicates that an internal error prevents the agent from performing the `set`, and that the agent couldn't return to its previous state.

Unfortunately, because the SNMPv1 error codes are ambiguous, there is no algorithmic mapping between the two sets of error codes. This means that when the API invokes a callback for a context procedure, the error code in the parameter list may be either an SNMPv1 error code or an SNMPv2 error code. As such, the callback procedure must be prepared to deal with both. Earlier on page 74 we had noted that the API's protocol engine attempts to provide a uniform interface which is independent of the SNMP version in use. However, this is one area in which the convergence rules defined in the SNMPv2 standard do not provide a means for mapping between the two. Fortunately, there are several examples throughout *The Networking Management Practicum* which show a callback procedure dealing with both kinds of error codes.

3.1.4   Agent Information

Several topics were not discussed when SNMP was introduced in Section 1.1. One of these is a means whereby the limitations of a particular agent implementation can be documented. In order to see why this is useful, we need to understand how agents might be limited:

- Objects in a MIB module are specified in groups. These groups can be thought of as "units of implementation" — if an agent implements one object in a group, it should implement every object in that group. Sometimes, however, this may not be possible. For example, the underlying instrumentation may not allow monitoring or control of an object in a MIB. In this case, when a management implementation communicates with a device, it may determine that not all of the objects it was expecting to find are present.

- The "MAX-ACCESS" property for an object indicates whether monitoring and control of the object should be allowed for authorized users. Sometimes an agent implementation can provide only partial access. For example, an object might have a "MAX-ACCESS" property of "read-write", but the underlying instrumentation allows only monitoring, and not control.

- The "SYNTAX" property for an object indicates the range of possible values that an object might take on. Sometimes an agent implementation can provide only a subset of these. For example, an object might have a "SYNTAX" property containing an enumerated integer, but only a subset of those enumerations may be available with the underlying instrumentation. To complicate matters, depending on whether the object is being monitored or controlled, a different subset might be available!

- Objects in a table may be defined so that a management application can create new instances of them, i.e., the agent should permit adding new rows to a table. Sometimes an agent might require that certain columns be specified in order to create a new row.

If information on the limitations of an agent were available, a management application could customize its behavior. For example,

procedure	arguments	returns
snmpinfo agentprop	`agent object` support	`string`
	return 1 if `object` is implemented by `agent`; otherwise, return 0	
snmpinfo agentprop	`agent entry` CREATION-REQUIRES	`list`
	return a list containing any columnar objects that must be supplied for creation of an `entry` row to succeeed	
snmpinfo agentprop	`agent object` ACCESS	`string`
	return the maximum level of access that `agent` can provide to `object`	
snmpinfo agentprop	`agent object` SYNTAX	`list`
	return the `SYNTAX` restriction for reading (and perhaps writing) `object`	
snmpinfo agentprop	`agent object` WRITE-SYNTAX	`list`
	return the `SYNTAX` restriction for writing `object`	

Table 3.2: The `snmpinfo agentprop` Command Procedure

suppose the user wants to change the value of an object. If that object has a "SYNTAX" property containing an enumerated integer, the management application might display a menu and allow the user to choose one of the enumerations. If the management application knew *a priori* that the agent would allow setting the object to only a subset of the enumerations, then the menu displayed to the user could be altered accordingly. However, it should be noted that this facility was added in the SNMPv2 framework and, as of this writing, few agent implementors are distributing this information.

Nonetheless, the API provides a command procedure, "`snmpinfo agentprop`", to find out about this information. The syntax of this command procedure is shown in Table 3.2.

In order to understand how this command procedure works, the
first thing to realize is that each agent implementation knows what
collection of objects it implements. This collection is termed "the MIB
held in the agent" or, more properly, the agent's *object resources*. The
agent keeps track of this by using an OBJECT IDENTIFIER. (As one
might expect, two agents running the same software will use the same
OBJECT IDENTIFIER.) In the SNMPv2 framework, the agent uses a
table of OBJECT IDENTIFIERs — this allows agents with dynamic
components to keep track of precisely those components which are
active.

So, information on the limitations of an agent is keyed by OBJECT
IDENTIFIER. Once you know the object resources for an agent, you can
check a database to see if information is known about the limitations
of that agent.

Let's consider a few examples. To keep things simple, these examples assume that only one OBJECT IDENTIFIER is used to identify the
agent's object resources, and that the corresponding value is stored
in a variable called "orid".

First, to see if the agent supported an object called printJName,

```
snmpinfo agentprop $orid printJName support
```

would be called. If the return value was "1", then the database of
agent information indicates that the agent should support it. Note
that if the database doesn't have any information on an agent implementation, then an error return is used. So, the best way to call this
command procedure is inside "catch", e.g.,

```
set support 0
catch { set support [snmpinfo agentprop $orid \
                     printJName support] }
```

If no information is available on an agent implementation, the set
command will never be executed.

Next, suppose a MIB module defined an object, `tcpConnState`, as "**read-write**", and we wanted to see if the agent implements it for both reading and writing, then

```
set access [snmpinfo agentprop $orid tcpConnState ACCESS]
```

would do the trick. Note that if this command procedure returns the empty string, then it indicates that the database of information on agent implementations does have information on the agent but that the agent doesn't have any limitations.

So, to determine the actual level of support, use

```
set access [snmpinfo mibprop tcpConnState MAX-ACCESS]
if {[set info [snmpinfo agentprop $orid tcpConnState \
                ACCESS]] != ""}
    set access $info
}
```

which first retrieves the value of the **MAX-ACCESS** property for the object, and then sees if the agent does anything different.

Suppose we wanted to find out which enumerations of an object, `printJAction`, were supported by an agent. Whilst the command

```
snmpinfo mibprop printJAction enums
```

returns a list containing:

```
{3 remove} {2 topq} {1 other}
```

the command

```
snmpinfo agentprop $orid printJAction SYNTAX
```

might return a list containing:

```
enums 1 2
```

which indicates that only enumerations 1 and 2 are supported by the agent implementation.

Similarly, if we were interested in range information about an object, the command

```
snmpinfo mibprop printJRank range
```

returns a list containing:

```
0 2147483647
```

whilst the command

```
snmpinfo agentprop $orid printJRank SYNTAX
```

might return a list containing:

```
range 0 255
```

which indicates the range is more restrictive than the one defined in the MIB module.

In both of these two examples, if the final argument was

```
WRITE-SYNTAX
```

instead of

```
SYNTAX
```

then the information returned would be about the agent's limitations when modifying the object. So, if the management application is interested in retrievals, it need check only "SYNTAX"; but, if it's interested in modifications, then it should first check "WRITE-SYNTAX", and if the return value is the empty string, then it should check "SYNTAX".

Finally, back on page 82, it was noted that a context procedure has a special configuration option, "resources", which is initialized to contain the identities of all the object resources in the agent, e.g., given a context procedure called "agent"

```
agent config resources
```

returns a list containing the OBJECT IDENTIFIERs used to identify the object resources contained in the agent. (Later, in Section 3.3.1, we'll see how this information is determined.)

So, a more realistic example to determine if there was any syntax restrictions when writing a variable, e.g., `ipDefaultTTL`, might look something like this:

```
set syntax ""
foreach orid [agent config resources] {
    if {[catch { set syntax [snmpinfo agentprop $orid \
                                       ipDefaultTTL \
                                       WRITE-SYNTAX] }]} {
        continue
    } elseif {$syntax == ""} {
        set syntax [snmpinfo agentprop $orid \
                             ipDefaultTTL SYNTAX]
        break
    }
    if {$syntax != ""} {
        break
    }
}
```

Note that the "`catch`" isn't necessary for the second call to "`snmpinfo agentprop`", because we already know that the database has information on the agent implementation.

Even in a more perfect world, there would be a need for a "snmpinfo agentprop" command procedure — experience with the SNMPv1 framework, which has no such capability, suggested this addition. So, the authors hope that agent implementors will now make this information widely available. As a reader of *The Networking Management Practicum*, you can help by asking your agent suppliers to do their share: just indicate that you want them to publish the `AGENT-CAPABILITIES` definition of their agents!

3.2 Objects

Recall from page 98, that objects in a MIB module are specified in groups. A group is a "unit of implementation" — if an agent implements one object in a group, it should implement every object in that group.

In this chapter, we'll look at two groups which every agent must implement. These groups aren't used for agent management (discussion on that topic is postponed until Chapter 9). Instead, these groups are used to make sense of the information returned by the agent.

However, before we look at these two groups, it's useful to introduce a modeling technique used when studying MIB objects.

3.2.1 Case Diagrams

It is often useful to pictorially represent the relationship between MIB objects in a protocol entity. A useful tool, the *Case Diagram*, was developed for this purpose [21].[1]

When designing a MIB module, it is often considered good practice to avoid defining objects which can be derived from other objects. In the case of counter objects, this means that the objects must not be (easily) related arithmetically. Case Diagrams are used to visualize the flow of management information in a layer and thereby mark where counters are incremented. This helps to decide if an object meets the arithmetic-derivability criterion.

Consider an example of a Case Diagram shown in Figure 3.1. According to this diagram, two invariants hold:

- the number of packets received from the layer below is equal to:

$$inErrors + forwPackets + inDelivers$$

- the number of packets sent to the layer below is equal to:

$$outRequests + forwPackets$$

---

[1]The term Case Diagram is named after the eminent Professor Case. The term was coined by Craig Partridge, then-chair of the working group which produced MIB-I.

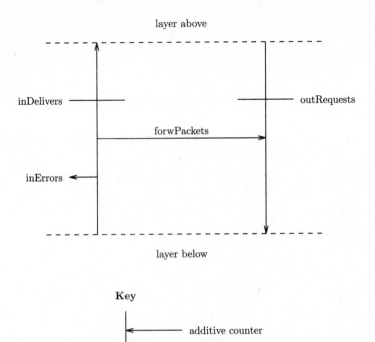

Figure 3.1: Example of a Case Diagram

In addition, the diagram also indicates that inErrors is checked before forwPackets, and so on.

The limitation of Case Diagrams is that they imply a sequential flow. Many error-counting objects can be incremented from anywhere inside a protocol entity. From a visual perspective, however, the error counter is incremented only in one place. Of course, since they are meant to be pictorially simple, they cannot convey any complex semantics. Thus, a Case Diagram is an aid to, not a substitute for, a textual MIB description.

Now we can proceed to look at some objects.

3.2.2   The system Group

All agents must implement the **system** group. This group is defined in a MIB module called MIB-II, or the Internet-standard MIB [3].

The objects in this group are:

sysUpTime (TimeTicks): the agent's epoch;

sysObjectID (OBJECT IDENTIFIER): the identity of the agent's object resources;

sysDescr (DisplayString): description of device;

sysServices (INTEGER sum): services offered by device;

sysContact (DisplayString): name of contact person;

sysName (DisplayString): device name; and,

sysLocation (DisplayString): device's physical location.

By now, the first two of these should be very familiar to the reader: **sysUpTime** indicates how long ago the management subsystem last restarted; and **sysObjectID** is used when finding out if an agent is limited in some way. (**sysDescr** can be thought of as the textual equivalent of **sysObjectID** — something meaningful to a human.)

sysServices is a concise means of determining the set of services which corresponds to the device's primary purpose. It is an integer-value, initially zero. Then for each layer, L, in the range 1 through 7, for which the device performs transactions, the number 2^{L-1} is added to the value. For example, a device which performs only routing functions would have a value of $2^{3-1} = 4$. The layers are:

layer	functionality	2^{L-1}
1	physical (e.g., repeaters)	1
2	data-link (e.g., bridges)	2
3	internet (e.g., supports IP)	4
4	end-to-end (e.g., supports TCP)	8
7	application (e.g., supports SMTP)	64

(Back on page 12, we saw an example of how this summed integer might be expressed using the BIT STRING syntax.)

3.2.3 The snmpOR Group

The definition of `sysObjectID` assumes that the agent's object resources, "the MIB held by an agent", are rather static. Some agents, however, are able to dynamically acquire new object resources.

To model this, all SNMPv2 agents must implement the `snmpOR` group from the `SNMPv2-MIB` [14]. This group contains two top-level objects: a timestamp, called `snmpORLastChange`, indicating the last time the table of dynamic object resources changed, and a single table containing information on those dynamic object resources. Each row of the table has three columns:

snmpORIndex (positive `INTEGER`): the index of this entry in the table;

snmpORID (`OBJECT IDENTIFIER`): the identity of a subset of the agent's object resources, analogous to `sysObjectID`; and,

snmpORDescr (`DisplayString`): a textual description of a subset of the agent's object resources, analogous to `sysDescr`.

In an agent which can't acquire new object resources, this table is usually empty. However, some static agents might have exactly one row in this table, which duplicates the information found in `sysObjectID` and `sysDescr`. (In fact, this is a desirable strategy for an SNMPv2 agent, in that the earliest SNMPv1 agents used `sysObjectID` to refer to the hardware configuration of the device running the agent.)

3.3   Applications

Finally, we get to look at some application fragments. Let's start by looking at four activities that form the core of most browsers, to illustrate all of the concepts throughout Part I.

Note that the application fragments in this chapter are considerably different from the fragments in the chapters which follow. The reason is that this chapter focuses not on managing agents, but on using SNMP to talk to an agent. As such, all of these fragments are fairly low-level. In contrast, the application fragments in later chapters will focus on using SNMP for management. So, think of the remainder of this chapter as unifying all the themes we've introduced throughout Part I.

Finally, don't bother typing in any of the application fragments which are in *The Networking Management Practicum* — on page 492 there's information on how to retrieve everything.

set	snmptcl_var_sysObjectID	[snmpinfo mibprop sysObjectID value]
set	snmptcl_var_sysUpTime	[snmpinfo mibprop sysUpTime value]
set	snmptcl_var_snmpORID	[snmpinfo mibprop snmpORID value]
agent	config	resources ""
agent	bulk	snmptcl_callback_getresources \
		[**list** [**list** $snmptcl_var_sysObjectID] \
		[**list** $snmptcl_var_snmpORID]] \
		−maxrept 10 −nonrptr 1

10

Figure 3.2: Initializing the `resources` Configuration Option

3.3.1 Determining an Agent's Object Resources

The first thing a browser normally does is start talking to an agent. Let's assume that a new context procedure, called "`agent`", has been defined, and we want to to initialize the "`resources`" configuration option for this context procedure.

Figure 3.2 shows how the process begins. First, three global variables are initialized to contain the `OBJECT IDENTIFIER` values of three MIB objects. Then, the "`resources`" configuration option is set to the empty string. Finally, the context procedure is invoked to perform a `get-bulk` operation, retrieving:

- the first variable in the agent after `sysObjectID` (which should be `sysObjectID.0`); and,

- no more than ten variables after `snmpORID` (which should be any instances of this column).

The choice of ten is based on a heuristic — most agents have only a few (if any) entries in this table.

All the work is done in "snmptcl_callback_getresources", which is shown in Figure 3.3. (You might want to refer back to Table 2.12 on page 79 to recall how a callback procedure is invoked.)

First, it uses the "global" command procedure to access the OBJECT IDENTIFIER variables defined earlier in Figure 3.2. Next, the error-status of the response is consulted to see if it's noSuchName. If so:

- we know we're talking to an SNMPv1 agent (so the get-bulk was mapped automatically by the API's protocol engine to a get-next);

- if the error-index doesn't refer to the second variable binding, then the agent is claiming that it has no variables after sysObjectID — that is, the agent claims it can't return sysObjectID.0 — which means that something is very, very wrong; otherwise,

- the agent has indicated that there aren't any variables after snmpORID, which, for an SNMPv1–only agent, is usually the case. So, the context procedure (passed as the "pHandle" parameter), is again invoked, this time to perform a get-next operation, hopefully to retrieve sysObjectID.0 and sysUpTime.0 (which follows it), objects which all agents are required to implement.

Regardless, if an error-status other than noError is returned, the callback procedure returns.

Otherwise, we loop through the variable bindings ("vBinds"). Recall that each variable binding consists of a triple:

- the OBJECT IDENTIFIER naming the variable;

- the syntax associated with the variable; and,

- the value associated with the variable.

So, the first test is to see if an exceptional value was returned for the variable. For example, if no variables following snmpORID were in the MIB view, then an SNMPv2 agent would return the exceptional value of endOfMibView. This would likely be the case for an SNMPv2 agent

```
proc snmptcl_callback_getresources {pHandle iHandle eStatus eIndex vBinds} {
    global     snmptcl_var_sysObjectID snmptcl_var_snmpORID
    global     snmptcl_var_sysUpTime

    switch -- $eStatus {
        noSuchName {
            if {$eIndex == 2} {
                $pHandle     next   snmptcl_callback_getresources \
                                    [list [list $snmptcl_var_sysObjectID] \
                                          [list $snmptcl_var_sysUpTime]]          10
            }
        }
    }
    if {$eStatus != "noError"} {
        return
    }

    set     reslist     ""
    set     lastvar     ""
    foreach   vb          $vBinds {                                               20
        if {(([set syntax [lindex $vb 1]] == "exception") \
                || ($syntax == "error"))} {
            continue
        }

        set   var          [lindex $vb 0]
        if {(("$snmptcl_var_sysObjectID.0" == $var) \
                || ([snmptcl_proc_oidcontains $snmptcl_var_snmpORID $var]))} {
            lappend   reslist [lindex $vb 2]
            set            lastvar    $var                                        30
        } else {
            set        lastvar ""
            break
        }
    }

    set     resources    [$pHandle config resources]
    foreach   res          $reslist {
        if {[lsearch -exact $resources $res] < 0} {
            lappend   resources    $res                                           40
        }
    }
    $pHandle   config       resources $resources

    if {$lastvar != ""} {
        $pHandle     bulk    snmptcl_callback_getresources \
                            [list [list $lastvar]] \
                            -maxrept 10 -nonrptr 0
    }                                                                             50
}
```

Figure 3.3: The `snmptcl_callback_getresources` procedure

which isn't able to dynamically acquire new object resources. (Of course, the API's protocol engine could have encountered a difficulty in understanding the value, so a check is made for "error" in addition to "exception".) Next, the variable's name is extracted and a test is made to see if it is either sysObjectID.0 or an instance of snmpORID. (Notice how *Tcl*'s variable-substitution rules are used:

```
$snmptcl_var_sysObjectID.0
```

says to append ".0" to the value of the variable

```
snmptcl_var_sysObjectID
```

in the comparison statement.) If so, the value associated with the variable is appended to the list "reslist", and the variable "lastvar" is set to the name of the variable. Otherwise, the variable "lastvar" is set to the empty string, and the loop terminates.

When the loop terminates, one of two conditions holds:

- all instances of snmpORID were retrieved (and "lastvar" is set to the empty string); or,

- additional instances of snmpORID may still be unknown (and "lastvar" is set to the name of the last instance retrieved).

Next, each OBJECT IDENTIFIER value retrieved is compared to the existing "resources" configuration option, and any values not present are added.

Finally, if additional instances of snmpORID may still be unknown, then another get-bulk is invoked, using the last instance retrieved as the starting point. Note that the first variable returned by this request will be the first variable after the last instance retrieved — which will be the next instance of snmpORID, if one exists!

In addition to demonstrating how get-bulk (or get-next) can be used to retrieve all instances (if any) of a variable, this application fragment also illustrates the difference between error responses and responses containing exceptional values. If a non-zero error-status is returned, the response has very little useful information — so when talking to an SNMPv1 agent, an additional request is issued; but, if the response doesn't indicate an error, then any non-exceptional values in the variable bindings can be used.

```
proc snmptcl_proc_oidcontains {parent child} {
    if {[string match $parent.* $child]} {
        return  1
    }
    if {"$parent" == "$child"} {
        return  1
    }
    return        0
}
```

Figure 3.4: The snmptcl_proc_oidcontains procedure

So, how can we tell if a variable is an instance of an object? Figure 3.4 shows a command procedure which returns 1 if its "child" parameter is an instance of its "parent" parameter.

The algorithm is based on two observations:

- the API represents OBJECT IDENTIFIERs as a sequence of integers separated by dots, e.g., the OBJECT IDENTIFIER for snmpORID is "1.3.6.1.6.3.1.1.3.2.1.2"; and,

- an instance of an object is formed by starting with the object's OBJECT IDENTIFIER.

Hence, the check is as simple as calling "string match" which checks to see if the "child" string starts with "parent".[2]

---

[2]Because this command procedure is invoked in the inner-loop of many management applications, in the authors' implementation "snmptcl_proc_oidcontains" is coded in *C* and then exported into the *Tcl* interpreter.

```
set        iHandle  [agent get snmptcl_getscalar_callback \
                         [list [list [snmpinfo mibprop $descr value].0]]]
set        snmptcl_info($iHandle) [list $descriptor]
```

Figure 3.5: Getting the Value of a Scalar

3.3.2   Getting, then Setting, a Scalar

Suppose we want to define a command procedure which will display
the value of a scalar variable to the user and then ask for a new value.
Figure 3.5 shows how the process begins. We assume that the variable
"`descr`" contains the descriptor of the object to be retrieved and then
set. The context procedure is invoked to perform a `get` operation,
retrieving the ".0" instance (the one and only instance for a scalar
object). Then the array "`snmptcl_info`" is used to store information
for the callback procedure "`snmptcl_getscalar_callback`".

Figure 3.6 starting on page 115 shows the callback procedure.
First, the information passed in "`snmptcl_info`" is retrieved, and
that element in the array is removed (as it will no longer be referenced). Next, a check is made that an exceptional value isn't present
and that the API's protocol engine could understand the value. If all
is well, then "`value`" is set to the value associated with the variable,
and a check is made to see if the object is an enumerated integer,
and, if so, "`value`" is set to the corresponding textual enumeration.
Otherwise, if there was a problem with the value, "`value`" is set to
the empty string.

The next step is to see if this agent implementation has any
syntax restrictions when writing this variable. An algorithm similar
to the one shown earlier on page 103 is used to initialize the variable
"`srs`" accordingly. If the object is an enumerated integer, and an
enumeration restriction is present, then the list of enumerations is
trimmed accordingly. Similarly, a check is made to see if the object
is an integer range, and a range restriction is present; if so, the value
of "`range`" is updated accordingly.

```
proc snmptcl_getscalar_callback {pHandle iHandle eStatus eIndex vBinds} {
    global          snmptcl_info

    set             data      $snmptcl_info($iHandle)
    unset           snmptcl_info($iHandle)

    set             vb        [lindex $vBinds 0]
    set             var       [lindex $vb 0]
    if {($eStatus == "noError") \
            && ([set syntax [lindex $vb 1]] != "exception") \            10
            && ($syntax != "error")} {
        set         value     [lindex $vb 2]
        if {([set enums [snmpinfo mibprop [lindex $vb 0] enums]] != "") \
                && ([set enum [lsearch −glob $enums "$value *"]] >= 0)} {
            set             value     [lindex [lindex $enums $enum] 1]
        }
    } else {
        set         value     ""
    }
                                                                         20
    set             srs                 ""
    foreach         resource            [set resources [$pHandle config resources]] {
        catch { set srs [snmpinfo agentprop $resource $var WRITE−SYNTAX] }
        if {$srs == ""} {
            catch { set srs [snmpinfo agentprop $resource $var SYNTAX] }
        }
        if {$srs != ""} {
            break
        }
    }                                                                    30

    if {(([set enums [snmpinfo mibprop $var enums]] != "") \
            && ([lindex $srs 0] == "enum")} {
        set         enew                ""
        foreach sr                      $srs {
            if {[set enum [lsearch −glob $enums "$sr *"]] >= 0} {
                lappend enew            [list $sr [lindex [lindex $enums $enum] 1]]
            } else {
                lappend enew            [list $sr $sr]
            }                                                            40
        }
        set         enums               $enew
    }

    set             range               [snmpinfo mibprop $var range]
    if {[lindex $srs 0] == "range"} {
        set         range               [lrange $srs 1 end]
    }
```

Figure 3.6: The **snmptcl_getscalar_callback** procedure

```
# create a new top-level window, $w

    set         array           snmptcl_array[join [split $w "."] "_"]
    global      $array
    upvar #0    $array          varinfo
    catch { unset varinfo }

    set         varinfo(pHandle) \
                                $pHandle
    set         varinfo(w)       $w                                              10
    set         varinfo(title)   ...
    set         varinfo(descr)   $descr
    set         varinfo(var)     $var
    set         varinfo(syntax)  [snmpinfo mibprop $var SYNTAX]
    set         varinfo(value)   $value
    set         varinfo(enums)   $enums

    if {$enums == ""} {
# create a label containing the descriptor
    } else {                                                                     20
# create a menu-button with a menu for each enumeration
# if the user selects one, call snmptcl_proc_setscalar
# with the corresponding value
    }
# to the right of this create an entry widget for the user to
# type in a new value

    if {$range != ""} {
# create a slider going from the smallest acceptable value
# to the largest                                                                 30
    }

# finally, create Confirm and Cancel buttons
# on confirmation, call snmptcl_proc_setscalar with the value
# entered by the user
}
```

Figure 3.6: The `snmptcl_getscalar_callback` procedure (cont.)

For example, if the value of "**enums**" initially was:

    {3 remove} {2 topq} {1 other}

and the value of "**srs**" was:

    enums 1 2

then the new value of "**enums**" would be:

    {1 other} {2 topq}

Then, a unique window name is created, and a unique array name, known locally as "**varinfo**", is generated from that. The array is initialized to store information used later on. Finally, some GUI code is performed to build a window hierarchy. This is omitted from the application fragment because it adds nothing to the discussion on management. However, Figures 3.7 through 3.9 on page 118 show what the user might see. The first figure shows what a window for **sysLocation** looks like. The second figure, Figure 3.8, shows what a window for the enumerated integer **ipForwarding** looks like. Because the "**ipForwarding:**" button is a menu, if the user click-holds on it, then the

menu appears, allowing the user to click-release over one of the choices. Finally, Figure 3.9 shows what a window for an integer range looks like. If the user click-releases over the "**Cancel**" button of any of these windows, no further action is taken. Otherwise, if the user clicks on "**Confirm**", then "**snmptcl_proc_setscalar_aux**" is invoked.

Figure 3.10 on page 119 shows the command procedure which is invoked when the user clicks on the "**Confirm**" button. First, the private array is accessed as "**varinfo**". If the object is an enumerated integer, and the user supplied a textual enumeration, then the numeric value is retrieved. Then, the context procedure is invoked to set the variable. If an error is generated, then a dialog box is presented to the user explaining the reason ("**result**"); otherwise, if the **set** operation was accepted by the API, then the global array "**snmptcl_info**" is used to pass information to the callback procedure.

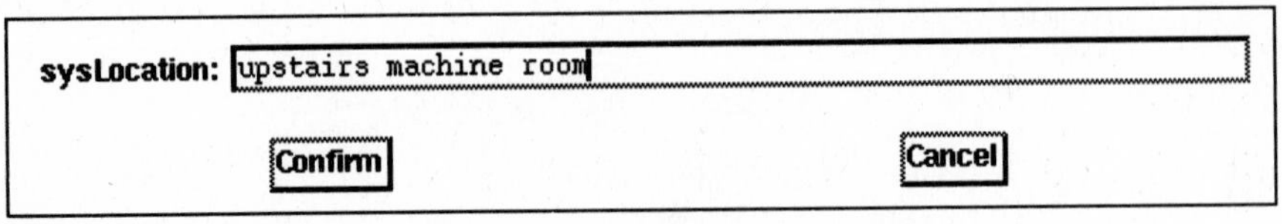

sysLocation: upstairs machine room

[Confirm]   [Cancel]

Figure 3.7: A Window to Set sysLocation

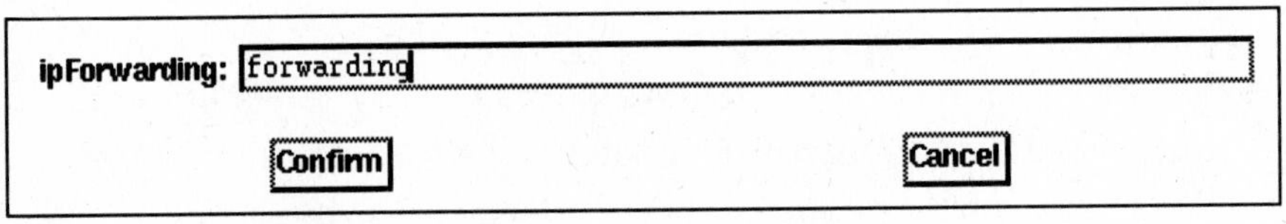

ipForwarding: forwarding

[Confirm]   [Cancel]

Figure 3.8: A Window to Set ipForwarding

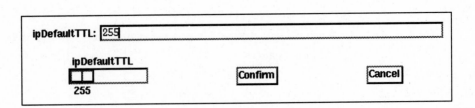

ipDefaultTTL: 255

ipDefaultTTL

255   [Confirm]   [Cancel]

Figure 3.9: A Window to Set ipDefaultTTL

```
proc snmptcl_proc_setscalar_aux {w array} {
    global          snmptcl_info

    global          $array
    upvar #0        $array              varinfo

    set             value   $varinfo(value)
    foreach         enum    $varinfo(enums) {
        if {[lindex $enum 1] == "$value"} {
            set     varinfo(value)      [lindex $enum 0]
            break
        }
    }

    if {[catch { set iHandle [$varinfo(pHandle) set \
                            snmptcl_setscalar_callback \
                            [list [list $varinfo(var).0 \
                                        $varinfo(syntax) \
                                        $varinfo(value)]]] } result]} {
        snmptcl_dialog  $varinfo(title) $result questhead 0 Abort
        unset           varinfo
    } else {
        set             snmptcl_info($iHandle)       $array
    }

# finally, destroy window which invoked us
}
```

Figure 3.10: The **snmptcl_proc_setscalar_aux** procedure

The callback procedure is shown in Figure 3.11 starting on page 121. It begins by accessing the private array as "`varinfo`". Then the **error-status** is consulted. If there was no error reported by the agent, a success window is displayed to the user. Otherwise, the routine decides if the error is permanent or transient. Based on this, it will present a dialog box to the user with the appropriate action selected as the result, either "`Retry`", "`Try New Value`", or "`Abort`". Figure 3.12 on page 122 shows what such a dialog box might look like (when the default action is the final alternative of the three).

```
proc snmptcl_setscalar_callback {pHandle iHandle eStatus eIndex vBinds} {
    global          snmptcl_info snmptcl_browsing_icon

    set             data    $snmptcl_info($iHandle)
    unset           snmptcl_info($iHandle)
    set             array   [lindex $data 0]

    global          $array
    upvar #0         $array              varinfo

    switch -- $eStatus {                                             10
        noError {
# create a new top-level window indicating success...

            unset           varinfo
            return
        }

        genErr
        -
        resourceUnavailable                                          20
        -
        commitFailed
        -
        undoFailed
        -
        timeout {
            set             offset   0
        }

        wrongValue {                                                 30
            set             offset   1
        }

        default {
            set             offset   2
        }
    }
}
```

Figure 3.11: The `snmptcl_setscalar_callback` procedure

```
switch [snmptcl_dialog "Agent Error for $varinfo(title)" \
                $eStatus question $offset Retry "Try New Value" Abort] {
    0 {
        set      iHandle      [$varinfo(pHandle) set \
                              snmptcl_setscalar_callback \
                              [list [list $varinfo(var).0 \
                                         $varinfo(syntax) \
                                         $varinfo(value)]]]
        set      snmptcl_info($iHandle) \
                      $array                                          10
    }

    1 {
        set          iHandle  [$varinfo(pHandle) get \
                              snmptcl_getscalar_callback \
                              [list [list $varinfo(var).0]]]
        set      snmptlc_info($iHandle) \
                      [list $varinfo(descr)]
        unset    varinfo
    }                                                                20

    default {
        unset    varinfo
    }
  }
}
```

Figure 3.11: The `snmptcl_setscalar_callback` procedure (cont.)

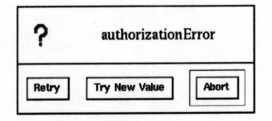

Figure 3.12: A Dialog Box

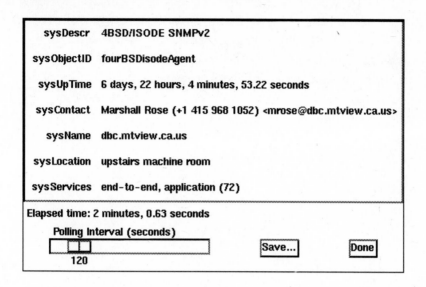

Figure 3.13: A Window Browsing the `system` Group

3.3.3 Polling Selected Instances

Suppose we want to poll a collection of instances on a regular interval and display those values to the user. For example, Figure 3.13 shows what a window displaying the `system` group might look like. So, let's take a look at how to build a routine that implements the basic polling algorithm. This is going to be a lengthy and detailed application fragment, so readers who don't really care about the "fine print of SNMP coding" may wish to skip ahead to Section 3.3.5 starting on page 148. Otherwise, turn the page...

Figure 3.14 shows how the process begins. A unique window name is created, and a unique array name, known locally as "`ainfo`", is generated, and some GUI code is performed to build a window hierarchy. Next, `sysUpTime.0` is put at the front of the list of variables to poll. The context procedure is invoked to perform a **get** operation, and "`ainfo(segs)`" is incremented to keep track of the number of requests outstanding. Finally, "`snmptcl_info`" is used to pass information to the callback procedure, specifically the name of the array and the list of variables that were requested (excluding `sysUpTime.0`).

```
# create a new top-level window, $w

    set         array          snmptcl_array[join [split $w "."] "_"]
    global      ${array}_info
    upvar #0    ${array}_info   ainfo

    set         ainfo(toplevel)  $w
    set         ainfo(title)     ...

# list of OIDs to poll
    set         ainfo(vars)      $vars

# how many seconds between polls
    set         ainfo(interval)  $interval

# iteration number
    set         ainfo(iter)      0

# number of requests in progress for this iteration
    set         ainfo(segs)      0

# the left-edge of the current sampling continuity
    set         ainfo(startime)  ""

# the right-edge of the current sampling continuity
    set         ainfo(lastime)   ""

# command to evaluate each time an iteration completes
    set         ainfo(command)   $command

# create four sub-windows:
#    one for the actual information (initially empty)
#    a label for the elapsed time
#    a slider for the polling interval
#    a command-button for Done

    set         vars             [concat $snmptcl_var_sysUpTime.0 $vars]
    set         iHandle          [agent get snmptcl_poll_callback $vars]
    incr        ainfo(segs)
    set         snmptcl_info($iHandle) \
                                 [list $array [lrange $vars 1 end]]
```

10

20

30

40

Figure 3.14: Preparing to Poll Selected Instances

Figure 3.15 starting on page 127 shows the callback procedure. First, the information passed in "`snmptcl_info`" is retrieved:

array: the prefix of the global name of the private array used to keep information between polling intervals; and,

lvars: the list of variables that the agent was asked to return for this request.

Then the element in the "`snmptcl_info`" array containing that information is removed. Next, the private array is accessed as "`ainfo`", and a check is made to see if the array still exists. If not, then after the polling interval began, but before the agent returned a response, the user clicked on the "`Done`" button. In this case, the response is irrelevant. Otherwise, some more information is extracted from the private array, and the number of outstanding requests is decremented. Next, a second private array, which holds information about each variable we've seen, is accessed as "`avar`".

```
proc snmptcl_poll_callback {pHandle iHandle eStatus eIndex vBinds} {
    global          snmptcl_info snmptcl_var_sysUpTime

    set             data            $snmptcl_info($iHandle)
    unset           snmptcl_info($iHandle)
    set             array           [lindex $data 0]
    set             lvars           [lindex $data 1]

    global          ${array}_info
    upvar #0        ${array}_info   ainfo                              10
    if {![info exists ainfo(toplevel)]} {
# user clicked on Done
        return
    }
    set             w               $ainfo(toplevel)
    set             iter            $ainfo(iter)
    incr            ainfo(segs)     −1

    global          ${array}_var
    upvar #0        ${array}_var    avar                               20
```

Figure 3.15: The `snmptcl_poll_callback` procedure

Then, a check is made to see if the response is really a timeout. If so, a simple heuristic is applied:

- if this request asked for at least 20 variables,

- then it is possible that the request we sent was too large for the agent to receive, so the agent couldn't even send back a `tooBig` error in response.

So, the heuristic says to pretend that the agent did send back a `tooBig`. Next, the `error-status` is checked:

- if a `noSuchName` was returned for something other than the first variable (`sysUpTime.0`), then we retry the request, removing the offending variable; otherwise,

- if a `tooBig` was returned for a request asking for more than one variable, then we split the request into two requests.

For either situation, "`ainfo(segs)`" is incremented, and the array "`snmptcl_info`" is updated accordingly. The `tooBig` situation makes it clear why we need to keep track of the number of requests outstanding, whilst both situations make it clear why we keep track both of the variables we asked for in the request, and the variables we're interested in polling for!

```
if {($eStatus == "timeout") && ([llength $lvars] >= 20)} {
    set      eStatus           tooBig
}
switch -- $eStatus {
    noSuchName {
        if {$eIndex > 1} {
            incr      eIndex    -2
            set       vars      [concat $snmptcl_var_sysUpTime.0 \
                                   [lreplace $lvars $eIndex $eIndex]]
            set       iHandle   [$pHandle get snmptcl_poll_callback $vars]   10
            incr      ainfo(segs)
            set       snmptcl_info($iHandle) \
                                [list $array [lrange $vars 1 end]]
            return
        }
    }

    tooBig {
        if {[set eIndex [llength $lvars]] > 1} {
            set       hIndex    [expr $eIndex/2]                             20

            set       vars      [concat $snmptcl_var_sysUpTime.0 \
                                   [lrange $lvars 0 [expr $hIndex-1]]]
            set       iHandle   [$pHandle get snmptcl_poll_callback $vars]
            incr      ainfo(segs)
            set       snmptcl_info($iHandle) \
                                [list $array [lrange $vars 1 end]]

            set       vars      [concat $snmptcl_var_sysUpTime.0 \
                                   [lrange $lvars $hIndex end]]              30
            set       iHandle   [$pHandle get snmptcl_poll_callback $vars]
            incr      ainfo(segs)
            set       snmptcl_info($iHandle) \
                                [list $array [lrange $vars 1 end]]
            return
        }
    }
}
```

Figure 3.15: The `snmptcl_poll_callback` procedure (cont.)

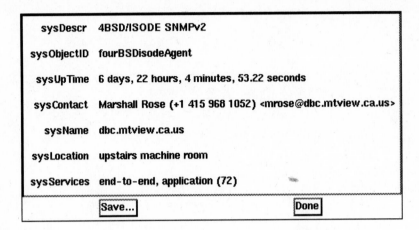

Figure 3.16: A Window Orphaned when Browsing the `system` Group

Next, the `error-status` is checked again:

- if the context procedure was `destroyed` (by the user), then the window is "orphaned" — the polling process is terminated, but the window containing the information remains (e.g., see Figure 3.16); or,

- on any other error, a dialog box is presented to the user, asking whether the operation should be retried, or the window should be orphaned, or the polling process should be terminated and the window destroyed.

```
switch -- $eStatus {
    noError {
    }

    destroyed {
# remove label for the elapsed time
# remove slider for the polling interval
# delete private arrays
        return
    }                                                                    10

    default {
        switch [snmptcl_dialog "Agent Error for $ainfo(title)" \
                $eStatus question 0 Retry Orphan Abort] {
            0 {
                set     vars        [concat $snmptcl_var_sysUpTime.0 \
                                    $lvars]
                set     iHandle     [$pHandle get snmptcl_poll_callback \
                                    $vars]
                incr    ainfo(segs)                                       20
                set     snmptcl_info($iHandle) \
                                    [list $array [lrange $vars 1 end]]
                return
            }

            1 {
# remove label and slider, delete private arrays
                return
            }
                                                                         30
            default {
# destroy window, delete private arrays
                return
            }
        }
    }
}
```

Figure 3.17: The `snmptcl_poll_callback` procedure (cont.)

Next, the first variable binding is examined. If the binding isn't `sysUpTime.0`, a dialog box is presented to the user indicating the agent is *hosed*. Otherwise, a check is made to determine whether an exceptional value is present or the API's protocol engine couldn't understand the value. If so, `sysUpTime` is treated as not available, and the largest possible value will be remembered for the next iteration in order to force a sampling discontinuity. If all is well:

- if this is the first value of `sysUpTime` we've retrieved, we note that we are starting a new sampling continuity; otherwise,

- if the current value is smaller than the value retrieved on the previous iteration, we note that a sampling discontinuity has occurred due to agent re-start; otherwise,

- once we have completed the first iteration, we note the length of the current sampling continuity.

Regardless, we remember the new value as the right-edge of the current sampling continuity.

```
    set         vb        [lindex $vBinds 0]
    if {"$snmptcl_var_sysUpTime.0" != [lindex $vb 0]} {
        snmptcl_dialog    "Agent Error for $ainfo(title)" \
      "instead of sysUpTime.0, got [snmptcl_proc_oid2ode [lindex $vb 0]]" \
                            warning 0 Abort
# destroy window, delete private arrays
        return
    }
    if {(([set syntax [lindex $vb 1]] == "exception") \
         || ($syntax == "error")} {                                       10
        set       sysUpTime     4294967296.0
        set       ainfo(startime)    ""
        set       ainfo(lastime)     ""
# set elapsed time label to
#      "sysUpTime not available, so no information on counters"
    } else {
        set       sysUpTime     [lindex $vb 2]
        if {[set startime $ainfo(startime)] == ""} {
            set       ainfo(startime)        $sysUpTime
# set elapsed time label to
#      "just started, so information on counters is unavailable"        20
        } elseif {$ainfo(lastime) > $sysUpTime} {
            set       ainfo(startime)        $sysUpTime
# set elapsed time label to
#      "agent re-started, so information on counters is unavailable"
        } elseif {$iter} {
# set elasped time label to $sysUpTime-$startime
        }
        set       ainfo(lastime)     $sysUpTime
    }                                                                      30
```

Figure 3.17: The **snmptcl_poll_callback** procedure (cont.)

Next, we cycle through the remaining variable bindings for each, making sure that the agent returned the right variable. If an exceptional value is encountered, or the API's protocol engine couldn't understand the value, that variable is skipped. Otherwise, the element in the "avar" array which corresponds to this variable is updated:

lindex 0: the number of the current iteration;

lindex 1: the variable's value for the previous iteration;

lindex 2: the value of sysUpTime for the previous iteration;

lindex 3: the variable's value at the beginning of the sampling continuity;

lindex 4: the variable's value for the current iteration;

lindex 5: the value of sysUpTime for the current iteration; and,

lindex 6: the variable's syntax.

The update rules are simple:

- if we haven't created an element for this variable in the array "avar", then we create an entry for it; otherwise,

- if the value of sysUpTime for the previous iteration is larger than the current value, then the entry is updated for a sampling discontinuity; otherwise,

- the entry is updated for the current iteration.

These entries will be used when the variables are displayed to the user.

```
        set       ivars   0
        set       nvars   [llength $lvars]

        foreach   vb      [lrange $vBinds 1 end] {
            set   var     [lindex $vb 0]

            if {$ivars >= $nvars} {
                snmptcl_dialog          "Agent error for $ainfo(title)" \
                    "retrieval botched, got back too many variables" \
                                        warning 0 Abort
# destroy window, delete private arrays                                          10
                return
            }

            set   lvar    [lindex $lvars $ivars]
            incr  ivars

            if {[snmptcl_proc_oidcmp $lvar $var] != 0} {
                snmptcl_dialog          "Agent Error for $ainfo(title)" \
                                        "retrieval botched, got back wrong variable"      20
                                        warning 0 Abort
# destroy window, delete private arrays
                return
            }

            if {(([set syntax [lindex $vb 1]] == "exception") \
                    || ($syntax == "error")} {
                continue
            }
                                                                                 30
            set   value   [lindex $vb 2]
            if {![info exists avar($var)]} {
                set       avar($var)    [list $iter "" 0 $value \
                                            $value $sysUpTime $syntax]
            } elseif {[lindex [set data $avar($var)] 2] > $sysUpTime} {
                set       avar($var)    [lreplace $data 0 6 $iter "" 0 $value \
                                            $value $sysUpTime $syntax]
            } else {
                set       avar($var)    [lreplace $data 0 5 $iter \
                                            [lindex $data 4] [lindex $data 5] \    40
                                            [lindex $data 3] $value $sysUpTime]
            }
        }
    }
    if {$ivars < $nvars} {
        snmptcl_dialog          "Agent error for $ainfo(title)" \
                                "retrieval botched, got back too few variables" \
                                warning 0 Abort
# destroy window, delete private arrays
        return
    }                                                                            50
```

Figure 3.17: The `snmptcl_poll_callback` procedure (cont.)

Finally, a check is made to see if other requests are still outstanding for this iteration. If so, the callback procedure returns. Otherwise, each element in "avar" is checked to see that a value was returned by the agent for this iteration. If not, the entry for the variable is removed. Then, the command to display the values to the user is evaluated. After this, the iteration number is incremented, and the next polling interval is scheduled.

Before finishing this application fragment, the use of "eval" should be explained. Observant readers might wonder why

```
eval $ainfo(command) [list $w $array]
```

was used instead of

```
$ainfo(command) $w $array
```

These two commands can be quite different. The second command invokes a command procedure ("$ainfo(command)") with exactly two parameters. In contrast, the first command performs command-substitution and variable-substitution and then evaluates the result — the first word in "$ainfo(command)" will be the command procedure that is called, and the last two arguments to this command procedure will be "$w" and "$array". However, if "$ainfo(command)" contains more than one word, the second and subsequent words will be passed as the initial arguments to the command procedure. So, the first command provides an easy way for the caller to provide additional parameters to the command which is run at the end of each iteration.

Whew! That's quite an application fragment, but we've seen how to write some robust code when using get:

- dealing with noSuchName and tooBig errors;

- dealing with agent errors; and,

- maintaining a sampling continuity.

```
if {$ainfo(segs)} {
     return
}

if {[info exists avar]} {
     foreach element [array names avar] {
         if {[lindex $avar($element) 0] != $iter} {
             unset    avar($element)
         }
     }                                                                      10
}

eval          $ainfo(command)          [list $w $array]

incr          ainfo(iter)

set           vars          [concat $snmptcl_var_sysUpTime.0 $ainfo(vars)]

# schedule evaluation of
#    set       iHandle       [$pHandle get snmptcl_poll_callback $vars]      20
#    incr      ainfo(segs)
#    set       snmptcl_info($iHandle) \
#                            [list $array [lrange $vars 1 end]]
# for $ainfo(interval) seconds in the future
}
```

Figure 3.17: The `snmptcl_poll_callback` procedure (cont.)

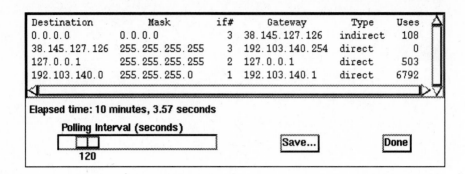

Destination	Mask	if#	Gateway	Type	Uses
0.0.0.0	0.0.0.0	3	38.145.127.126	indirect	108
38.145.127.126	255.255.255.255	3	192.103.140.254	direct	0
127.0.0.1	255.255.255.255	2	127.0.0.1	direct	503
192.103.140.0	255.255.255.0	1	192.103.140.1	direct	6792

Elapsed time: 10 minutes, 3.57 seconds

Polling Interval (seconds)

120

Save...   Done

Figure 3.18: A Window Browsing parts of the ipRoutingTable

3.3.4   Polling All Instances

Suppose we want to poll all instances of some variables, instead of some well-known instances. For example, Figure 3.18 shows what a window displaying portions of the ipRoutingTable might look like. This is another "classic" browsing activity — polling a table.

Figure 3.19 shows how the process begins, which is similar to the one in Figure 3.14 back on page 125. The only difference is that a second array, known locally as "ancol", is also created. For each instance-identifier (row) we encounter, this array will tell us how many variables we've seen in that row. In addition, instead of get, the context procedure is invoked to perform a get-bulk operation, and some different information is stored in the array "snmptcl_info".

```
# create a new top-level window, $w

    set         array          snmptcl_array[join [split $w "."] "_"]
    global      ${array}_info
    upvar #0    ${array}_info   ainfo

    global      ${array}_ncol
    upvar #0    ${array}_ncol   ancol
    set         ancol("")       ""
                                                                        10
    set         ainfo(toplevel) $w
    set         ainfo(title)    ...

# list of OID prefixes to poll
    set         ainfo(cvars)    $cvars

# how many seconds between polls
    set         ainfo(interval) $interval

# iteration number                                                      20
    set         ainfo(iter)     0

# number of requests in progress for this iteration
    set         ainfo(segs)     0

# the left-edge of the current sampling continuity
    set         ainfo(startime) ""

# the right-edge of the current sampling continuity
    set         ainfo(lastime)  ""                                      30

# command to evaluate each time an iteration completes
    set         ainfo(command)  $command

# create four sub-windows:
#    one for the actual information (initially empty)
#    a label for the elapsed time
#    a slider for the polling interval
#    a command-button for Done
                                                                        40
    set         vars            [concat $snmptcl_var_sysUpTime $cvars]
    set         maxrept         10
    set         iHandle         [agent bulk snmptcl_polltable_callback \
                                    $vars -maxrept $maxrept -nonrptr 1]
    incr        ainfo(segs)
    set         snmptcl_info($iHandle) \
                                [list $array [lrange $vars 1 end] \
                                    [lrange $vars 1 end] $maxrept]
```

Figure 3.19: Preparing to Poll All Instances

Figure 3.20 starting on page 141 shows the callback procedure (which, as you might expect, is similar to Figure 3.15 back on page 127). The callback begins with the usual unpacking of information from "snmptcl_info":

array: the prefix of the global name of the private arrays used to keep information between polling intervals;

lvars: the list of variables that the agent was asked to return for this request;

xvars: the list of OID prefixes that we're interested in polling for with this request (each element in "lvars" is either an instance of, or identical to, the corresponding element in "xvars"); and,

maxrept: the maximum number of repetitions requested.

This is followed by a check to see if the user clicked on "Done", and the unpacking of some information from "ainfo", and two other private arrays, "avar", which holds information about each variable we've seen, and, "ancol", which keeps track of how many variables we've seen in each row. (This latter array will be maintained by the command which displays values to the user.)

Following this, the tooBig heuristic is applied for a timeout response.

Then the error-status check is made to see if the context procedure was destroyed, or to ask the user for a decision on how to proceed.

Following this, the examination of sysUpTime.0, the first variable binding, is made.

```
proc snmptcl_polltable_callback {pHandle iHandle eStatus eIndex vBinds} {
    global          snmptcl_info snmptcl_var_sysUpTime

    set       data          $snmptcl_info($iHandle)
    unset     snmptcl_info($iHandle)
    set       array         [lindex $data 0]
    set       lvars         [lindex $data 1]
    set       xvars         [lindex $data 2]
    set       maxrept       [lindex $data 3]

    global    ${array}_info
    upvar #0  ${array}_info     ainfo
    if {![info exists ainfo(toplevel)]} {
# user clicked on Done
        return
    }
    set       w             $ainfo(toplevel)
    set       iter          $ainfo(iter)
    set       cvars         $ainfo(cvars)
    incr      ainfo(segs)       -1

    global    ${array}_var
    upvar #0  ${array}_var      avar

    global    ${array}_ncol
    upvar #0  ${array}_ncol     ancol
```

Figure 3.20: The `snmptcl_polltable_callback` procedure

```tcl
    if {($eStatus == "timeout") && ([llength $lvars] >= 20)} {
        set     eStatus         tooBig
    }
    switch -- $eStatus {
        noSuchName {
            if {$eIndex > 1} {
                incr    eIndex   -2
                set     vars        [concat $snmptcl_var_sysUpTime \
                                        [lreplace $lvars $eIndex $eIndex]]
                set     iHandle     [$pHandle next snmptcl_polltable_callback \
                                        $vars]                                      10
                incr    ainfo(segs)
                set     snmptcl_info($iHandle) \
                                    [list $array [lrange $vars 1 end] \
                                        [lreplace $xvars $eIndex $eIndex] \
                                        $maxrept]
                return
            }
        }
                                                                                    20
        tooBig {
            if {[set eIndex [llength $lvars]] > 1} {
                set     hIndex      [expr $eIndex/2]

                set     vars        [concat $snmptcl_var_sysUpTime \
                                        [lrange $lvars 0 [expr $hIndex-1]]]
                set     iHandle     [$pHandle next snmptcl_polltable_callback \
                                        $vars]
                incr    ainfo(segs)
                set     snmptcl_info($iHandle) \                                     30
                                    [list $array [lrange $vars 1 end] \
                                        [lrange $xvars 0 [expr $hIndex-1]] \
                                        $maxrept]

                set     vars        [concat $snmptcl_var_sysUpTime \
                                        [lrange $lvars $hIndex end]]
                set     iHandle     [$pHandle next snmptcl_polltable_callback \
                                        $vars]
                incr    ainfo(segs)
                set     snmptcl_info($iHandle) \                                     40
                                    [list $array [lrange $vars 1 end] \
                                        [lrange $xvars $hIndex end] \
                                        $maxrept]
                return
            }
        }
    }

    switch -- $eStatus {
        noError {                                                                   50
        }

        destroyed {
# orphan the window
            return
        }
```

Figure 3.20: The snmptcl_polltable_callback procedure (cont.)

```tcl
            default {
                switch [snmptcl_dialog "Agent Error for $ainfo(title)" \
                        $eStatus question 0 Retry Orphan Abort] {
                    0 {
                        set     vars            [concat $snmptcl_var_sysUpTime $lvars]
                        set     iHandle         [$pHandle bulk \
                                                    snmptcl_polltable_callback \
                                                    $vars −maxrept $maxrept \
                                                    −nonrptr 1]
                        incr    ainfo(segs)
                        set     snmptcl_info($iHandle) \
                                            [list $array [lrange $vars 1 end] \
                                                $xvars $maxrept]
                        return
                    }

                    1 {
# remove label and slider, delete private arrays
                        return
                    }

                    default {
# destroy window, delete private arrays
                        return
                    }
                }
            }
    }

    set     vb      [lindex $vBinds 0]
    if {"$snmptcl_var_sysUpTime.0" != [lindex $vb 0]} {
        snmptcl_dialog              "Agent Error for $ainfo(title)" \
        "instead of sysUpTime, got [snmptcl_proc_oid2ode [lindex $vb 0]]" \
                                warning 0 Abort
# destroy window, delete private arrays
        return
    }
    if {([set syntax [lindex $vb 1]] == "exception") \
            || ($syntax == "error")} {
        set     sysUpTime       4294967296.0
        set     ainfo(startime)     ""
        set     ainfo(lastime)      ""
# update elapsed time label
    } else {
        set     sysUpTime       [lindex $vb 2]
        if {[set startime $ainfo(startime)] == ""} {
            set     ainfo(startime)     $sysUpTime
# update elapsed time label
        } elseif {$ainfo(lastime) > $sysUpTime} {
            set     ainfo(startime)     $sysUpTime
# update elapsed time label
        } elseif {$iter} {
# set elasped time label to $sysUpTime−$startime
        }
        set     ainfo(lastime)      $sysUpTime
    }
```

Figure 3.20: The **snmptcl_polltable_callback** procedure (cont.)

Finally, things get interesting as we cycle through the remaining variable bindings — a ring is maintained because the response to a `get-bulk` might not have the same number of variables as the request. The variables used are:

ivars: the offset into the ring;

mvars: the variables requested;

nvars: the number of variables requested; and,

evars: variables returned with exceptional responses.

For each variable binding returned by the agent, the variable supplied to the `get-bulk` is retrieved from the ring, and then that position in the ring is updated to the variable returned.

A check is then made to make sure that the ordering semantics of `get-next` and `get-bulk` were adhered to by the agent. If the variable returned isn't an instance of the corresponding element in "xvars", then no further processing occurs for that variable binding. Otherwise, if an exceptional value is encountered, or the API's protocol engine couldn't understand the value, then that variable is appended to the "evars" list.

Following this, the position of the variable in the master list of OID prefixes ("cvars") is calculated. (Recall that "xvars" could be a subset of "cvars" — if a `noSuchName` or `tooBig` was encountered earlier.) Just as the instance-identifier of the variable can be thought of as identifying the table-row for the variable, the position in "cvars" can be thought of as identifying the table-column.

Then, the usual update is made of the element in "avar" which corresponds to the variable. However, there is one bit of additional information — the column number.

```
set          ivars     0
set          nvars     [llength [set mvars $lvars]]
set          evars     ""

foreach      vb        [lrange $vBinds 1 end] {
    set      var       [lindex $vb 0]

    set      mvar      [lindex $mvars [set icol $ivars]]
    set      mvars     [lreplace $mvars $ivars $ivars $var]
    if {[incr ivars] >= $nvars} {                                    10
        set      ivars     0
    }

    if {[snmptcl_proc_oidcmp $mvar $var] >= 0} {
        snmptcl_dialog          "Agent Error for $ainfo(title)" \
                                "lexicographic ordering botched" \
                                warning 0 Abort
# destroy window, delete private arrays
        return
    }                                                                20

    if {![snmptcl_proc_oidcontains [set xvar [lindex $xvars $icol]] $var]} {
        continue
    }

    if {([set syntax [lindex $vb 1]] == "exception") \
         || ($syntax == "error")} {
        lappend      evars     $var
        continue
    }                                                                30

    set      icol      0
    foreach cvar       $cvars {
        if {$xvar == $cvar} {
            break
        }
        incr         icol
    }

    set      value     [lindex $vb 2]                                40
    if {![info exists avar($var)]} {
        set          avar($var)        [list $iter "" 0 $value \
                                        $value $sysUpTime $syntax $icol]
    } elseif {[lindex [set data $avar($var)] 2] > $sysUpTime} {
        set          avar($var)        [lreplace $data 0 7 $iter "" 0 $value \
                                        $value $sysUpTime $syntax $icol]
    } elseif {[lindex $data 0] == $iter} {
        continue
    } else {
        set          avar($var)        [lreplace $data 0 5 $iter \           50
                                        [lindex $data 4] [lindex $data 5] \
                                        [lindex $data 3] $value $sysUpTime]
    }
}
```

Figure 3.20: The `snmptcl_polltable_callback` procedure (cont.)

Next, a check is made to see if additional instances may still need to be retrieved. For each variable originally requested ("`lvars`"), the last variable retrieved is extracted from "`mvars`". If an exceptional value was returned for the variable, or if the variable isn't an instance of the corresponding element of "`xvars`", then no other instances of that OID prefix remain to be retrieved. Otherwise, we build up two lists, one containing the variables we will ask for, the other containing the corresponding OID prefixes.

If additional work remains to be done, then the context procedure is invoked to perform a `get-bulk` operation, "`ainfo(segs)`" is incremented, and the array "`snmptcl_info`" is updated accordingly, before the callback procedure returns. Because we have no way of knowing how many instances there may be, "`maxrept`" is simply set to the number of rows we've seen thus far (or multiplied by 10 if we're still on the first sweep).

Finally, a check is made to see if other requests are still outstanding for this iteration. If so, the callback procedure returns. Otherwise, the command to display the values to the user is evaluated. (Unlike the earlier application fragment, variables which have disappeared are not removed — the display command is responsible for this.) After this, the iteration number is incremented, and the next polling interval is scheduled.

Hopefully this application fragment wasn't as daunting as the preceding one. However, it does illustrate how to write some robust code when using `get-next` and `get-bulk`. When sweeping a table:

- never expect a response to contain variables related all to one row (even when using `get-next`);

- never expect all columns to come back in a single request;

- be prepared to deal with `noSuchName` errors when talking to an agent using SNMPv1; and,

- be prepared to deal with `tooBig` errors.

The key to successfully sweeping a table with SNMP is to maintain both a ring to keep track of the last variable retrieved, and a corresponding list of OID prefixes.

```
set        vars      $snmptcl_var_sysUpTime
set        ivars     0
set        yvars     ""
foreach    lvar      $lvars {
      set        mvar      [lindex $mvars [set icol $ivars]]
      incr       ivars

      if {([lsearch −exact $evars $mvar] >= 0) \
              || ![snmptcl_proc_oidcontains [set xvar [lindex $xvars $icol]] \
                      $mvar]} {                                                      10
          continue
      }

      lappend vars      $mvar
      lappend yvars     $xvar
}

if {[llength $vars] > 1} {
      if {$iter} {
          set    maxrept              [array size ancol]                            20
      } else {
          set    maxrept              [expr $maxrept*10]
      }
      set        iHandle              [$pHandle bulk snmptcl_polltable_callback \
                                          $vars −maxrept $maxrept −nonrptr 1]
      incr    ainfo(segs)
      set        snmptcl_info($iHandle)      \
                                   [list $array [lrange $vars 1 end] $yvars \
                                          $maxrept]
      return                                                                        30
}

if {$ainfo(segs)} {
      return
}

eval        $ainfo(command)          [list $w $array]

incr        ainfo(iter)
                                                                                    40
set        vars      [concat $snmptcl_var_sysUpTime $cvars]
set        maxrept   [array size ancol]
# schedule evaluation of
#    set        iHandle          [$pHandle bulk snmptcl_polltable_callback \
#                                    $vars −maxrept $maxrept −nonrptr 1]
#    incr    ainfo(iter)
#    set        snmptcl_info($iHandle) \
#                                 [list $array [lrange $vars 1 end] \
#                                        [lrange $vars 1 end] $maxrept]             50
# for $ainfo(interval) seconds in the future
}
```

Figure 3.20: The `snmptcl_polltable_callback` procedure (cont.)

3.3.5   Putting It All Together

Since browsers are all about displaying things to the user, let's look a
little bit at how the command which does the actual displaying might
work. One could imagine that such a command procedure might use
the syntax of the object to determine how to display it, e.g.,

```
set     snmptcl_print_syntax(Counter32) \
             snmptcl_print_Counter32

...

foreach var $ainfo(vars) {
    set     data     $avar($var)
    set     syntax   [lindex $data 6]
    set     value    [$snmptcl_print_syntax($syntax) $var \
                         avar($var)]
# do something with value
}
```

(For those readers who skipped the previous two sections, back on
page 134 we discussed the format of the information kept in the
"avar" array.)

Figure 3.21 shows how counters might be processed. Each command procedure begins by using "upvar" to access an element in the
caller's array, "avar", locally as "info".

The rules are simple:

- if a value was not retrieved on the previous iteration, the empty
  string is returned (remember that two samples are needed to
  make sense of a counter); otherwise,

- the current value is retrieved ("value"), along with the first
  value retrieved for this sampling continuity ("initvalue");

- if the current value is less than the value retrieved on the previous iteration ("prevalue"), then the counter has wrapped and
  the left-edge of this sampling continuity is moved further left by
  the width of the counter; finally,

- the difference between the current value and the first value is
  returned.

```
proc snmptcl_print_Counter32 {var data} {
    upvar          $data    info

    if {[set prevalue [lindex $info 1]] == ""} {
        return    ""
    }
    set            value            [lindex $info 4]
    set            initvalue        [lindex $info 3]
    if {$prevalue > $value} {
        set        initvalue        [expr $initvalue−4294967296.0]          10
        set        info             [lreplace $info 3 3 $initvalue]
    }
    if {[string match *.0 [set value [expr $value−$initvalue]]]} {
# since the arguments to expr are floating point numbers,
# expr will return a floating pointer number,
# so we strip off any trailing ".0" from expr's result
        set        value            [string range $value 0 \
                                        [expr [string length $value]−3]]
    }
    return         $value                                                    20
}


proc snmptcl_print_Counter64 {var data} {
    upvar          $data    info

    if {[set prevalue [lindex $info 1]] == ""} {
        return    ""
    }
    set            value            [lindex $info 4]                         30
    set            initvalue        [lindex $info 3]
    if {$prevalue > $value} {
        set        initvalue        [expr $initvalue−18446744073709551616.0]
        set        info             [lreplace $info 3 3 $initvalue]
    }
    if {[string match *.0 [set value [expr $value−$initvalue]]]} {
        set        value            [string range $value 0 \
                                        [expr [string length $value]−3]]
    }
}                                                                            40
```

Figure 3.21: Processing Counter Objects

The only tricky part is the third step, where the left-edge is moved. Because the value returned is the difference between the left- and right-edges, a counter wrapping can be modeled by moving either edge away from the other.

Figure 3.22 shows how other kinds of objects might be processed:

INTEGER-values: a check is made to see if this object is an enumerated integer, and if so, if the current value is one of those enumerations — in this case, the textual enumeration is returned instead;

OCTET STRING-values: the initial "0x" is removed; and,

OBJECT IDENTIFIER-values: a check is made to see if the value is "0.0" and, if so, the string "null" is returned; otherwise, "snmpinfo mibprop" is invoked to see if the value corresponds to an object and, if so, the corresponding descriptor property is used as the prefix of the string returned, followed by an instance-identifier.

```
proc snmptcl_print_Integer32 {var data} {
    upvar        $data    info

    set          value          [lindex $info 4]
    if {(([set enums [snmpinfo mibprop $var enums]] != "") \
            && ([set enum [lsearch -glob $enums "$value *"]] >= 0)} {
        return   [lindex [lindex $enums $enum] 1]
    }

    return       $value                                            10
}


proc snmptcl_print_Octets {var data} {
    upvar        $data    info

    set          value          [lindex $info 4]
    if {[string range $value 0 1] != "0x"} {
        return   $value
    }                                                              20
    return       [string range $value 2 end]
}


proc snmptcl_print_ObjectID {var data} {
    upvar        $data    info

    set          value          [lindex $info 4]
    if {$value == "0.0"} {
        return   "null"                                           30
    }
    return       [snmptcl_proc_oid2ode $value]
}


proc snmptcl_proc_oid2ode {oid} {
    if {[catch { set full [snmpinfo mibprop $oid full] }]} {
        return   $oid
    }                                                             40
    set          i        [llength [set elemi [split $oid "."]]]
    set          j        [llength [set elemj [split [lindex $full 2] "."]]]

    set          descr    [lindex $full 0]
    for {} {$j < $i} {incr j} {
        append descr    "."      [lindex $elemi $j]
    }

    return       $descr
}                                                                 50
```

Figure 3.22: Processing Other Kinds of Objects

```
proc snmptcl_graph_Counter32 {var data} {
    upvar          $data    info

    if {[set prevalue [lindex $info 1]] == ""} {
        return  ""
    }
    if {$prevalue > [set value [lindex $info 4]]} {
        set        diff               [expr $value+(4294967296.0−prevalue)]
    } else {
        set        diff               [expr $value−$prevalue]
    }
    if {[set delta [expr [lindex $info 5]−[lindex $info 2]]] == 0} {
        set        delta              1
    } else {
        set        delta              [expr $delta]
    }
    return         [expr ($diff*100)/$delta]
}
```

10

Figure 3.23: Calculating Rates using Counters

Of course, other kinds of processing might take place instead. For example, given the information gathered by the polling command procedures, it's trivial to calculate rates using counter objects. Figure 3.24 shows the number of SNMPv2 packets received each second. Figure 3.23 shows how a rate is calculated:

- if a value was not retrieved on the previous iteration, the empty string is returned (which isn't drawn, resulting in a discontinuity in the curve); otherwise,

- to calculate the numerator for the rate, if the current value is less than the value retrieved on the previous iteration ("**prevalue**"), then the counter has wrapped, so add the maximum value of the counter to the current value, and subtract the previous value; otherwise, just subtract the previous value from the current value;

- to determine the denominator for the rate, just calculate the elapsed **TimeTicks** between the two samples;

- do the division and multiply the result by 100 to convert to units per second (recall that **TimeTicks** are in hundredths of a second).

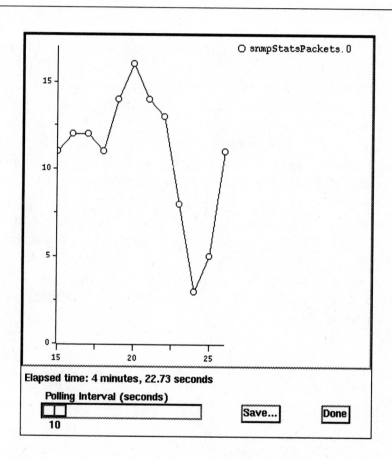

Figure 3.24: A Window Graphing snmpStatsPackets

3.3.6   Testing Agents

Some readers might wonder if the agent error-checking in these application fragments is really necessary. The answer, sadly, is yes. It is the authors' experience that some deployed agents simply don't work right. So, it is critical that a management application thoroughly check each response it receives to make sure that the right variables are returned, the values make sense, and so on. (Even if all deployed agents worked correctly, detailed checking is an invaluable part of network programming.)

Of course, it makes sense to test an agent before you deploy it for production use. To help, the authors have made available an implementation of an agent test suite, built on top of the API. Remember Figure 2.1 way back on page 65? That's it! As of this writing, the agent test suite implements sixty different tests, and uses the information in the database on agent implementations whenever it can. (Two tests even try to check the consistency of the database with the agent.) While it doesn't test everything that can go wrong, the agent test suite does look for many of the most common problems.

So, if you do retrieve the software which goes with *The Networking Management Practicum*, you might want to run the agent test suite against your agents. If you find a problem, then you might want to contact your agent supplier!

Part II

Managing Wires

Chapter 4

Interface Management

This chapter discusses the management of network interfaces at the internet layer and below. For the layers below the internet layer, this chapter covers those aspects of management common to all interfaces; management of specific types of interfaces is covered in later chapters.

For the internet layer itself, this chapter specifically refers only to the Internet Protocol (IP) [22] of the Internet protocol suite. However, SNMP MIB modules (both standard and enterprise-specific) have been defined for a number of other internet layer protocols, and typically these MIB modules follow the same general model as that described in this chapter. Thus, many of the concepts and applications described here can also be applied to other internet layer protocols. For example, [23] specifies an SNMP MIB module for OSI's Connectionless-mode Network Protocol (CLNP). The management objects in this MIB module were purposely defined to be as similar as possible to the standard management objects for IP, to promote commonality within management applications.

4.1   Concepts

The architectural model for the Internet suite of protocols is espoused
in [24]. With this model, the Internet suite of protocols is viewed as
having four layers:

- the *interface* layer, which describes physical and data-link technologies used to realize transmission at the hardware (media)
  level;

- the *internet* layer, which describes the internetworking technologies used to realize the internetworking abstraction;

- the *transport* layer, which describes the end-to-end technologies
  used to realize reliable communications between hosts; and,

- the *application* layer, which describes the technologies used to
  provide end-user services.

The major emphasis of the Internet suite is on the connection
of diverse network technologies. As such, the current generation of
protocols is *primarily* based on:

- a connection-oriented transport service, provided by the
  Transmission Control Protocol (TCP) [25]; and,

- a connectionless-mode (inter)network service, provided by the
  Internet Protocol (IP) [22].

Figure 4.1 provides a simple representation of IP's relationship
to the Internet suite's two common transport protocols, and several
of its most common application protocols. As well as TCP, the
other transport protocol shown in the figure is the User Datagram
Protocol (UDP), a connectionless-mode transport protocol providing
little more than a simple multiplexing function on top of IP. The
application protocols shown are: the Simple Mail Transfer Protocol
(SMTP) [26,27], the File Transfer Protocol (FTP) [28], TELNET [29],
the Domain Name System (DNS) [30,31], and the Simple Network
Management Protocol (SNMP) [4,5] itself. Also shown is the Internet
Control Message Protocol (ICMP), which is used to report on the
"health" of the internet layer, as explained later in this section.

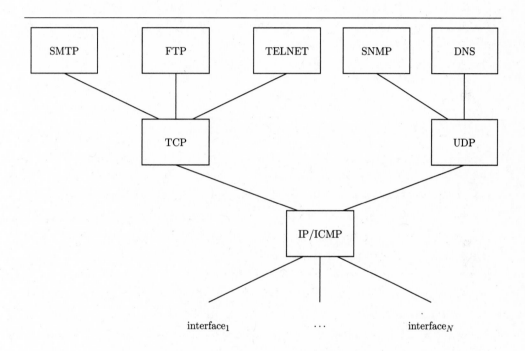

Figure 4.1: Brief Overview of Internet Protocols

It should be noted that other descriptions of the Internet suite of protocols use similar (or slightly different) terminology to describe the architecture. The authors feel that this organization strikes a useful balance between historical perspective (from the original Internet research) and "modern" terminology (from the OSI Reference Model).

To briefly remind the reader about layering, when referring to a particular layer, one usually refers to the *entities* residing at that layer. For example, at the internet layer, one refers to the IP entity. This entity provides the internet service to the entities at the layer above. Similarly, the entity uses the interface service provided by the entities at the layer below.

The lower two layers, which are of relevance to this chapter, are now examined in turn.

4.1.1   Interface Layer

One of the strengths of IP (and other similar internet protocols) is that it is designed to run over any network interface.[1] In achieving this, IP considers any and all protocols it runs over as a single interface layer. As such, IP has a generic view of the interface layer. In practice, the interface layer may consist of several individual sub-layers, each implementing its own protocol and providing its own functions. The lowest sub-layer controls the physical connection to the media.

Ethernet is an example of an interface layer which consists of just a single sub-layer. In contrast, an X.25 interface consists of multiple sub-layers, including an X.25 packet layer, a LAPB sub-layer, and a physical interface sub-layer (e.g., RS-232).

As a whole, the interface layer is responsible for taking a "packet", consisting of multiple octets (simply termed "bytes") of data, provided to it from above (e.g., from IP), and transmitting it over the physical medium. At the destination, the interface layer is responsible for receiving the packet and delivering it to the layer above (e.g., to IP).

Thus, the interface layer corresponds to the two lowest layers of the OSI model, the physical and data-link layers. The purist will observe that this also covers part of OSI's network layer, but that distinction is ignored in this text.

---

[1]A humorous example of this is the RFC published on 1 April 1990 [32]

The majority of packets are transmitted from one system to exactly one other system. Such packets are called unicast packets. Alternatively, a single transmitted packet can be delivered to multiple other systems. Such packets are called broadcast packets if they are delivered to all other systems reachable via the interface, or multicast packets if delivered to a subset of those systems.

Interfaces connect to one of the following categories of media:

point-to-point media: exactly two systems are connected to the medium; all packets are unicast and transmitted by one of the systems to be received by the other (a serial line is an example of a point-to-point media);

broadcast media: multiple systems can be reached via the interface; a packet can be unicast, multicast or broadcast (an Ethernet is an example of a broadcast media); and,

non-broadcast / multiple-access media: multiple systems can be reached via the interface, but a single packet cannot be delivered to all the other systems, i.e., broadcast is not possible even though multicast may or may not be; (ATM, SMDS and Frame Relay are examples of this category).

The non-broadcast/multiple-access category typically has an underlying point-to-point sub-layer by which the system gets access to the non-broadcast/multiple-access network.

Except for point-to-point, just about all interfaces have an address.[2] Indeed, for interfaces which consist of multiple sub-layers, several of the sub-layers may have their own addresses. For connectionless-mode interfaces, each transmitted packet contains the address of the system(s) to which it is to be delivered. For connection-oriented interfaces, packets are transmitted on a connection and contain a connection-identifier rather than an address. However, the establishment of a connection is typically performed by specifying the addresses of the interfaces between which the connection is to be established. The format of an address is specific to the type of media.

---

[2]Even interfaces to point-to-point media sometimes have an address.

For broadcast media, a system normally receives only traffic with specific destination addresses. However, many such interfaces can be configured to be in *promiscuous* mode in which case they receive all traffic on the media, regardless of destination address.

The above descriptions apply to interface types which transmit data as packets. For interfaces which consist of multiple sub-layers, there are some types of lower sub-layers which have no knowledge of packets. RS-232 is an example of an interface sub-layer which transmits characters, and needs a packetizing sub-layer on top of it in order to be used as a network interface by IP. Another example is a Time-Division Multiplexing interface such as a DS-1 line, where the unit of data transmission is in bits.

4.1.2   Independence of the Interface Layer

The interface layer was introduced above as the undercarriage by which IP (and/or other internet layer) packets are transmitted from one system to another. In addition, the interface layer and its sub-layers are also used in other situations. It is the use of layering which makes this possible, since each layer/sub-layer provides its services to the layer above in a manner which is independent of the above layers.

In particular, there are networking protocols which do not have an internet layer and, even for those that do, there are interface layer devices, (e.g., MAC layer bridges, see chapter 5) which forward data without regard for whether or not the data contains an IP packet. By keeping the interface layer independent of IP, the interface layer can be managed in these situations in the same way as when IP is situated directly above it in the protocol stack.

4.1.3   Mapping IP to the Interface Layer

IP is termed a connectionless-mode (CL-mode) network protocol. This means that it is *datagram-oriented*. The basic unit of commerce in IP is the datagram. Each datagram consists of one or more bytes of *user-data*. Associated with each datagram is an address indicating where the datagram should be delivered. This address consists of an *IP address*, and an *upper-layer protocol* (ULP) number. The syntax and semantics of IP addresses are considered later on. For now, simply think of IP as delivering datagrams to arbitrary addresses.

When IP has some user-data to send, it takes that user-data and encapsulates it in an IP datagram, which contains all the information necessary to deliver the datagram to the IP entity at the destination. The remote IP entity will examine the IP datagrams it receives, and then strip off the header and pass the data up to the appropriate upper-layer protocol.

Since IP must run over multiple types of interfaces, its addresses must be independent of the format of the various interface layer addressing schemes. Further, although an IP address indicates where a network device resides in an internet, the IP address needn't (and normally shouldn't) have any relationship to the corresponding media address where the device is physically attached. This indirection is important for two reasons:

- media addresses are often assigned administratively by the manufacturer, so there can be no correlation between network attachment and media address; and,

- media addresses can change when interface hardware changes (e.g., to replace a broken board); this shouldn't result in a change in the IP address.

Given this rather simplistic, yet particularly elegant design, it appears that two services are needed in order to map IP onto an interface layer:

- mapping from IP addresses to interface-specific addresses; and,

- encapsulation of IP datagrams for transmission over a specific interface.

For each interface type which can be used to transmit IP datagrams, there is a document which specifies how these services are provided. On page 475, a list of defined mappings is presented. In general, the mechanisms used by these documents fall into one of two categories:

- if the underlying technology is connectionless-mode, the mechanism is straightforward: IP datagrams are encapsulated in media frames; otherwise,

- if the underlying technology is connection-oriented, the interface layer must perform connection management in order to find an underlying connection over which to send the IP datagram.

In either case, address translation occurs through one of three mechanisms:

- *algorithmically*, if there is a deterministic method for achieving a one-to-one mapping between IP addresses and media addresses;

- *statically*, if a table is built during system configuration; or,

- *dynamically*, if a protocol is used to determine the mappings.

Of the three approaches, the dynamic mechanism is clearly the best as it determines the address mappings in a decentralized fashion.

IP datagrams over Ethernet

To conclude this section on mapping IP to the interface layer, we now examine one particular mapping, specifically, how IP packets are encapsulated on Ethernet networks [33].

Each IP datagram is encapsulated in the data field of an Ethernet frame. Since the maximum size of this data field is 1500 octets, if the IP datagram is larger, the IP datagram must be *fragmented* prior to transmission. (This topic is discussed in greater detail in Section 4.1.5 starting on page 180.)

Since the minimum size of the frame's data field is 46 octets, if the IP datagram is smaller, the sending process adds *padding* after the IP datagram to bring the data field to the minimum length. Note that this padding is transparent to IP. When the data field is extracted on the remote system, the IP entity will consult a count in the IP header indicating the actual length of the datagram. Thus, the octets used for padding will be ignored. The frame format is shown in Figure 4.2, and is used for all Ethernet packets, regardless of whether they carry IP or something else.

Because IP addresses are 32 bits in length and Ethernet addresses are 48 bits in length, an algorithmic mechanism cannot achieve a one-to-one mapping between them. This leaves either a static approach or the use of a protocol to achieve a dynamic mapping.

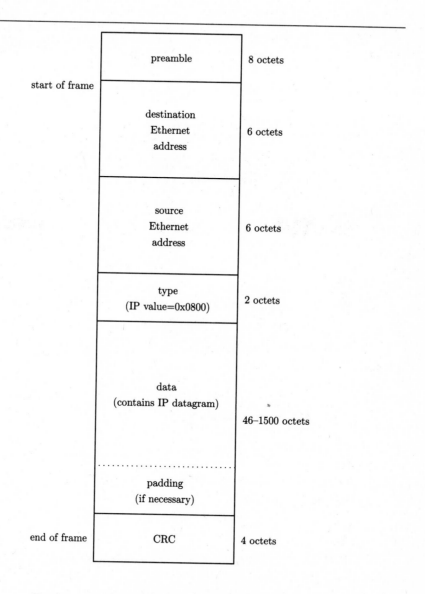

Figure 4.2: IP datagrams over Ethernet

In the case of **Ethernet**, the *Address Resolution Protocol* (ARP), defined in [34], is the dynamic mechanism used in virtually all implementations. ARP makes use of the *broadcasting* facilities of **Ethernet** technology. When the local IP determines that it must send a packet to a device on an attached **Ethernet**, the interface layer consults its ARP cache to see if the address mapping from the remote IP address to an **Ethernet** address is already known. If so, the IP datagram can be sent in an **Ethernet** packet to the corresponding media address.

If not, the interface layer constructs an ARP request packet. The format of an ARP packet is shown in Figure 4.3. Note that the format of ARP packets is actually media-independent.[3] The "media type" field indicates what kind of hardware is being used. The value 1 is used for **Ethernet**. Similarly, the "network type" field indicates which networking protocol is being translated. Since IP datagrams are transmitted using the value 0x0800 over **Ethernet**, this value is used.

An ARP request uses a value of 1 for the operation code. All fields in the packet, except for the target media address (obviously), are filled in by the sender. The ARP packet is placed in the data field of an **Ethernet** packet (**Ethernet** type 0x0806 is used), and the packet is then sent to the **Ethernet** *broadcast* address.[4]

Upon receiving an ARP packet, the interface layer verifies that it supports the media type and protocol type described. If not, the packet is discarded. Otherwise:

1. A check is first made to see if the sender's protocol address is already in the local ARP cache and, if so, the corresponding media address is updated.

2. A check is then made to see if the target's protocol address corresponds to the local IP address. If not, the packet is discarded.

---

[3]The ARP specification uses the term "hardware address" when referring to media addresses. In striving for consistency with the previous discussion, the authors have chosen to use the term "media" instead.

[4]Back in the days when ARP was invented, implementations of multicasting were few and far between.

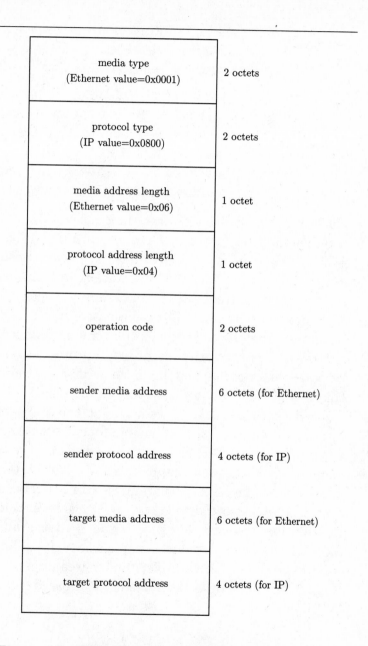

Figure 4.3: Format of ARP packets

3. Otherwise:

    (a) If the sender's protocol address was not already in the local
        ARP cache (the first check), then a media/protocol address
        mapping for the sender is now added to the cache.

    (b) If the operation code of the ARP packet indicated "ARP
        request", then an "ARP response" packet is formed (usu-
        ally by reusing the incoming ARP packet), with all of the
        fields filled in. This response packet is then sent on the
        same physical interface as the original request packet to the
        Ethernet address of the original sender (i.e., not broadcast).

Note that one of the very last things checked for in the algorithm is
whether the ARP packet is a request or a reply. The rationale for this
is quite clever: when the local interface layer consults its ARP cache
and doesn't find the desired information, in addition to generating and
sending an ARP request, it could simply discard the IP datagram it
was going to send. As will be discussed in the next section, inherent
to the internet layer is the notion of unreliability. Thus, if the IP
datagram is gratuitously discarded, a protocol somewhere above IP is
responsible for retransmitting it as necessary at a later time. Usually,
this will be TCP at the transport layer, but this needn't be the case
(e.g., if the application uses UDP at the transport layer, then the
application protocol is responsible for retransmission). Regardless of
whether or not the IP datagram was discarded, when an ARP packet
containing the desired mapping arrives, the ARP cache is updated.
Thus, when the next IP datagram (e.g., a retransmission) is to be
sent to that remote device, the ARP cache should have the desired
information. Since holding onto the IP datagram while waiting for
an ARP reply has resource implications (i.e., buffering), the ARP
algorithm allows for a simpler, buffer-free implementation. Although
this latter behavior is permitted, the *Host Requirements* documents
[35,36] strongly discourage its use.

4.1.4 Internet Layer

The internet layer is responsible for providing transparency over both the topology of the Internet and the transmission media used in each physical network comprising the Internet. To achieve this, the internetwork service must provide:

- a common level of *delivery service* which is independent of the capabilities of the underlying media;

- a global *addressing* mechanism; and,

- a *routing* scheme to transfer data through the concatenation of physical networks.

All of these issues are fundamental if the internetworking abstraction is to be realized. This allows network devices to view an internet as homogeneous in nature.

Delivery Service

At the internet layer, the delivery service is connectionless in nature. User-data is sent as packets, termed *datagrams*, containing an integral number of octets. Further, from the perspective of the internet layer, there is no explicit relationship between the datagrams. That is, the internet layer is inherently *stateless*.[5] As a consequence, the service is said to be unreliable, because the internet layer doesn't keep track of the datagrams it has previously sent. It is up to the upper-layer protocols to implement the desired level of reliability.

Naturally, a stateless model implies that datagrams may be lost, re-ordered, excessively delayed, or (even) duplicated. Further, data contained within a datagram might be corrupted. It is the responsibility of other portions of the protocol suite (at some higher layer) to deal with these conditions.

It is important to appreciate that the extremely modest demands made by the internet layer is one of the primary strengths of the

---

[5]The research community is currently investigating the possibility of having some IP datagrams be part of "flows", as a means of providing bandwidth reservation as a future capability. For such flows, the internet layer would have a so-called "soft-state", which is a state that, if lost, can be recovered, albeit with a reduction in performance in the interim.

protocol suite. By minimizing expectations of the interface layer, the largest number of different media may be easily accommodated. Further, by placing reliability concerns at a layer above, these functions may be centralized at one layer for both efficiency and robustness. However, this argument, usually termed the *end-to-end* argument [37], must be qualified: there are several kinds of reliability. One is data integrity; the other is recovery from lost, duplicated, or mis-ordered datagrams. The philosophy of the Internet suite of protocols is that data integrity is best performed at the physical layer where there are usually powerful checksum algorithms implemented in hardware. In contrast, reliability above the physical layer is best achieved at the transport or application layer. (Of course, both the internet and transport layers include a modest checksum, efficiently implementable in software, to provide a simple "sanity check" against potential misbehavior at the layers below.[6])

IP Addressing

As foreshadowed above, an IP address is a 32–bit quantity, divided into two fields: a *network-identifier*, and a *host-identifier*. The network-identifier refers to a particular physical network in an internet, and the host-identifier refers to a particular device attached to that physical network. Because of this, an IP address precisely identifies where a network device is attached to an internet. Thus, a network device with multiple attachments will have multiple IP addresses associated with it (usually one IP address per attachment). Such a device is termed a *multi-homed* device. Finally, note that unlike a media address, an IP address is said to be a *logical* artifact. It bears no relation to hardware, media, or any other physical artifact.

The choice of 32 bits was both lucky and *problematic*. The lucky part is that it allows for extremely efficient implementation of software at the internet layer. The problematic part is that a 32–bit address space, whilst sufficient for the needs of the 80's, is expected to be too small for all the devices attached to the Internet by the end of the 90's. The problem is made harder by the fact that the 32 bits must

---

[6]The internet layer's checksum calculation is only performed on the IP-specific information in the datagram's header.

be divided between network- and host-identifiers. Whilst the original designers of the IP address developed a flexible scheme for allocating the 32 bits using address *classes*, the amount of flexibility has proved to be insufficient to cope with the phenomenal success and explosive growth of the Internet.

In late 1991, a working group was formed to examine the situation. As a result, an immediate solution, called Classless Inter-Domain Routing (CIDR) [38], was devised, and several parallel efforts began to devise a long-term solution. Before we look at CIDR, let's first examine the original address structure provided by classes.

IP addresses are divided into five classes, of which only three are germane to the topic at hand:

	bits for identifying	
class	network	host
A	7	24
B	14	16
C	21	8

Thus, there are potentially 128 class A networks, each containing up to $2^{24}-2$ hosts; potentially 16384 class B networks, each containing up to 65534 hosts; and, potentially 2^{21} class C networks, each containing up to 254 hosts. As one might expect, due to the small amount of class A network numbers possible, it is quite difficult to successfully petition the Internet Assigned Numbers Authority (IANA) for such a number — even class B network petitions receive extensive scrutiny!

In each address class, there are two special values for the host-identifier. If all the bits are zero, then the resulting 32–bit quantity refers precisely to the network identified in the IP address, and not to any host attached to the network. Similarly, if all the bits in the host-identifier are one, then the resulting IP address refers to *all* hosts attached to the network (the IP broadcast address for that network).[7]

---

[7]Some early versions of Internet software used all zeroes for the broadcast address, and a few such systems are still in use. As long as all the devices on an IP network honor the same convention, few problems ensue, but having both conventions in use on the same network can lead to disastrous anomalies, termed *broadcast storms*. However, because of the multi-vendor, heterogeneous nature of IP networks, a single convention (all ones) was chosen.

Finally, by convention, an IP address with all bits set to one refers to all hosts on the local network (another form of the IP broadcast address).

Address Encodings

As one might expect, choice of a fixed length address allows for an efficient encoding:

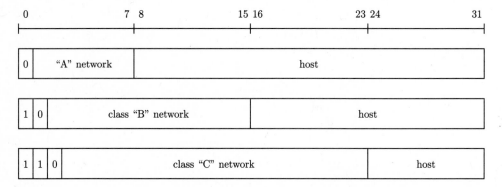

These 32–bit quantities appear in many packets: it is crucial that the ordering of the octets is consistent among implementations. In the Internet suite of protocols, the term *network byte order* is used to refer to the octet ordering which is used by *all* implementations. When an IP address is transmitted, a "big endian" scheme is used. The most significant byte (the one with bit number 0 in the figure above) is sent first, then the next significant byte, and so on.

The implications of this should be well-understood: if a network device treats IP addresses as unsigned, 32–bit integer quantities, and if it represents integers in a different format, then, prior to transmission it must perform the appropriate conversion when stuffing IP addresses into packets. Similarly, upon receipt of a packet, the device must perform the appropriate conversion from the network byte order to the local format, prior to performing any manipulations.

Finally, when describing addresses as printable strings (e.g., for use by humans), the *dotted quad* (or *dotted decimal*) notation is used: each octet is expressed as a decimal number, separated by a dot, e.g.,

```
192.33.4.21
```

Routing

Given that IP addresses allow globally unique addresses to be assigned to each network device in an internet, the next question is, how is data transferred between two devices? That is, how is routing accomplished?

To begin, the local IP entity must decide the "next hop". If the destination is on the same IP network (determined by comparing the network-identifier portion of the relevant IP addresses), then choosing the next hop is simple: it is the destination IP address. This is termed *direct* routing. Otherwise, the next hop must be to a *router*[8] on the same IP network as the local device, which is somehow "closer" to the destination device. This is termed *indirect* routing.

In the interest of clarity, the discussion will use the term *host* when referring to either the source or destination device, and the term *router* when referring to an intermediary device. The term *network device* will continue to refer to any device attached to the network.

First, note that the routing responsibilities of hosts and routers differ considerably: a host typically has only one interface and needs routing information only to make a simple determination of the next hop on that interface. The routers need much more routing information since they have multiple interfaces, and in order to forward a datagram they need to choose a next interface and a next hop.

Each network device maintains a *routing table* containing, among other things, a list of addresses reachable via routers on an attached IP network. It is often convenient to think of the routing table as being an associative array keyed by destination IP network numbers.[9] The other columns in a row in the array contain the IP address of the router and various routing metrics.

Given this terse discussion, two questions present themselves:

- How does a host find out about the routers on its IP network?

- How do routers find out about one another?

---

[8]The term *IP gateway*, or sometimes just *gateway* was used in the early days of TCP/IP.

[9]By routing based on IP network numbers, rather than IP addresses, the size of the routing table is dramatically reduced.

Usually both hosts and routers start with some initial configuration information on stable storage (e.g., a local disk). Then, they dynamically learn about the network topology through protocol interactions. In addition, there is also the notion of a *default route*, which can be used to reach a destination if its IP network isn't in the routing table.

It is beyond the scope of this edition of *The Networking Management Practicum* to discuss specific routing protocols, other than to note that routing has been the subject of intense investigation for over a decade, with each new advance leading to a re-occurrence of the "horizon effect" (i.e., every time one problem is solved, another more complicated one arises).

Two-level internets

In the mid-80's, when the Internet was beginning to enter a period of fantastic growth, it was based on a two-level connection scheme:

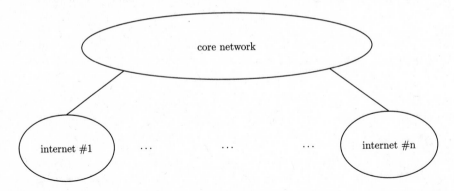

In this scheme, internets are connected to the Internet through a collection of *backbone routers*, and the backbone network is used for *all* traffic between these internets (i.e., the resulting topology is an acyclic graph). As a consequence, the backbone routers are required to have routing information on all networks available in the entire topology.

Each internet connected to the backbone is termed an *Autonomous System*, which underscores the notion that each is under a single administrative control and uses the same routing procedures.

In such a scheme, the routers in each Autonomous System need different kinds of information about a network. If the network is inside the same Autonomous System, then routing information is needed. Otherwise, if the network lies outside the Autonomous System, then only *reachability* information is needed (since the only way to route traffic is through the backbone).

To exchange reachability information between Autonomous Systems and the backbone, a special protocol, the *Exterior Gateway Protocol* (EGP) [39] was developed. Although the needs of the Internet have long since outgrown the capabilities of EGP, it provided a much-needed service for several years. The successor to EGP is the *Border Gateway Protocol* (BGP) [40].

Addressing Revisited: Subnetting

Although the two-level addressing hierarchy seems reasonable at first glance, in practice many sites have found a need to have multiple physical networks. Earlier we noted that the network-identifier corresponds to precisely one physical network. A logical conclusion (no pun intended) is that if a site was running several physical networks, then it would need several IP network-identifiers, one for each physical network.

Unfortunately, this solution isn't scalable since it increases the size of the routing tables with semantically redundant information. A better solution is to introduce extra levels in the addressing hierarchy. In particular, a three-level hierarchy allows each site to partition the host-identifier portion of its IP network address. A network so sub-partitioned is termed a *subnet*, and the mechanisms used to achieve subnetting are described in [41], which is now an Internet-standard.[10]

The idea behind subnetting is simple: outside of a site using subnets, the IP address appears to have two components, the network- and host-identifiers. Inside the site, the host-identifier is further divided into two parts: a *subnet-number*, and a *host-number*. The subnet-number refers to a particular physical network within the site's IP network, and the host-number refers to a particular device on that subnet:

---

[10]The name chosen (*subnet*) for this concept is unfortunate. In OSI parlance, the term *subnetwork* is used to denote a physical network. Needless to say, the similarity of these terms causes endless confusion and consternation.

network-identifier	host-identifier	
network-identifier	subnet-number	host-number

As with "ordinary" addresses, the question arises as to how the bits in the host-identifier should be divided between the subnet- and host-numbers. To provide maximum flexibility, a *subnet-mask* is used. This is a 32–bit quantity which is logical-ANDed with an IP address in order to derive the actual physical network being identified:

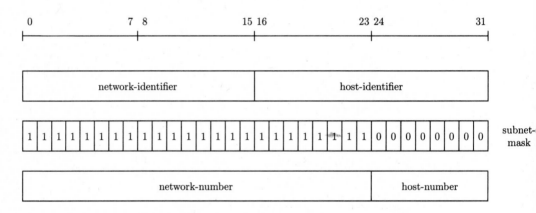

So, a new column is added to the routing table, the subnet-mask. As a default condition, if the network device doesn't know if an IP network is subnetted, the subnet-mask consists of a 32–bit quantity in which all of the bits corresponding to the network-portion of the IP address are set to one.

In such an architecture, the routing table is no longer considered as an associative array. Rather, when the next hop for an address, say A, must be determined, the device scans its routing table: for each entry, it logically-ANDs A with the subnet-mask associated with that entry. It then checks to see if the resulting quantity is equal to the destination address in the entry. If only one entry matches, then it forwards the packet to the IP router recorded as the next hop in that entry. If multiple entries match, then the longest match is chosen (i.e., the one with the most ones in its subnet-mask).[11]

Note that this approach generalizes quite nicely with the addressing architecture: if the network device is connected to a non-subnetted network, the mask is set to extract just the network-identifier, and this algorithm is equivalent to scanning the routing table sequentially, comparing A to the destination address in each entry. Of course, it is slightly slower since an additional 32-bit logical operation is performed for each entry.

Finally, one might wonder how information about subnet-masks is determined. The same mechanisms are used as with the routing table: usually there is some initial configuration from stable storage; following this, there is usually some dynamic learning through protocol interactions.

Classless Inter-Domain Routing

Even the introduction of the three-level address hierarchy described above is proving inadequate to cope with the explosive growth of the Internet. The problems occur in two ways.

- inefficient usage of the address space, and

- a rapid increase in the size of the routing tables in backbone routers.

The inefficiency in usage of the address space can be seen from the following two examples. An organization obtaining a class C network number, with 254 usable host addresses, might use only 10 of those addresses, leading to an efficiency of only 4%. Similarly, a site needing 600 addresses would obtain a class B network number and choose an appropriate subnet mask; here, less than 1% of the addresses are used.

To see how the size of backbone routers' routing tables increases, observe that if all class B network numbers were assigned, then each backbone router would need 16384 entries in its routing tables. Further, if all class C network numbers were assigned, each backbone router would need more than 2 million entries in its routing tables!

---

[11]As one might imagine, the default route in such a scheme consists of an entry with both the destination address and subnet-mask set to all zeros.

The long-term solution to this is to use more than 32 bits for an
IP address. In the meantime, a scheme called Classless Inter-Domain
Routing (CIDR) has been introduced. CIDR extends the notion
of subnets beyond the boundaries of the A, B, and C classes. For
example, a set of 65536 addresses which could only have been previously assigned as a class B address, can now be assigned to several
organizations. One organization wanting 600 host addresses can be
assigned the subnet mask 255.255.252.0 (0xFFFFFC00), which was
previously 4 class C network numbers, leaving the remaining 64512
addresses free to be assigned to other organizations. This not only
increases the usage efficiency of the address space, but also allows
one entry in a router's routing table to represent one site, no matter
how many class C network numbers it would have previously taken.
Indeed, the judicious assignment of consecutive network numbers to
multiple sites which are topologically "close" can provide even further
aggregation of routing information, and thus a further reduction in the
need for routing table entries.

Furthermore, since CIDR works based on the same subnet masks
that were already introduced by subnetting, it is largely an administrative issue of how addresses are assigned. It has no effect on
host implementations, and its principal effect on routers is how they
aggregate routing information.

Devices Revisited: Routers or Hosts

Earlier it was noted that all routers and some hosts have multiple network attachments and as such have multiple IP addresses. This leads to the obvious question as to how one distinguishes between a router and multi-homed host.

At the highest level, the distinction is simple: routers forward packets, whilst hosts don't. Therefore, routers have additional requirements placed on their internet layer. Of course, a network device might function in both capacities, and the distinction can be made only from context of usage.

Although one might view participation in a routing protocol as the only requirement, the difference is much more fundamental:

> *If a device isn't configured to act as a router, then it should never forward datagrams.*

Thus, if a host receives a datagram for a remote IP address, it should discard the datagram.[12] This behavior is critical in determining problems at the internet layer. If a failure is due to transient causes, a protocol above IP will cause a retransmission and communications will resume. Otherwise, the failure will become visible and network management tools can be used to determine the cause of the problem.

In order to heal transient problems, routers use both ICMP (a protocol discussed in Section 4.1.6) and routing protocols to synchronize their view of the internet. A host doesn't employ these mechanisms, and therefore can only *contribute* to the problem by forwarding the IP datagram. In particular, it is difficult to see how any good can result when a host, with only a single network attachment, decides to forward some of the IP datagrams it receives.

---

[12]There is one exception. An IP datagram can contain an option for source-routing indicating the path that a datagram should take through an internet. So, if an IP datagram with such an option is received, it should be forwarded according to the source route, regardless of whether the IP entity is functioning as a host or router.

4.1.5   The Internet Protocol

We finally come to the actual protocol used in the internet layer, the *Internet Protocol* (IP) [22]. For our purposes, little need be said. Each IP datagram contains a header containing addressing and other information, followed by user-data:

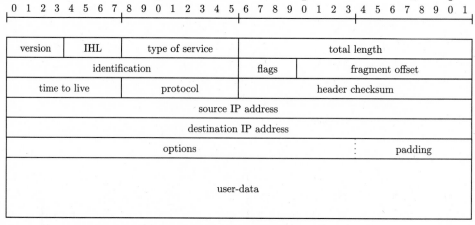

The meaning of these fields is straightforward:

version: identifies the format used. The current number is 4.

IHL: the length of IP header in 32–bit words (the minimum allowed value is 5).

type of service: indicates the quality of service (precedence, delay, throughput, and reliability) desired for the datagram.

total length: the length of the datagram (both header and user-data), measured in octets. As noted earlier, this is necessary since some types of interfaces (e.g., Ethernet) require padding if a small amount of data is transferred.

identification: a 16–bit value assigned by the originator of this datagram. It is used during reassembly (discussed below).

flags: control bits determining if this datagram may be fragmented and, if so, whether other later fragments exist.

fragment offset: a 13–bit value indicating the position of this fragment, in units of 8 octets, in the original datagram.

time to live: the upper bound (in seconds) that the datagram may be processed within the internet. Each time the datagram passes through the internet layer on any network device, the IP entity must decrement this field by at least one. If the field reaches zero at a router, the datagram is discarded. In practice, this field is actually a hop-count, and not a timer.

protocol: identifies the upper-layer protocol using IP.

header checksum: a one's-complement arithmetic sum, computed over the header of the IP datagram. This value is re-calculated each time the datagram is sent (originated or forwarded) by the IP entity on any network device.

source IP address: the IP address of the initial sender.

destination IP address: the IP address of the final recipient.

options: a collection of zero or more options.

padding: zero to three octets used to pad the datagram header to a 32–bit boundary.

user-data: zero or more octets of data from the upper-layer protocol. (Note that it is an artifact of the convention used in producing the figure above that this field appears to be a multiple of four octets in length. No such requirement is made by IP.)

As noted earlier in the discussion of the interface layer, each type of interface has a maximum size for the data field used to encapsulate an IP datagram. This is termed the *Maximum Transmission Unit* (MTU). The interface layer communicates this information to the internet layer using a local mechanism.

When the local IP entity (either a host or a router) wishes to send a datagram larger than the interface's MTU, it must *fragment* the datagram prior to transmission.

Here's how fragmentation works: Each datagram generated by an IP entity is assigned an identification number, which is carried in the IP header. When an IP entity attempts to send the datagram, it checks the MTU of the associated interface. If the MTU is greater than or equal to the size of the datagram, then no further processing is required. Otherwise, the IP entity checks to see if the **flags** field in the datagram permits fragmentation. If not, the datagram is discarded, and an ICMP message is sent to the originator. Otherwise, the IP entity generates two or more fragments. Each fragment contains a portion of the user-data from the original datagram: the user-data portion in each fragment, except the last, is a multiple of 8 octets. The **fragment offset** field contains a number corresponding to the position of the user-data, in 8–octet increments, in the original datagram. Then, for each fragment except the last in the sequence, the *more fragments* bit is set in the **flags** field.

IP fragments are treated just like IP datagrams when they are in transit. When they arrive at the destination IP address, the IP entity must buffer the fragments until it has received all of them.[13] At that point it can reassemble the original datagram. Of course, since fragments may be routed over different paths, the fragments may arrive out of order. Further, some of the fragments may be lost or corrupted. In this case, the datagram cannot be reassembled and the fragments which did arrive intact are discarded. Because IP fragmentation has no concept of selective retransmission of fragments (this would be contrary to the stateless behavior described earlier), it is up to the protocols above to retransmit the original datagram.

Although necessary to provide the internetworking abstraction, fragmentation has its drawbacks. If repeated fragmentation occurs and if the network experiences only modest congestion, the likelihood that a single fragment will be lost is alarmingly high. Even so, the entire datagram will be discarded, presumably causing retransmission by the protocols above. Of course, if only one small part of the datagram is lost, this is a rather inefficient use of resources.

To avoid fragmentation, an MTU must be chosen which is no greater than the minimum of the MTUs of each subnetwork in the path. In a large richly-connected internet, there may be several potential paths between two devices, each with different MTUs. Until recently, the "rule of thumb" was to assume an intervening MTU size of 576 octets if the first hop is to a router. However, a *Path MTU*

---

[13]Routers don't reassemble fragments as they may be sent over different paths.

Discovery algorithm is now standardized [42] by which a host may determine a reasonable lower-bound on the minimum MTU along the path. Briefly, the host guesses what the Path MTU might be, using the MTU of the first hop as its starting guess. It then sends a "probe" packet of that size with the Don't Fragment flag set in its IP header. If the path contains a subnetwork with a lower MTU, then an ICMP Destination Unreachable message will be returned, and another attempt is made with a new reduced guess. The standard provides a set of values for use as guesses.

4.1.6   The Internet Control Message Protocol

Associated with IP is another protocol providing low-level feedback about how the internet layer is operating. This protocol is termed the *Internet Control Message Protocol* (ICMP) [43]. ICMP provides very simple advice as to how the internet layer might tailor its behavior.

For now, it is important to understand that ICMP provides a modest number of basic control messages for error-reporting. Even though IP and ICMP are both part of the internet layer, ICMP uses the delivery services of IP. If the **protocol** field of an IP datagram has the value 1, the user-data contained in the datagram is an ICMP packet. Although the format of ICMP packets varies with each control message, the first 32 bits contain the same three fields:

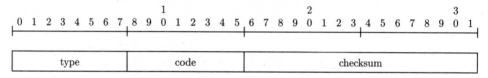

The meaning of these fields is straightforward:

type: identifies which control message is being sent (and thereby defines the format of the rest of the packet).

code: identifies a basic parameter for the control message (the semantics depend on the value of the **type** field).

checksum: a one's-complement arithmetic sum, computed over the entire ICMP packet. (Recall that the IP checksum is calculated *only* for the IP header, not the user-data.)

The control messages supported by ICMP include:

destination unreachable: to report that a datagram couldn't be delivered because a network or host was unreachable, a protocol was not running, or fragmentation was necessary but not allowed by the **flags** field.

time exceeded: to report that a datagram was discarded because its **time to live** field reached zero, or a fragment was discarded because it was on the reassembly queue too long.

parameter problem: to report an error in an IP header.

source quench: to report that a network device is discarding datagrams, especially due to lack of resources (e.g., buffers).

redirect: to report to a host the address of a router closer to a destination IP address. This is the recommended means whereby a host can learn about routers: the host starts with a default router, and performs all indirect routing through it. If the router knows of another router on the same IP network which is closer to the desired destination, it can generate an ICMP redirect message to inform the host.

echo/echo reply: to test reachability of an IP address, an echo message is sent. Upon receiving such a message, the local IP entity responds by sending an echo reply message.

timestamp/timestamp reply: to sample the delay in the network between two network devices.

information request/information reply: to determine the address of the local IP network.[14]

address-mask request/address-mask reply: to determine the subnet-mask associated with the local IP network. (These two messages are defined in [41].)

router advertisement/router solicitation: to aid in router discovery. (These two messages are defined in [44].)

The first four of these are ICMP error messages. Note that it is a fundamental principle that an ICMP error message is never sent in response to an ICMP error message.

---

[14]The Host Requirements documents [35,36] advises against implementing these.

4.2   Objects

This section describes the management instrumentation for network interfaces. It serves as both commentary text on the overall structure of the information, as well as a reference section where the meaning of specific objects can be found when they are mentioned later in this and other chapters. Thus, some readers will only want to read the commentary text in this section, and skip over the explanations of specific objects. When a specific object is referenced later in *The Networking Management Practicum*, the page number with an explanation of the object can be found by searching for the object's descriptor in the Index starting on page 537.

4.2.1 The Interfaces Group

The `interfaces` group contains generic information on the entities at the interface layer. This group was originally defined in MIB-II [3]. An evolution of the group has more recently been defined in [45]. However, as of this writing, most agents have not yet been updated with the evolution, and still implement the MIB-II definitions. Thus, let's look first at the MIB-II definition of the `interfaces` group. It contains a table, called the `ifTable`, containing one row for each of a device's network interfaces, plus a scalar object. The scalar is:

ifNumber (`INTEGER`): the number of network interfaces attached to the device.

Thus, `ifNumber` gives the number of rows in the `ifTable`.

To provide a common naming scheme applicable to all devices, each interface is identified by a unique integer value, called `ifIndex`. That is, the `ifTable`'s row template (`ifEntry`) has the property:

```
INDEX { ifIndex }
```

So, an interface's row in the `ifTable` is identified by its value of the `ifIndex` object. Values of `ifIndex` start at 1 and are typically (but not always) contiguous.

Figure 4.4 shows a Case Diagram relating the counters in each row:

ifInOctets: the total number of octets received by the interface;

ifInUcastPkts: the number of input unicast packets delivered to a higher-layer;

ifInNUcastPkts: the number of input broadcast/multicast packets delivered to a higher-layer;

ifInDiscards: the number of input packets discarded due to resource limitations;

ifInErrors: the number of input packets discarded due to any error;

ifInUnknownProtos: the number of input packets destined for an unknown higher-layer;

ifOutOctets: the total number of octets transmitted by the interface;

ifOutUcastPkts: the number of output unicast packets from a higher-layer;

ifOutNUcastPkts: the number of output broadcast/multicast packets from a higher-layer;

ifOutDiscards: the number of output packets discarded due to resource limitations; and,

ifOutErrors: the number of output packets discarded due to error.

The six traffic counters

```
ifInOctets
ifInUcastPkts
ifInNUcastPkts
ifOutOctets
ifOutUcastPkts
ifOutNUcastPkts
```

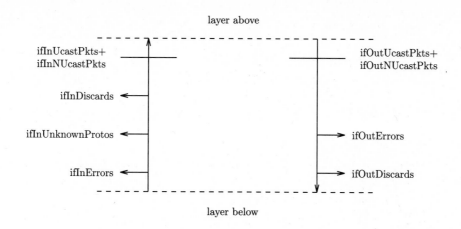

Figure 4.4: Case Diagram for the `interfaces` Group

reflect the traffic sent/received on the interface by the one system. For point-to-point interfaces, these counters give the total of the traffic on the network. In contrast, for a broadcast or multiple-access media, the counters only reflect the traffic on the device's interface, not on the whole network, except when the interface is in promiscuous mode. The other (error and discard) counters always reflect only the errors on the interface, even when an interface is in promiscuous mode.

The ifTable also has the following objects in each row:

ifIndex (INTEGER): the interface number;

ifDescr (DisplayString): a description of the interface;

ifType (enumerated INTEGER): the type of interface;

ifMtu (INTEGER): the MTU size of the interface in octets;

ifSpeed (Gauge32): the transmission rate in bits/second;

ifPhysAddress (PhysAddress): the interface-layer (media-specific) address;

ifAdminStatus (enumerated INTEGER): the desired interface state;

ifOperStatus (enumerated INTEGER): the current interface state;

ifLastChange (TimeStamp): the time when the interface last changed state;

ifOutQLen (Gauge32): the current number of packets in the interface's output queue; and,

ifSpecific (OBJECT IDENTIFIER): a media-specific pointer to a MIB module.

Figure 4.5 illustrates what a window displaying most of these objects might look like.

These objects are generic, and although MIB-II specifies that all of them apply to all interfaces regardless of type, we'll see in the next section that this is no longer the case. Objects specific to particular types of interface are supported by using the ifSpecific object as a "pointer" to an appropriate media-specific MIB module. (A selection of media-specific MIB modules is explained in Chapters 5 and 6.) If no media-specific MIB module is supported, the ifSpecific object has the value 0.0.

The ifAdminStatus object is a means for conveying an imperative action to the agent. For example, if the value is changed from down to up, the agent understands this to mean that the interface should be initialized and brought into the ready state, if possible. The result of

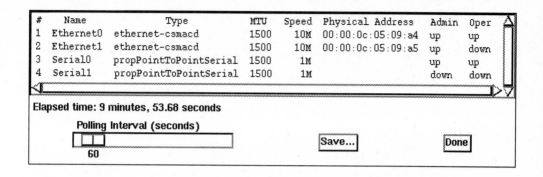

Figure 4.5: A Window Browsing parts of the `ifTable`

the action is subsequently available as the value of the `ifOperStatus` object.

It is also useful to inspect `ifOperStatus` and `ifLastChange` at other times. Differing values of `ifOperStatus` and `ifAdminStatus`, and/or a value of `ifLastChange` which is "recent", are typically indicators that there is or has recently been a problem.

4.2.2 Evolution of the Interfaces Group

Since the standardization of MIB-II, many media-specific MIB modules have been written. These contain the management information specific to particular types of interfaces. Experience in defining and using these media-specific MIB modules showed the need to distinguish between the multiple sub-layers beneath the internetwork layer. In addition, there is a need to manage these sub-layers in devices (e.g., MAC layer bridges) unaware of which, if any, internetwork protocols run over the sub-layers. For example, for an interface consisting of the Point-to-Point Protocol (PPP) [46] running over an HDLC/LAPB link and using an RS232-like connector, each of the three sub-layers has its own media-specific MIB module. Thus, not only is it useful for each of these sub-layers to be represented by a row in the `ifTable`, but a mechanism is also needed to describe the relationship between them, particularly when the sub-layers perform upward or downward multiplexing.

An example of *upward multiplexing* is MLP (Multi-Link Procedure) [47] which provides load-sharing over several serial lines by appearing as a single point-to-point link to the sub-layer(s) above. An example of *downward multiplexing* would be several instances of PPP, each framed within a separate X.25 virtual circuit, all of which run over one fractional T1 channel, concurrently with other uses of the T1 link.

To address these and other issues, the `IF-MIB` module [45] defines an evolution of the `interfaces` group, which

- retains the definition of `ifNumber`;

- updates the columnar objects of the `ifTable`; and,

- defines four additional tables.

The updates to the `ifTable` are:

- `ifType` is now defined using the

      `IANAifType`

  textual convention thereby allowing the IANA to assign new enumerated values for new interface types; and,

- four objects have been deprecated:

  ifInNUcastPkts and ifOutNUcastPkts: are replaced by four new counters in the new tables which count multicast and broadcast packets separately (see below);

  ifOutQLen: was difficult to implement on some systems, and not sufficiently detailed on others; and,

  ifSpecific: became redundant with each sub-layer having its own row in the `ifTable`, since `ifType` indicates which media-specific MIB module is relevant.

  (Deprecated objects are obsolescent — while they are still used and may still be implemented to foster interoperability with older implementations, they will become obsolete over time.)

The new tables also make use of a new textual convention, `RowStatus`, which is an enumerated `INTEGER` allowing the status of a row to be monitored/controlled through having one of the following values:

active	row is in use
notInService	ready for, but not in use
notReady	incomplete
createAndGo	create new row in one-shot
createAndWait	create new row in multiple steps
destroy	delete row

The status of a row normally corresponds to one of the first three values; all values except `notReady` can be `set` to cause the row's state to change. When `set` to `createAndGo`, the row is created and enters the `active` state, if that is possible; if not, the `set` fails.

The new `ifStackTable` provides the means to represent the relationships between multiple sub-layers, including the representation of upward and downward multiplexing. A row in the `ifStackTable` is identified by two `INTEGER`s:

> INDEX { ifStackHigherLayer, ifStackLowerLayer }

such that one row represents the relationship of two sub-layers, one running "on top" of the other. The `ifStackHigherLayer` object has the `ifIndex` value of the higher sub-layer, and `ifStackLowerLayer` has the `ifIndex` value of the lower sub-layer. The table contains one accessible object

ifStackStatus (`RowStatus`): the status of the row.

Note that although this textual convention allows new rows to be created, most implementations of `ifStackStatus` will support only one value, `active`, and not provide write-access to the object.

The second new table, the `ifXTable`, defines new generic objects for each interface. Effectively, it augments the `ifTable`, and thus, as one would expect, its row template has the property:

> AUGMENTS { ifEntry }

That is, it is indexed in the same way as the `ifTable`, by the `ifIndex` value of the interface. Four of the new objects are the counters which replace `ifInNUcastPkts` and `ifOutNUcastPkts`. These are:

ifInMulticastPkts: the number of input multicast packets delivered to a higher-layer;

ifInBroadcastPkts: the number of input broadcast packets delivered to a higher-layer;

ifOutMulticastPkts: the number of output multicast packets from a higher-layer; and,

ifOutBroadcastPkts: the number of output broadcast packets from a higher-layer.

The `ifXTable` also contains eight "high capacity" 64–bit counters, specifically defined for use on higher-speed interfaces. For such interfaces, 32–bit counters have the potential to wrap around in a shorter amount of time than it is reasonable to expect a management application to poll them twice. For SNMPv2 agents, the octet counters `ifHCInOctets` and `ifHCOutOctets` are required for interfaces greater than 20Mb/s, whilst the packet counters,

```
ifHCInUcastPkts
ifHCInMulticastPkts
ifHCInBroadcastPkts
ifHCOutUcastPkts
ifHCOutMulticastPkts
ifHCOutBroadcastPkts
```

are required for interfaces greater than 650Mb/s.

In addition, the `ifXtable` contains five other new objects:

ifName (`DisplayString`): the name of the interface (as used by humans);

ifLinkUpDownTrapEnable (enumerated `INTEGER`): indicates whether linkUp/linkDown traps are enabled for the interface;

ifHighSpeed (`Gauge32`): the speed of the interface in Mb/s;

ifPromiscuousMode (`TruthValue`):   indicates whether the interface is in promiscuous mode; and,

ifConnectorPresent (`TruthValue`):   indicates whether the interface has a physical connector;

The value of ifName is the name of the interface as known by the local device, for example, "1e0" or simply the port number. If several rows in the ifTable together represent a single interface as named by the device, then they will typically all have the same value of ifName.

The third new table is the ifTestTable. It is defined to allow diagnostic or other tests (e.g., loopback) to be performed on an interface.

ifTestId (TestAndIncr): a test invocation number for the next test;

ifTestStatus (enumerated INTEGER): an indication of whether a test is currently in progress;

ifTestType (AutonomousType): the type of test to be run;

ifTestResult (enumerated INTEGER): a standard set of results;

ifTestCode (OBJECT IDENTIFIER): a pointer to test-specific results; and,

ifTestOwner (OwnerString): an indication of who invoked the current test.

The last new table, the ifRcvAddressTable, is used when there are multiple media addresses in use on an interface. In such a situation, the primary address is held by ifPhysAddress, and the additional addresses are recorded in this table. For example, for systems which receive packets sent to one or more multicast addresses, this table records the current set of multicast addresses. Each row in the table represents one such media address on a particular interface, and is identified by the interface number and the media address:

```
INDEX  { ifIndex, ifRcvAddressAddress }
```

The table contains two accessible objects:

ifRcvAddressStatus (RowStatus): the current status of the row;

ifRcvAddressType (enumerated INTEGER): an indication of whether this address will be retained after the next restart of the system.

4.2.3 Conformance Levels for the Interfaces Group

Table 4.1 shows how the objects described above are organized into object groups for the purposes of conformance.

Two groups are applicable to all interfaces: the `ifGeneralGroup` and the `ifStackGroup`. Two other groups apply according to the type of interface: the `ifFixedLengthGroup` for those which are character-oriented or transmit data in fixed-length transmission units; and the `ifPacketGroup` for packet-oriented interfaces. Variations on these latter two groups are further defined according to the speed of the interface, as mentioned above.

4.2.4 The Address Translation Group

Information on address resolution is contained in MIB-II's address translation group. The group consists of a single table, the `atTable`, used for mapping IP addresses into media-specific addresses. Each row of the table contains three columns:

atIfIndex (INTEGER): the interface number on which the mapping is valid;

atPhysAddress (PhysAddress): the media address of the mapping; and

atNetAddress (NetworkAddress): the IP address of the mapping.[15]

Two of the three columns are used to uniquely identify a row:

    INDEX { atIfIndex, atNetAddress }

The address translation group is marked *deprecated*, since information on address resolution was moved (in the evolution of MIB-I to MIB-II) to each network protocol group. For IP, the information is contained in the `ipNetToMediaTable`, explained on page 204.

---

[15]Note that the `NetworkAddress` syntax is deprecated by SNMPv2.

group	objects
ifGeneralGroup	ifAdminStatus
	ifConnectorPresent
	ifDescr
	ifHighSpeed
	ifLastChange
	ifLinkUpDownTrapEnable
	ifName
	ifOperStatus
	ifPhysAddress
	ifSpeed
	ifType
ifFixedLengthGroup	ifInErrors
	ifInOctets
	ifInUnknownProtos
	ifOutErrors
	ifOutOctets
ifPacketGroup	ifInBroadcastPkts
	ifInDiscards
	ifInErrors
	ifInMulticastPkts
	ifInOctets
	ifInUcastPkts
	ifInUnknownProtos
	ifMtu
	ifOutBroadcastPkts
	ifOutDiscards
	ifOutErrors
	ifOutMulticastPkts
	ifOutOctets
	ifOutUcastPkts
	ifPromiscuousMode
ifStackGroup	ifStackStatus

Table 4.1: Conformance Levels for the Interfaces Group

4.2.5   The IP Group

The ip group contains information about the IP subsystem of a managed node. The group contains several scalars and four tables. Figure 4.6 shows a Case Diagram relating the scalar counters:

ipInReceives: the total number of datagrams from below;

ipInHdrErrors: the number of datagrams discarded due to format error;

ipInAddrErrors: the number of datagrams discarded due to misdelivery;

ipForwDatagrams: the number of datagrams forwarded;

ipInUnknownProtos: the number of datagrams for unknown protocols;

ipInDiscards: the number of datagrams discarded due to resource limitations;

ipInDelivers: the number of datagrams delivered to the layer above;

ipOutRequests: the number of datagrams received from the layer above;

ipOutDiscards: the number of datagrams discarded due to lack of resources;

ipOutNoRoutes: the number of datagrams discarded due to the absence of applicable routing information;

ipReasmReqds: the number of fragments received needing reassembly;

ipReasmOKs: the number of datagrams successfully reassembled;

ipReasmFails: the number of reassembly failures;

ipFragOKs: the number of datagrams successfully fragmented;

ipFragFails: the number of datagrams needing fragmentation when not allowed; and,

ipFragCreates: the number of fragments created.

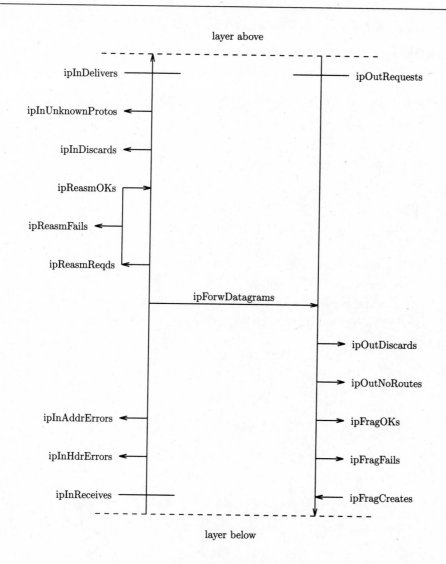

Figure 4.6: Case Diagram for the IP Group

The other scalars in the `ip` group are:

ipForwarding (enumerated `INTEGER`): an indication of whether
the device is acting as a router or a host;

ipDefaultTTL (`INTEGER`): the default TTL for IP packets;

ipReasmTimeout (`INTEGER`):   the timeout value (in seconds)
for the reassembly queue.

For fragmentation, the counters

```
ipReasmReqds
ipFragCreates
ipReasmOKs
ipFragOKs
```

give an indication of how much fragmentation is occurring, whereas
`ipReasmFails` and `ipFragFails` give an indication of how much of
the efficiency of the network is being wasted as a result of fragmentation. If the wastage is significant, the best remedy is to upgrade the
system performing the fragmentation to use Path MTU Discovery.
If this is not possible, then the system reporting excessive values of
`ipReasmFails` may be able to be configured with a larger value of
`ipReasmTimeout`.

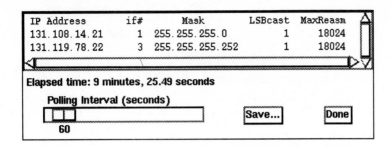

Figure 4.7: A Window Browsing the `ipAddrTable`

The IP address table, `ipAddrTable`, keeps track of the IP addresses associated with the managed node. Each row of the table contains:

ipAdEntAddr (`IpAddress`): the IP address of this row;

ipAdEntIfIndex (`INTEGER`): the interface number on which this IP address is valid;

ipAdEntNetMask (`IpAddress`): the subnet-mask for this IP address;

ipAdEntBcastAddr (`INTEGER`): the least significant bit of the IP broadcast address;

ipAdEntReasmMaxSize (`INTEGER`): the largest IP datagram that can be reassembled.

Each row is identified by the IP address it represents:

```
INDEX { ipAdEntAddr }
```

Figure 4.7 shows what a window displaying these objects might look like. While it might be surprising that the value of `ipAdEntBcastAddr` is a single bit, recall from page 172 that there was originally some confusion as to whether all-zeros or all-ones were used in the host-identifier of the IP broadcast address. The single bit serves to distinguish these two cases.

The **ipRouteTable** keeps track of the IP routes in the managed node's IP routing table. This table has since been replaced by a new table discussed in Section 4.2.7 starting on page 208. Each row of the table contains several columns:

ipRouteDest (`IpAddress`): the destination IP address;

ipRouteIfIndex (`INTEGER`): the interface used by this route;

ipRouteMetric1 (`INTEGER`): the routing metric #1;

ipRouteMetric2 (`INTEGER`): the routing metric #2;

ipRouteMetric3 (`INTEGER`): the routing metric #3;

ipRouteMetric4 (`INTEGER`): the routing metric #4;

ipRouteMetric5 (`INTEGER`): the routing metric #5;

ipRouteNextHop (`IpAddress`): for an indirect route, the IP address of the next hop router;

ipRouteType (enumerated `INTEGER`): the type of route: `direct`, `indirect` or `invalid`;

ipRouteProto (enumerated `INTEGER`): the mechanism by which the route was learned;

ipRouteAge (`INTEGER`): the age of the route in seconds;

ipRouteMask (`IpAddress`): the subnet-mask for the route; and,

ipRouteInfo (enumerated `INTEGER`): a pointer to a protocol-specific MIB module.

The destination IP address is used to uniquely identify a row:

```
INDEX { ipRouteDest }
```

New routes are entered into the table either through a **set** which creates a new row (often called a static route), or through being learned via a routing protocol. Rows created by network management are distinguished by **ipRouteProto** having the value **netmgmt**. Routes can also be deleted by **ipRouteType** being **set** to "invalid".[16] Note

---

[16]This usage of the **invalid** value was the norm before the introduction of the RowStatus textual convention.

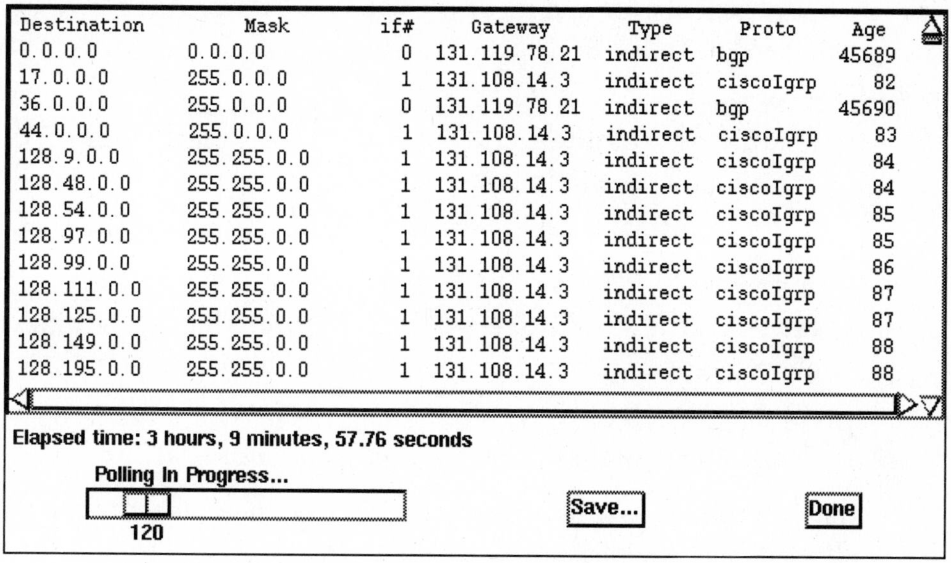

Destination	Mask	if#	Gateway	Type	Proto	Age
0.0.0.0	0.0.0.0	0	131.119.78.21	indirect	bgp	45689
17.0.0.0	255.0.0.0	1	131.108.14.3	indirect	ciscoIgrp	82
36.0.0.0	255.0.0.0	0	131.119.78.21	indirect	bgp	45690
44.0.0.0	255.0.0.0	1	131.108.14.3	indirect	ciscoIgrp	83
128.9.0.0	255.255.0.0	1	131.108.14.3	indirect	ciscoIgrp	84
128.48.0.0	255.255.0.0	1	131.108.14.3	indirect	ciscoIgrp	84
128.54.0.0	255.255.0.0	1	131.108.14.3	indirect	ciscoIgrp	85
128.97.0.0	255.255.0.0	1	131.108.14.3	indirect	ciscoIgrp	85
128.99.0.0	255.255.0.0	1	131.108.14.3	indirect	ciscoIgrp	86
128.111.0.0	255.255.0.0	1	131.108.14.3	indirect	ciscoIgrp	87
128.125.0.0	255.255.0.0	1	131.108.14.3	indirect	ciscoIgrp	87
128.149.0.0	255.255.0.0	1	131.108.14.3	indirect	ciscoIgrp	88
128.195.0.0	255.255.0.0	1	131.108.14.3	indirect	ciscoIgrp	88

Elapsed time: 3 hours, 9 minutes, 57.76 seconds

Polling In Progress...

120

Save... Done

Figure 4.8: A Window Browsing parts of the `ipRouteTable`

however, that if the route was learned through a routing protocol, the route might immediately be re-learned through the same routing protocol. For this reason, some agents only allow static routes to be deleted.

Use of the routing metric objects varies. Hosts do not use them at all; routers use them according to the routing protocol by which the route was learned; and most routing protocols use fewer than five metrics. For each metric which is unused, the relevant object takes the value '-1'. Where they are valuable is in comparing two routes learned via the same routing protocol (typically, metrics of different protocols are not directly comparable).

Figure 4.8 shows what a window displaying some of these objects might look like.

The IP address translation table, `ipNetToMediaTable`, keeps track of the mapping between IP and media-specific addresses: It replaces the deprecated `atTable` for IP addresses. Each row of the table contains four columns:

ipNetToMediaIfIndex (`INTEGER`): the interface number on which the mapping is valid;

ipNetToMediaPhysAddress (`PhysAddress`): the media address of the mapping;

ipNetToMediaNetAddress (`IpAddress`): the IP address of the mapping;

ipNetToMediaType (enumerated `INTEGER`): the type of mapping: `static`, `dynamic`, `other` or `invalid`.

The `ipNetToMediaTable` is indexed by the interface number and the IP address of the mapping:

```
INDEX { ipNetToMediaIfIndex, ipNetToMediaNetAddress }
```

If the value of the **ipNetToMediaType** is set to "invalid", then the corresponding row is invalidated. Figure 4.9 shows what a window displaying these objects might look like.

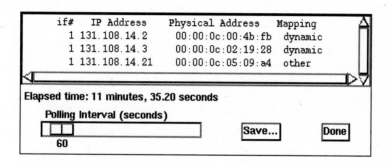

Figure 4.9: A Window Browsing the ipNetToMediaTable

4.2.6   The ICMP Group

The `icmp` group consists of 26 counters. In the interest of brevity, this
group can be summarized as:

- for each ICMP message type, two counters exist, one counting
  the number of times the message type was generated by the
  local ICMP entity; the other counting the number of times the
  message type was received by the local ICMP entity; and,

- there are four additional counters which keep track of the total
  number of ICMP messages received, sent, received in error, or
  not sent due to error.

Figure 4.10 shows a Case Diagram relating these objects.

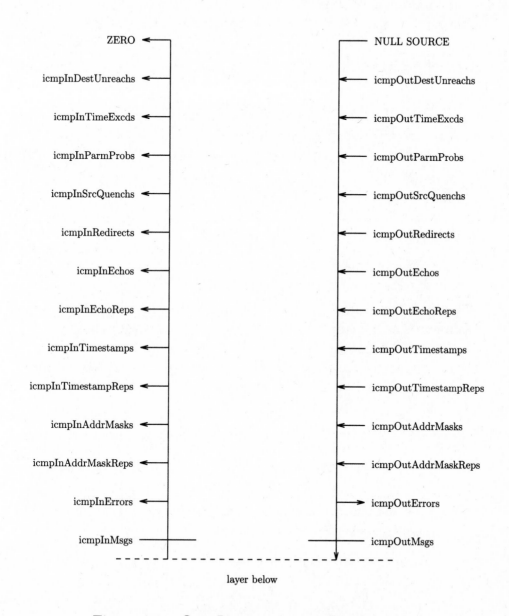

Figure 4.10: Case Diagram for the ICMP Group

4.2.7   The IP Forwarding Table MIB

Refinements in the IP routing algorithm led to MIB-II's `ipRouteTable`
being inadequate for its intended task. In particular, it did not
allow representation of multiple routes to the same destination, which
occurs quite often in modern routers. So, the IP Forwarding Table
MIB module [48] was defined as a replacement. It contains two
top-level objects:

> **ipForwardNumber** (`Gauge32`): the number of entries in the
> routing table,

and a single table, the `ipForwardTable`, containing information on
those routes.

The table's biggest difference from the `ipRouteTable` is how the
rows are identified. In the `ipForwardTable`, four values are used to
identify a particular row:

```
INDEX { ipForwardDest, ipForwardProto,
        ipForwardPolicy, ipForwardNextHop }
```

With these four values, multiple rows for the same destination can be
represented no matter whether they were learned via different protocols, are used according to a different routing policy, or are routed via
a different next hop. The columns of the table are mostly the same
as those in the `ipRouteTable`, but there are a few refinements:

> **ipForwardDest** (`IpAddress`): same as `ipRouteDest`;

> **ipForwardMask** (`IpAddress`): same as `ipRouteMask`;

> **ipForwardPolicy** (`INTEGER`): the policy associated with this
> route, used when there are multiple routes to the same
> destination. By default, the policy refers to the IP type
> of service field (introduced earlier on page 180);

> **ipForwardNextHop** (`IpAddress`): this is equivalent to
> `ipRouteNextHop`;

> **ipForwardIfIndex** (`INTEGER`): same as `ipRouteIfIndex`;

> **ipForwardType** (enumerated `INTEGER`): this is equivalent to
> `ifRouteType`;

ipForwardProto (enumerated INTEGER): this is the same as ipRouteProto but with enumerations for more routing protocols;

ipForwardAge (INTEGER): same as ipRouteAge;

ipForwardInfo (OBJECT IDENTIFIER): same as ipRouteInfo;

ipForwardNextHopAS (INTEGER): the autonomous system number (see page 174) associated with the next hop;

ipForwardMetric1 (INTEGER): same as ipRouteMetric1;

ipForwardMetric2 (INTEGER): same as ipRouteMetric2;

ipForwardMetric3 (INTEGER): same as ipRouteMetric3;

ipForwardMetric4 (INTEGER): same as ipRouteMetric4; and,

ipForwardMetric5 (INTEGER): same as ipRouteMetric5.

4.3   Applications

Now it's time to turn our attention to applications for interface management. Before looking at some specific applications, let's consider how we can use some of the 135 MIB objects introduced in the previous section.

The first thing to observe is that about half of those MIB objects are counters of "interesting" events. Such events are counted only so that they can be monitored as a part of determining the health and performance of the interfaces. The events can be categorized as follows:

problem conditions: which indicate a problem that requires attention — the seriousness of the problem, and the urgency of fixing the problem, varies by condition;

unusual conditions: which can and do occur at some low frequency as a part of the normal operation of the network, but each of these becomes a problem when it occurs too frequently; and,

workload events: which count the normal activity of an interface in performing its regular functions, and are used to determine how much and how well the interfaces are performing. In addition, they can also be used to recognize problems, for example:

- when the workload of the network is reaching its capacity, and thus is close to becoming overloaded; or,

- when part of the network is under-utilized, which could mean that there is a problem somewhere else preventing the normal workload from being present.

For the `interfaces` group, guidelines on what are good/bad values for particular objects vary according to the type of interface. In particular, one counter might be a problem condition on one interface but an unusual condition on another. However, there are some generic relationships which hold and can be useful to apply. As explained earlier in Section 3.1.2 on page 94, a management application uses counters to calculate rates. For the `interfaces` group, the `ifInErrors` and `ifOutErrors` counters give input and output error rates; `ifInDiscards` and `ifOutDiscards` give discard rates. The input packet rate is the sum of `ifInUcastPkts` and `ifInNUcastPkts`; the output rate is the sum of `ifOutUcastPkts` and `ifOutNUcastPkts`. With these rates,

- the input and output error rates should be relatively low and much smaller than the input and output packet-rates respectively,

- the discard rates should be relatively low and much smaller than the corresponding packet-rate,

- unless the interface is relatively idle, the broadcast rate should always be, and the multicast rate should normally be, much smaller than the packet-rate.[17]

`ifInUnknownProtos` is a problem condition for just about all types.

For the `ip` group, `ipInDelivers` and `ipOutRequests` are workload events. In a router, `ipForwDatagrams` is also a workload event, but not in a host, where it is typically a problem condition, suggesting that the manager should check the value of `ipForwarding`. `ipInAddrErrors` and `ipOutNoRoutes` are just about always problem conditions. `ipInHdrErrors`, `ipInUnknownProtos`, `ipInDiscards` and `ipOutDiscards` are unusual conditions. For the `icmp` group, `icmpInTimeExcds` and `icmpOutTimeExcds` are unusual conditions. In contrast, `icmpInParmProbs` and `icmpOutParmProbs` are normally problem conditions.

---

[17]Network applications which make extensive use of multicast are relatively rare these days. Even if this changes in the future, it is still of value for a network manager to know that such applications are in use on the network.

4.3.1   Specific Applications

Let's start our application fragments by looking at how the simple browsing application introduced in Section 3.3.5 on page 148 can be customized for some of the network interface objects.

Suppose we modified the browser to check for an object-specific formatting procedure when it has an object's value to be displayed. When the elements of the array **avar** have the structure described on page 134, and **var** is one of those array elements, then we can append the object's descriptor as a new list element (at offset 7) to **var**, like this:

```
set     data      $avar($var)
if {[set object [lindex $data 7]] == ""} {
    lappend    avar($var)     \
        [set object [snmpinfo mibprop $var descriptor]]
}
set     value     [lindex $data 4]
if {[info exists snmptcl_print_object($object)]} {
    set     value \
        [$snmptcl_print_object($object) $var avar($var)]
}
```

Then, to get a more readable format for, say, **ifSpeed**, all we have to do is provide the procedure shown in Figure 4.11, and do the initialization:

```
set     snmptcl_print_object(ifSpeed) \
            snmptcl_print_ifSpeed
```

Earlier in this section, an interface's packet rates, discard rates, and error rates were mentioned. The same technique shown in Figure 3.24 on page 153 can be used to graph these.

But suppose we want to go further and show the utilization of the the interface. We could use the formula given by Leinwand in [49] and in Volume 1, Number 4, of *The Simple Times* [50]:

```
if-utilization =
    100 * 8 * (!serial ? ifInOctets + ifOutOctets
                      : ifInOctets > ifOutOctets
                            ? ifInOctets : ifOutOctets)

        / ifSpeed
```

```
proc snmptcl_print_ifSpeed {var data} {
    upvar $data info

    set    value   [lindex $info 4]
    set    i       0
    if {[string first . $value] >= 0} {
        incr  i
        set    value   [expr int($value/1024)]
    }
    for {} {$value > 999} {set value [expr $value/1000]} {          10
        incr  i
    }
    switch $i {
        0
            _

        1
            _

        2
            _

        3 {                                                         20
            return [format "%s%s" $value [lindex [list "" "K" "M" "G"] $i]]
        }

        default {
            return "huge"
        }
    }
}
```

Figure 4.11: **Formatting** `ifSpeed`

where the `serial` variable indicates whether the interface is half-
or full-duplex; for half-duplex interfaces[18] the sum of the input and
output bytes is used; for full-duplex, the number of input or output
bytes is used, whichever is larger. The interface's utilization as a
percentage is produced as the result multiplying by 8 (to get the
number of bits) and dividing by the interface's speed.

A procedure called `snmptcl_graph_command` was used to draw the
graph in Figure 3.24 on page 153. By modifying this procedure to take
the name of another procedure as an extra optional parameter, which
it will call before graphing the values, we can then supply a procedure
to apply the formula to the retrieved values in order to calculate the
utilization percentage to be displayed in the graph.

The supplied procedure, `snmptcl_graph_ifutil`, is shown in Figure 4.12 starting on page 215.

This procedure is called with three parameters, the first parameter
contains the `ifIndex` value of the interface, except on the first call
when it has the special value "labels"; the second and third parameters
are the window name and the base for the names of the global arrays.
The first call does initialization; succeeding calls are to obtain a value
to be plotted on the graph.

After setting up the global variables, the procedure examines the
value of `idx` to determine if this is the first call. If so, the elements
of the array `avar` are extracted, sorted, and all except those which
are instances of `ifDescr` are discarded. For each instance of `ifDescr`,
its value (the interface description) is used to format a label for the
graph's legend and is stored in `ainfo(objs)`. The `ainfo(idx)` list
is initialized to contain one element for each line to be drawn on
the graph; the values of these elements will be passed as the first
parameter on succeeding calls to this procedure. The `afnx` array is
also initialized to be used by the calling procedure to record how far
along the x-axis the plot has progressed.

---

[18]Half-duplex interfaces (such as regular Ethernet) can only send or receive, not
both, at any given moment in time; full-duplex interfaces (such as serial lines) can
send and receive at the same time.

```
proc snmptcl_graph_ifutil {idx w array} {
  global    snmptcl_var_ifDescr snmptcl_var_ifType
  global    snmptcl_var_ifSpeed
  global    snmptcl_var_ifInOctets snmptcl_var_ifOutOctets

  global    ${array}_info
  upvar #0  ${array}_info    ainfo

  global    ${array}_var
  upvar #0  ${array}_var     avar                                      10

  global    ${array}_fnx
  upvar #0  ${array}_fnx     afnx

  switch $idx {
    labels {
        set       ainfo(objs)    ""
        set       ainfo(idx)     ""
        foreach   var  [lsort -command snmptcl_proc_oidcmp \
                        [array names avar]] {                          20
      if {![snmptcl_proc_oidcontains $snmptcl_var_ifDescr $var]} {
              break
      }
        set     idx       [lindex [snmpinfo mibprop $var full] 3]
        lappend   ainfo(objs)   "#$idx:  [lindex $avar($var) 4]"
        lappend   ainfo(idx)    $idx
        set     afnx($idx)     $avar($var)
    }

# add "Help" button to window to explain Leinwand's formula...         30
  }
```

Figure 4.12: The `snmptcl_graph_ifutil` procedure

On subsequent calls, the values retrieved from the device for each of the interface objects needed to calculate the formula are extracted from the `avar` array, and stored in local variables. Two of the techniques here deserve special mention:

- to execute the same loop for all four objects, four local variables are stored in a list so that each one can be extracted by the `foreach`; and,

- `eval` is used to construct the object descriptor from the local variable.

Next, after a check to ensure that values for all the objects were obtained, the values on the previous iteration are extracted, and a sanity check is performed on the value of `ifSpeed`. Providing all these checks are successful, the increments of `ifInOctets` and `ifOutOctets` over the previous period are calculated (with appropriate care for the case where the counter values roll-over). Note the way that `0.0` is used to convert the values to floating point so that precision will not be lost in later calculations:

```
set     diffInOctets \
           [expr 0.0+$curInOctets-$prevInOctets]
```

For each counter, the `sysUpTime` at the beginning and end of the period is also extracted, in order to convert the increments to bits per second rates (multiplying by 100 since `sysUpTime` is in hundredths of a second). Then, `ifType`'s value is inspected to determine whether to take the larger of the two increments, or their sum. Finally, the value is converted to bits, multiplied by 100 to convert to a percentage, and divided by the interface's speed.

The result is a graph like the one shown in Figure 4.13 on page 218.

```tcl
default {
    set     ifOutOctets    ""
    foreach  var   [list ifType ifSpeed ifInOctets ifOutOctets] {
        eval    set obj \$snmptcl_var_$var
        if {(![info exists avar($obj.$idx)]))} {
            break
        }
        set     $var   $avar($obj.$idx)
    }
    if {($ifOutOctets == "") \                                                     10
        || ([set prevInOctets [lindex $ifInOctets 1]] == "") \
        || ([set prevOutOctets [lindex $ifOutOctets 1]] == "") \
        || ([set speed [lindex $ifSpeed 4]] <= 0)} {
        return    ""
    }
    if {$prevInOctets > [set curInOctets [lindex $ifInOctets 4]]} {
        set     diffInOctets \
                    [expr $curInOctets+(4294967296.0-$prevInOctets)]
    } else {
        set     diffInOctets \                                                     20
                    [expr 0.0+$curInOctets-$prevInOctets]
    }
    if {[set delta [expr [lindex $ifInOctets 5] - \
                        [lindex $ifInOctets 2]]] == 0} {
        set     delta    1
    }
    set     diffInOctets  [expr 100*$diffInOctets/$delta]
    if {$prevOutOctets > [set curOutOctets [lindex $ifOutOctets 4]]} {
        set     diffOutOctets \
                    [expr $curOutOctets+(4294967296.0-$prevOutOctets)]           30
    } else {
        set     diffOutOctets \
                    [expr 0.0+$curOutOctets-$prevOutOctets]
    }
    if {[set delta [expr [lindex $ifOutOctets 5] - \
                        [lindex $ifOutOctets 2]]] == 0} {
        set     delta    1
    }
    set     diffOutOctets  [expr 100*$diffOutOctets/$delta]
    switch -- [lindex $ifType 4] {                                                40
                  2 - 3 - 4 - 5 -
                                     16 - 17 - 18 - 19 -
        20 - 21 - 22 - 23 -              28 -
        30 -    32 - 33 - 34 -          38 -
        40 -            45 -       48 {
            if {[set octets $diffInOctets] < $diffOutOctets} {
                set   octets    $diffOutOctets
            }
        }
                                                                                  50
        default {
            set   octets   [expr $diffInOctets+$diffOutOctets]
        }
    }
    return    [expr 800*$octets/$speed]
}
}
}
}
```

Figure 4.12: The `snmptcl_graph_ifutil` procedure (cont.)

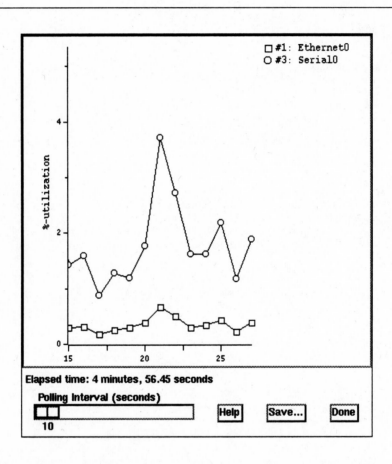

Figure 4.13: A Window Graphing Interface Utilization

4.3.2 History Data

It is often useful to collect values over a period of time and store them in a file, so that they can be processed later. Such later processing might be to produce reports, for example, on network usage, or to analyze the data to determine how the network operates. An example of the need for the latter is to handle the counters in the unusual conditions category, mentioned earlier.

Recall that this unusual conditions category refers to conditions which occur naturally during the normal operation of the network, but can indicate a problem if a condition is occurring too frequently. Where is the dividing line between normal operation and a problem condition? Unfortunately, even for the most specific counters, the answer can vary significantly depending on the topology of the network, the types of devices, and the applications in use on the network. Thus, it's necessary to collect sample values over a period of time and then analyze them to find what values are typical for specific devices in the network.

So, let's look at two applications:

data collector: an application to collect *history* data; and,

history display: an application to produce a histogram of the collected data.

A Data Collector

For the data collector, we can use the same polling procedure introduced in Section 3.3.3 on page 123, but instead of just displaying
the values as the browsing application did, we'll store them in a file.
Thus, when the collector starts, it interacts with the user to choose
a filename, and allows the user to select which objects are to be collected, and then calls the polling procedure to start collecting values,
specifying `snmptcl_collect_command` as the callback procedure to
be called when the values are available. `snmptcl_collect_command`
is shown in Figure 4.14 starting on page 221.

The procedure starts by checking if this is the first time it has
been called. If so, then it opens the selected file; if the open fails,
an appropriate dialog box is displayed to the user. Otherwise, the
file-identifier is saved and some header records are written to the file to
identify it as a collection file, and to record the context and the objects
being collected. For subsequent calls, the file-identifier is recovered
from the global array.

```
proc   snmptcl_collect_command  {w array} {
   global          snmptcl_collect_object snmptcl_collect_syntax

   global          ${array}_info
   upvar #0        ${array}_info      ainfo

   global          ${array}_var
   upvar #0        ${array}_var       avar

   global          ${array}_collect                                10
   upvar #0        ${array}_collect          lvars

   if {![info exists ainfo(onceonly)]} {
          set      ainfo(onceonly)   1

          if {[catch { set fileid [open $ainfo(filepath) w] } result]} {
                 snmptcl_dialog          [wm title $w] $result questhead 0 Abort
# destroy window, delete private arrays
                 return
          }                                                        20
          set       ainfo(fileid)     $fileid
          puts      $fileid           "Data file produced by snmptcl_collect"
          puts      $fileid           [$ainfo(pHandle) config name]

# setup button in window for user to terminate collection

          foreach var   $ainfo(vars) {
              set       full          [snmpinfo mibprop $var full]
              puts      $fileid       [join [list [lindex $full 2] \
                                                  [lindex $full 3]]]    30

              lappend   lvars         $var
          }
          puts      $fileid           ""
   } else {
          set       fileid            $ainfo(fileid)
   }
```

Figure 4.14: **The snmptcl_collect_command procedure**

Next, the current date and time are obtained through the `exec` system call and the important fields stored in the file. Then, for each object, two records are written to the file:

- the length of the period; and,

- the value for the period.

If no value was retrieved, the length of the period is set to zero and the value to the empty string. Otherwise, the value is processed through any object-specific, or syntax-specific special routines supplied. In particular, Figure 4.14 shows a syntax-specific routine for `Counter32` which calculates the increment in the counter's value for the period.

```
set          date            [exec date]
puts         $fileid         [join [list [lindex $date 5] [lindex $date 1] \
                                    [lindex $date 2] [lindex $date 3]]]
foreach      var             $lvars {
    if { ![catch { set data $avar($var) }] } {
        set      value    [lindex $data 4]
        set      period   [expr [lindex $data 5]−[lindex $data 2]]
        set      full     [snmpinfo mibprop $var full]
        set   object  [lindex $full 0]
        set   syntax  [lindex $data 6]                               10

        if {[info exists snmptcl_collect_object($object)]} {
            set value   [$snmptcl_collect_object($object) $var \
                                              avar($var)]
        } elseif {[info exists snmptcl_collect_syntax($syntax)]} {
            set value   [$snmptcl_collect_syntax($syntax) $var \
                                              avar($var)]
        }
        puts     $fileid   $period
        puts     $fileid   $value                                    20
    } else {
        puts     $fileid   "0"
        puts     $fileid   ""
    }
}
flush        $fileid
}


# syntax−specific routines to return interval counts                 30

set      snmptcl_collect_syntax(Counter32)          snmptcl_collect_Counter32

proc     snmptcl_collect_Counter32        {var data} {
    upvar       $data    info

    if {[set prevalue [lindex $info 1]] == ""} {
        return  ""
    }
    set      value      [lindex $info 4]                             40
    set      initvalue  [lindex $info 3]
    if {$prevalue > $value} {
        set      prevalue   [expr $prevalue−4294967296.0]
        set      initvalue  [expr $initvalue−4294967296.0]
        set      info       [lreplace $info 3 3 $initvalue]
    }
    return       [expr $value−$prevalue]
}
```

Figure 4.14: The `snmptcl_collect_command` procedure (cont.)

A History Displayer

Once we have collected the data, the best way to analyze it is to look at the range and dispersion of the collected values. The first order of importance here is the specific values which occur and their frequency. When they occur is of secondary importance. Thus, a convenient way to summarize them is in a histogram.

This application starts by having the user select a particular history file. On opening the file, the initial records are read, and the user queried to select one of the objects for which the file contains values. Then, the whole file is read and the values for the selected object are processed through object-specific or syntax-specific procedures and saved. For counters, the syntax-specific procedures convert the values into per-second rates. Minimum and maximum values for the processed values are maintained in order to determine how many bars to show in the histogram and the range of values covered by each bar. Then, the saved values are retrieved and compared with the bar ranges, to determine the number of occurrences for each bar range. Finally, the histogram is produced. Figure 4.15 shows a sample histogram for values of `ifInUcastPkts` for interface number 3, collected over a period of 13 days.

This sample histogram shows a roughly exponential distribution, with few occurrences of the higher values. For these higher values, it is useful to know when they occurred, for example, to determine any correlation between these higher values and the time of a specific network problem condition. For this purpose, the application can be enhanced with the further capability of allowing the user to request a display of the values represented by a particular bar and their time of occurrence. A convenient method is to display a dialog box containing the values and times for the occurrences represented by a particular bar when the user clicks the mouse pointer over that bar. Figure 4.16 on page 226 shows the dialog box for the bar at the far right of Figure 4.15. By examining the times of occurrences for various bars, exceptional situations which were known to have occurred at particular times can be discounted. Using this output, a network manager could conclude that an exceptional situation is occurring when the input packet rate exceeds 1500 packets/second;

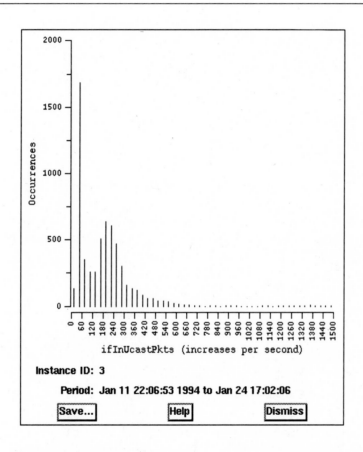

Figure 4.15: A Histogram of Unicast Packets/second

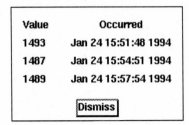

Figure 4.16: Times and Values for one Histogram Bar

alternatively, a rate at a slightly lower value, say 1400 packets/second, could be chosen.

4.3.3   Monitoring for Problem Conditions

The applications in the previous section provide the means to collect and display the range and dispersion of the values of various objects, and thereby determine which values are typical, and which are not, for specific devices in a particular network. So, for our last application in this chapter, we'll discuss an "alert" application to monitor the values of specific objects in respect to given thresholds.

The procedure for this monitoring application is very similar to the `snmptcl_graph_command` discussed earlier on page 214, and used to draw the graph in Figure 3.24 back on page 153. However, instead of graphing the values, it compares them with a threshold value. The first time a particular object exceeds its threshold, it is inserted as a new row in a window displayed to the user. Each row in the window contains the particular object and its instance information, together with the number of times it has exceeded its threshold,[19] the time of the most recent occurrence, the value at that time, and the threshold value. The thresholds are passed through to the command procedure as parameters using the technique discussed on page 136. Given this, the procedure can be invoked with a specific list of interface

---

[19]An alternate would be to count only the threshold-exceeded occurrences for which the previous sample did not exceed the threshold.

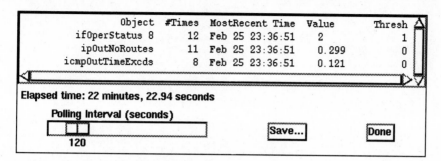

```
        Object    #Times  MostRecent Time   Value      Thresh
ifOperStatus 8        12   Feb 25 23:36:51   2               1
  ipOutNoRoutes       11   Feb 25 23:36:51   0.299           0
icmpOutTimeExcds       8   Feb 25 23:36:51   0.121           0
```

Elapsed time: 22 minutes, 22.94 seconds

Polling Interval (seconds)

120   Save...   Done

Figure 4.17: A Window Monitoring Network Interface Objects

management objects. For those objects in the problem conditions category, a threshold of zero will cause any occurrence of the condition to be displayed in the application's window. For those objects in the unusual conditions category, a threshold set to a value obtained from an analysis of history data will cause the window to display only the exceptional situations where the condition is occurring too frequently. Figure 4.17 shows a sample output window.

Further, this alert application can be given the same extension as discussed in Section 4.3.1 for `snmptcl_graph_command`, i.e., to take a procedure such as `snmptcl_graph_ifutil` as an extra optional parameter. With this extension, we now have an application which can monitor an interface for excessive utilization, and display when and by how much the utilization exceeds a configured value. Figure 4.18 on page 228 demonstrates this with the utilization threshold set at 5%. (In practice, a higher threshold would typically be used, especially for serial interfaces.)

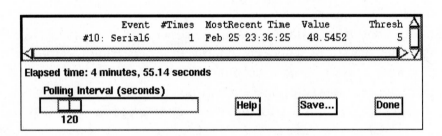

Figure 4.18: A Window Monitoring Interface Utilization

Chapter 5

LAN Management

This chapter discusses the management of local area networks. Specifically, it covers the media-specific information for the two most popular types of standard LANs:

- IEEE 802.3/Ethernet; and,
- IEEE 802.5/Token Ring.

It also covers management information for three types of physical and MAC-layer devices used in LANs:

- a MAC-layer bridge;
- a physical-layer repeater; and,
- a Medium Attachment Unit (MAU).

5.1   Concepts

A LAN serves to interconnect multiple systems within a constrained geographical area, typically within a single site or campus, using a particular subnetwork technology. All of today's popular subnetwork technologies are multi-megabit/second, shared-media networks. A system connected to a LAN is normally referred to as a *station.*

Prior to the early 1980's, when LANs first started appearing, connections between systems physically close to each other were normally point-to-point. Since then, three basic topologies have been used for LANs, as illustrated in Figure 5.1:

ring: each station is connected to two neighbors, one upstream and one downstream; a station transmits to its downstream neighbor which forwards to its downstream neighbor, and so on, until the transmission arrives back at the original sender; and,

star: the stations are connected via a central point; stations transmit to the central point which normally forwards to all other stations;

bus: each station is connected to a single transmission medium; stations transmit to the transmission medium, all other stations receive from that same transmission medium.

Each topology has its strengths and weaknesses and, over the years, hybrid approaches of using different topologies at the various sub-layers of the protocol stack have been introduced as attempts to combine the strengths of each topology. Thus, the first thing we must examine is the protocol layering.

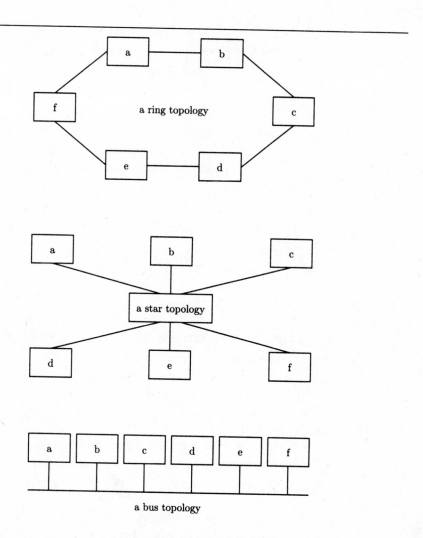

Figure 5.1: **Basic LAN Topologies**

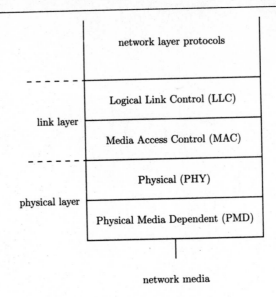

Figure 5.2: LAN Protocol Layering

5.1.1   Protocol Layering

A LAN subnetwork technology represents two layers of the OSI Reference Model: the data link layer, and the physical layer. Within each of these layers, a LAN normally has two sub-layers as shown in Figure 5.2. The roles played by these sub-layers are:

Logical Link Control (LLC) provides multiplexing to allow one LAN interface to be used concurrently by multiple network-layer protocols; it can also provide link-layer reliability and flow control;

Media Access Control (MAC) provides the arbitration mechanism to determine when a station can transmit on the media; it also defines the format of transmitted frames, and the addressing that enables a transmitted frame to be directed to one or more of the receiving stations;

Physical (PHY) provides framing and encoding/decoding of the transmitted/received data; and,

> **Physical Media Dependent (PMD)** isolates the sub-layers above it from the specifics of the particular type of transmission media in use.

5.1.2   Media Access Control

The two basic types of MAC protocol are:

- Carrier Sense Multiple Access with Collision Detection (CS-MA/CD); and,

- Token Passing.

CSMA/CD assumes it is running over a *multiple access* transmission medium, i.e., a bus topology, such that a transmission by any station on the medium is heard by all other stations. *Carrier sense* is the ongoing activity of a station detecting whether one or more other stations are transmitting. A *collision* occurs when more than one station concurrently transmits on the physical medium. With CSMA/CD, when a station wishes to transmit, it waits for the medium to become idle and then starts transmitting. If two or more stations happen to begin transmitting at the same time, then a collision occurs, and each transmission must be retried at a later time. CSMA/CD is used by Ethernet and by the IEEE 802.3 standard [51] defined by the Institute of Electrical and Electronics Engineers (IEEE).

In contrast, Token passing uses a deterministic protocol to pass a logical *token* amongst the stations, whereby a station can only transmit when it holds the token. Both 802.5 [52], the Token Ring protocol defined by IEEE, and the Fiber Distributed Data Interface (FDDI) [53], the higher-speed token ring protocol defined by the American National Standards Institute (ANSI), specify the use of a token on rings.

All of the above MAC protocols use the MAC addressing defined by IEEE. IEEE MAC addresses are defined to be either 16-bits or 48-bits in length. However, all stations of a specific Token Ring or Ethernet must use the same length, and 16-bit addresses are rarely used these days.[1] The structure of a MAC address is shown in Figure 5.3. The first (transmitted) bit of an address is the I/G bit which is 0 for an individual (i.e., unicast) address, and 1 for a group (i.e., multicast) address.[2] For 48-bit addresses, the second (transmitted) bit is the U/L bit which is 0 if the address is globally unique, or 1 if the address is assigned by a local LAN administration.[3] A LAN can use a mixture of globally-unique addresses and locally-administered addresses, although most systems use globally-unique addresses.[4] The address for which all 48 bits are 1 is the broadcast address.

While having this standard for addressing across the different types of LANs is advantageous, much of the benefit is lost because of the unfortunate lack of a common standard for which bit is transmitted first. For each octet of 802.5 and FDDI frames, including the octets of all addresses, the *most significant bit* (MSB) is transmitted first, whereas for 802.3/Ethernet, the *least significant bit* (LSB) is transmitted first. Thus, when addresses are written, the I/G and U/L bits appear in different places for the different LAN types, as shown in Figure 5.3. Of these different orderings, IEEE 802.1a specifies the 802.3/Ethernet format as the *canonical* bit order.

To support globally-unique addressing, a manufacturer can apply to the IEEE to be assigned a unique 24-bit identifier for use as the first three octets of globally-unique individual addresses.[5] In addition, the manufacturer is responsible for assigning a unique serial number to each manufactured LAN interface. Then, a globally-unique address for the interface is formed by combining the manufacturer's identifier in the first 24-bits with the interface's serial number in the last 24-bits.

---

[1]In fact, the use of 16-bit addressing has been officially deprecated by the IEEE.

[2]Note that source addresses are required to be individual addresses, but see page 260 for how Source Routing uses the I/G bit in source addresses.

[3]16-bit addresses are always locally administered.

[4]An exception is DECnet which embeds a hierarchical address structure inside a locally-assigned address.

[5]All such identifiers assigned by IEEE have zero in their U/L and I/G bits.

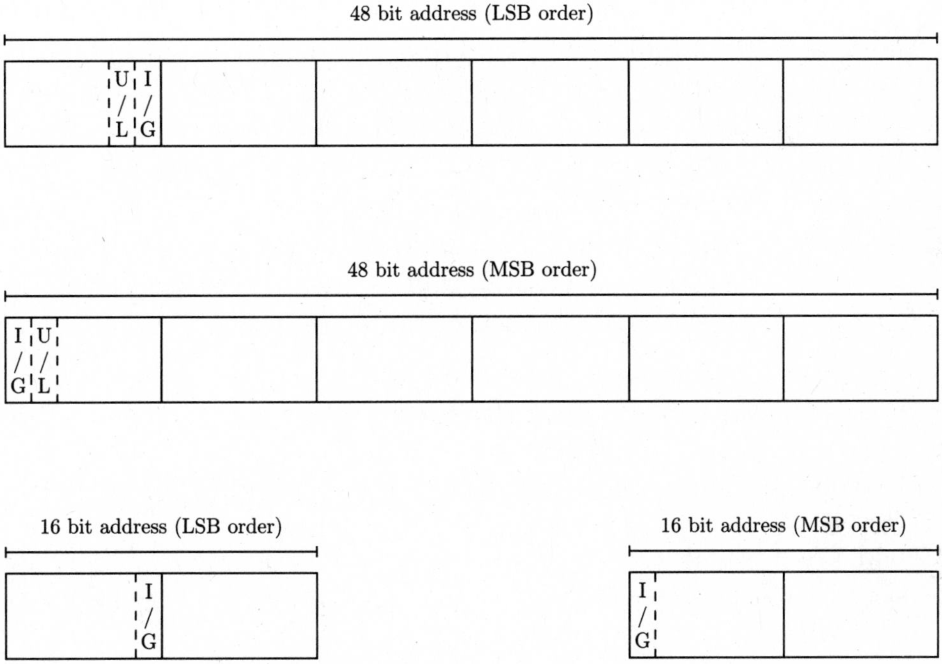

48 bit address (LSB order)

	U / L	I / G					

48 bit address (MSB order)

I / G	U / L					

16 bit address (LSB order)

	I / G	

16 bit address (MSB order)

I / G	

Legend	
I/G	address is individual(0) or group(1)
U/L	address is administered globally(0) or locally(1)
MSB	most significant bit, order used by 802.5
LSB	least significant bit, order used by Ethernet

Figure 5.3: IEEE MAC Addresses

Many products have their assigned address "burned-in" (e.g., in a ROM).

5.1.3   802.2 Logical Link Control

IEEE 802.2 [54] specifies a standard for the LLC sub-layer. This standard is used on 802.3, 802.5, and FDDI networks. One of 802.2's functions is to identify the network-layer protocol to/from which a frame is sent. In addition, 802.2 has several modes, including LLC Type I and LLC Type II. All stations are required to support LLC Type I. LLC Type II is modeled after HDLC/SDLC in that it provides for flow control and retransmission. LLC Type II is used by network-layer protocols, such as IBM's SNA, which require reliable delivery by the link-layer. LLC Type I is a subset of LLC Type II which supports only "unnumbered information" frames, thereby bypassing the extra overhead of Type II's flow control and retransmission.

5.1.4   Ethernet and 802.3

Ethernet, sometimes call *DIX Ethernet* in recognition of the contributions to its definition made by Digital Equipment Corporation, Intel and Xerox, was specified prior to 802.3. In practice, the only difference between the two specifications is their interpretations of the third field in the header of a MAC frame.

The format of a 802.3/Ethernet MAC frame is shown in Figure 5.4. The preamble is a specified pattern which allows the receiver to synchronize to the start of a frame. The first two fields in the frame header are the Destination Address field and the Source Address field. The third field is interpreted by Ethernet as a *type* field containing a value, sometimes called an *Ethertype* value, to identify the type of packet carried in the remainder of the frame. In contrast, 802.3 uses the third field as a *length* field containing the length of the packet carried in the remainder of the frame. As a result of this difference, Ethernet with its type field has no need of a separate LLC protocol, but does require each packet type (e.g., an IP packet) to have its own length field(s).

Fortunately, all Ethertype values now assigned to identify packet

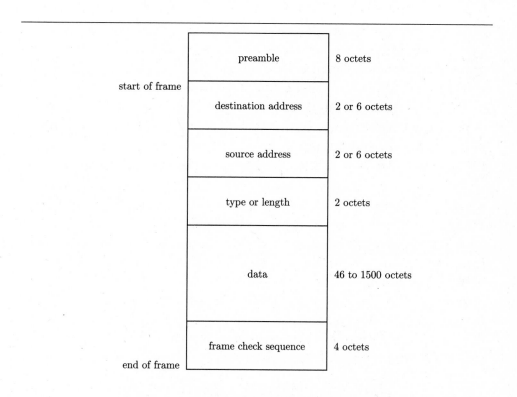

Figure 5.4: Ethernet/802.3 MAC Frame

types are greater than the maximum legal size of a frame. Thus, it's easy to distinguish an 802.3 frame from an Ethernet frame, and even though they cannot interoperate, the two protocols can happily run alongside each other on the same "wire".

Valid frames are always an integral number of octets, ending with a 32-bit *Frame Check Sequence* (FCS) field containing a cyclic redundancy check (CRC) code to protect against bit errors. After the transmission of a frame, an *inter-frame gap* of 9.6 microseconds occurs before any station with a frame to send attempts to transmit.

The minimum length of a frame, 64 octets, is governed by the maximum propagation time over the medium, to ensure that two colliding stations will hear each other's transmission before their transmission ends. The maximum length of a frame is standardized as 1518 octets.[6]

When a transmitting station detects a collision, it continues transmitting for a small number of bits to ensure that the other transmitting station also detects the collision, and schedules a retransmission of its frame according to a "truncated binary exponential backoff" algorithm. This algorithm selects a delay time which is a random multiple of the minimum frame time, to decrease the odds that the colliding stations will retransmit at the same time. If 16 successive collisions occur in trying to transmit a frame, then the transmission of that frame fails.

One of the "features" of CSMA/CD is its simplicity. There are no control frames transmitted on the medium; all frames carry user data, either LLC frames or network-layer packets. We'll see later how the 802.5 MAC protocol is different.

Physical Layer

The medium-independent PHY sub-layer for Ethernet and 802.3 uses an encoding known as "Manchester" encoding, in which the waveform transitions from high-to-low (for a 0) or low-to-high (for a 1) in the middle of a bit-time. If the PHY sub-layer detects improper signals on the medium, it generates a *signal quality error* (SQE) indication. A collision is one of the conditions which causes an SQE indication. Thus, if an SQE indication occurs during transmission, the MAC layer

---

[6]A few protocols still exist which use larger non-standard length frames.

knows that a collision has occurred. On the other hand, there is a particular situation immediately after completing a transmission, for which an SQE indication should always occur. The 802.3 standard takes advantage of this situation by using it as a test, called the *SQE Test*, of the collision detection circuitry. If no SQE indication occurs when it should, an SQE Test error occurs.

Some Ethernet interfaces for some types of media have a capability to perform a test on the network cabling, called a *Time-domain Reflectometry* (TDR) test. A TDR test returns as its result the time interval, measured in 10 MHz ticks (i.e., each tick is 100 nanoseconds), between the start of the TDR test transmission and the subsequent detection of a collision or the deassertion of carrier. Some systems can run this test on demand; other systems run the test during inter-frame gaps. The TDR value is quite useful for physical bus topologies in determining the approximate distance from the transmitting station to a cable fault. It is advisable to run this test multiple times to check for consistency in the resultant TDR value, to verify that there really is a fault.

The PHY sub-layer defines an (optional) interface to the medium called the *Attachment Unit Interface* (AUI). On some devices the AUI is an exposed external interface; on others, the AUI is either internal to the device or non-existent.

Thick and Thin Ethernet

The original physical media defined for Ethernet was a co-axial cable, colloquially known as *thick net*, using the standard designated as 10BASE5. This designation is derived from the standard being 10 Mb/s, using baseband transmission, and capable of driving up to 500 meters of cable. Using this media, all stations connect to the co-axial cable (i.e., a bus topology). Connections to the cable, called *taps*, occur at regular intervals in the length of the cable. Standard cables are available to connect a station's AUI interface to a cable tap.

The next physical media to be defined was given the designation 10BASE2, i.e., it can drive up to 200 meters of cable. This media uses less bulky cable and more convenient connectors, and thus is colloquially known as *thin net*, but the media is still configured as a physical bus topology.

5.1.5 Repeaters

In order to extend the physical network beyond the length imposed by the cable transmission technology, a device called a multi-port *repeater* is defined. The basic functions of a repeater are to receive bits on one port, regenerate the amplitude and timing of the signal, and then to transmit them on *all* of its other ports. Since repeaters can have any number of ports, each of which can be connected to a cable at any valid position for a station, they allow the topology to become a tree, rather than a simple bus.[7] Each section of cable joined to other sections by a repeater is called a *segment.*

A repeater must also detect the simultaneous receipt of input on two or more of its ports as a collision. When this occurs, the repeater must propagate the collision event throughout the physical network by transmitting a *jam* signal for at least 96 bit times on *all* of its ports. Other repeaters detect such propagations as short "frames" called collision fragments or *runts*. Since the jam signal is transmitted for at least 96 bit times, runts are always at least 96 bits long. A repeater will occasionally receive a transmission even shorter than a runt. These are called *short events* and normally indicate externally-generated noise hits. A repeater reacts to the receipt of a runt or a short event in the same way as to the receipt of a regular frame, except that it extends short events to be at least 96 bits in length. Note that this extension of a short event into a runt has the result that whenever a short event is detected, its cause is local to the segment on which it is detected.

To maintain the timing dependencies which allow stations to detect collisions within the length of a minimum-sized frame, there can be a maximum of five segments (i.e., four repeaters) between any two stations connected to the physical network. Figure 5.5 shows an example of using a repeater to connect two segments.

---

[7]Note that it is the regeneration of received bits to all other ports which maintains the extended topology as a logical bus.

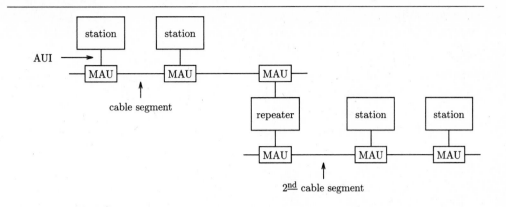

Figure 5.5: Ethernet/802.3 Topology Example

10BASET and FOIRL

With the introduction of repeaters, it now becomes useful to have point-to-point segments within the physical network. One such technology, used for point-to-point fiber connections between repeaters, is the *Fiber Optic Inter-Repeater Link* (FOIRL).

Another is 10BASET which provides for the use of Unshielded Twisted Pair (UTP) cabling. Not only is UTP inexpensive and much more convenient than "thick" or "thin" cables, but it is often already installed in buildings for use by the phone system.

Other Media Types

More recently, many other types of physical media have been defined, including IEEE standards for:

10BASEFP: passive fiber;

10BASEFB: synchronous fiber;

10BASEFL: asynchronous fiber; and,

10BROAD36: broadband.

The observant reader will notice that with the exception of the last type, none of the designators for these additional types conforms to

the original convention whereby the last digit(s) of the 10BASE5 and
10BASE2 designators referred to the maximum length of cable.

Medium Attachment Units

For each type of media, the function of connecting the PHY sub-layer
(or AUI interface) to the specific medium is performed by a device
known as a transceiver or a *Medium Attachment Unit* (MAU). For
example, for fiber media, it is the MAU which generates the optical
signals. All MAUs are required to prevent the transmission of *jabber*
onto the media. Jabber occurs when malfunctioning hardware results
in output by the PHY sub-layer of a continuous stream of bits which
is far longer than the maximum length of a frame.

MAUs also have various other capabilities, depending on the type
of media; for example, the ability to perform link testing and loop-
backs. Sometimes, a single interface has multiple MAUs to enable it
to be connected to any one of several types of media.

Additional Repeater Functions

Repeaters are also defined to have two other features which are useful
to prevent the propagation of errors:

MAU Jabber Lockup Protection (MJLP): a repeater will
interrupt its output if it has transmitted continuously for
longer than the maximum jabber timeout (approximately
50,000 bit times); this prevents malfunctioning MAUs from
taking the whole network down; and,

Auto-partitioning: a repeater will remove a port from the
network if the port exhibits either too many consecutive
collisions, or a single collision lasting an excessive length of
time; this condition can occur due to cable breaks, faulty
connectors, or even due to a mis-connection which results
in a loop in the topology.

Star Wiring

There are two situations where the physical bus topology of the original 10BASE5 and 10BASE2 media has inherent problems for network managers:

cable problems: a problem such as a break anywhere in the cable; and,

adds, moves and changes: a temporary disruption to the network when a new user is added, or an existing user is removed from the network.

In both of these situations, the network is unusable for all stations connected to the affected section of cable.

The introduction of repeaters and the 10BASET technology provided the means to overcome these problems through the use of *star wiring*. The MAU jabber lockup protection and auto-partitioning capabilities of a repeater isolate these problems to an individual section of cable. With star wiring, they can be further isolated so as to affect only a single station.

Star wiring is typically implemented by installing the repeaters in *wiring closets*, typically one (or more) on each floor of a building, and installing UTP wiring from each office to the nearest wiring closet. In the wiring closet, the wire from each office is connected to a port on the repeater, possibly via a patch-panel.

Hubs

As a further aid to efficient management of the network, the repeater function in the wiring closet can be packaged, not as a stand-alone repeater, but rather as a card in a modular chassis. Such a chassis can contain multiple repeater cards, each with some number (e.g., 12 or 24) of ports,[8] and each interconnected via the backplane of the chassis. Such a chassis performs a concentration function, and is known as a concentrator, or more usually as a *hub*. The latter term is consistent with its role as a central element of a star-wired network.

---

[8]A larger number of ports reduces the per-port cost of the repeater.

Typically, such repeater cards are designed so that a MAC frame entering through a port on one card and exiting through a port on another card counts as having been processed by only one repeater, i.e., it counts as only one of the maximum of four repeaters between any two stations. Thus, the set of cards interconnected via the backplane together constitute a single repeater.

To get access to a repeater's network management information, each repeater card will sometimes have its own SNMP agent, or, alternatively, an additional management card will be installed in another slot of the same chassis. Management features normally include the ability to monitor and control the status of ports, e.g., to watch for auto-partitioning and to enable/disable ports. Note that a repeater port is also an ideal location for tracking the number of collisions occurring on the physical network.

5.1.6   Transparent Bridges

Whereas a repeater extends the network at the physical layer by interconnecting multiple segments within a LAN, a *bridge* extends the network at the MAC layer, by interconnecting multiple LANs to form an *extended LAN*. The repeater does nothing to increase the bandwidth of the network. In contrast, the bridge can *filter* frames, i.e., not forward them onto a particular LAN, when it knows that the destination MAC address is reached via a different LAN. Thus, the total bandwidth on an extended LAN can be greater than the capacity of any individual LAN segment.

To perform filtering, a bridge processes frames according to the content of their MAC headers, and thus typically operates in a store-and-forward fashion, receiving a whole frame prior to beginning to re-transmit it. While this has the minor disadvantage that the source-to-destination latency of frame transmission increases slightly, it does permit error-checking, e.g., for FCS errors prior to retransmission, thereby avoiding the propagation of errors across the network. Note also that a bridge does not propagate collisions from one LAN to another.

For 802.3/Ethernet, the standard bridge is a *transparent* bridge, as defined by the IEEE 802.1d standard [55]. The insertion of such a

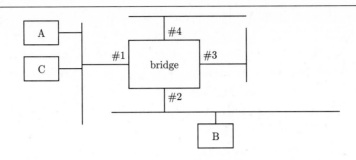

Figure 5.6: A Simple Bridge Topology

bridge between any two LANs is entirely transparent to the stations on the physical network, in that the MAC frames sent/received by stations do not contain the address of the bridge, and the bridge performs no modification of the frames it forwards.

In order to know the LAN to which a frame should be forwarded, a transparent bridge has a *forwarding database*. The forwarding database contains a set of MAC addresses and, for each address, it identifies the port on that bridge to which frames with that destination MAC address should be forwarded. The forwarding database is populated either through *learning* or through network management. Learning occurs by observing the source MAC addresses in frames the bridge receives. If the destination MAC address in a received frame is not presently in the forwarding database, the bridge *floods* the frame by forwarding it to all ports other than the one on which it was received. Of course, only unicast addresses can be learned in this manner; multicast and broadcast frames are always flooded (unless otherwise configured by network management) to all ports other than the receiving port.

To illustrate the learning process, consider the topology shown in Figure 5.6, and suppose that stations A and B have not previously sent any frames. Then, if station A sends a frame to station B, the bridge receiving the frame on port 1 will not know where station B is and so will forward the frame to ports 2, 3 and 4, but by examining the source address, it will learn that A is reached via port 1. If station B responds by sending a frame back to station A, the bridge will now

have A in its forwarding database, and so will only forward the frame
to port 1, and by examining the source address will learn that B is
reached via port 2. From now on, for all frames which A and B send
to each other, the bridge will forward them only to the appropriate
port. Further, if station C (on the same LAN as A) now sends a frame
to station A, the bridge will know to discard the frame, and will also
learn that station C is reached via port 1.

After an initial exchange, the operation of a transparent bridge
results in unicast frames only being sent over the LANs required for
it to reach its destination. This can significantly reduce the amount
of unicast traffic on most LANs of the network, particularly for stub
LANs (i.e., those with only one connection to the rest of the network). It does nothing, however, to reduce the load of multicast
and broadcast traffic on the LANs. Thus, the use of bridges allows
the network to be expanded up to the limit at which the amount of
multicast/broadcast traffic becomes burdensome.

Learned entries in the forwarding table are aged, i.e., they are
deleted after being unused for some period of time, in order to:

- support stations which are moved from one LAN to another;
  and,

- reduce the size of the forwarding table to contain only the addresses currently in use on the network.

In contrast, *static* entries are created and deleted only by network
management, and can be configured for multicast/broadcast addresses
as well as for unicast addresses.

Spanning Tree Protocol

The method described above of extending LANs via bridges requires
that the extended topology is a tree, i.e., there can be no loops in
the connectivity. Otherwise, frames within the network would get
replicated (many times!), and bridges would get confused as to which
of their ports to use to reach the source address of looping frames.

The need for a tree topology causes two problems:

- there is no backup path to maintain connectivity when a LAN
  or bridge in the middle of the tree fails; and,

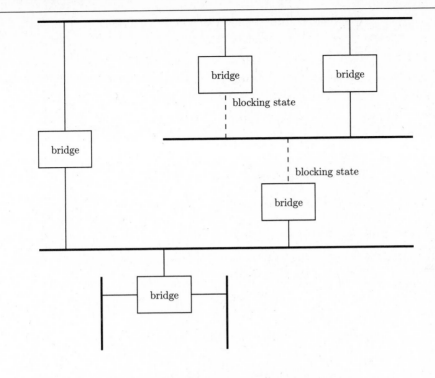

Figure 5.7: A Spanning Tree Network

- inadvertent misconnections can cause loops.

To address these problems, a standard *Spanning Tree Protocol* (STP) is defined by 802.1d. An earlier proprietary version of STP was defined for use by Digital's LANbridge 100 product; however, the two versions are not compatible. STP allows the connected topology to contain multiple physical paths between two stations, but constrains the active topology to be a single spanning tree. That is, there can be loops in the connected topology, but there are none in the active topology. Figure 5.7 shows an example topology.

When multiple paths exist, some ports on some bridges are set into a *blocking* state, i.e., they are not forwarding frames. Thus, when an active link or bridge within a loop fails, one or more of the ports in the blocking state transition to the *forwarding* state and connectivity between stations is restored. Also, if a misconnection causes a loop, then the operation of STP causes a port to enter the blocking state and thereby prevents a loop in the active topology.

To achieve this, the bridges exchange data in STP protocol packets, called *Bridge Protocol Data Units* (BPDUs). BPDUs are always transmitted to a destination multicast MAC address, and are received but never forwarded by all other STP bridges on the same LAN. Each bridge has a Bridge-id, consisting of a bridge priority, and the MAC address of the lowest numbered port on the bridge. The bridge with the lowest Bridge-id becomes the *root* of the tree. Ports on a bridge are in the forwarding state only if they are:

- the *root port* of a bridge; or,

- the *designated port* of a LAN.

On each bridge, the port which is "closest" to the root is the *root port* for that bridge. On each LAN interconnected by the bridges, the bridge which is "closest" to the root is the *designated bridge* for that LAN, and the designated bridge's port on that LAN is the LAN's *designated port*. The notion of "closest" is determined through each LAN having a *path cost*, and each bridge having a *root path cost* which is the sum of the path costs of the LANs in the path to the current root.

Each bridge begins by assuming it is the root. It then transmits BPDUs on each of its ports containing, amongst other parameters:

- its own Bridge-id and the Bridge-id which it believes to be the root; and,

- the root path cost and port identifier of the transmitting port.

This is sufficient for receiving bridges to determine if the receiving port should transition to become either the LAN's designated port, or the receiving bridge's root port. The port identifier for a port is the combination of a port priority and the port number.

In the stable state, the information in all bridges is consistent. When a segment or a bridge comes up or goes down, a change occurs in the topology, and for a short while, the information in the bridges is inconsistent. To prevent these inconsistencies from causing loops in the active topology, STP defines two additional transitional port states between blocking and forwarding. The full set of states is:

disabled: disabled by management;

blocking: BPDUs are being received but both forwarding and learning are disabled;

listening: BPDUs are being exchanged but both forwarding and learning are disabled;

learning: BPDUs are being exchanged and learning is enabled but forwarding is disabled; and,

forwarding: BPDUs are being exchanged and both forwarding and learning are enabled.

The state diagram is shown in Figure 5.8 on the next page.

Priorities and path costs can be configured by network management. When multiple bridges have the same root path cost, the bridge priority allows management to specify which bridge will have precedence when the root, the root port and the designated port are chosen. When multiple ports on the same bridge have the same root path cost, the port priority allows management to specify which port will have precedence when the root port and the designated port are chosen. In the absence of management configuration, lower bridge addresses and lower port numbers take precedence, and path costs are recommended as:

```
path-cost = 1000 / LAN-speed-in-Mbs
```

which makes path costs inversely proportional to speed, and thus, LANs with higher bandwidths are preferred.

Various timers can also be configured by network management. However, it is important that all bridges in the network use the same values for these timers. To ensure this, only the values which are configured at the root bridge are actually used. These values are distributed to all other bridges by being included in BPDUs.

5.1.7   802.5/Token Ring

In a fashion similar to the 802.3 versus Ethernet relationship, the IBM specification for Token Ring [56] was defined prior to its adoption by IEEE as the 802.5 standard [52]. In this case, however, some of the

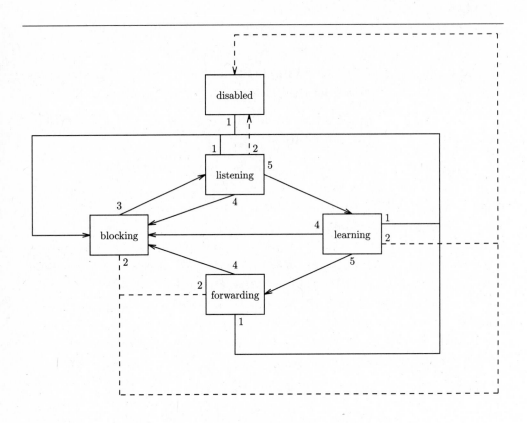

Figure 5.8: STP Protocol State Diagram

details (especially for the use of MAC frames) are contained only in the IBM specification.

Logically, a Token Ring network is a ring in which each station receives from its upstream neighbor, and transmits to its downstream neighbor.[9] However, it would be most undesirable if the whole ring were to stop functioning just because a station was powered off without first being disconnected from the ring. Thus, physically, it is the Medium Attachment Units (MAUs) which are connected in a ring, and each station is connected to its MAU via a short cable,[10] called a *lobe*. The MAUs are often housed in hubs/concentrators, and the hubs interconnected via their "ring-in" and "ring-out" ports.[11]

A MAU not only supports a particular cable type, but also inserts a station into the ring or bypasses an inactive station. When a station wishes to be inserted into the ring, it introduces a *phantom* circuit on its lobe cable.[12] Upon detection of the phantom voltage, the MAU momentarily breaks the ring, and then inserts the station. Upon cessation of the phantom voltage, the MAU momentarily breaks the ring, re-connects the ring thereby bypassing the station, and cross-connects the input and output wires from the station forming a loopback, as shown in Figure 5.9 on the next page. The station's interface is said to be in an *opened* state when inserted into the ring, and a *closed* state when removed/bypassed. Since the lobe cable is looped when its interface is closed, it is common for a station to perform a series of loopback tests on its lobe cable prior to introducing the phantom circuit.

Once inserted, a station is required to transmit a data signal on its lobe cable. When the station is not originating frames, it *repeats* the signal it receives from the cable. Before it can transmit its own frames, the station must hold the logical token. A station obtains the token by receiving a special frame: the token frame. Once the token is received, the station transmits its own frame, and *strips* the incoming signal from the ring. A station with multiple frames awaiting

---

[9]On rings with only one station, that station is its own upstream and downstream neighbor.

[10]Normally, Shielded Twisted Pair (STP) or Unshielded Twisted Pair (UTP).

[11]Often using fiber optic cables.

[12]The phantom circuit has DC voltage; data signals use AC voltage.

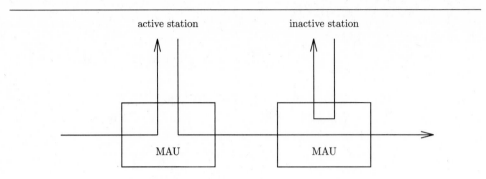

Figure 5.9: Connection to a Token Ring

transmission can send as many of them as it can within a time interval
called the *Token Holding Timer*. After completing its transmissions,
a station transmits an idle pattern until all the transmitted frames
have circulated the ring and have been stripped; it then transmits a
token frame to allow other stations to transmit. An option, called
Early Token Release, permits any station to release the token as soon
as it finishes transmitting. This option is useful on networks with a
high ring latency.

Token Ring Frames

Token Ring frames are transmitted using a Manchester encoding sim-
ilar to that used for **Ethernet** as described on page 238. For Token
Ring, all frames begin with a *Start Delimiter* (SD) and end with an
End Delimiter (ED).[13] The ED delimiter also contains a bit called the
E bit which is set if an error is detected in the frame. There are three
kinds of frames:

a token frame: a single octet between the SD and ED;

MAC frames: used by the ring-management protocol; and,

data frames: used to carry LLC frames (see Figure 5.10).

---

[13]These delimiters are encoded differently from data since they contain some
symbols with no transition in the middle of the bit-time.

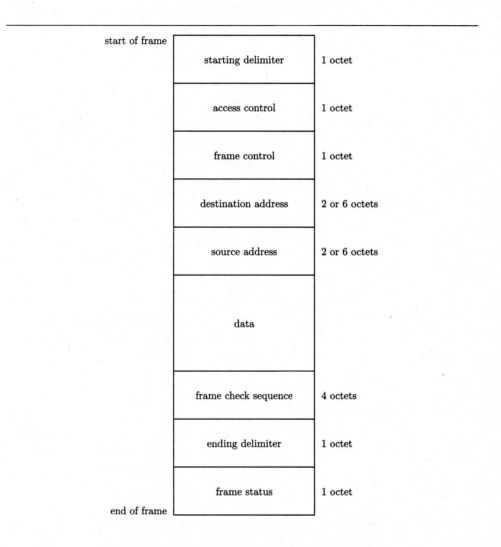

Figure 5.10: **Token Ring Frame Format**

The Access Control field frame contains a *Token* bit to identify a token frame, a *Monitor* bit (see below) and an indication of priority. The use of priority allows a station to obtain the token ahead of any lower priority station, but there are few Token Ring applications which make use of this feature. The Frame Control field distinguishes MAC frames from data frames.

Token Ring uses a subset of the locally-administered group addresses (see page 234) as *Functional Addresses*. Each bit within a Functional Address is associated with a particular ring management functional entity, e.g., the Active Monitor (explained momentarily).

The Frame Check Sequence field contains the CRC of the frame, using the same CRC algorithm as **Ethernet**. The frame ends with the Frame Status field which contains the *Address Recognized* (A) bit and the *Frame Copied* (C) bit. While not holding the token, a station is always comparing the Destination Address field of incoming frames against its own MAC address. If a match is found, the A bit is set in that frame, and if the frame can be received then the C bit is also set. Note that the A and C bits are not covered by the FCS calculation and can be modified without requiring the FCS to be re-calculated.

Unlike **Ethernet**, Token Ring does not have a fixed maximum frame size. 64 different valid values ranging from 516 up to 65535 are defined by IEEE, but values below 2052 or above 18000 are rarely, if ever, used.

Ring Management

One of the stations on the ring must perform the role of the *Active Monitor*. The (non-deterministic) choice of which station performs this role occurs through use of *Claim Token* MAC frames. While being the Active Monitor does require extra processing, it's typically not significant which station is the Active Monitor, since practically all stations interface to Token Ring via a special-purpose microprocessor-based MAC chip which includes the necessary logic and processing resources.

The functions of the Active Monitor are to:

- monitor the ring for lost or corrupted tokens;

- generate a new token when necessary;

- monitor the ring for re-circulating frames;

- purge the ring when certain error conditions occur;

- generate timing for the ring; and,

- initiate ring polls.

One of the bits in the Access Control field is the *Monitor* bit. Frames are always transmitted with the Monitor bit set to 0. When it repeats a frame, the Active Monitor sets this bit, such that it can monitor for frames with the Monitor bit already set. This occurs either because a frame is circulating on the ring for a second time, or because some other station is also acting as an Active Monitor. In response to this error, the Active Monitor purges the ring. It will also purge the ring if it fails to see a valid token within a particular timer interval. The ring is purged by the Active Monitor transmitting one or more Ring Purge MAC frames.

A Token Ring can operate at 4Mb/s or 16Mb/s.[14] The Active Monitor generates the timing for the ring based solely on its own internal clock. All other stations use the timing of the signal they receive to clock the signal they transmit. In practice, *jitter* gets introduced as the data proceeds around the ring, such that the signal received by the Active Monitor may be slower or faster than that which it is generating. To account for this, the Active Monitor contains a 24-bit elastic buffer. If the received signal is faster than its clock generation rate, the excess bits get added to the buffer (the buffer expands). If the received signal is slower, then the additional bits required for transmission are obtained from the buffer (the buffer contracts). A Frequency Error occurs if the buffer overflows or underflows.

In addition to the Active Monitor, three other ring management functional entities are defined:

- the Configuration Report Server (CRS);

- the Ring Parameter Server (RPS); and,

- the Ring Error Monitor (REM).

---

[14] A 1Mb/s rate is also defined but rarely used.

These entities are particularly important when the Token Ring is managed using the IBM-defined "LAN Network Management" scheme, and tied into IBM's NetView management products.

Ring Poll

The *ring poll* process occurs at periodic intervals (e.g., every 3 seconds). This process is vital to the proper functioning of the ring since it provides each station with its *Upstream Neighbor Address* (UNA).[15] This information is also extremely useful in determining the offending station for certain types of errors on the ring.

The process begins by the Active Monitor transmitting an *Active Monitor Present* (AMP) MAC frame. When the first station downstream from the Active Monitor sees this frame with its A and C bits not set, it sets these bits, copies the frame, and updates its recorded UNA to be the frame's Source Address. This station then waits for a timer interval (e.g., 10 milliseconds) and then transmits its own *Standby Monitor Present* (SMP) frame. An SMP frame performs the same function as the AMP, except that it is not transmitted by the Active Monitor. The timer ensures that SMP and AMP frames have negligible effect on the bandwidth available to data frames.

This process iterates with each successive station downstream receiving an SMP frame with the A and C bits clear, setting them, updating its recorded UNA, waiting for the timer, and then sending out its own SMP frame. Finally, when the Active Monitor receives an SMP frame with the A and C bits clear, the Ring Poll terminates.

Soft Errors

There are ten types of Soft Errors reported by stations on a ring. None of these types is severe enough to interrupt the operation of the ring. Rather, the detecting station just updates the appropriate error counter and continues. Periodically, non-zero counters are reported to ring management via a Report Error MAC frame. Five of the errors

---

[15]The UNA is also known as the *Nearest Active Upstream Neighbor* (NAUN) address.

are called isolating errors, since they can be isolated to a particular location on the ring. The other five are non-isolating errors.

The five isolating errors are:

Line Error: a FCS error or a coding violation;

> Line Errors are caused by a bad cable, or by having the cable too close to a source of Electro Magnetic Interference (EMI). As a frame travels around the ring, each station checks for a Line Error. The first station to detect a Line Error sets the E bit in the End Delimiter. Only the station setting the E bit increments its counter. Thus, the fault which caused the error occurred immediately upstream of that station, between it and its upstream neighbor;

Burst Error: an error of longer duration than a single coding violation, but not long enough to cause a signal loss error (see below);

> A Burst Error can be caused by a momentary disconnection in the cable, e.g., when a lobe is inserted/removed from the ring, or by a brief surge of EMI. Burst errors also cause the E bit to be set, and thus can also be isolated to an immediately upstream location.

A/C Error: an AMP or SMP frame was received with an invalid setting of the A and C bits;

Internal Error: an internal recoverable error occurred in the station's interface; and,

Abort Delimiter Transmitted: a recoverable error occurred while transmitting a frame which forced the transmission to be aborted.

Whereas a few Burst Errors and even Line Errors are common occurrences, the other three errors above normally indicate that a station's interface is faulty and should be replaced. For an A/C Error, the problem is with the station upstream from that which increments its counter. For an Internal Error or the Abort Delimiter Transmitted, it is the station reporting the error which is suspect.

The non-isolating errors are:

Receiver Congestion: a station recognized its address as the destination of a frame but did not have sufficient unused buffer space to receive it. This typically occurs because a file server or bridge is temporarily overloaded;

Lost Frame Error: the station transmitted a frame onto the ring, but did not receive it back. This often happens when a station is inserted/removed from the ring, because of the momentary break in ring connectivity;

Token Error: the Active Monitor did not see a valid token within the required time interval. This can also happen when a station is inserted/removed from the ring;

Frequency Error: the signal received by the Active Monitor differed too much from its own internal clock. One cause of this error is exceeding the limit of the number of stations on the ring (e.g., 72 stations for UTP cabling); and,

Frame Copied Error: a station recognized its own address in the destination address of a frame, but the frame already had its A bit set. This can be caused by having multiple stations with the same address on the ring, or by a line hit on the Frame Status field.

Hard Errors

In addition to the various Soft Errors, errors which have a more serious effect on the operation of the ring can also occur. Such errors can be caused by a bad interface on a station, a cable break between two hubs, or a frayed lobe cable. Note that a clean break in a lobe cable will not cause this type of error since it will result in the station being removed from the ring.

When such a condition occurs, the station downstream from the problem will no longer be receiving a valid signal from the ring. This could result either from the upstream station sending garbage, which is called a *streaming signal* error, or from a frayed lobe cable at the upstream neighbor or at the station itself, causing a *signal loss* error. The downstream station reacts by periodically transmitting a *Beacon*

MAC frame to the local broadcast address, containing the address of its upstream neighbor.

When a station receives a Beacon frame, if its own address is given as the upstream neighbor, then the station removes itself from the ring, and performs a test on itself and its lobe cable.[16] If the test fails, then the station remains disconnected from the ring. Otherwise, it will re-insert itself into the ring.

If this hard error condition still exists after an interval (e.g., 26 seconds) given by the Beacon Transmit Timer, then the station that started beaconing will remove itself from the ring and perform the same diagnostics. For a frayed lobe cable, this procedure will isolate the particular station and operation of the ring can continue. However, for a cable problem between hubs, the problem must be fixed before the whole ring can successfully operate again.

5.1.8   Source Routing Bridges

As with Ethernet, Token Ring networks can also be expanded using bridges. However, the normal type of bridges used to interconnect multiple rings is the *source routing bridge* defined by IEEE [57] and IBM [56]. Whereas transparent bridges hide their existence from the stations on the extended LAN and implement their own STP protocol, the use of source routing extends the LAN protocol through the participation of both the stations and the bridges on the LAN.

Theoretically, transparent bridges can operate over Token Ring, and source routing bridges can operate over Ethernet. In practice, however, there are some problems. As a result, Ethernet almost always uses transparent bridging, and until recently, Token Ring almost always used source routing. To address the problems, the IEEE has more recently been standardizing procedures for *Source Routing Transparent* (SRT) [58], for Token Ring bridges with the combined functionality of source routing bridges and transparent bridges.

Source routing extends the LAN protocol by assigning a unique *ring number* to each ring within the extended LAN, and a *bridge number* to each source routing bridge's connection to a ring. Two

---

[16]Recall that when a station is removed from the ring, its lobe cable is looped.

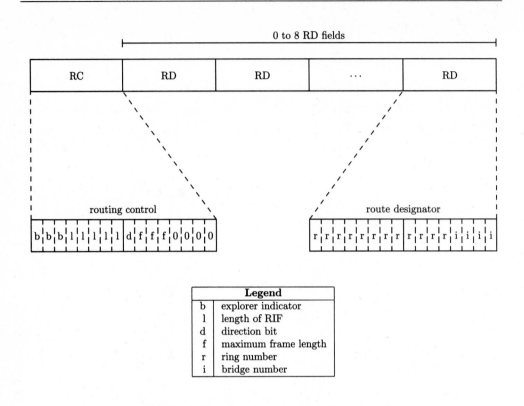

Figure 5.11: **Routing Information Field**

bridges connected to the same ring must have different bridge numbers on that ring if they both connect to the same other ring. The ring number is also known as a *segment number* or *LAN-id*.

Frames which have their source and destination on the same ring can be sent exactly as before, but those which need to traverse multiple rings have an additional field, the *Routing Information Field* (RIF), placed in front of the LLC data within an LLC frame. The presence of a RIF is indicated by the I/G bit being set in the frame's source address.[17] The format of the RIF is shown in Figure 5.11. The initial Routing Control (RC) field contains an explorer indicator, a direction bit and a maximum length sub-field.[18] Following the RC

---

[17]Recall that source addresses cannot be group addresses.

[18]The maximum length sub-field has recently been expanded from 3-bits to 6-bits.

field, there are from zero to eight Route Designator (RD) fields. Thus, a source routed frame can traverse at most 8 rings. Each RD field represents one hop, where each hop is a triplet:

(ring number, bridge number, ring number)

The RD field contains only the bridge number and the second ring number. The first ring number is implicitly the ring which the frame is traversing, or the ring number of the previous RD field.

In order to discover routes, there are three types of "broadcast":

all-stations broadcast frames are sent with the destination MAC address as the broadcast address, and either no RIF, or a RIF with the explorer indicator set to zero (i.e., not an explorer frame) and no RDs; such frames are copied once by all stations on the local ring, but not forwarded by (source routing) bridges;

all-paths explorer frames[19] are sent with the RIF containing the all-paths explorer indicator; a bridge forwards these to all rings for which the appropriate triplet was not previously present as one of the RDs, adding an RD field for the appropriate triplet prior to forwarding to each ring; multiple copies of an all-paths explorer frame are delivered to the destination, one for each distinct non-repeating route the frame may follow to a particular ring; and,

spanning tree explorer frames[20] are sent with the spanning-tree explorer indicator; a bridge forwards these on each of its ports which are part of an active spanning tree, adding an RD field with the appropriate value; exactly one copy of a spanning tree explorer frame is received by all stations on the multi-ring network.

Note that all-paths explorer and spanning tree explorer frames can have unicast destination MAC addresses.

---

[19]All-paths explorer frames, also known as all-routes explorer frames, were previously known as all-routes broadcast frames.

[20]Spanning tree explorer frames were previously known as single-route broadcast frames.

Originating stations do not generate RD fields; they merely use the source route (the set of RDs) received in a previous broadcast frame from a particular address. A bridge will forward a frame which has a source route but is not an explorer to one of its attached rings if the appropriate triplet appears as one of the RDs. The RC's direction bit specifies whether the source route is to be read front-to-back or vice-versa, thereby allowing the same source route to be used in both directions between the same two stations. The maximum length sub-field is used for route discovery to require the route to support a particular length of frame.

Typically, a source routing bridge will have hardware support to receive frames with RIFs only if they contain an RD field with an appropriate "target" ring number. However, early hardware support assumed that a bridge had only two ports and, thus, it could only recognize one target ring number (the ring number of the other port). In order to use this hardware support on bridges with more than two ports, many vendors implemented a scheme of having a *virtual* ring inside the bridge, so that the hardware could be set up with the virtual ring's number as the target ring, with the bridge adding two RD fields when forwarding explorers. While this mechanism works, it reduces the maximum number of rings between any two stations. The IEEE has recently clarified this issue by explicitly specifying the direct multiport model of source route bridging, in which each pair of ports is directly connected by the bridge.

5.1.9　Other LAN Devices

In addition to those devices specifically described in this chapter, several other types of devices are relevant to LAN management.

RMON Probes

The advent of SNMP management introduced a new type of device into LANs. This device attaches to one or more network segments with its interface(s) in promiscuous mode for the sole purpose of monitoring the traffic on the segment. The information collected is represented by its MIB objects, available for retrieval, not just from an NMS local to the LAN, but also from an NMS situated anywhere on the internet. This type of device is called a Remote network MONitoring probe, or an *RMON probe*. The standard MIB modules developed for use by RMON probes are beyond the scope of the current edition of *The Networking Management Practicum*.

Brouters

Both transparent and source routing bridges forward MAC frames irrespective of the types of packets they contain. In contrast, a router (see page 173) forwards packets according to their internet-layer protocol. For some protocols, either a bridge or a router can be used; other protocols have no internet-layer and so cannot be routed. Thus, the choice of whether a frame received from an interface should be bridged or routed needs to be determined on a per-protocol basis. Devices which can perform both bridging and routing on the same interface(s) are sometimes termed *brouters*.

5.2 Objects

This section describes the management instrumentation for the LAN types and LAN devices introduced in the previous section. It serves as both commentary text on the overall structure of the information, as well as a reference section where the meaning of specific objects can be found when they are mentioned later in this chapter. Thus, some readers will want to read only the commentary in this section, and skip over the explanations of specific objects. When a specific object is referenced later in *The Networking Management Practicum*, the number of the page containing an explanation of the object can be found by searching for the object's descriptor in the Index starting on page 537.

The `interfaces` group, described starting on page 196, defines generic information for all types of interfaces. Since all LAN interfaces are packet-oriented, all the objects in the `ifTable` apply to each type of LAN interfaces. In addition, media-specific information is defined for many types of LAN interfaces.

One textual convention is used in many LAN management MIB modules:

> **MacAddress:** a 6 octet address in the "canonical" order, i.e., as if it were transmitted least significant bit first.

5.2.1 Ether-like LANs

The 802.3 MIB module [59] captures the media-specific information for 802.3 and other similar types of CSMA/CD interfaces. This MIB module contains a mandatory Statistics group for general statistics and an optional Collision Statistics group for more detailed information on collisions.

The Statistics group contains one table, the `dot3StatsTable`, for which the row template (`dot3StatsEntry`) has the property:

```
INDEX { dot3StatsIndex }
```

where the value of `dot3StatsIndex` for an interface has the same value as `ifIndex` (see page 187) for that interface. The table contains 12 counters, seven of which are concerned with frame transmission,

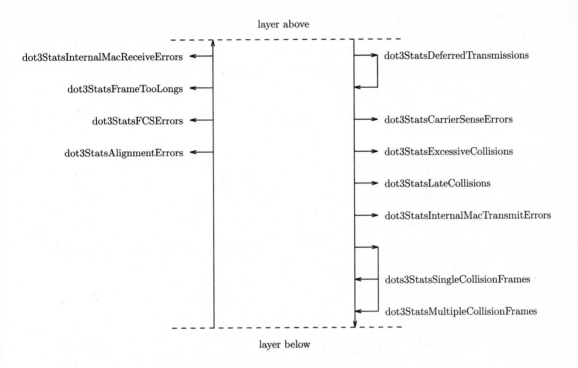

Figure 5.12: Case Diagram for the `dot3StatsTable`

and four with frame reception. A Case Diagram for these is shown in Figure 5.12. The transmission-related counters are:

dot3StatsSingleCollisionFrames: the number of frames successfully re-transmitted on the interface after one and only one collision;

dot3StatsMultipleCollisionFrames: the number of frames successfully re-transmitted on the interface after more than one collision;

dot3StatsDeferredTransmissions: the number of frames for which the first transmission attempt on the interface was delayed because the medium was busy;

dot3StatsLateCollisions: the number of times that a collision was detected on the interface after the minimum length of

a frame, i.e., at a time later than is legal for a properly
operating network;

dot3StatsExcessiveCollisions: the number of frames for which
transmission on the interface failed due to excessive (16)
collisions;

dot3StatsInternalMacTransmitErrors: the number of
frames for which transmission on the interface failed due
to an internal MAC sub-layer transmit error; and,

dot3StatsCarrierSenseErrors: the number of times that
the carrier sense condition was lost or never asserted when
attempting to transmit a frame on the interface.

The receive-related errors are:

dot3StatsAlignmentErrors: the number of frames received
on the interface that were not an integral number of octets
in length and did not pass the FCS check;

dot3StatsFCSErrors: the number of frames received on the
interface that were an integral number of octets in length
but did not pass the FCS check;

dot3StatsFrameTooLongs: the number of frames received
on the interface that exceed the maximum permitted frame
size; and,

dot3StatsInternalMacReceiveErrors: the number of frames
for which reception failed due to an internal MAC sub-layer
receive error.

The final counter is:

dot3StatsSQETestErrors: the number of SQE Test errors
detected on the interface.

Figure 5.13 shows a window browsing the values.[21]

---

[21]In this particular example, the number of deferred transmissions shown is too
large to be consistent with the values of the collision-related counters; this probably
indicates the agent is counting incorrectly.

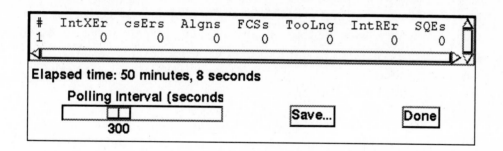

Figure 5.13: A Window Browsing Ethernet Statistics

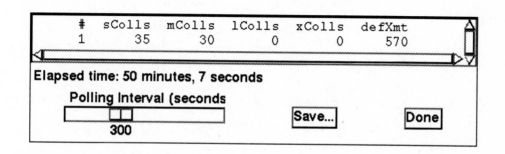

Figure 5.13: A Window Browsing Ethernet Statistics (cont.)

Note that

dot3StatsSingleCollisionFrames

and

dot3StatsMultipleCollisionFrames

represent frames which were successfully transmitted, and thus such frames are also counted by ifOutUcastPkts or ifOutNUcastPkts.

The Ethernet-like Collision Statistics group contains one table, the `dot3CollTable`. It represents a set of collision histograms, one for each interface. Each histogram has 16 elements, with each element representing a particular number of (per-frame) collisions. With each row in the table representing one element in the histogram, the row template (`dot3CollEntry`) has the property:

    INDEX   { dot3CollIndex, dot3CollCount }

where `dot3CollIndex` has the `ifIndex` value of the interface and `dot3CollCount` is the number of collisions, ranging from 1 through 16. The table contains one other column:

> **dot3CollFrequencies:** the number of frames having the given number of collisions.

Note that the count of frames having 16 collisions is equivalent to `dot3StatsExcessiveCollisions`; the count for frames having one collision is equivalent to `dot3StatsSingleCollisionFrames`; and the sum of the remaining elements in the histogram is equivalent to `dot3StatsMultipleCollisionFrames`.

Two tests are defined for use with the `ifTestTable` (see page 195) for Ethernet-like interfaces:

> **testFullDuplexLoopBack:** this test configures the MAC chip and executes an internal loopback test of memory and the MAC chip logic. This loopback test can only be executed if the interface is offline; and,

> **dot3TestTdr:** a TDR test. On successful completion, the appropriate instance of `ifTestCode` contains a pointer to the MIB object which contains the time interval.

5.2.2   802.3 repeaters

The first definition of management instrumentation for 802.3 repeaters was produced by the IEEE 802.3 committee[60]. The SNMP MIB module for Repeaters [61] was purposely developed as an SNMP equivalent to the IEEE's definition, so that the same instrumentation can be used to implement both the IEEE and Internet management standards.

Since repeaters are often packaged as cards housed in a modular chassis, [60] defines the term *group* as a related collection of repeater ports. Through the use of such groups, each port within the repeater is uniquely identified by a combination of its group number and port number. For example, in a modular chassis where a repeater port is naturally identified by its card number and port number on that card, it is convenient to represent all the ports on one card as a group, and to number the groups according to the slot number of the corresponding card. This results in the identification of MIB objects being aligned with the natural port numbering of the modular hardware implementation.

Unfortunately, this usage of the term "group" clashes with the standard SNMP usage of the same term. This resulted in the developers of the SNMP MIB module having to choose between the potential confusion of having two meanings for the same term, or the use of different terminology from the IEEE specification. The former course was chosen. In this and the following section, the terms *MIB group* and *port-group* will be used to distinguish the two meanings where the intended meaning would not otherwise be clear from the context.

The SNMP MIB module defines three MIB groups:

the Basic Group: a mandatory MIB group containing the objects which are applicable to all repeaters. It contains status, parameter and control objects for the repeater as a whole, for the port-groups within the repeater, as well as for the individual ports themselves;

the Monitor Group: an optional MIB group containing monitoring statistics for the repeater as a whole and for individual port-groups and ports; and,

the Address Tracking Group: an optional MIB group containing objects for tracking the MAC addresses of the stations attached to the ports of the repeater.

The Basic Group

The Basic MIB group consists of six scalars and two tables: a port-group table, and a port table. The scalars are:

rptrGroupCapacity (INTEGER):   the maximum number of port-groups that can be contained within the repeater. The actual number of groups present may be less than this number;

rptrOperStatus (enumerated INTEGER): indicates the current operational state of the repeater:

ok	no known failures
other	undefined or unknown state
rptrFailure	repeater-related failure
groupFailure	port-group-related failure
portFailure	port-related failure
generalFailure	unspecified type of failure

rptrHealthText (DisplayString): a textual description of the operational state of the repeater;

rptrReset (enumerated INTEGER):   this object may be **set** to cause the repeater to reset itself (and perform a self-test);

rptrNonDisruptTest (enumerated INTEGER): this object may be **set** to cause the repeater to perform an agent-specific non-disruptive self-test; and,

rptrTotalPartitionedPorts (Gauge32):   the total number of ports in the repeater which are present and enabled but are currently auto-partitioned.

Figure 5.14 shows how a window displaying these values might look. The port-group table, `rptrGroupTable` has a row template of

```
INDEX    { rptrGroupIndex }
```

where `rptrGroupIndex` identifies a group of ports. The table contains:

rptrGroupDescr (DisplayString):   a textual description of the port-group;

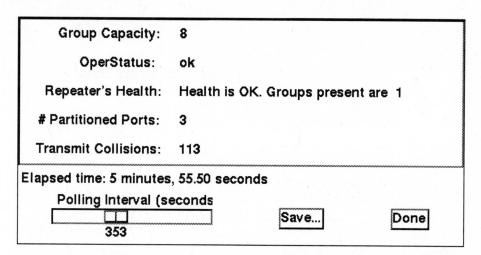

Figure 5.14: A Window Browsing Repeater Information

rptrGroupObjectID (OBJECT IDENTIFIER): an authoritative identification of the type of port-group, e.g., if a group comprises all the ports on a card, then this value would identify the type of card; values for this object are typically assigned by the manufacturer from within an enterprise subtree (see section B.4 on page 482);

rptrGroupOperStatus (enumerated INTEGER):   the operational status of the port-group:

other
operational
malfunctioning
notPresent
underTest
resetInProgress

The notPresent state indicates that the port-group is temporarily or permanently physically and/or logically not a part of the repeater;

rptrGroupLastOperStatusChange (TimeTicks):   the value of sysUpTime at the time when the value of the

rptrGroupOperStatus last changed; and,

rptrGroupPortCapacity (INTEGER): the number of ports that can be contained within the port-group.

Figure 5.17 on page 279 shows a window displaying these and other values for a repeater group.

The port table, **rptrPortTable**, has a row template of

```
INDEX    { rptrPortGroupIndex, rptrPortIndex }
```

where

    rptrPortGroupIndex

identifies a port-group, and

    rptrPortIndex

identifies a port in that port-group. The table contains:

rptrPortAdminStatus (enumerated INTEGER):   this object may be **set** to enable or disable the port;

rptrPortAutoPartitionState (enumerated INTEGER):   which indicates whether the port is currently partitioned by the repeater's auto-partition protection; and,

rptrPortOperStatus (enumerated INTEGER):   indicates the port's operational status: operational, notOperational, or notPresent.

Figure 5.15 shows how a window displaying these values might look.

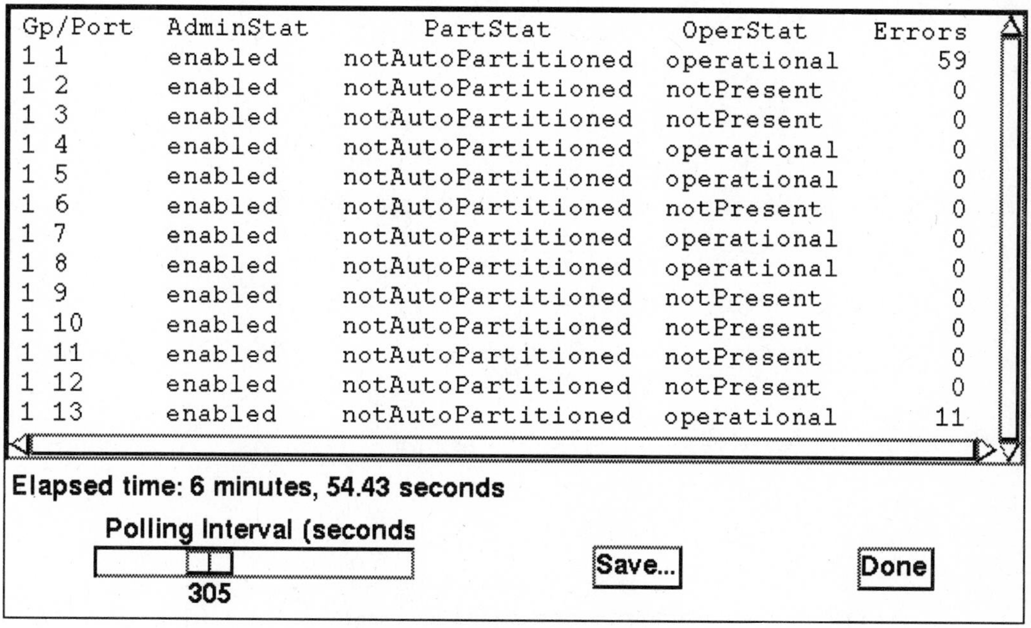

Gp/Port	AdminStat	PartStat	OperStat	Errors
1 1	enabled	notAutoPartitioned	operational	59
1 2	enabled	notAutoPartitioned	notPresent	0
1 3	enabled	notAutoPartitioned	notPresent	0
1 4	enabled	notAutoPartitioned	operational	0
1 5	enabled	notAutoPartitioned	operational	0
1 6	enabled	notAutoPartitioned	notPresent	0
1 7	enabled	notAutoPartitioned	operational	0
1 8	enabled	notAutoPartitioned	operational	0
1 9	enabled	notAutoPartitioned	notPresent	0
1 10	enabled	notAutoPartitioned	notPresent	0
1 11	enabled	notAutoPartitioned	notPresent	0
1 12	enabled	notAutoPartitioned	notPresent	0
1 13	enabled	notAutoPartitioned	operational	11

Elapsed time: 6 minutes, 54.43 seconds

Polling Interval (seconds

305

Save...   Done

Figure 5.15: A Window Browsing Repeater Port Status

The Monitor Group

The Monitor MIB group consists entirely of counters: one for the whole repeater, and the others for each port-group and each port. These counters provide a means of tracking the performance and health of the networked devices attached to the repeater. The counters for each port-group are redundant in the sense that they are the summations of the values of the counters for each port in the group. However, these sums provide a considerable optimization of network management traffic over the otherwise necessary retrieval of the individual counters included in each sum.

There is one counter which is an overall counter for the whole repeater:

rptrMonitorTransmitCollisions: the number of collisions that occurred within the repeater because there was incoming activity on two or more of its ports simultaneously.

The `rptrMonitorPortTable` contains the counters for each port, and so has a row template of:

```
INDEX   { rptrMonitorPortGroupIndex, rptrMonitorPortIndex
}
```

where `rptrMonitorPortGroupIndex` identifies a port-group, and

```
rptrMonitorPortIndex
```

identifies a port. The counters are:

rptrMonitorPortReadableFrames: the number of valid frames received on this port;

rptrMonitorPortReadableOctets: the number of octets contained in valid frames received on this port;

rptrMonitorPortAlignmentErrors: the number of frames received on this port which were not a whole number of octets in length and which had an FCS error;

rptrMonitorPortFCSErrors: the number of frames which were a whole number of octets in length and which had an FCS error;

rptrMonitorPortFrameTooLongs: the number of frames received on this port with a length greater than the maximum frame size;

rptrMonitorPortRunts: the number of runts received on the port (runts usually indicate collision fragments, a normal network event, not an error);

rptrMonitorPortShortEvents: the number of (non-)frames received which were shorter than a runt, and thus too short to be a legal collision fragment;

rptrMonitorPortCollisions: the number of collisions that occurred within the repeater because there was incoming activity on this port and on one or more other ports simultaneously;

rptrMonitorPortLateEvents: the number of collisions which were detected after already receiving the minimum number of octets of a frame;

rptrMonitorPortVeryLongEvents: the number of (non-) frames which lasted longer than the MAU Jabber Lockup Protection timeout;

rptrMonitorPortDataRateMismatches: the number of frames received on this port which were long enough to be valid frames, but for which the data rate did not match the local transmit frequency;

rptrMonitorPortAutoPartitions: the number of times this port has been automatically partitioned; and,

rptrMonitorPortTotalErrors: the total number of errors which have occurred on this port. This value is the summation of the values of other error counters (for the same port), namely:

```
rptrMonitorPortFCSErrors
rptrMonitorPortAlignmentErrors
rptrMonitorPortFrameTooLongs
rptrMonitorPortShortEvents
rptrMonitorPortLateEvents
```

```
rptrMonitorPortVeryLongEvents
rptrMonitorPortDataRateMismatches
```

`rptrMonitorPortTotalErrors` is valuable in that it alone needs to be polled on a regular basis. When `rptrMonitorPortTotalErrors` is not increasing, no errors are occurring; otherwise, the other error counters can be polled to investigate. For example, in Figure 5.15 on page 273 the error counters for port-1 are worth investigating; Figure 5.16 on the next page shows the corresponding set of individual error counters, which reveals a combination of Frame Check Sequence errors, alignment errors and data rate mismatches, resulting from the transmission of very few frames. This suggests a cable problem or a faulty adaptor card on that segment. Note that an increase in `rptrMonitorPortFCSErrors` indicates that bits within a frame were changed during transmission, whereas

```
rptrMonitorPortAlignmentErrors
```

indicates that bits were inserted or dropped.

```
rptrMonitorPortDataRateMismatches
```

detected at one repeater will often become

```
rptrMonitorPortAlignmentErrors
```

at the next repeater; this occurs because a repeater always transmits at the "proper" rate and thus, may need to insert/drop bits when receiving at an invalid rate, i.e., a repeater "fixes" the data rate but may corrupt the packet in doing so.

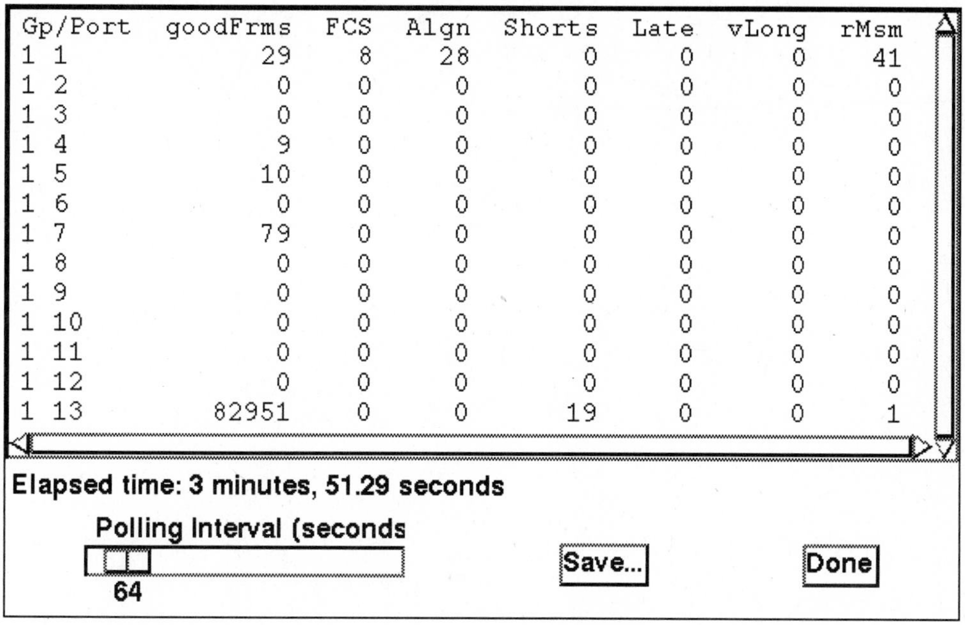

Gp/Port	goodFrms	FCS	Algn	Shorts	Late	vLong	rMsm
1 1	29	8	28	0	0	0	41
1 2	0	0	0	0	0	0	0
1 3	0	0	0	0	0	0	0
1 4	9	0	0	0	0	0	0
1 5	10	0	0	0	0	0	0
1 6	0	0	0	0	0	0	0
1 7	79	0	0	0	0	0	0
1 8	0	0	0	0	0	0	0
1 9	0	0	0	0	0	0	0
1 10	0	0	0	0	0	0	0
1 11	0	0	0	0	0	0	0
1 12	0	0	0	0	0	0	0
1 13	82951	0	0	19	0	0	1

Elapsed time: 3 minutes, 51.29 seconds

Polling Interval (seconds

64   Save...   Done

Figure 5.16: A Window Showing Repeater Port Statistics

The `rptrMonitorGroupTable` contains the counters for each port-group, and so has a row template of:

```
INDEX     { rptrMonitorGroupIndex }
```

where `rptrMonitorGroupIndex` identifies a group of ports.

rptrMonitorGroupTotalFrames: the total number of valid frames that have been received on the ports in this port-group. This counter is the summation of the values of `rptrMonitorPortReadableFrames` for all the ports in the port-group;

rptrMonitorGroupTotalOctets: the total number of octets contained in the valid frames that have been received on the ports in this port-group. This counter is the summation of the values of `rptrMonitorPortReadableOctets` for all ports in the port-group; and,

rptrMonitorGroupTotalErrors: the total number of errors which have occurred on all ports in this port-group. This counter is the summation of the values of `rptrMonitorPortTotalErrors` for all ports in the port-group.

Figure 5.17 shows a window displaying these statistics and other group-related information.

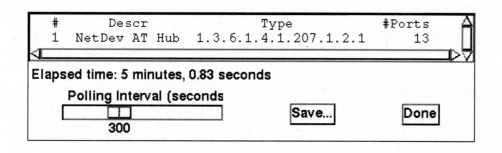

Figure 5.17: A Window Browsing Repeater Group Information

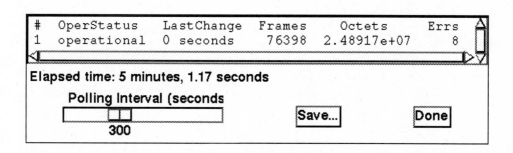

Figure 5.17: A Window Browsing Repeater Group Information (cont.)

The Address Tracking Group

This MIB group provides a probabilistic means of determining the list of active stations which are "behind" a port on the repeater. It is probabilistic in the sense that it contains only the most recent address. By reading the most recent address a number of times, a management application can build a list of most of the active stations. The more times it is read, the more probable it becomes that the list is complete.

The MIB group consists of one table, the `rptrAddrTrackTable` having a row template of:

```
INDEX { rptrAddrTrackGroupIndex, rptrAddrTrackPortIndex }
```

where `rptrAddrTrackGroupIndex` identifies a group of ports, and `rptrAddrTrackPortIndex` identifies a port.

rptrAddrTrackLastSourceAddress (MacAddress):   the source MAC address of the last readable frame received by this port. This object has been deprecated because its definition did not define its value when no frames have been observed on the port. The replacement object is `rptrAddrTrackNewLastSrcAddress`;

rptrAddrTrackSourceAddrChanges (Counter32):   the number of times that `rptrAddrTrackLastSourceAddress` (or `rptrAddrTrackNewLastSrcAddress`) for this port has changed; and,

rptrAddrTrackNewLastSrcAddress (OCTET STRING):   the source MAC address of the last readable frame received by this port. If no frames have been received by this port since the agent began monitoring the port activity, the value is the string of length zero.

5.2.3   802.3 Medium Attachment Units

The SNMP MIB module for 802.3 MAUs [62] was developed in the same fashion as the MIB for 802.3 Repeaters. Management instrumentation for MAUs was first defined by the IEEE 802.3 committee[63] and, subsequently, an equivalent SNMP MIB module was defined, allowing the same instrumentation to be used to implement both.

This MAU MIB module is most useful for repeaters. However, it is specified as a separate MIB module in recognition of the fact that interfaces on stations also have MAUs, and thus the equivalent instrumentation is applicable to stations.

There are three MIB groups each containing one table.

the **Repeater MAU Group:** configuration, status, and control information for MAUs attached to repeaters;

the **Interface MAU Group:** configuration, status, and control information for MAUs attached to station interfaces; and,

the **Broadband MAU Group:** broadband-specific configuration information for 10BROAD36 MAUs.

The Repeater MAU Group

The `rpMauTable` has a row template of:

    INDEX   { rpMauGroupIndex, rpMauPortIndex, rpMauIndex }

where `rpMauGroupIndex` identifies a group of ports, `rpMauPortIndex` identifies a port, and `rpMauIndex` identifies a MAU on that port.

rpMauType (`OBJECT IDENTIFIER`): the type of MAU:

```
dot3MauTypeAUI
dot3MauType10Base5
dot3MauTypeFoirl
dot3MauType10Base2
dot3MauType10BaseT
dot3MauType10BaseFP
dot3MauType10BaseFB
dot3MauType10BaseFL
dot3MauType10Broad36
```

rpMauStatus (enumerated `INTEGER`): the current state of the
MAU:

`other`
`unknown`
`operational`
`standby`
`shutdown`
`reset`

This object may be `set` to alter the state of the MAU;

rpMauMediaAvailable (enumerated `INTEGER`): an indication
of whether the MAU is providing access to the media:

`other`	
`unknown`	
`available`	the link and/or light and loopback state is normal.
`notAvailable`	link loss, low light or a loopback problem.
`remoteFault`	fault detected at remote end of the link.
`invalidSignal`	invalid signal received from other end of the link

Some of these states are only valid for particular types of
media;

rpMauMediaAvailableStateExits (`Counter32`): the number
of times that `rpMauMediaAvailable` for this MAU has
transitioned out of the available state;

rpMauJabberState (enumerated `INTEGER`):   an indication of
the jabber state of the MAU:

`other`	normal for AUI type
`unknown`	
`noJabber`	normal for other types
`jabbering`	error state

> **rpMauJabberingStateEnters** (Counter32): the number of
> times that **rpMauJabberState** has entered the jabbering
> state.

The Interface MAU Group

The **ifMauTable** has a row template of:

```
INDEX  { ifMauIfIndex, ifMauIndex }
```

where **ifMauIfIndex** has the **ifIndex** value of the interface, and
ifMauIndex identifies a MAU on that interface. The columns in this
table have identical syntax and semantics to those in the **rpMauTable**.
They are:

```
ifMauType
ifMauStatus
ifMauMediaAvailable
ifMauMediaAvailableStateExits
ifMauJabberState
ifMauJabberingStateEnters.
```

The Broadband MAU Group

Since there is no IEEE standard definition for a broadband repeater,
this group typically applies only to 10BROAD36 MAUs attached to
station interfaces and supplements the Interface MAU Group.

The **broadMauBasicTable** has a row template of:

```
INDEX  { broadMauIfIndex, broadMauIndex }
```

where **broadMauIfIndex** has the **ifIndex** value of the interface, and
broadMauIndex identifies a MAU on that interface. The columns in
this table are:

> **broadMauXmtRcvSplitType** (enumerated INTEGER):
> the type of frequency multiplexing/cabling system used
> to separate the transmit and receive paths for the
> 10BROAD36 MAU (other, single or dual);

> **broadMauXmtCarrierFreq** (INTEGER): the transmit carrier
> frequency of the 10BROAD36 MAU in units of 250 KHz;
> and,

broadMauTranslationFreq (INTEGER): the translation offset frequency of the 10BROAD36 MAU in units of 250 KHz.

5.2.4   Bridges

The SNMP MIB module for bridges[64] associates each port on a bridge with one interface of the `interfaces` group (see page 187). Each port is normally associated with a different interface, although there are situations in which multiple ports are associated with the same interface; for example, several ports, each corresponding to a different X.25 virtual circuit, but all on the same X.25 interface. Each port is uniquely identified by a port number greater than zero. A port number has no mandatory relationship to an interface number, but in the normal case a port number will have the same value as its corresponding interface's `ifIndex` value.

For a device which bridges some protocols and routes others, the objects in this MIB module apply only to its operation as a bridge. Thus, for example, the counters described in this section apply only to that subset of frames on the device's interfaces which are sent/received for a protocol being bridged. All such frames are sent/received via the ports of the bridge.

There are three groups in this MIB module:

the Base Group: basic information applicable to all types of bridges;

the Transparent Group: status and configuration information for transparent bridges;

the STP Group: status and configuration information for the Spanning Tree Protocol; and,

the Static Group: configuration information for static entries in the forwarding database.

A separate MIB module (see page 294) contains management information for Source Route and SRT bridging.

Textual Conventions

Two textual conventions are used in this MIB module:

BridgeId: an `OCTET STRING` containing the Bridge-id used by STP to uniquely identify a bridge. Its first two octets contain a priority value and its last six octets contain a MAC address; and,

Timeout: an STP timer in units of 10 milliseconds. Note, however, that some agents will support only values representing whole numbers of seconds.

The Base Group

This group contains three scalars and a table. The scalars are:

dot1dBaseBridgeAddress (`MacAddress`): a MAC address used by this bridge, normally its numerically smallest MAC address;

dot1dBaseNumPorts (`INTEGER`): the number of ports controlled by this bridge; and,

dot1dBaseType (enumerated `INTEGER`): the types of bridging this bridge can perform: `unknown`, `transparent-only`, `sourceroute-only` or `srt`.

Figure 5.18 on page 288 shows how these might be included in a window with other bridge information.

The `dot1dBasePortTable` has one row per port on the bridge, and thus its row template is:

```
INDEX  { dot1dBasePort }
```

where `dot1dBasePort` identifies the port. The columns in this table are:

dot1dBasePortIfIndex (`INTEGER`): the value of `ifIndex` for the corresponding interface;

dot1dBasePortCircuit (`OBJECT IDENTIFIER`): whenever multiple ports have the same value of

```
dot1dBasePortIfIndex
```

this object names an object instance unique to this port; otherwise, this object can have the value `0.0`;

dot1dBasePortDelayExceededDiscards (`Counter32`): the number of frames discarded by this port due to excessive transit delay through the bridge; and,

dot1dBasePortMtuExceededDiscards (`Counter32`): the number of frames discarded by this port because their size exceeded the maximum on the attached segment.

The STP Group

This group contains 14 scalars and a port table. The scalars are:

dot1dStpProtocolSpecification (enumerated `INTEGER`): the version of the Spanning Tree Protocol being run:

`unknown`	
`decLb100`	DEC LANbridge 100
`ieee8021d`	IEEE standard

dot1dStpPriority (`INTEGER`): the bridge's priority; this object can be **set** to change the priority;

dot1dStpTimeSinceTopologyChange (`TimeTicks`): the time since this bridge last detected a topology change;

dot1dStpTopChanges (`Counter32`): the number of topology changes detected by this bridge;

dot1dStpDesignatedRoot (`BridgeId`): the bridge identifier of the root of the spanning tree as determined by this bridge;

dot1dStpRootCost (`INTEGER`): the root path cost from this bridge;

dot1dStpRootPort (`INTEGER`): the port on this bridge which leads to the root; and,

dot1dStpHoldTime (`INTEGER`): the interval at which the bridge transmits BPDUs when it is not the root;

There are three timers which must be the same in all bridges. Each bridge has a configured value, but only the values configured at the root bridge are used, and these are distributed to each bridge via BPDUs. The values in use are:

dot1dStpMaxAge (`Timeout`): the age at which STP information learned from BPDUs is discarded;

dot1dStpHelloTime (`Timeout`): the interval between the transmission of BPDUs by this bridge when it is (or is attempting to become) root; and,

dot1dStpForwardDelay (`Timeout`): the length of time a port stays in each of the Listening and Learning states before transitioning toward the Forwarding state; this value is also used when a topology change has been detected to age all dynamic entries in the Forwarding Database.

The values which would be in use if this bridge were the root are:

dot1dStpBridgeMaxAge (`Timeout`): the value used for `dot1dStpMaxAge` (this value may be `set`);

dot1dStpBridgeHelloTime (`Timeout`): the value used for `dot1dStpHelloTime` (this value may be `set`); and,

dot1dStpBridgeForwardDelay (`Timeout`): the value used for `dot1dStpForwardDelay` (this value may be `set`).

Figure 5.18 on the next page shows how these STP parameters might look when combined with other bridge parameters.

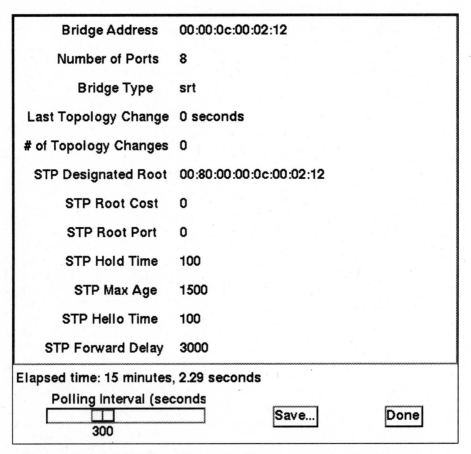

Figure 5.18: A Window Browsing Transparent Bridge Parameters

The `dot1dStpPortTable` has one row per port on the bridge, and thus its row template is:

INDEX   { dot1dStpPort }

where `dot1dStpPort` identifies the port. The columns in this table are:

dot1dStpPortPriority (INTEGER): the port priority (this value may be set);

dot1dStpPortState (enumerated INTEGER): the port's current state:

disabled	
blocking	
listening	
learning	
forwarding	
broken	malfunctioning

dot1dStpPortEnable (enumerated INTEGER): this value may be set to disabled or enabled;

dot1dStpPortPathCost (INTEGER): the path cost of this port if used in the path to the root (this value may be set);

dot1dStpPortDesignatedBridge (BridgeId): the designated bridge for the LAN connected to this port;

dot1dStpPortDesignatedRoot (BridgeId): the root as indicated in BPDUs received from the designated bridge for the LAN connected to this port;

dot1dStpPortDesignatedPort (OCTET STRING): the port identifier of the designated port for the LAN connected to this port;

dot1dStpPortDesignatedCost (INTEGER): the path cost of the designated port of the LAN connected to this port; and,

dot1dStpPortForwardTransitions (Counter32): the number of times this port has transitioned from the Learning state to the Forwarding state.

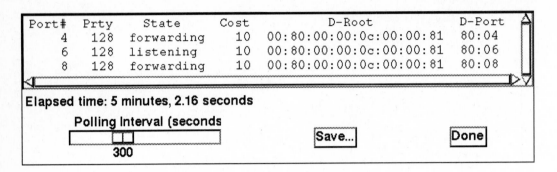

Figure 5.19: STP Status for Bridge Ports

Figure 5.19 shows what some of the STP status information for a bridge's ports might look like.

The Transparent Group

This group contains two scalars and two tables. The scalars are:

dot1dTpLearnedEntryDiscards (`Counter32`): the number of Forwarding Database entries which (would) have been learned, but have been discarded due to a lack of space in the forwarding data base; and,

dot1dTpAgingTime (`INTEGER`): the timeout for aging out dynamically learned forwarding information (this value may be `set`).

The `dot1dTpFdbTable` object represents the bridge's forwarding database. It has one row for each MAC address for which the bridge has forwarding information; its row template is:

```
    INDEX   { dot1dTpFdbAddress }
```

where `dot1dTpFdbAddress` identifies the MAC address. The two columns in this table are:

dot1dTpFdbPort (`INTEGER`): either the port number learned for the MAC address, or the value '0' indicating the bridge has non-learned information for this address (e.g., in the dot1dStaticTable); and,

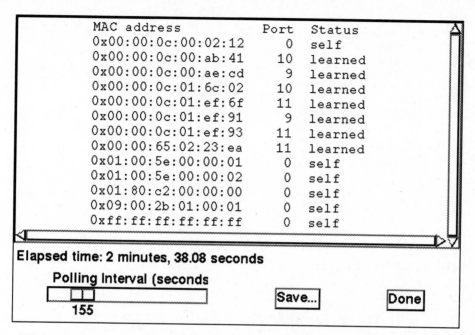

```
    MAC address                    Port    Status
    0x00:00:0c:00:02:12              0     self
    0x00:00:0c:00:ab:41             10     learned
    0x00:00:0c:00:ae:cd              9     learned
    0x00:00:0c:01:6c:02             10     learned
    0x00:00:0c:01:ef:6f             11     learned
    0x00:00:0c:01:ef:91              9     learned
    0x00:00:0c:01:ef:93             11     learned
    0x00:00:65:02:23:ea             11     learned
    0x01:00:5e:00:00:01              0     self
    0x01:00:5e:00:00:02              0     self
    0x01:80:c2:00:00:00              0     self
    0x09:00:2b:01:00:01              0     self
    0xff:ff:ff:ff:ff:ff              0     self
```

Elapsed time: 2 minutes, 38.08 seconds

Polling Interval (seconds

155 | Save... | | Done |

Figure 5.20: A Window Browsing a Bridge's Forwarding Database

dot1dTpFdbStatus (enumerated `INTEGER`): the status of this
row:

other	none of the following
invalid	no longer valid
learned	a learned row
self	an address of the bridge
mgmt	contained in dot1dStaticTable

The value `invalid` may be `set` to remove a row.

A sample forwarding database is shown in Figure 5.20.

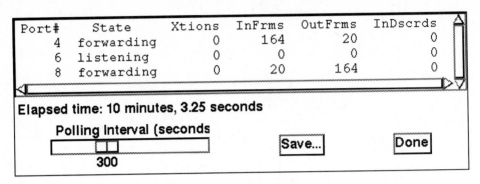

Figure 5.21: A Window Browsing Bridge Port Statistics

The `dot1dTpPortTable` contains information on each port of the bridge. Its row template is:

```
INDEX   { dot1dTpPort }
```

where `dot1dTpPort` identifies the port. The columns in this table are:

dot1dTpPortMaxInfo (`INTEGER`):   the maximum length of data in a MAC frame on this port;

dot1dTpPortInFrames (`Counter32`):   the number of frames that have been received on this port;

dot1dTpPortOutFrames (`Counter32`): the number of frames that have been transmitted on this port; and,

dot1dTpPortInDiscards (`Counter32`):   the number of valid frames received on this port which were filtered by the bridge's forwarding process.

Figure 5.21 shows what these might look like when combined with some STP information.

The Static Group

The `dot1dStaticTable` provides the means for (local or network) management to create static entries in the bridge's forwarding database. Specifically, it allows management to indicate the set of ports to which frames received from specific ports and containing specific destination addresses are allowed to be forwarded; the destination addresses can be either unicast or group/broadcast addresses.

The table has a row for each specified destination address and port, and so its row template is:

```
INDEX  { dot1dStaticAddress, dot1dStaticReceivePort }
```

where `dot1dStaticAddress` identifies the destination MAC address, where `dot1dStaticReceivePort` identifies the receiving port. Rows for which the port number is zero provide a default value for that address applicable to any port which is not specifically configured. The columns in this table are:

dot1dStaticAllowedToGoTo (`OCTET STRING`):   the set of ports to which frames are allowed to be forwarded. The value is a string of octets with each bit representing a port; a bit has the value 1 to allow a frame to be forwarded. The first octet specifies ports 1 through 8, with the most significant bit representing port 1, and so on (this value may be `set`); and,

dot1dStaticStatus (enumerated `INTEGER`):   the status of this row (this value may be `set`):

other	
invalid	deletes the row
permanent	will be retained after next reset of the bridge
deleteOnReset	will be deleted at next reset of the bridge
deleteOnTimeout	may be aged out

Source Routing

The MIB module for Source Routing bridges [65] contains status values, parameters, and counters for both SRT and Source Route only bridges. The Source Route group applies to all Source Routing bridges, whereas the optional Port-Pair group applies to bridges which support the direct multiport model of source route bridging.

Source Routing — The Source Route Group

This group has one scalar:

>   **dot1dSrBridgeLfMode** (enumerated `INTEGER`): an indication of whether this bridge generates/expects to receive RIFs using the older 3-bit maximum length sub-field (`mode3`), or the newer 6-bit maximum length sub-field (`mode6`); bridges supporting both lengths may allow this value to be `set`.

The `dot1dSrPortTable` has one row for each port which supports source routing; its row template is:

```
INDEX    { dot1dSrPort }
```

where `dot1dSrPort` identifies the port. The columns in this table are:

>   **dot1dSrPortHopCount** (`INTEGER`):   the maximum number of RDs allowed in All Paths Explorer and Spanning Tree Explorer frames (this value may be `set`);

>   **dot1dSrPortLocalSegment** (`INTEGER`):   the ring number of the segment to which this port is connected; the value 65535 signifies that no segment number is assigned to this port (this value may be `set`);

>   **dot1dSrPortTargetSegment** (`INTEGER`):   the ring number of the target segment (typically, a virtual ring inside the bridge) to which the bridge connects this port; the value 65535 signifies that no target segment is assigned to this port (this value may be `set`);

>   **dot1dSrPortBridgeNum** (`INTEGER`): the bridge number used between the local segment and the target segment; the value

65535 signifies that no bridge number is assigned for this purpose (this value may be `set`);

dot1dSrPortLargestFrame (`INTEGER`): the maximum size of the data field of a MAC frame on this port; 64 valid values (between 516 and 65535 octets) are defined by the IEEE; this value may be `set`, but not all bridges will accept all values;

dot1dSrPortSTESpanMode (enumerated `INTEGER`): this port's method of processing Spanning Tree Explorer frames:

> `disabled`: the port will not accept or send Spanning Tree Explorer frames;
>
> `forced`: the port will always accept and propagate Spanning Tree Explorer frames, as required by a manually configured Spanning Tree; or
>
> `auto-span`: when STP is enabled on this port, Spanning Tree Explorer frames are processed according to the value of `dot1dStpPortState` for the port.

This value may be `set`, but not all bridges will accept all values;

dot1dSrPortSpecInFrames (`Counter32`): the number of Source Routed frames received from this port;

dot1dSrPortSpecOutFrames (`Counter32`): the number of Source Routed frames transmitted to this port;

dot1dSrPortApeInFrames (`Counter32`): the number of All Paths Explorer frames received from this port;

dot1dSrPortApeOutFrames (`Counter32`): the number of All Paths Explorer frames transmitted to this port;

dot1dSrPortSteInFrames (`Counter32`): the number of Spanning Tree Explorer frames received from this port;

dot1dSrPortSteOutFrames (`Counter32`): the number of Spanning Tree Explorer frames transmitted to this port;

dot1dSrPortSegmentMismatchDiscards (Counter32):
the number of Explorer frames received from this port
and discarded because the RD field contained an invalid
adjacent ring (segment) number;

dot1dSrPortDuplicateSegmentDiscards (Counter32): the
number of frames received from this port and discarded
because the RD field contained a duplicate ring (segment)
number;

dot1dSrPortHopCountExceededDiscards (Counter32):
the number of Explorer frames received from this port but
discarded because the RIF exceeded or would have exceeded
the maximum number of RDs;

dot1dSrPortDupLanIdOrTreeErrors (Counter32):   the
number of duplicate LAN-id or Tree errors; this is useful
in detecting problems in networks containing older IBM
Source Routing Bridges; and,

dot1dSrPortLanIdMismatches (Counter32): the number of
All-Routes Explorer and Spanning Tree Explorer frames
received from this port but discarded because the ring
(segment) number in the last RD did not equal the port's
local ring (segment) number.

Sample values for the parameter and the status objects are shown in
Figure 5.22, and for the statistics objects (in an idle network!) in
Figure 5.23.

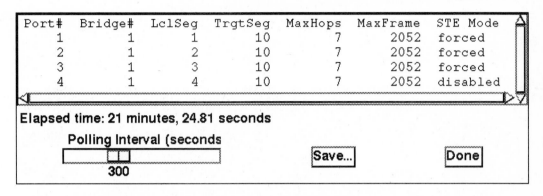

Figure 5.22: Source Route Bridge Port Parameters

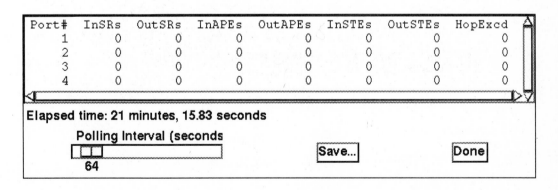

Figure 5.23: Source Route Bridge Port Statistics

Source Routing — The Port-Pair Group

This group applies to bridges that support the direct multiport model of Source Route bridging as defined in [58]. Ports on bridges supporting the direct multiport model do not have a single target ring, and thus, `dot1dSrPortTargetSegment` and `dot1dSrPortBridgeNumber` (described on page 294) should have the value 65535. The group has one scalar:

dot1dPortPairTableSize (`Gauge32`):   the total number of entries in the bridge's Port-Pair database.

The `dot1dPortPairTable` represents the Port-Pair database, and has one row for each pair of ports. Each row represents a (ring number, bridge number, ring number) triplet, where one port of the pair connects to one of the ring numbers, and the other port connects to the other ring number. The row template is:

INDEX   { dot1dPortPairLowPort, dot1dPortPairHighPort }

where `dot1dPortPairLowPort` identifies the lower-numbered port of the pair, and `dot1dPortPairHighPort` identifies the higher-numbered port of the pair. The columns in this table are:

dot1dPortPairBridgeNum (`INTEGER`): the bridge number of the (ring number, bridge number, ring number) triplet (this value may be **set**); and,

dot1dPortPairBridgeState (enumerated `INTEGER`): the state of the bridge's interconnection of the port-pair:

invalid	remove this port-pair
enabled	
disabled	

This object may be **set** to alter the current state;

5.2.5   Token Ring

The 802.5 MIB module [66] captures the media-specific information for Token Ring interfaces. It contains a mandatory group and an optional Timer group containing values of 802.5 timers. The mandatory group contains two tables: one for status and parameter values, and one for statistics.

Token Ring Status and Parameters

The `dot5Table` contains status and parameter values, with one row per 802.5 interface. Thus, the row template is:

    INDEX   { dot5IfIndex }

where `dot5IfIndex` is the `ifIndex` value of the interface. The columns in this table are:

dot5Commands (enumerated `INTEGER`):   this object may be **set** to issue control commands to the interface:

open	insert into ring
reset	reset interface
close	remove from ring
no-op	no effect

dot5RingStatus (`INTEGER`):   the current interface status, expressed as the sum of multiple possible states:

0	no problems detected
32	ring recovery
64	single station
256	remove received
512	reserved
1024	auto-removal error
2048	lobe wire fault
4096	transmit beacon
8192	soft error
16384	hard error
32768	signal loss
131072	open not completed

dot5RingState (enumerated `INTEGER`):   the current interface state with respect to entering or leaving the ring:

`opened`
`closed`
`opening`
`closing`
`openFailure`
`ringFailure`

dot5RingOpenStatus (enumerated `INTEGER`): the success, or the reason for failure, of the station's most recent attempt to enter the ring:

`open`	last open successful
`noOpen`	no open attempted
`badParam`	
`lobeFailed`	
`signalLoss`	
`insertionTimeout`	
`ringFailed`	
`beaconing`	
`duplicateMAC`	
`requestFailed`	
`removeReceived`	

dot5RingSpeed (enumerated `INTEGER`): the ring's bandwidth, one of:

unknown
oneMegabit
fourMegabit
sixteenMegabit

(Some agents will allow this value to be **set**);

dot5UpStream (`MacAddress`):   the MAC-address of the upstream neighbor station in the ring;

dot5ActMonParticipate (enumerated `INTEGER`): whether this interface will participate in the Active Monitor selection process; some agents will allow this value to be **set**; and,

dot5Functional (`MacAddress`): a bit mask indicating a set of Token Ring functional addresses, where each bit is a 1 if the interface accepts frames addressed to the functional address associated with that bit; some agents will allow this value to be `set`.

Figure 5.24 on the next page shows what these might look like.

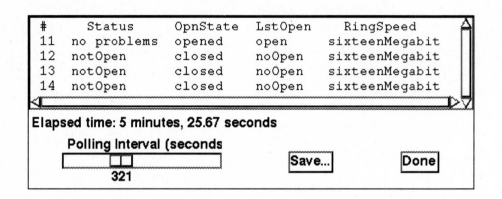

Figure 5.24: A Window Showing Token Ring Interface Status

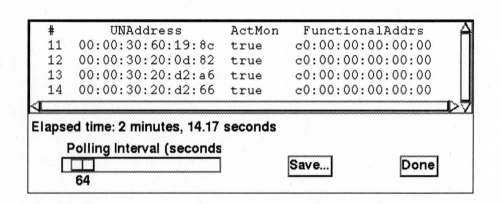

Figure 5.24: A Window Showing Token Ring Interface Status (cont.)

Token Ring Statistics

The `dot5StatsTable` contains statistics and error counters which are specific to 802.5 interfaces. Thus, the row template is:

        INDEX   { dot5StatsIfIndex }

where `dot5StatsIfIndex` has the `ifIndex` value of the interface. The counters in this table are:

dot5StatsLineErrors: the number of times this station detected a Line Error in a frame which did not have its E bit set;

dot5StatsBurstErrors: the number of burst errors;

dot5StatsACErrors: the number of times an AMP or SMP frame was received with an invalid setting of the A and C bits;

dot5StatsAbortTransErrors: the number of times a transmission was aborted;

dot5StatsInternalErrors: the number of internal errors on this interface;

dot5StatsLostFrameErrors: the number of Lost Frame Errors;

dot5StatsReceiveCongestions: the number of times this station recognized a frame addressed to its specific address, but had no available buffers to receive it;

dot5StatsFrameCopiedErrors: the number of times this station recognized a frame addressed to its specific address with the A bit set to 1, indicating a possible line hit or duplicate address;

dot5StatsTokenErrors: the number of times when this station acting as the Active Monitor recognized an error condition that required a new token to be transmitted;

dot5StatsSoftErrors: the number of Report Error MAC frames (to report Soft Errors) that this interface has transmitted;

dot5StatsHardErrors: the number of times this interface has detected an immediately recoverable fatal error because it was either transmitting or receiving beacon MAC frames;

dot5StatsSignalLoss: the number of times this interface has detected the loss of signal condition from the ring;

dot5StatsTransmitBeacons: the number of times this interface has transmitted a beacon frame;

dot5StatsRecoverys: the number of Claim Token MAC frames received or transmitted after the interface has received a Ring Purge MAC frame, which signifies the ring has been purged and is being recovered back into a normal operating state;

dot5StatsLobeWires: the number of times the interface has detected an open or short circuit in its lobe data path. On detecting this condition, the interface will be removed from the ring;

dot5StatsRemoves: the number of times the interface has received a Remove Ring Station MAC frame request. On receiving this frame, the interface will be removed from the ring;

dot5StatsSingles: the number of times the interface has sensed that it is the only station on the ring. If the station is not the only station on the ring, there is a hardware problem; and,

dot5StatsFreqErrors: the number of Frequency Errors.

Note that `dot5StatsSoftErrors` does not count the total number of soft errors, but it does get incremented at least once whenever a group of soft errors occurs. Thus, the individual counters for soft error conditions need only be investigated if `dot5StatsSoftErrors` increases. Figures 5.25 and 5.26 shows what these statistics counters might look like. Note that the number of soft errors in Figure 5.25 is equal to the sum of the individual soft errors in Figure 5.26.

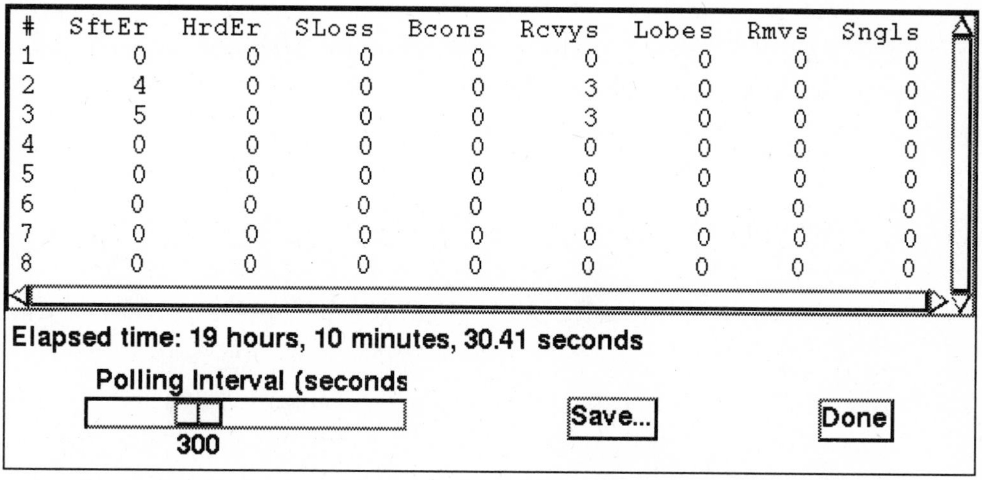

#	SftEr	HrdEr	SLoss	Bcons	Rcvys	Lobes	Rmvs	Sngls
1	0	0	0	0	0	0	0	0
2	4	0	0	0	3	0	0	0
3	5	0	0	0	3	0	0	0
4	0	0	0	0	0	0	0	0
5	0	0	0	0	0	0	0	0
6	0	0	0	0	0	0	0	0
7	0	0	0	0	0	0	0	0
8	0	0	0	0	0	0	0	0

Elapsed time: 19 hours, 10 minutes, 30.41 seconds

Polling Interval (seconds

300   Save...   Done

Figure 5.25: A Window Showing Token Ring Statistics

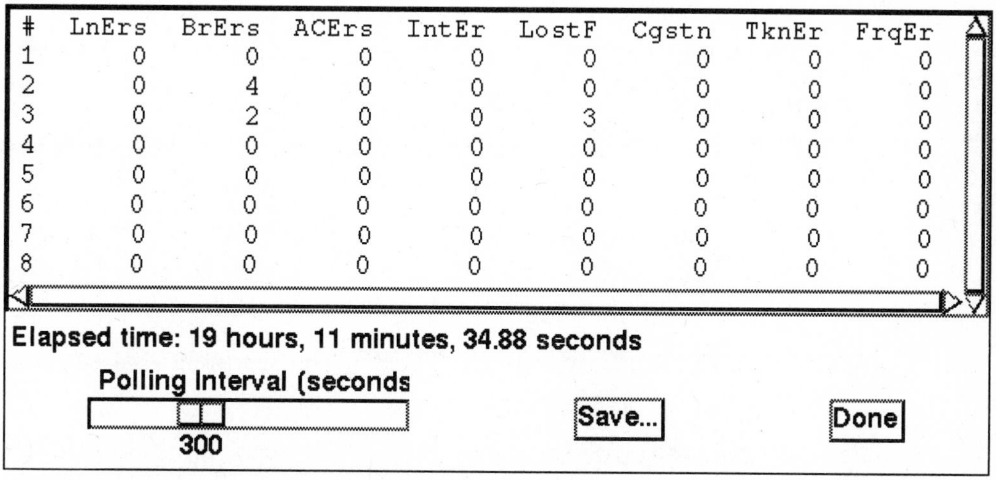

#	LnErs	BrErs	ACErs	IntEr	LostF	Cgstn	TknEr	FrqEr
1	0	0	0	0	0	0	0	0
2	0	4	0	0	0	0	0	0
3	0	2	0	0	3	0	0	0
4	0	0	0	0	0	0	0	0
5	0	0	0	0	0	0	0	0
6	0	0	0	0	0	0	0	0
7	0	0	0	0	0	0	0	0
8	0	0	0	0	0	0	0	0

Elapsed time: 19 hours, 11 minutes, 34.88 seconds

Polling Interval (seconds

300   Save...   Done

Figure 5.26: A Window of Token Ring Soft Error Counts

Token Ring Timers

This optional group contains the values of the timers defined by the IEEE 802.5 specification. However, experience indicates there is little value in having these timers represented as MIB objects, and few agents provide access to this group.

The group contains the `dot5TimerTable` with a row template of:

```
INDEX   { dot5TimerIfIndex }
```

where `dot5TimerIfIndex` has the `ifIndex` value of the interface. The columns in this table are:

dot5TimerReturnRepeat (INTEGER): the timer value used to ensure the interface will return to Repeat State;

dot5TimerHolding (INTEGER): the maximum period of time a station is permitted to transmit frames after capturing a token;

dot5TimerQueuePDU (INTEGER): the timer value for enqueuing of an SMP PDU after reception of an AMP or SMP frame in which the A and C bits were equal to 0;

dot5TimerValidTransmit (INTEGER): the timer value used by the Active Monitor to detect the absence of valid transmissions;

dot5TimerNoToken (INTEGER): the timer value used to recover from various error situations;

dot5TimerActiveMon (INTEGER): the timer value used by the Active Monitor in generating AMP frames;

dot5TimerStandbyMon (INTEGER): the timer value used by the Standby Monitors to ensure that there is an Active Monitor on the ring;

dot5TimerErrorReport (INTEGER): the frequency of sending Report Error MAC frames;

dot5TimerBeaconTransmit (INTEGER): how long to transmit Beacon frames before leaving the ring; and,

dot5TimerBeaconReceive (INTEGER): how long to receive Beacon frames before leaving the ring.

Token Ring Tests

Two tests are defined for use with the `ifTestTable` (see page 195) for Token Ring interfaces:

testFullDuplexLoopBack: this test configures the MAC chip and executes an internal loopback test of memory and the MAC chip logic. This loopback test can only be executed if the interface is offline; and,

testInsertFunc: the Insert Function test, which tests the insert ring logic of the hardware; note that this command inserts the station into the network, and thus could cause disruption if the station is connected to an operational network.

5.3   Applications

In this section, we'll consider how to use some of the more than 150 MIB objects introduced in the previous section.

- first, recall the categorizations introduced earlier in Section 4.3 on page 210:

  - problem conditions;

  - unusual conditions; and,

  - workload events.

- second, observe that error counters can indicate either:

  a local problem in the station which detects the error; or,

  a non-local problem which exists in another station.

For non-local problems, it is very useful to know the topology of the network. However, it is often quite difficult to discover the topology of a LAN network, so let's first explore topology-discovery applications.

5.3.1   Discovering Topology

On a Token-Ring network, the value of `dot5UpStream` in each station provides the MAC address of its upstream neighbor. Thus, each station can be queried in turn to find the topology of the ring. A quicker way to discover all the MAC addresses on a ring is to have an RMON probe connected to the Token-Ring network; the Token-Ring RMON MIB module [67] contains a single table which provides the order of the MAC addresses around the ring. Unfortunately, the MAC address is rarely sufficient to allow a station to be queried via SNMP; normally, at least the IP address is required in order to send SNMP requests. A possible way to obtain the IP address from a MAC address is to inspect the `ipNetToMediaTable` (see page 204) of stations with which it is communicating (e.g., a router on that network).

On an Ether-like network, it is practically impossible to discover the relative positions of the stations on a segment. However, when the network is divided up into segments through the use of repeaters and/or bridges, these devices can be queried to discover which stations are reached via which of their ports, and thus which stations are on which segments. For repeaters, the information is available in

> `rptrAddrTrackLastSourceAddress`

or

> `rptrAddrTrackNewLastSrcAddress`

for each port on a repeater. Use of this value depends upon the topology:

- for a port which connects to a single station (the normal case when using 10BASET and star-wiring), the value can be used directly as the address of that single station;

- when multiple stations are "behind" a repeater port, then

  > `rptrAddrTrackLastSourceAddress`

  provides only the source MAC address of the last frame received on that port; or,

- when one of the multiple stations behind a repeater port is another repeater, further investigation is required.

The first of these cases can be distinguished by observing that the corresponding value of `rptrAddrTrackSourceAddrChanges` is not increasing. For the other cases, it is necessary to have an application which retrieves the value of `rptrAddrTrackLastSourceAddress` multiple times in order to build a list of the addresses behind a port. The more times that a port's value is read, the greater the probability that the list of addresses will contain the addresses of all stations behind that port. For example, for a station which transmits only one out of every 50 frames received on the port, reading the value 100 times has an 87% probability of obtaining that station's address; reading the value 300 times increases the probability to 99.8%.[22]

The multiple repeaters on a segment case can be distinguished either by the value of the port's `rpMauType` indicating a point-to-point

---

[22]This assumes the receipt of SNMP requests and the recording of the source address of the last frame are not inter-related events, which may not be true for port(s) through which the SNMP requests are transmitted!

link between two repeaters (e.g., `dot3MauTypeFoirl`), or through having the same MAC address appear on the lists of multiple repeaters. In the latter situation, when two MAC addresses are on different ports of one repeater but also appear to be behind a single port of a second repeater, then the single port of the second repeater provides connectivity to the first repeater, and those MAC addresses can be deleted from the list of the single port of the second repeater.

A similar application is possible for determining which stations are on which LANs of an extended LAN, by retrieving the

> `dot1dTpFdbAddress`

and

> `dot1dTpFdbPort`

objects in the forwarding database of each transparent bridge. Here, multiple values of `dot1dTpFdbAddress` are retained for each port, and so the probabilistic mechanism of polling multiple times is not required. However, entries in the forwarding database are aged out, and so complete information for one address may be available only after a station sends a frame (e.g., an ARP request) to the broadcast or a multicast address.

The algorithms just discussed have assumed that the NMS can query the repeaters and/or bridges. This requires that the NMS know the addresses of the repeaters and bridges. Since these devices are transparent to the stations, this is non-trivial. In fact, the repeaters themselves do not have addresses, and their management agents are not necessarily connected to the same segment as the repeater itself. Thus, it is normally necessary for their IP addresses to be entered into the NMS manually. The situation for transparent bridges is a little better since they generally transmit STP protocol BPDUs to other bridges. Unfortunately, the information recorded in MIB objects is not sufficient to allow the NMS to communicate with all the bridges on the extended LAN:

- the bridges only record the MAC addresses which are significant in the STP topology; in particular, they record the address of the root and the designated bridge on each LAN (in

  > `dot1dStpDesignatedRoot`

and

> `dot1dStpPortDesignatedBridge`

respectively);

- an RMON probe can be used to record the MAC addresses of all frames sent to the multicast destination address of BPDUs; recall, however, that BPDUs are never forwarded by bridges participating in STP, and thus, recording every bridge's address would require an RMON probe to be connected to every LAN within the extended topology; and

- even if all MAC addresses were recorded, it is still necessary in the normal case that the NMS needs an IP address in order to send an SNMP request; since SNMP messages are the only IP datagrams which most bridges send/receive, it's unlikely that any other agent's `ipNetToMediaTable` will provide the information to determine their IP addresses.

Thus, in general, the IP address of every bridge also has to be entered into the NMS manually.

The applications described above were aimed at discovering which stations were connected to which segments/LANs. To discover the inter-connection topology of the repeaters and bridges themselves requires a little more work since repeaters/bridges are connected to multiple segments/LANs. For bridges, given that the IP addresses of the bridges are known, then:

- first, retrieve

> `dot1dBaseBridgeAddress`

and

> `dot1dBaseNumPorts`

to obtain the MAC address and number of ports on each bridge;

- second, find which ports are used on each bridge to reach every other bridge, by retrieving from each bridge the instance of `dot1dTpFdbPort` for the MAC address of every other bridge, making sure to check the values of `dot1dTpFdbStatus` to ensure the rows are valid; and,

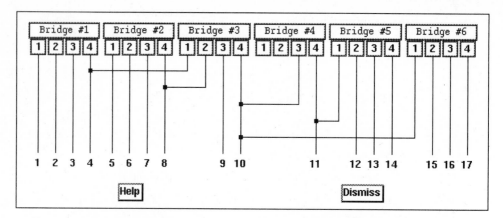

Figure 5.27: A Window Displaying Bridge Topology

- then, make use of the fact that two bridges, A and B, are on the same LAN if A and B are reached via the same port on every other bridge.

Through this procedure, the number of LANs and the interconnections of the bridges to those LANs can be determined and displayed in a window to the network operator. An example of such a window is shown in Figure 5.27. The bridges are depicted across the width of the top of the window, with their ports being represented in ascending order across the bottom of each bridge. Extending down from each port is a line representing that port's connection to a LAN segment. For the left-most occurrence of each LAN, the line is extended vertically to the bottom of the window. Where a port connects to a LAN which has already been extended to the bottom of the window, its line is curved around to run horizontally to the left, to connect to that LAN's fully vertical line.

Note that as well as producing a display of the topology, it is of significant value to store the topology in a topology database for use by other applications.

5.3.2   Ethernet Errors

Having explored applications for determining the topology of the network, let's return to the categorization of conditions counted by the various counter objects. First, recall that

>   ifInErrors

and

>   ifOutErrors

count the number of errors on an interface. Thus, the Ethernet-specific error counters need only be referenced when it's necessary to investigate increases in `ifInErrors` or `ifOutErrors`.

Several of the Ethernet-specific error counters are local problem conditions:

>   dot3StatsInternalMacTransmitErrors
>   dot3StatsInternalMacReceiveErrors
>   dot3StatsSQETestErrors
>   dot3StatsCarrierSenseErrors

The first two indicate a probable fault in the local adaptor card; **dot3StatsSQETestErrors** indicates a fault in the local station's collision detection circuitry; and **dot3StatsCarrierSenseErrors** normally indicates a bad transmit or receive lead.

Of the others, **dot3StatsFrameTooLongs** indicates either a non-local software error or that a protocol using non-standard frame lengths is in use; and **dot3StatsLateCollisions** indicates either that the network has too large a propagation delay between the reporting station and some other station(s), or that some other station is not detecting/responding to collisions correctly. **dot3StatsAlignmentErrors** is also typically a non-local problem condition. Examination of the corresponding counter for the port of a repeater/bridge connected to the same segment can help in determining whether these are local or non-local problems. Assuming the discovered topology has been stored in a topology database, then the retrieval of the corresponding counter from the appropriate repeater/bridge can be done automatically by an application.

dot3StatsFCSErrors is an unusual condition, but should never exhibit a significant rate of increase. If it does, then there is a non-local problem, and the detecting station's MIB objects provide no means of determining which station is sending the erroneous frames. The best approach to diagnose such a problem is to determine the stations with which the station reporting the errors is communicating. For each of these stations, if the station is attached to a repeater port's segment, inspect the `rptrMonitorPortFCSErrors` object for that port; if the station is attached to a bridge port's LAN/segment, inspect the `dot3StatsFCSErrors` object for that port. If either of these objects indicates a significant number of FCS errors, then the source has been isolated to a particular segment. If that segment has lots of stations, then a further reduction of the candidate list can be achieved by inserting an extra bridge/repeater in an appropriate location.

Note that this type of isolation technique is useful in other situations as well, and is more effective when there are fewer stations on each segment.

The other counters for Ether-like interfaces are unusual conditions concerned with collisions:

```
dot3StatsDeferredTransmissions
dot3StatsSingleCollisionFrames
dot3StatsMultipleCollisionFrames
dot3StatsExcessiveCollisions
```

These counters do not count all collisions on the network, but rather only the collisions which occurred when that station was attempting to transmit. So, the important ratio is the number of collisions to the number of frames sent (`ifOutUcastPkts` plus `ifOutNUcastPkts`), and it should normally be much less than one. High collision rates do not normally indicate equipment failure, but rather a performance problem; in particular, that the stations on the network have more traffic to send than the network can support. When

```
dot3StatsExcessiveCollisions
```

is increasing, not only is traffic being delayed, but data is actually being lost. However, if only one station on a segment has a high collision ratio, then a faulty adaptor card in that station is a possibility.

The `rptrMonitorTransmitCollisions` counter for repeaters also does not count all the collisions on the network, but rather only those between two or more ports of the repeater and not those which occur only on an individual segment. However, these latter collisions are detected by each repeater as runts, and thus, the total number of collisions on the network can be determined (at least to a first-order approximation) by the formula:

$$\texttt{rptrMonitorTransmitCollisions} + \sum_{\text{all ports}} \texttt{rptrMonitorPortRunts}$$

This value should be the same in all repeaters within the same LAN.

Even so, the total number of collisions still doesn't give the best indication of the overall condition of the LAN. A better indication is the ratio of the total number of collisions to the total number of frames, i.e.,

$$\frac{\texttt{rptrMonitorTransmitCollisions} + \sum_{\text{all ports}} \texttt{rptrMonitorPortRunts}}{\sum_{\text{all groups}} \texttt{rptrMonitorGroupTotalFrames}}$$

Producing a graph is just a simple matter of modifying `snmptcl_graph_ifutil` (see page 215) to implement the above formula. A sample graph is shown in Figure 5.28 on the next page. This graph shows a LAN which initially has only background traffic, and the effect (at polling interval 52) of starting up several traffic generators each producing about 200 frames/second.

If the above formula produces a result greater than one, i.e., more collisions than frames, then the network is definitely overloaded (and the users on the network will not be getting much work done!). If this condition occurs without being caused by some unusual event (e.g., a misbehaving station), then the network needs to be divided up with more bridges and/or routers.

Other important objects for repeaters are those concerned with auto-partitioned ports. A port can become auto-partitioned either due to cable breaks, faulty connectors, or a mis-connection which causes a loop in the topology.

> `rptrTotalPartitionedPorts`

gives the current number of ports which are auto-partitioned on the repeater; the specific ports are those for which

> `rptrPortAdminStatus`

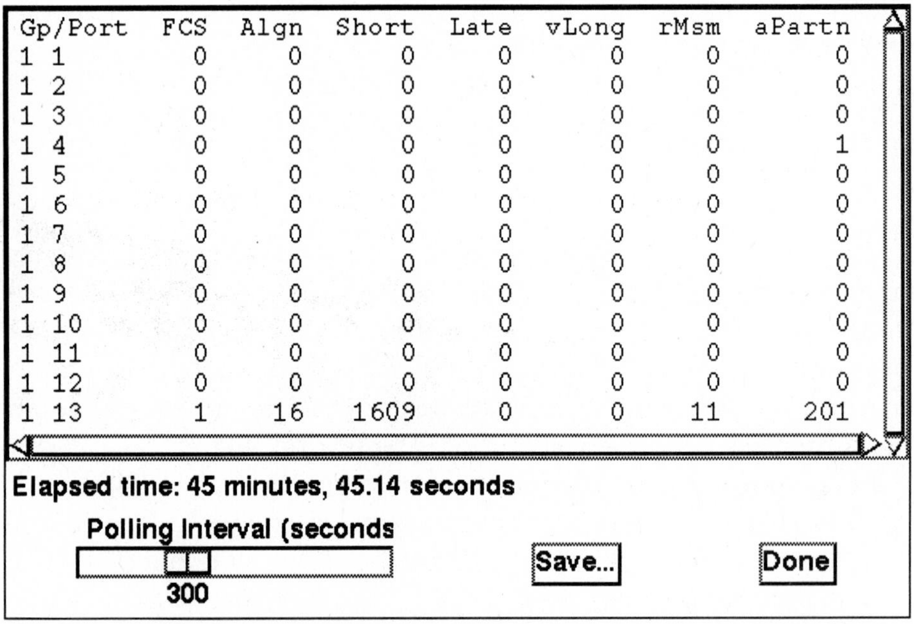

Gp/Port	FCS	Algn	Short	Late	vLong	rMsm	aPartn
1 1	0	0	0	0	0	0	0
1 2	0	0	0	0	0	0	0
1 3	0	0	0	0	0	0	0
1 4	0	0	0	0	0	0	1
1 5	0	0	0	0	0	0	0
1 6	0	0	0	0	0	0	0
1 7	0	0	0	0	0	0	0
1 8	0	0	0	0	0	0	0
1 9	0	0	0	0	0	0	0
1 10	0	0	0	0	0	0	0
1 11	0	0	0	0	0	0	0
1 12	0	0	0	0	0	0	0
1 13	1	16	1609	0	0	11	201

Elapsed time: 45 minutes, 45.14 seconds

Polling Interval (seconds

300

Save...   Done

Figure 5.28: A Window Graphing Collisions/Frame

has the value `enabled`,

> `rptrPortOperStatus`

is either `operational` or `notOperational`, and

> `rptrPortAutoPartitionState`

is `autoPartitioned`.

> `rptrMonitorPortAutoPartitions`

counts the transitions into the auto-partitioned state, and normally indicates an intermittent problem. For ports which are `notPresent`, the value of `rptrPortAutoPartitionState` indicates its partitioned state when it was last installed.

Lastly, recall that `ifInErrors` and `ifOutErrors` are defined to count the number of input and output errors on the interface. So, any problem which can be identified through increasing values of the error counters in the Ethernet (or any other) media-specific MIB module, will also cause an increase in the corresponding instance(s) of `ifInErrors` or `ifOutErrors` as appropriate. Thus, it is valuable to have a management application which:

- begins by retrieving `ifType` for each interface and, then, the values of the particular set of interesting counters according to each value of `ifType`;

- periodically polls to check for significant increases in the values of `ifInErrors` and `ifOutErrors`; and

- when an increase in `ifInErrors` or `ifOutErrors` occurs, expands the poll to include the appropriate set of interesting counters again and displays their increasing values to the operator.

The equivalent application for repeaters would always poll for increases in

> `rptrMonitorGroupTotalErrors`

retrieving

> `rptrMonitorPortTotalErrors`

for all ports in a group having a significant number of errors, and then the set of individual error counters (see page 275) for the offending ports. All of these individual errors are problem conditions, of which

> `rptrMonitorPortDataRateMismatches`

or

> `rptrMonitorPortVeryLongEvents`

normally indicates an error in one of the adaptors on that port's segment. Of course, these errors could also indicate a problem with the repeater itself or one of its port. If this is suspected, the value of `rptrHealthText` can be examined, possibly after a `set` to `rptrReset` to cause the repeater to reset and perform a self-test,

5.3.3   Transparent Bridge Statistics

The statistics available from a bridge can be used in various ways:[23]

- detecting instabilities in the spanning tree;
- measuring LAN utilization;
- determining non-optimal bridge placement; and,
- other performance problems.

Let's look at each of these in turn.

It is vital to have a stable STP Spanning Tree in an extended LAN. During any topology change, most bridge ports go through a period where they are not forwarding any traffic, and then through a period where they are flooding more frames than necessary. Multiple topology changes can and do happen when bridges and/or links come up/down, but within some number of seconds, the topology should stabilize. If and when topology changes occur with any frequency, it is very disruptive to the network. `dot1dStpTopChanges` counts the number of topology changes, and `dot1dStpTimeSinceTopologyChange` indicates the time of the last change. Whenever `dot1dStpTopChanges` increases, the network manager should investigate the cause of the topology change. `dot1dStpPortForwardTransitions` gives an indication of the ports and, thus, which parts of the network have been affected by the occurrence of topology changes.

LAN interfaces in general, and the two described in this chapter, are all broadcast media. However, LAN interface counters reflect the

---

[23]A number of these are taken from [68].

traffic specific to the interface, which is less than the traffic for the whole LAN, except when the interface is in promiscuous mode. Transparent bridges run in promiscuous mode and, thus, can effectively provide a minimal subset of the information available from an RMON probe. However, there are certain types of hardware-assist capabilities for bridges which result in some frames being discarded without being processed by software and, thus, the counters of a transparent bridge may or may not reflect the total traffic on the network. Talk to your vendor to find out if your bridges' counters reflect the total traffic on their attached LAN.

It is also useful to compare the amount of forwarded traffic to the amount of filtered traffic. The sum of

        `dot1dTpPortInFrames`

over all ports is the total number of frames accepted by a bridge's forwarding entity, while the sum of

        `dot1dTpPortInDiscards`

over all ports is the number of filtered frames. A constant low ratio of filtered frames to received frames indicates poor isolation of traffic. This often indicates non-optimal placement of the bridge(s). For example, consider the topology shown in Figure 5.6 on page 245: if stations A and B are generating lots of traffic between themselves, but relatively little to all the other stations on the network, then their traffic is being transmitted on both LANs. If the bridge were moved so that A and B were on the same LAN, then their traffic would be isolated to that single LAN. When poor isolation of traffic is indicated, the information on how many frames a station is sending to which other stations can be obtained by connecting an RMON probe to the relevant LAN.

The total number of frames transmitted by the bridge on any given port, `dot1dTpPortOutFrames`, should similarly be a fairly small percentage of the number of frames received. Comparing the rate of increase of `dot1dTpPortOutFrames` across multiple ports can help in revealing "funneling" syndromes.

Performance problems can also be caused by a number of other factors. Both

```
dot1dTpLearnedEntryDiscards
```

and

```
dot1dBasePortDelayExceededDiscards
```

indicate problem conditions. If `dot1dTpLearnedEntryDiscards` is increasing, it indicates that the forwarding database is regularly becoming full. This condition will only happen on large networks where the number of stations exceeds the size of the bridge's forwarding database. If and when it does occur, it results in a performance impact on the network since it causes an increase in the number of frames which the bridge floods unnecessarily. If this happens, there are three possible courses:

- determine if the number of entries in the bridge's forwarding table can be increased;

- check if the value of `dot1dTpAgingTime` is unnecessarily high; or,

- consider partitioning the network with extra bridges, or with routers.

`dot1dBasePortDelayExceededDiscards` is a count of frames that the bridge was required to discard since it was not able to forward them within a reasonable period of time, typically on the order of two seconds. This most likely indicates congestion on the LAN to which these frames would have been transmitted. When investigating performance problems, it is always worthwhile to inspect the value of

```
dot1dStpTimeSinceTopologyChange
```

to determine whether STP topology changes may be contributing to the problem.

5.3.4   Bridge Filtering

For security or other reasons, it is sometimes valuable to specify fixed restrictions on the forwarding decisions by a bridge for particular frames, rather than to have the bridges operate their normal learning algorithm. While there are several fields in a frame's header upon which these decisions can be based, the `dot1dStaticTable` allows the restrictions to be specified based on the destination address of a frame, and on a per-receive port basis. For a frame received from a particular port (`dot1dStaticReceivePort`) and addressed to a particular destination address (`dot1dStaticAddress`), `dot1dStaticAllowedToGoTo` specifies a restricted set of ports to which that frame may be forwarded. When `dot1dStaticReceivePort` is zero, the restriction applies to all ports other than those for which a restriction has been explicitly specified.

As well as the obvious security purposes, these filters are the only means to prevent multicast traffic from being distributed across the whole extended LAN. For example, filters can prevent AppleTalk® multicast frames from reaching a LAN with no AppleTalk® stations.

If frames with a particular destination address are not being received across an extended LAN, the information in this table in each bridge should be inspected to determine if such a filter is causing that bridge to drop those frames.

5.3.5   Tuning a Spanning Tree

There are several ways to improve the run-time characteristics and, thus, the stability of an extended LAN's Spanning Tree:

choosing the root: when one LAN is used as a backbone of the extended LAN, a bridge connected to the backbone should be chosen to be the root. This avoids having bridges further away from the backbone forwarding traffic at the expense of bridges connected to the backbone. Also, if and when the chosen root fails, another bridge will take over as root. The perturbations in the topology when this happens can be minimized by selecting a bridge adjacent to the root as the one which will take over. To choose the root and its backup explicitly, set the value of `dot1dStpPriority` in all bridges, so that the desired root has the lowest value and the desired backup has the second lowest value;

adjusting path costs: the default algorithm (see page 249) sets path costs to be inversely proportional to their line speed; to give preference to one of several links with the same line speed, or to prefer a lower-speed link over a higher-speed link, adjust the values of `dot1dStpPortPathCost` for the ports which connect to the relevant links;

tuning the timers: the global node parameters of the spanning tree

> `dot1dStpBridgeHelloTime`
> `dot1dStpBridgeMaxAge`
> `dot1dStpBridgeForwardDelay`

determine the Spanning Tree's timing characteristics. By adjusting these timers, the delay in switching over to a backup link may be tuned. However, these parameters should be changed only if the topology allows it; they are based on the diameter of the extended LAN. To effect a change, the values of these objects must be set at the root (and the backup root for use when it takes over as root). Recommended values for these parameters are given in [55];

disabling a port: if a particular bridge port is (suspected to be) causing oscillations in the tree, it can be isolated by setting `dot1dStpPortEnable` to `disabled`.

5.3.6 Token Ring Errors

`dot5RingState` and `dot5RingOpenStatus` objects provide for debugging problems when a station cannot even enter the ring.[24] After a station has successfully been added to the ring, `dot5RingStatus` can be used to diagnose fluctuating problems on the ring.

The causes of the Token Ring error counters were explained in some detail starting on page 256. The two categories of errors are hard errors and soft errors. An application which polls the Token Ring interface counters on a periodic basis need retrieve only

    dot5StatsHardErrors

and

    dot5StatsSoftErrors.

Only if these indicate a significant number of errors, do the other error counters need to be examined. For these others,

    dot5StatsLostFrameErrors
    dot5StatsTokenErrors
    dot5StatsFrameCopiedErrors
    dot5StatsBurstErrors
    dot5StatsLineErrors
    dot5StatsRecoverys

are unusual conditions; whereas

    dot5StatsACErrors
    dot5StatsInternalErrors
    dot5StatsFreqErrors
    dot5StatsAbortTransError
    dot5StatsRemoves
    dot5StatsLobeWires
    dot5StatsSignalLoss

---

[24]Of course, these objects will only be accessible when the device has another interface through which to receive SNMP queries.

are normally problem conditions; `dot5StatsReceiveCongestions` is a workload condition.

5.3.7   Source Routing Bridge Statistics

Section 5.3.3 on page 318 contained a description of how the statistics available from transparent bridges can be used to measure ring utilization, to detect non-optimal placement of the bridges and to reveal funnels in the topology. Performing this same set of functions is more difficult with source routing bridges, because source routing bridges do not operate in promiscuous mode. To perform the same calculations, `dot1dSrPortSpecInFrames` and `dot1dSrPortSpecOutFrames` provide counts for the individual ports of number of frames forwarded, but a promiscuous monitor such as a Token-Ring RMON probe is required to determine the total amount of traffic on the ring, so that the applicable ratios can be calculated.

Finally,

```
dot1dSrPortDuplicateSegmentDiscards
dot1dSrPortHopCountExceededDiscards
dot1dSrPortLanIdMismatches
```

are all problem conditions which often indicate that different bridges on the network have inconsistent configurations of their ring and/or bridge number parameters, i.e., inconsistent values of:

```
dot1dSrPortLocalSegment
dot1dSrPortTargetSegment
dot1dSrPortBridgeNum
```

or inconsistent rows in the `dot1dPortPairTable`. The first place to look for an inconsistency is between the bridge at which the counter is being incremented and another bridge on the ring connected to the port for which the counter is incrementing. Whether or not the inconsistency is found amongst the bridges on that ring, the configuration of all bridges on the network should be checked for consistency whenever this error occurs. If the counter being incremented is `dot1dSrPortHopCountExceededDiscards`, the problem condition can also be caused by one or more bridge's having a value of `dot1dSrPortHopCount` which is smaller than the diameter of the network. In this situation, either the value of `dot1dSrPortHopCount` needs to be increased in the appropriate bridges, additional bridges need to be added in order to reduce the diameter of the network, or the network needs to be partitioned with routers.

Chapter 6

WAN Management

This chapter discusses the management of Wide-Area Networks. It briefly discusses WANs in general and how they differ from LANs, and then delves into the media-specific information for two types: DS1 and DS3 interfaces. Discussion of other types of WAN interfaces and WAN devices, (e.g., Frame Relay, modems, and so on) is beyond the scope of the current edition of *The Networking Management Practicum*.

Since the original DS1 design in the early 1960's, several line disciplines have been defined for DS1 and DS3 lines, initially by AT&T, and later by the Amercian National Standards Institute (ANSI). Fortunately, most of these differences are buried in the details of the interfaces and it is not necessary from a management perspective to understand the nitty-gritty details for most of them. Thus, this chapter will not describe the various disciplines in any great detail.

In Europe, different standards, defined by the International Telecommunication Union (ITU),[1] are used. The greatest difference between the North American DS1 and DS3 lines and their approximate European equivalents, E1 and E3, are differences in line speed. Otherwise, the differences between the North American and European standards are no greater than the differences between two North American line disciplines. Thus, the DS1 media-specific MIB module applies to both DS1 and E1 lines; similarly, the DS3 media-specific MIB module applies to both DS3 and E3.

---

[1]In particular, by the ITU-T which was formerly known as the International Consultative Committee on Telephony and Telegraphy (CCITT).

6.1   Concepts

A wide-area network (WAN) is a network which connects two or more geographically-distant sites together via a particular subnetwork technology. Unlike LANs, the basic transmission *facilities* of a WAN are normally owned by a carrier (e.g., a telephone company). Various options exist on top of the basic transmission facilities concerning the level of *service* provided by a *service provider*. The service provider might be the telephone company itself, or some other company which leases transmission facilities from the telephone company. The options range from:

dedicated lines: all of the lines' bandwidth is available to the user, and the user typically pays a fixed monthly charge; to,

shared public service: a user gets access to a network carrying the traffic of many users, and usually pays a (smaller) fixed charge plus a usage charge based on the individual user's amount of traffic.

The availability of intermediate options, such as virtual private networks, varies according to the provider and the geographic area.

Because each of these options involves a non-trivial charge (e.g., thousands of dollars per month), there is a much greater incentive for efficiency than exists for LANs. The charges, normally set according to tariffs approved by regulatory agencies, are almost always cheaper per bit for higher bandwidth lines. Thus, one efficiency incentive is to procure fewer higher bandwidth lines and increase the number of streams of traffic carried over each line. This, of course, requires a means of multiplexing the streams.

So, let's first look at the types of traffic which might be multiplexed over a single line, and then at how multiplexing is achieved on DS1 and DS3 lines.

6.1.1   Different Types of Traffic

Originally, the type of traffic with the highest volume was voice. Today, the multiplexing of voice traffic over a single line is typically from a Private Branch Exchange (PBX) system installed at the user's premises to a Local Exchange Carrier (LEC) or Interexchange Carrier (IXC).[2] Each external phone line supported by the PBX occupies 64Kb/s of bandwidth, as required for the normal Pulse Code Modulation (PCM) encoding technique used for voice.[3]

The fastest growing type of traffic is for data communications. Each WAN site will often have multiple local systems connected together via one or more local area networks. The WAN provides the means to carry traffic between the LANs at different sites. In general, LANs and WANs use different subnetwork technologies.[4] Thus, a device, such as a router or a MAC layer bridge, is needed which implements both the LAN and the WAN subnetwork technologies, and forwards packets between them. Providing all the traffic can be routed, a router is the natural device to use in this situation, especially for large networks. The use of a bridge causes all of the LAN broadcast/multicast traffic to be sent over the WAN, irrespective of whether any system at a remote site needs to receive the traffic. This inefficiency can be ameliorated by various types of filtering, but this reduces the simplicity of use which is one of the bridge's advantages.

Video is another type of traffic with small but increasing usage. Various forms of video encoding and compression produce different qualities and require different bandwidths, ranging from 384Kb/s up to 100Mb/s.

6.1.2 DS1/DS3 Multiplexing

In North America, the basic unit of multiplexing is the 64Kb/s DS0 channel. A DS0 channel, often referred to as a "voice grade" channel, was originally designed to carry one PCM-encoded voice connection of 8-bit samples at 8000 samples per second. DS1 and DS3 lines use Time Division Multiplexing (TDM) to carry multiple DS0 channels, where the line's bit rate is shared by allocating individual time slots to each separate DS0 channel.

---

[2]These terms are US-centric; in other countries, there is generally no distinction.

[3]Voice can also be carried on lesser bandwidth channels, e.g., Adaptive Differential PCM (ADPCM) uses 32Kb/s.

[4]Asynchronous Transfer Mode (ATM) promises to be an exception to this.

A DS1 line can carry 24 DS0 channels, and in its basic form, the transmission consists of a succession of 193-bit frames, transmitted at a rate of 8000 frames per second, with each frame consisting of eight bits from each channel followed by a framing bit, as shown in Figure 6.1. Thus, the DS1 bandwidth is:

$$((24 * 8) + 1) * 8000 = 1.544 \text{Mb/s}$$

A DS3 line carries the equivalent of 28 DS1 links, and requires a bandwidth of 44.736 Mb/s. As one might expect, a DS2 line is also defined, and forms part of the North American TDM Digital Signal Hierarchy [69]:

hierarchy designator	# DS0-channels	line bit rate
DS0	1	64Kb/s
DS1	24	1.544Mb/s
DS1C	48	3.152Mb/s
DS2	96	6.312Mb/s
DS3	672	44.736Mb/s
DS4	4032	274.176Mb/s

However, DS4 is not used, and DS1C and DS2 rarely so.

For the European standards, a similar hierarchy is defined but with different line speeds. In particular, an E1 line is 2.048 Mb/s and consists of 31 64Kb/s channels plus another 64Kb/s channel to carry *signaling* information used to establish and terminate connections. An E3 line is 34.368 Mb/s and consists of 16 E1 channels. For specific details, consult [70], [71] and [72].

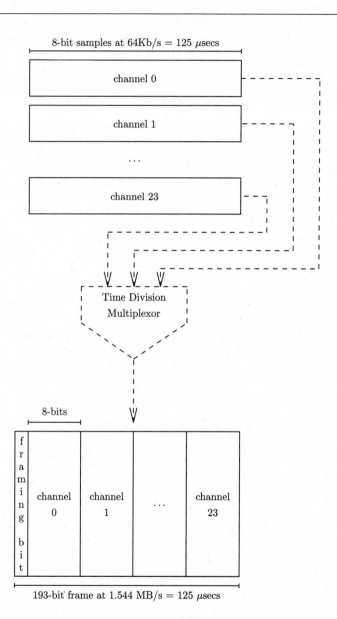

Figure 6.1: Time Division Multiplexing

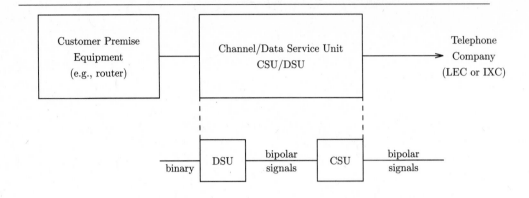

Figure 6.2: The Role of CSU/DSUs

6.1.3   Channel/Data Service Units

A DS1/DS3 link connects the user's premises to the telephone company's facilities. A Channel Service Unit (CSU) at least, and possibly a Data Service Unit (DSU) as well, are required at the user's premises to connect the user's equipment, often termed the Customer Premise Equipment (CPE), to the DS1/DS3 service, as shown in Figure 6.2.

CSUs terminate telephone company digital circuits, and must be designed in accordance with the appropriate regulations. Other CSU functions include:

- line conditioning and equalization (which concern the use of amplifiers to compensate for signal loss);

- error control; and,

- the ability to respond to local and network loopback circuit testing commands.

DSUs provide frame synchronization and, for DS1 lines, timing recovery. They also convert ordinary binary signals generated by user equipment into the *bipolar signals* required by the phone company's DS1 equipment. The DSU function is often combined with the CSU function into a single device.

6.1.4 DS1 Links

For bipolar signals, a line coding technique called Alternate Mark Inversion (AMI) specifies that a 1 bit is represented by either a positive or negative pulse, and a 0 bit by the absence of a pulse. Each pulse has the opposite polarity from its preceding and succeeding pulses, i.e., after a positive pulse, the next 1 bit is represented by a negative pulse, and vice-versa. This allows all single-bit errors to be detected (as *bipolar violations*) and corrected. However, this scheme degrades when the data contains a long sequence of 0's due to the lack of pulses for recovering timing. As a result, various *zero suppression coding* techniques are normally used. One example is *binary eight zero substitution* (B8ZS) where a sequence of eight 0's is replaced (on transmission) by a special code which can be recognized (on reception) as having a particular pattern of bipolar violations and replaced by the original sequence rather than being counted as an error.[5] While B8ZS imposes no restrictions on the data content and no reduction in available bit rate, other techniques do impose such restrictions and/or reduce the bit rate.

Today, the two most common framing formats for DS1 links are:

- the T1 Superframe, commonly known as the D4 format; and,

- the T1 Extended Superframe (ESF).

The D4 format has a *superframe* consisting of 12 regular 193-bit frames, such that the 12 framing bits (the first bit in each frame) have specific patterns which can be used to maintain frame synchronization. For more detailed information, see [73].

The ESF format extends the superframe to be 24 frames, instead of 12 frames, to take advantage of the fact that modern technology requires fewer bits for frame synchronization. Of the 24 framing bits in each extended superframe:

- six are used for frame synchronization;

- six contain a CRC code for the superframe; and

- twelve are used for a *facility data link*.

---

[5] When a zero suppression encoding scheme is used, an excessive string of zeros counts as a bipolar violation.

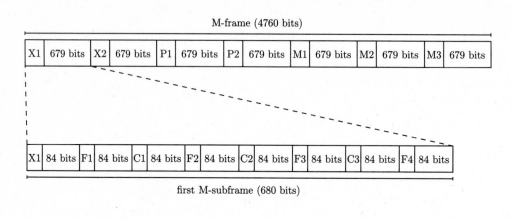

$$
\begin{array}{l}
\text{overhead bits per M-frame:} \quad \text{C1, X2, P1, P2, M1, M2, M3} \\
\text{overhead bits per M-subframe:} \quad \text{F1, F2, F3, F4, C1, C2, C3} \\
\text{data bits per M-subframe:} \quad \ \ \text{672 bits} \quad (8*84) \\
\text{data bits per M-frame:} \quad \ \ \ \text{4704 bits} \quad (7*672)
\end{array}
$$

Figure 6.3: DS3 Framing Structure

The CRC is fairly weak by data communications standards, but even so, it significantly improves error detection. The facility data link (FDL) is an in-band communications link to the CSU, through which error counts and alarm indications can be exchanged, and the operational and test modes of the CSU can be controlled. For more detailed information, see [74] and [75].

E1 links use a different framing structure (see [76]), for which a CRC code can also be present (see [77]).

6.1.5 DS3 Links

DS3 links have a more complicated framing structure, in which the "overhead" bits are spread throughout the frame. As shown in Figure 6.3, the DS3 signal is partitioned into *M-frames* containing 4760 bits. Each M-frame consists of 7 *M-subframes*, each having 680 bits. Each M-subframe consists of 8 blocks of 85 bits, with 84 bits of data, called the *payload*, and one overhead bit. Thus, there are 56 overhead bits (one in each block) in an M-frame.

The use of the overhead bits varies according to the line discipline.[6] The particular disciplines provide different capabilities in terms of how the DS3 line is to be sub-divided into DS0, DS1, or other channel rates. For example, the M13 multiplex format, also known as *SYNTRAN*, and the C-bit Parity disciplines contain 28 DS1 channels. In all disciplines, the first overhead bit in the third and fourth M-subframes are the *P-bits* (P1 and P2); these are used to holds the parity of the 4704 bits of the previous M-frame's payload. Twenty-one of the other overhead bits are C-bits. For C-bit Parity, a subset of the C-bits, known as the CP-bits, also hold the parity of the previous M-frame. The difference between the P-bits and the CP-bits is that the P-bits may get re-calculated as the frame passes through the network, whereas the CP-bits will pass through the network unchanged.

For more information on DS3 framing, see [78] and [79]. For E3 links, see [72].

6.1.6   Timing

A clock is used to generate a signal that provides a timing reference for functions, such as establishing bit rates and timing the duration of bit intervals. In a completely synchronous TDM network, all participating devices must use the timing provided by a single master clock. However, this is not the case in many of today's networks. For minor variations, a bit-stream being passed through the network from one link to another can be buffered; this is particularly useful for satellite circuits for which the line "rate" appears to vary as the propogation delay to the satellite varies. Buffering does not, however, solve the problem when one link's rate is consistently faster/slower than the other's. For DS1/E1, such ever-increasing differences are handled by generating a *controlled slip* error, for which a frame is deleted or replicated, as necessary.[7] An upper bound on the number of controlled slips per unit time can be calculated given the tolerance on the "lowest quality" clock source allowed in the network. For DS2 and above, the frame formats include additional "overhead" bits in

---

[6]In the telecom world, a particular discipline is known as a DS3 "application".

[7]Obviously, the deletion or replication of a DS1 frame introduces errors into the data stream.

order to obviate the need for controlled slips.

6.1.7 DS1/E1 Errors

Error counts on DS1 and E1 lines fall into three categories:

- counts of occurrences of particular types of errors;

- counts of time intervals in which particular types of errors occurred; and,

- counts of time intervals in which a particular severity of errors occurred.

The highest level of severity is "unavailable". While at this level, no count except the number of unavailable seconds is incremented.

The particular types of errors are:

Line Coding Violations (LCV): errors which are detected within a received frame, either bipolar violations or too many successive 0 bits;

Path Coding Violations (PCV): errors which are detected on received frames, such as CRC errors;

Controlled Slips (CS): errors introduced into the received data to correct for timing variations; and,

framing errors: errors in recovering frames from the incoming bit stream; a framing error is refered to as a *defect*, and multiple consecutive framing errors cause a *failure condition*. The various types of defects include: OOF (Out Of Frame), LOS (Loss Of Signal), and AIS (Alarm Indication Signal), which if they persist cause: LOF (Loss Of Frame), LOS and AIS failure conditions, respectively.

The idea behind these types is to identify the cause of a fault condition, and thereby help to isolate the problem. Controlled Slips indicate a clock speed problem; if there isn't an unbuffered satellite in the path, then there's probably a clock crystal or signal repeater about to fail. A large number of coding violations indicates a probable wiring fault, either a broken wire[8] (caused, for example, by dropping a floor tile on the cable), or one that's not adequately shielded.

The time intervals in which particular types of errors occurred are all counted in seconds:[9]

Errored Seconds (ES): the number of seconds in which any error occurred;

Controlled Slip Seconds (CSS): the number of seconds in which a controlled slip occurred;

Line Errored Seconds (LES): the number of seconds in which a line coding violation occurred; and,

Bursty Errored Seconds (BES): the number of seconds in which many path coding violations occurred.

These counts reflect that the time intervals over which errors occur have greater significance than the particular number of errors. The persistent occurrence of a few coding violations per second affects voice and data differently. The loss of a few bits every second is insignificant for voice because only one or two samples are corrupted. In contrast, for data, each bit error probably causes the loss of a whole packet and, thus, the persistent loss of a bit or two every second can cause a serious performance degradation for data and indicates that something is wrong with the line and it needs to be fixed. On the other hand, if practically every bit of each frame is in error, but only for a few seconds each day, then it's a major annoyance when it happens, but there's not a significant loss of service. The count of Bursty Errored Seconds is intended to help distinguish between these cases, but is probably more relevant to voice than data.

Another factor is that, particularly for older types of cabling, the quality of a DS1/DS3 line can degrade over time. Thus, an increasing number of errors, even when the number of them is still relatively low, is a warning to call the maintenance staff before the problem gets worse.

---

[8]Note that broken wires do not necessarily cause a complete loss of signal, since the two ends which were originally joined are often still close enough that most of the pulses can bridge the gap simply as a result of electro-magnetic radiation.

[9]Some of these descriptions have been simplified for clarity. For more detailed information, see [80] and [81].

The time intervals in which a particular severity of errors occurred are:

Severely Errored Framing Seconds (SEFS):   the number of seconds in which one or more framing errors occurred;

Severely Errored Seconds (SES): the number of seconds in which "too many" errors occurred;[10]

Unavailable Seconds (UA): the number of seconds for which the line was unavailable; a line is unavailable from the start of:

- ten consecutive SES seconds; or,
- a persistent framing error condition;

and until

- ten consecutive non-SES seconds; and,
- the framing error condition is cleared.

Degraded Minutes (DM): the number of "minutes" in which the estimated bit error rate exceeded 1E-6 but not 1E-3; unavailable and severely errored seconds are disregarded in counting the 60 seconds of a "minute".

These severity levels are important because the tariffs typically specify a reduced charge for periods with high levels of severity.

A simplified view of the relationships between all the above error counts is summarized in Figure 6.4.

6.1.8   DS3/E3 Errors

Since different framing formats are used, a few of the error types and the way they are detected on DS3 and E3 lines are different from those described above for DS1 and E1. However, the inherent causes of errors are basically the same, and thus the reporting of errors is handled in a very similar manner.

The categories of errors are the same, and unavailable seconds are treated the same. The particular types of errors are:

---

[10]The definition of "too many" varies according to the framing fromat.

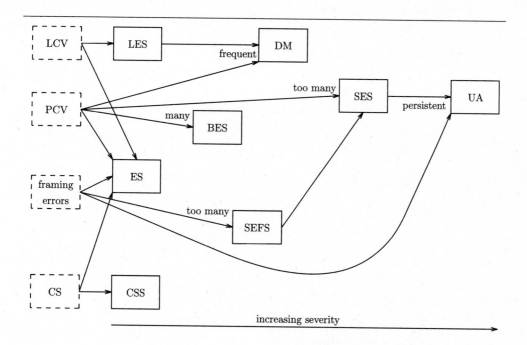

Figure 6.4: Simplified Relationships of DS1/E1 Error Counts

Legend		
Errors	CS	Controlled Slips
	LCV	Line Coding Violations
	PCV	Path Coding Violations
Types	BES	Bursty Errored Seconds
	CSS	Controlled Slip Seconds
	DM	Degraded Minutes
	ES	Errored Seconds
	LES	Line Errored Seconds
	SEFS	Severely Errored Framing Seconds
	SES	Severely Errored Seconds
	UA	Unavailable Seconds

Line Coding Violations (LCV): same as DS1/E1;

P-bit Coding Violations (PCV): P-bit parity errors (not to be confused with DS1 path coding violations);

C-bit Coding Violations (CCV): C-bit parity errors; and

framing errors: similar to DS1/E1.

The types of errored seconds are:

Line Errored Seconds (LES): same as DS1/E1;

P-bit Errored Seconds (PES): the number of seconds in which a P-bit coding violation occurred; and

C-bit Errored Seconds (CES): the number of seconds in which a C-bit coding violation occurred.

The time intervals in which a particular severity of errors occurred are:

Severely Errored Framing Seconds (SEFS): same as DS1/E1.

P-bit Severely Errored Seconds (PSES): the number of seconds in which "too many" P-bit coding violations occurred;

C-bit Severely Errored Seconds (CSES): the number of seconds in which "too many" C-bit coding violations occurred; and,

Unavailable Seconds (UA): same as DS1/E1, except that ten consecutive PSESs are required (rather than ten consecutive SESs).

6.1.9   Line Testing

Two types of loopback tests are defined:

Line Loopback: the signal received from the line does not go through the local device, but instead is looped (with minimum penetration) back to the line; and,

Payload loopback: the signal received from the line is looped through the device (maximum penetration) and transmitted back out to the line.

There are a number of standard data patterns for use in loopback tests.

6.1.10   Interval Counters

As was evident from the discussion of errors in the previous sections, the treatment of error counts for DS1/E1 and DS3/E3 lines differs from the typical SNMP usage of counters. Not only do the ANSI and ITU standards keep track of how many errors occurred in a particular time interval, but it is also important from a billing perspective that error counts (particularly, for high severity errors) are not lost through roll over, as might occur with SNMP counters. Whilst supporting the ANSI/ITU counts is a greater burden on agents, it is common practice when implementing ANSI/ITU standards, and thus it is appropriate that the SNMP MIB modules for these types of lines use the same style of counts.

Counts are kept for 15-minute intervals (which prevents them from rolling over), and in order for the counts to be available for subsequent retrieval, counts are kept not only for the current interval, but also for all previous 15-minute intervals in the last 24 hours, i.e., the agent must retain counts for a maximum of 96 intervals. In addition, total counts are kept for the whole of the last 24 hour period.[11]

As a 15-minute interval ends, the counts for the current interval are transferred into the counts for the most recently completed 15-minute interval, and the counts for each other interval are aged; i.e., each count is transferred to its next older interval, with the oldest counts being discarded. Thus, the individual MIB object values which contain these counts will increase or decrease every 15-minutes. For this reason, the appropriate "SYNTAX" for these counts is `Gauge32`, rather than the `Counter32` used for regular SNMP counters.[12]

---

[11]Some products only retain 8 hours worth of counts.

[12]Recall that the value of a `Counter32` or `Counter64` object is monotonically increasing.

6.1.11   Proxying to CSUs

As mentioned earlier, a CSU is required between the user's equipment, e.g., a router, and the telephone company's facilities. Thus, network management needs to access the DS1/DS3 management information available not only from the router, but also from the CSU. However, a CSU often has no "address", in which case, how can it receive SNMP requests sent by the management station?

This problem is normally solved by having the router perform a *proxy* function whereby the management station sends the requests to the router, and the router forwards them to the CSU, perhaps over a physically separate interface (e.g., an RS-232 connection between the router and the CSU).

6.1.12   An Example DS1 Configuration

Now that we've covered at some level of detail how the DS1/DS3 technology works, let's look at an example configuration. Let's suppose we have a DS1 line with the CSU at the user's premises connected to a router. Of the 24 DS0 channels, the router might use one for a LAPB Interface, another for a PPP Interface, a third for a Frame Relay Interface, a fourth for an SNA connection, and three others for an X.25 attachment using MLP to make them appear as a single 192Kb/s line. The remaining channels are "drop-and-inserted" to a PBX to be used for carrying voice.[13] Figure 6.5 shows the hardware and software configuration. In this example, there are four DS1 interfaces. The one which contains the most useful information for DS1 management purposes is the (public) network interface of the CSU.

6.1.13   Fractional DS1/DS3

So far, we have seen how a DS1 or DS3 link can be divided up into individual DS0 or DS1 channels. What if a particular application needs an intermediate bandwidth, e.g., greater than 64Kb/s but less

---

[13]Note that if this were an Integrated Services Digital Network (ISDN) Primary Rate interface, one of the 24 channels would be the D channel, and would be used for signaling the setup/tear-down of connections.

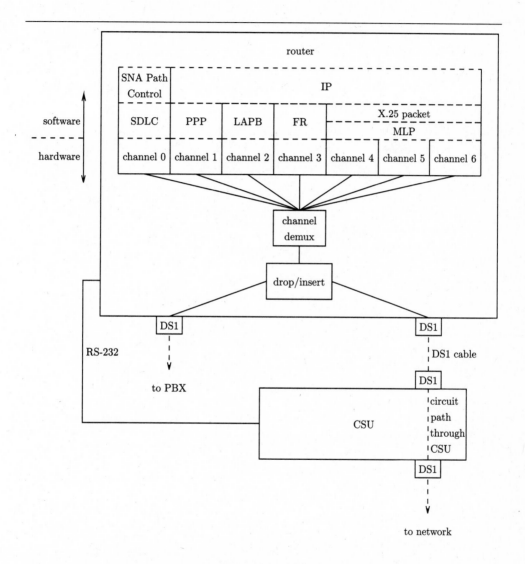

Figure 6.5: **Example of DS1 Configuration**

than 1.544 Mb/s? In the example configuration, we saw three DS0 channels combined through a software protocol (MLP) into a 192 Kb/s link. However, this is a software-intensive solution which can be applied only for data communications.

A hardware-based alternative is *fractional* DS1 or DS3. Fractional DS1 service provides a single logical interface to the combination of any number of DS0 channels on a DS1 interface. For example, not only can three DS0 channels be combined into one 192Kb/s interface, as in the example configuration, but also six DS0 channels can be combined into a 384 Kb/s interface to carry video. Similarly, fractional DS3 service provides a single logical interface to the combination of any number of DS1 channels on a DS3 interface.

6.2   Objects

The `interfaces` group described starting on page 196 defines generic information for all types of interface. Since DS1 and DS3 lines are bit-oriented interfaces, only these objects:

    ifIndex
    ifDescr
    ifType
    ifSpeed
    ifPhysAddress
    ifAdminStatus
    ifOperStatus
    ifLastChange
    ifLinkUpDownTrapEnable
    ifConnectorPresent
    ifHighSpeed
    ifName

apply to them.

6.2.1   Identifying DS1/DS3 interfaces

When a device, such as a router, is performing a proxy function for its local CSU, then the router needs to recognize that each DS1/DS3 MIB object has three separate instances for each line, one for the router's own interface, one for the router-side of the CSU, and one for the network-side of the CSU. To allow the router to distinguish between these three instances, a DS1/DS3 interface is identified not just by an `ifIndex` value but also by a `dsx1LineIndex` or `dsx3LineIndex` value.

When a device has a local SNMP agent, then:

- each local interface has a unique `ifIndex` value and the same value is used for `dsx1LineIndex` or `dsx3LineIndex`.

When a device is acting as a proxy for a CSU, then for each DS1/DS3 line which passes through the CSU:

- an even-numbered value greater than all of the proxy device's `ifIndex` values is chosen, together with the odd-numbered value one greater;

- the odd-numbered value is assigned to `dsx1LineIndex` or `dsx3LineIndex` to represent the CSU's network-side interface; and,

- the even-numbered value is assigned to `dsx1LineIndex` or `dsx3LineIndex` to represent the CSU's user-side interface.

In this proxy situation, all three interfaces (the one on the proxy device and the two on the CSU) are associated with the same `ifIndex` value.

Thus, in our example configuration in Figure 6.5 back on page 343, suppose that the router has only one other interface. Then, it could number the interfaces (in its own MIB) as follows:

	`ifIndex`	`dsx1LineIndex`
Other non-DS1 interface on router	1	–
DS1 interface on router	2	2
DS1 interface on CSU's router-side	2	4
DS1 interface on CSU's network-side	2	5

6.2.2   The DS1 MIB

The media-specific MIB module for DS1/E1 interfaces is [82]. It is divided into three groups:

- the DS1 Near End Group which provides configuration information and error counts for the local end of a DS1/E1 line;

- the DS1 Far End Group which provides error counts for the remote end of a DS1/E1 line; and,

- the DS1 Fractional Group which provides information on how DS0 channels are combined into logical interfaces.

For both the Near End Group and the Far End Group, the error counts are kept for the current 15-minute interval, previous 15-minute intervals, and the last 24-hour period;

Let's look at each of these groups in turn.

The DS1 Near End Group

The configuration information is contained in the `dsx1ConfigTable`, for which the row template has the property:

```
INDEX { dsx1LineIndex }
```

where the value of `dsx1LineIndex` identifies the DS1/E1 interface. The columns in this table are:

dsx1IfIndex (INTEGER): the value of `ifIndex` for this interface;

dsx1TimeElapsed (INTEGER):   the number of seconds that have elapsed since the beginning of the current 15-minute error-measurement period;

dsx1ValidIntervals (INTEGER):   the number of previous intervals for which valid data has been collected. The value will be 96 unless the interface was brought on-line within the last 24 hours, in which case the value will be the number of complete 15 minute intervals since the interface has been online;

dsx1LineType (enumerated `INTEGER`): the framing format in use on the line:

dsx1ESF	Extended SuperFrame DS1
dsx1D4	AT&T D4 format DS1
dsx1E1	ITU G.704 (Table 4a)
dsx1E1-CRC	ITU G.704 (Table 4b)
dsxE1-MF	G.704(4a) with TS16 multiframing
dsx1E1-CRC-MF	G.704(4b) with TS16 multiframing

This value may be **set**;

dsx1LineCoding (enumerated `INTEGER`): the type of zero-code suppression in use on the line:

dsx1AMI	no zero-code suppression
dsx1B8ZS	Binary Eight Zero Substitution
dsx1JBZS	Jammed Bit Zero Suppression
dsx1ZBTSI	Zero Byte Time Slot Interchange
dsx1HDB3	for E1 links
other	

This value may be **set**;

dsx1SendCode (enumerated `INTEGER`):   an indication of whether data, or a request code, or a test pattern is being transmitted on the line; in the latter two cases, the value indicates the type of code or pattern:

dsx1SendNoCode	looped or normal data
dsx1SendLineCode	request for line loopback
dsx1SendPayloadCode	request for payload loopback
dsx1SendResetCode	loopback termination request
dsx1SendQRS	Quasi-Random Signal (QRS) test pattern
dsx1Send511Pattern	511 bit fixed test pattern
dsx1Send3in24Pattern	fixed test pattern of 3 bits set in 24
dsx1SendOtherTestPattern	

This value may be **set**;

dsx1CircuitIdentifier (`DisplayString`): the name of the DS1/E1 line as known by the transmission vendor; this provides the means to identify a particular DS1/E1 line to the vendor when reporting a problem; This value may be `set`;

dsx1LoopbackConfig (enumerated `INTEGER`): the loopback configuration of the interface:

`dsx1NoLoop`	no loopback
`dsx1PayloadLoop`	loopback with maximum penetration
`dsx1LineLoop`	loopback with minimum penetration
`dsx1OtherLoop`	another type of loopback

This value may be `set`;

dsx1LineStatus (`INTEGER` sum): the line status of the interface:

`dsx1NoAlarm`	No alarm present
`dsx1LoopbackState`	Near End is looped
`dsx1RcvTestCode`	Near End detects a test code
`dsx1RcvFarEndLOF`	Far End LOF (Yellow Alarm)
`dsx1XmtFarEndLOF`	Near End sending LOF
`dsx1RcvAIS`	Far End sending AIS
`dsx1XmtAIS`	Near End sending AIS
`dsx1LossOfFrame`	Near End LOF (Red Alarm)
`dsx1LossOfSignal`	Near End Loss Of Signal
`dsx1T16AIS`	E1 TS16 AIS
`dsx1RcvFarEndLOMF`	Far End sending TS16 LOMF
`dsx1XmtFarEndLOMF`	Near End sending TS16 LOMF
`dsx1OtherFailure`	

dsx1SignalMode (enumerated `INTEGER`): the mode used for signaling in the line:

`none`	No signaling
`robbedBit`	Robbed Bit signaling
`bitOriented`	E1 Channel associated signaling
`messageOriented`	Common Channel signaling

This value may be `set`;

dsx1TransmitClockSource (enumerated `INTEGER`):   the
source of the Transmit Clock:

`localTiming`	local clock source
`loopTiming`	receive clock recovered from this line
`throughTiming`	receive clock recovered from another line

This value may be **set**;

dsx1Fdl (enumerated `INTEGER`):   the type of facility data link
on this line:

`dsx1Fdl-none`	no FDL in use
`dsx1Ansi-T1-403`	the ANSI standard
`dsx1Att-54016`	the ESF FDL
`other`	

This value may be **set**.

Figure 6.6 shows what some of these objects might look like.

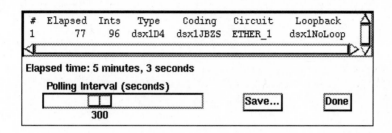

Figure 6.6: A Window Browsing Parts of the dsx1ConfigTable

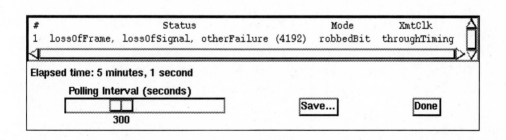

Figure 6.6: A Window Browsing Parts of the dsx1ConfigTable (cont.)

DS1 Near End Error Counts

The error counts for the local interface are kept in three tables:

dsx1CurrentTable for the current 15-minute interval;

dsx1IntervalTable   for the up to 96 previous 15-minute intervals; and,

dsx1TotalTable for the last 24-hour period.

All three tables contain the same ten error counts, as shown in the first column of Table 6.1. All of these error count objects are Gauge32.

The dsx1CurrentTable contains one value for each of the error counts for each interface. These counts are all zero when a 15-minute interval starts, and are incremented when the specific error condition occurs. The row template for this table is:

INDEX { dsx1CurrentIndex }

where the value of dsx1CurrentIndex is the value of dsx1LineIndex for the DS1/E1 interface.

The dsx1IntervalTable has one value for each of the error counts for each previous interval for each interface. These counts change only when a new 15-minute interval starts. The row template for this table is:

INDEX { dsx1IntervalIndex, dsx1IntervalNumber }

where dsx1IntervalIndex is the value of dsx1LineIndex for the DS1/E1 interface, and dsx1IntervalNumber is the interval number; intervals are numbered from 1 to 96, where 1 is the most recently completed interval, and higher numbered intervals are less recent.

The dsx1TotalTable contains one value for each of the error counts for each interface. These counts change only when a new 15-minute interval starts. The row template for this table is:

INDEX { dsx1TotalIndex }

where dsx1TotalIndex is the value of dsx1LineIndex for the DS1/E1 interface. Figure 6.7 on page 354 shows what a display of the current interval's error counts might look like.

near end object	far end object	error count
dsx1CurrentESs dsx1IntervalESs dsx1TotalESs	dsx1FarEndCurrentESs dsx1FarEndIntervalESs dsx1FarEndTotalESs	errored seconds

dsx1CurrentSESs
dsx1IntervalSESs
dsx1TotalSESs
	dsx1FarEndCurrentSESs
	dsx1FarEndIntervalSESs
	dsx1FarEndTotalSESs
		severely
		  errored
		    seconds

dsx1CurrentSEFSs
dsx1IntervalSEFSs
dsx1TotalSEFSs
	dsx1FarEndCurrentSEFSs
	dsx1FarEndIntervalSEFSs
	dsx1FarEndTotalSEFSs
		severely
		  errored
		    framing
		      seconds

dsx1CurrentUASs dsx1IntervalUASs dsx1TotalUASs	dsx1FarEndCurrentUASs dsx1FarEndIntervalUASs dsx1FarEndTotalUASs	unavailable seconds

dsx1CurrentCSSs
dsx1IntervalCSSs
dsx1TotalCSSs
	dsx1FarEndCurrentCSSs
	dsx1FarEndIntervalCSSs
	dsx1FarEndTotalCSSs
		controlled
		  slip
		    seconds

dsx1CurrentPCVs
dsx1IntervalPCVs
dsx1TotalPCVs
	dsx1FarEndCurrentPCVs
	dsx1FarEndIntervalPCVs
	dsx1FarEndTotalPCVs
		path
		  coding
		    violations

dsx1CurrentLESs
dsx1IntervalLESs
dsx1TotalLESs
	dsx1FarEndCurrentLESs
	dsx1FarEndIntervalLESs
	dsx1FarEndTotalLESs
		line
		  errored
		    seconds

dsx1CurrentBESs
dsx1IntervalBESs
dsx1TotalBESs
	dsx1FarEndCurrentBESs
	dsx1FarEndIntervalBESs
	dsx1FarEndTotalBESs
		bursty
		  errored
		    seconds

dsx1CurrentDMs dsx1IntervalDMs dsx1TotalDMs	dsx1FarEndCurrentDMs dsx1FarEndIntervalDMs dsx1FarEndTotalDMs	degraded minutes

dsx1CurrentLCVs
dsx1IntervalLCVs
dsx1TotalLCVs
		line
		  coding
		    violations

Table 6.1: DS1/E1 Error Counts

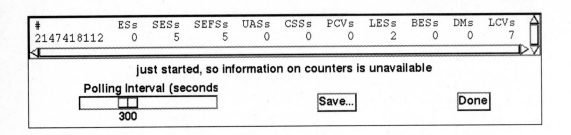

#	ESs	SESs	SEFSs	UASs	CSSs	PCVs	LESs	BESs	DMs	LCVs
2147418112	0	5	5	0	0	0	2	0	0	7

just started, so information on counters is unavailable

Polling Interval (seconds

300

Save...   Done

Figure 6.7: A Window Browsing DS1 Errors

The DS1 Far End Group

The DS1 Far End Group is optional since the information is obtained via the Facility Data Link which is not always available. This group contains three tables of error counts, exactly analagous to the three tables in the Near End Group; the only difference being that the number of LCVs is not available in this group. The specific objects in the three tables are shown in the second column of Figure 6.1 on page 353. Of course, there is a time descrepancy between the occurrence of an error at the Far End and the local agent learning of it; thus, an error which is counted at the Far End and an co-incident error at the Near End are not necessarily counted in corresponding intervals.

The dsx1FarEndCurrentTable has the row template:

    INDEX { dsx1FarEndCurrentIndex }

where dsx1FarEndCurrentIndex is the value of dsx1LineIndex for the local DS1/E1 interface connected to the Far End DS1/E1 interface. As well as the error counts, the dsx1FarEndCurrentTable contains:

dsx1FarEndTimeElapsed (INTEGER): the number of seconds since the beginning of the Far End's current 15-minute error-measurement period; and,

dsx1FarEndValidIntervals (INTEGER): the number of previous Far End intervals for which valid data is available.

The row template for the dsx1FarEndIntervalTable is

```
INDEX   { dsx1FarEndIntervalIndex,
          dsx1FarEndIntervalNumber }
```

where `dsx1FarEndIntervalIndex` is the value of `dsx1LineIndex` for the local DS1/E1 interface connected to the Far End DS1/E1 interface, and `dsx1FarEndIntervalNumber` is the interval number (from 1 to 96, where 1 is the most recently completely interval).

The row template for the `dsx1FarEndTotalTable` is:

```
INDEX { dsx1FarEndTotalIndex }
```

where `dsx1FarEndTotalIndex` is the value of `dsx1LineIndex` for the local DS1/E1 interface connected to the Far End DS1/E1 interface.

The DS1 Fractional Group

This group consists of one table to identify which channels on a DS1/E1 line are being combined to create a local logical interface. Devices, such as CSUs, which ignore the data content of a channel, generally do not support this group. Within the table, there is a row for each channel to identify the `ifIndex` value of the local logical interface which contains that channel.

The row template for the `dsx1FracTable` is:

```
INDEX   { dsx1FracIndex, dsx1FracNumber }
```

where `dsx1FracIndex` is the value of `dsx1LineIndex` for the DS1/E1 interface, and `dsx1FracNumber` is the channel number within the DS1/E1 interface. The table contains one column:

dsx1FracIfIndex (`INTEGER`): the value of ifIndex for the logical interface which contains the channel, or zero if the channel is not part of a local logical interface. This value may be **set** to change the logical configuration.

For example, for a link to a remote router, if six channels are being combined to form a 384Kb/s link and the link's `ifIndex` value is 8, then the value of `dsx1FracIfIndex` for each of those six channels is 8.

6.2.3   The DS3 MIB

The media-specific MIB module for DS3/E3 interfaces is [83]. Its
structure and overall semantics are identical to the DS1/E1 MIB,
except for an additional table for the Far End Group, and the use
of DS3/E3-specific configuration parameters, line status values and
error counts.

The DS3/E3 Near End Group

The `dsx3ConfigTable` has the row template:

```
INDEX   { dsx3LineIndex }
```

where `dsx3LineIndex` identifies the DS3/E3 interface. The table
contains:

dsx3IfIndex (`INTEGER`): same as dsx1IfIndex;

dsx3TimeElapsed (`INTEGER`): same as dsx1TimeElapsed;

dsx3ValidIntervals (`INTEGER`): same as dsx1ValidIntervals;

dsx3LineType (enumerated `INTEGER`): The type of DS3 or E3
    discipline in use on the line:

`dsx3M23`	ANSI T1.107-1988
`dsx3SYNTRAN`	ANSI T1.107-1988
`dsx3CbitParity`	ANSI T1.107a-1989
`dsx3ClearChannel`	ANSI T1.102-1987
`dsx3Other`	some other DS3 discipline
`e3Framed`	ITU G.751
`e3Plcp`	ETSI T/NA(91)18
`e3Other`	some other E3 discipline

dsx3LineCoding (enumerated `INTEGER`): the type of zero-code
    suppression in use on the line:

`dsx3B3ZS`	B3ZS on DS3
`e3HDB3`	HDB3 on E3
`dsx3Other`	some other scheme

dsx3SendCode (enumerated `INTEGER`):   an indication of whether data, a request code, or a test pattern is being transmitted on the line; in the latter two cases, the value indicates the type of code or pattern:

`dsx3SendNoCode`	looped or normal data
`dsx3SendLineCode`	request for line loopback
`dsx3SendPayloadCode`	request for payload loopback
`dsx3SendDS1LoopCode`	request to loopback a specific channel
`dsx3SendResetCode`	loopback termination request
`dsx3SendTestPattern`	test pattern

dsx3CircuitIdentifier (`DisplayString`): this is the same as `dsx1CircuitIdentifier`;

dsx3LoopbackConfig (enumerated `INTEGER`): this is the same as `dsx1LoopbackConfig`;

dsx3LineStatus (`INTEGER` sum): the line status of the interface:

`dsx3NoAlarm`	no alarm present
`dsx3LoopbackState`	Near End is looped
`dsx3RcvTestCode`	Near End receiving a test pattern
`dsx3RcvRAIFailure`	Far End sending Yellow Alarm
`dsx3XmitRAIAlarm`	Near End sending Yellow Alarm
`dsx3RcvAIS`	Far End sending AIS failure state
`dsx3XmitAIS`	Near End sending AIS
`dsx3LOF`	Far End sending LOF failure state
`dsx3LOS`	Far End sending LOS failure state
`dsx3OtherFailure`	

dsx3TransmitClockSource (enumerated `INTEGER`):   same as `dsx1TransmitClockSource`.

DS3/E3 Near End Error Counts

The three error count tables,

```
dsx3CurrentTable
dsx3IntervalTable
dsx3TotalTable
```

have the same semantics as their DS1/E1 equivalents, but hold different counts, as shown in the first column of Table 6.2.

The DS3/E3 Far End Group

The DS3/E3 Far End Group is optional since only C-bit Parity and SYNTRAN DS3 disciplines have the capability of providing the information. It contains a Far End Configuration Table, plus the same three error count tables as the DS1/E1 Far End Group, but with different error counts.

The dsx3FarEndConfigTable contains information which the local device sends in Path Identification Messages, in order to identify the local equipment. The row template is:

```
INDEX   { dsx3FarEndLineIndex }
```

where dsx3FarEndLineIndex has the value of dsx3LineIndex for the DS3/E3 interface. The information is:

dsx3FarEndEquipCode (DisplayString):   the Far End Equipment Identification code to describe the specific piece of local equipment;

dsx3FarEndLocationIDCode (DisplayString):   the Far End Location Identification code that describes the specific location of the local equipment;

dsx3FarEndFrameIDCode (DisplayString):   the Far End Frame Identification code that identifies where the local equipment is located within a building at the given location;

dsx3FarEndUnitCode (DisplayString):   the Far End code that identifies the local equipment location within a bay; and,

near end object	far end object	error count
dsx3CurrentPESs dsx3IntervalPESs dsx3TotalPESs		P-bit errored seconds
dsx3CurrentPSESs dsx3IntervalPSESs dsx3TotalPSESs		P-bit severely errored seconds
dsx3CurrentSEFSs dsx3IntervalSEFSs dsx3TotalSEFSs		severely errored framing seconds
dsx3CurrentUASs dsx3IntervalUASs dsx3TotalUASs	dsx3FarEndCurrentUASs dsx3FarEndIntervalUASs dsx3FarEndTotalUASs	unavailable seconds
dsx3CurrentLCVs dsx3IntervalLCVs dsx3TotalLCVs		line coding violations
dsx3CurrentPCVs dsx3IntervalPCVs dsx3TotalPCVs		P-bit coding violations
dsx3CurrentLESs dsx3IntervalLESs dsx3TotalLESs		line errored seconds
dsx3CurrentCCVs dsx3IntervalCCVs dsx3TotalCCVs	dsx3FarEndCurrentCCVs dsx3FarEndIntervalCCVs dsx3FarEndTotalCCVs	C-bit coding violations
dsx3CurrentCESs dsx3IntervalCESs dsx3TotalCESs	dsx3FarEndCurrentCESs dsx3FarEndIntervalCESs dsx3FarEndTotalCESs	C-bit errored seconds
dsx3CurrentCSESs dsx3IntervalCSESs dsx3TotalCSESs	dsx3FarEndCurrentCSESs dsx3FarEndIntervalCSESs dsx3FarEndTotalCSESs	C-bit severely errored seconds

Table 6.2: DS3/E3 Error Counts

dsx3FarEndFacilityIDCode (`DisplayString`):   the code
which locally identifies the specific Far End DS3 path.

DS3/E3 Far End Error Counts

The three Far End Group error count tables,

```
dsx3FarEndCurrentTable
dsx3FarEndIntervalTable
dsx3FarEndTotalTable
```

have the same semantics as their DS1/E1 equivalents, but hold different counts, as shown in the second column of Figure 6.2 on the previous page. All of these error count objects are `Gauge32`.

The DS3/E3 Fractional Group

This group consists of one table, the `dsx3FracTable`, to identify which channels on a DS3/E3 line are being combined to create a local logical interface. It has identical semantics and syntax to the DS1 Fractional Group.

6.3 Applications

A problem with a DS1/DS3 line can be reported in a number of ways:

- by receiving a phone call from a user;

- by noticing that `ifOperStatus` has the value `down`; or,

- by receiving a `linkDown` trap.

Each of these ways may occur at the DS1/DS3 layer, or at some higher-layer multiplexed on top of the DS1/DS3 line. For example, in the configuration shown in Figure 6.5 on page 343, the first report received might be for any of the uses of the line: SNA, IP, Frame Relay, X.25 or voice-traffic; and is likely to be quickly followed by one or more reports for each of the others.

On being alerted to a problem, the first thing to do is to check the value of `dsx1LineStatus` (or `dsx3LineStatus`) for each of the line's interfaces — those on the router and/or on the CSU. These values indicate if any alarms are present and if any of the interfaces are in a loopback state. If there are alarms on the CSU's network-side, then these should be reported to the service provider (identifying the line with the value of `dsx1CircuitIdentifier`). If there are alarms on the router or on the CSU's router-side, then the cabling between the router and the CSU should be checked.

The values `dsx1LoopbackState` or `dsx1RcvTestCode` (or their DS3 equivalents) indicates that a loopback is present or that testing is in progress. In this situation, `dsx1LoopbackConfig` should be inspected to determine the type of loopback, and other management personnel (e.g., the service provider) contacted to determine if anyone is running a test on the line.

If no loopback is present, then the error counts should be inspected, starting with those for the current interval, and if it has only just begun, the most recently completed 15-minute interval also. The Near End counts relate to occurrences in the receive direction; the Far End counts, if available, relate to the remote end's receive direction, The most useful counts are probably those on the CSU's network-side. To interpret the individual error counts, see the descriptions in Sections 6.1.7 and 6.1.8 starting on page 336.

Another possibility is that the line's configuration is incorrect. Checking for the desired configuration can be made easier by having an application which compares the current configuration with a stored copy of the intended configuration; in particular, the values of

```
dsx1LineType
dsx1LineCoding
dsx1SendCode
dsx1SignalMode
dsx1TransmitClockSource
dsx1Fdl
```

or their DS3 equivalents, should be checked for the router's interface, and for both of the CSU's interfaces. For a fractional DS1/DS3, the router's values of `dsx1FracIfIndex` are also applicable. When multiple lines are procured from the same service provider, it is probably best to store the values for each line identified by that line's value of `dsx1CircuitIdentifier`, since if that value is to fulfill its function, then it has to be unique, and it is probably more constant than the values of `dsx1LineIndex`.

Other useful applications are those which display the information in a graphical way:

- graphs of the last 96 intervals:
    - one line on the graph for each of the error counts (LCVs, PCVs, CSSs, LESs, ESs),
    - one line on the graph for each of the severity counts (BESs, SESs, SEFSs, UASs, DMs)

- a barchart for last 24 hours with bars for:
    - the percentage of time available, i.e.,

        24 hours minus `dsx1TotalUASs`

    - the percentage of time available and not-degraded, i.e.,

        24 hours minus (`dsx1TotalUASs`+`dsx1TotalDMs`)

    - the percentage of time available and not severely-errored, i.e.,

        24 hours minus (`dsx1TotalUASs`+`dsx1TotalSESs`)

    - the percentage of time available and error free, i.e.,

        24 hours minus (`dsx1TotalUASs`+`dsx1TotalESs`)

- a pictorial representation of how the channels of a fractional-DS1 (or fractional-DS3) are combined and used for various ifIndex interfaces.

Unfortunately, the authors could not locate any agents which both fully implemented these MIB modules and were in use in an operational environment. So, we have no interesting figures to include for these applications.

Part III

Managing Hosts and
Network Services

Chapter 7

Host Management

In this chapter, we consider how to manage hosts using SNMP, independent of whatever network services or protocols might be running on the host.

There is extensive experience in using SNMP to manage media devices and intermediate systems, as evidenced by the considerable attention that this topic received in Part II of *The Networking Management Practicum*. In contrast, using SNMP to manage hosts is a relatively new topic — the first MIB module defining managed objects for this purpose was standardized in September 1993, nearly five years after SNMP was initially developed. From the authors' perspective, this gap is due primarily to market pressures rather than technical difficulties — the original proponents of SNMP were working in network management, not systems management, so the initial set of MIB modules focused on managing wires instead of hosts and network services. However, today there is considerable interest in managing a wide variety of host- and service-related technologies using SNMP, so this chapter and the next two discuss those technologies that are already on the standards-track. The next edition of *The Networking Management Practicum* will likely contain many more chapters in this area.

7.1   Concepts

A *host* is a general-purpose computing device that consists of one or more components. A component is either:

- a hardware *device*, such as a video adaptor; or,

- a *software* package, such as a program or collection of programs.

As we have seen earlier with network interfaces, one could imagine that there are several generic properties which are shared by all hardware devices; similarly, there are also several generic properties which are shared by all software packages. However, as with network interfaces, within these broad categories, we'll see a lot of characteristics which are specific to individual sub-classes.

7.1.1   How Hosts Change the Rules

Recall from page 6, that SNMP's design is based on a *Fundamental Axiom*, namely, that the cost of adding management to a system must be minimal. This strategy has proven very effective in allowing SNMP to manage a wide range of devices. Fortunately, most hosts have a lot of "overhead" that we can exploit.

Time

Perhaps the most interesting of these is a "stable clock". Throughout Part II, SNMP's notion of time has always been *relative* to the last restart of the management subsystem. This is because it may be very expensive, for the devices discussed in those chapters, to maintain time across reboots. However, a host is usually able to do this. As such, we now have a second notion of time, one which is an *absolute* calendar time. However, not all of these hosts are knowledgeable as to their time-zone of operation. So, this absolute time contains a date (month, day, and year) and a time (hour, minutes, and seconds), plus optional time-zone information.

Character Sets

Another large difference is that hosts deal with "users". This means that issues of user-interaction begin to surface. The most important of these is the character set used to represent characters. Throughout Part II, SNMP's notion of characters has been embodied by the `DisplayString` textual convention, which uses the NVT ASCII repertoire — which defines a US-centric rendition of English language characters. Whilst the authors might argue that this choice is mandated by pragmatism — for better or worse, US-English[1] is the language of networking professionals — it is clear that such a limitation is inappropriate when dealing with users in general.

In the computer industry, the term *internationalization* (or *i18n*) is used to refer to making systems natural language-independent. Unfortunately, no consensus has arisen as to the solution to this problem. While there is some support for developing a "universal character set", there is also support for a "tag-based" approach, one in which an unambiguous identifier is associated with a string of octets, which are processed as a unit by the host which then renders the characters appropriately for the user.

Third-Party Vendors

Finally, hosts tend to be considerably more friendly toward "mixing and matching" components within a single system. While a particular media device might be highly modular, the individual components are usually proprietary to the vendor of that device, even if that vendor has extensive third-party relationships to supply additional components for the device.

In contrast, hosts are typically designed around interface standards to encourage the development of a plug-and-play third-party market, due to a number of economic and market realities. As such, it's not necessary to be able to remotely identify the manufacturer of a particular component within a media device, but this may be critical for managing hosts. Of course, regardless of whether a host or media device is being managed, it may be useful to be able to identify the

---

[1]As opposed to the UK-English currently spoken by one of the authors.

serial number or revision level of a component. Having said this, great care must be taken to avoid the "scratchpad phenomenon" — a desire to use SNMP to update arbitrary information about a component. It's one thing to use SNMP to retrieve information about a device, but it's quite another to use SNMP to store information about a device if that information doesn't affect the device's operation. Rather than using an agent as a database system, it may be better to use a database. In other words, we should focus our use of SNMP to managing component information which can be directly retrieved from the component.

7.1.2 Hardware Devices

Every distinct piece of hardware on a host is a device. This includes the host's processor, its network adaptors, any attached printers, local disks, and so on. Clearly, the list of device types is large and possibly open-ended.

There are at least three characteristics which are common to all devices, regardless of their function:

- an indication of the manufacturer and product model;

- a current status; and,

- the number of errors which the device has reported.

Beyond this, it is difficult to identify characteristics without focusing on the type of device. Since there's little point to reciting a litany of information on computer architectures, operating system principles, etc., let's cut to the chase and consider what's really interesting about four types of network devices, from the management perspective:

processors: processors execute programs, so it's useful to know how busy a processor is;

adaptors: network adaptors were discussed throughout Chapters 4, 5, and 6, so refer back to those chapters to find out what's useful to know about an interface;

printers: printers often require operator intervention (e.g., to add paper), so it's useful to know if the printer needs help; and,

disks: disks are usually divided into partitions, and these partitions are sometimes combined to form file-systems, so it's useful to know which partitions on a disk comprise a given file-system.

7.1.3 Software Packages

Even a stand-alone host runs a lot of different software, but these usually fall into three general categories:

operating system: a set of routines responsible for coordinating use of the host's resources, and providing a uniform interface regardless of the underlying hardware components;

device driver: routines used by the operating system to access a specific type of hardware component, such as a disk or network adaptor; and,

user application: a program, or collection of programs, which performs some distinct task for the user, such as a text editor or spreadsheet.

Note that although one usually doesn't think of an operating system or device driver as a distinct piece of software, it is useful to do so for management purposes. (Even so, these three concepts make sense only in the context of a particular operating system.)

For any program it is useful to know if it is currently running, or if it is waiting for some resource or event. Further, it is often useful to know how much system resources a particular program is consuming.

7.2   Objects

The `HOST-RESOURCES-MIB` [84] provides the basic framework for host management with SNMP. It is divided into three primary areas:

- the `hrSystem` group contains general information about the host;

- the `hrDevice` and `hrStorage` groups contain information about devices and file-systems; and,

- the `hrSWRun`, `hrSWRunPerf`, and `hrSWInstalled` groups contain information about running and installed software.

Before looking at each, let's consider four textual conventions that are used throughout this MIB module:

DateAndTime: this is an `OCTET STRING` which contains a date and time, and possibly a time-zone (see Table 7.1);

InternationalDisplayString: this is an `OCTET STRING` which contains one or more characters, each represented using one or more octets, and interpreted by the management application using "local knowledge";

ProductID: this is an `OBJECT IDENTIFIER` which unambiguously identifies a product (i.e., the "make and model"), and is (ideally) assigned by the manufacturer; and,

KBytes: this is a unit of 1024 octets.

Each of the first three of these is problematic in its own special way. For example, it's not really clear how useful knowing the time is when you don't know the time-zone. Similarly, at present, there is no `OBJECT IDENTIFIER` clearinghouse, so it's difficult for management application writers to find out what a particular `ProductID` means. Finally, since there isn't any way for the management application to determine, using SNMP, what character set is in use on the host, there is no standardized way to interpret an `InternationalDisplayString`, which henceforth we'll refer to as `IDisplayString`.

octets	contents	range
1–2	year (in network byte order)	0..65535
3	month	1..12
4	day	1..31
5	hour	0..23
6	minutes	0..59
7	seconds (use 60 for leap-second)	0..60
8	deci-seconds	0..9
9	direction from UTC	"+" / "–" (ASCII)
10	hours from UTC	0..11
11	minutes from UTC	0..59

Table 7.1: The `DateAndTime` Textual Convention

7.2.1   General Information

The `hrSystem` group, which must be implemented by all host agents, contains these scalars:

hrSystemUpTime (`TimeTicks`):   the host's epoch (how long ago the operating system was restarted);

hrSystemDate (`DateAndTime`):   the current date and time (which may be `set`);

hrSystemInitialLoadDevice (positive `INTEGER`): an index into the `hrDeviceTable` (discussed momentarily) indicating the default device for reloading the host's operating system (which may be `set`);

hrSystemInitialLoadParameters (`IDisplayString`):   the parameters used to reload the host's operating system (which may be `set`);

hrSystemNumUsers (`Gauge32`):   the number of users logged onto the host;

hrSystemProcesses (`Gauge32`):   the number of processes known to the operating system; and,

hrSystemMaxProcesses (non-negative `INTEGER`):   the maximum number of processes that the operating system allows (a value of 0 indicates there is no predetermined limit).

Note that the semantics of the latter four of these objects depend somewhat on the operating system used on the host.

Figure 7.1 shows what a window displaying the `hrSystem` group might look like.

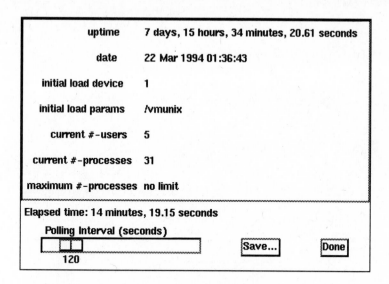

Figure 7.1: A Window Browsing the hrSystem Group

7.2.2 Hardware Devices

There are two groups dealing with devices which all host agents must implement:

- the hrStorage group which identifies the host's storage areas; and,

- the hrDevice group which identifies the devices attached to the host.

Let's look at each in turn.

Storage Areas

The `hrStorage` group consists of two top-level objects:

hrMemorySize (`KBytes`): the amount of physical memory on
the host; and,

hrStorageTable: a table containing an entry for each of the
host's logical storage devices.

This table has seven columns:

hrStorageIndex (positive `INTEGER`): the number used as the
`INDEX` for the table's row template (`hrStorageEntry`);

hrStorageType (`OBJECT IDENTIFIER`):   the type of logical
storage device:

`hrStorageRam`
`hrStorageVirtualMemory`
`hrStorageFixedDisk`
`hrStorageRemovableDisk`
`hrStorageFloppyDisk`
`hrStorageCompactDisc`
`hrStorageRamDisk`
`hrStorageOther`

hrStorageDescr (`DisplayString`): a textual description of the
logical storage device;

hrStorageAllocationUnits (positive `INTEGER`): the allocation
granularity, in octets, of the logical storage device;

hrStorageSize (non-negative `INTEGER`):   the total number of
allocation units contained within the logical storage device;

hrStorageUsed (positive `INTEGER`):   the number of units
currently allocated on the logical storage device; and,

hrStorageAllocationFailures (`Counter32`): the total number
of times that the logical storage device was unable to grant
a request for storage.

Figure 7.2 shows what a window displaying some of these objects
might look like.

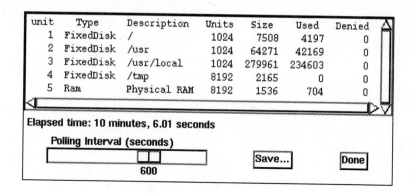

unit	Type	Description	Units	Size	Used	Denied
1	FixedDisk	/	1024	7508	4197	0
2	FixedDisk	/usr	1024	64271	42169	0
3	FixedDisk	/usr/local	1024	279961	234603	0
4	FixedDisk	/tmp	8192	2165	0	0
5	Ram	Physical RAM	8192	1536	704	0

Elapsed time: 10 minutes, 6.01 seconds

Polling Interval (seconds)

600

[Save...] [Done]

Figure 7.2: A Window Browsing the `hrStorageTable`

Hardware Devices

The `hrDevice` group consists of a generic table for all hardware devices, along with several others tables, each specific to a particular type of hardware device.

The `hrDeviceTable` contains generic information about a hardware device:

hrDeviceIndex (positive `INTEGER`):   the number used as the INDEX for the table's row template (`hrDeviceEntry`);

hrDeviceType (`OBJECT IDENTIFIER`):   the type of hardware device (see Table 7.2 for the list of standard values);

hrDeviceDescr (`DisplayString`): a textual description of the hardware device;

hrDeviceID (`ProductID`):   the hardware device's product identity;

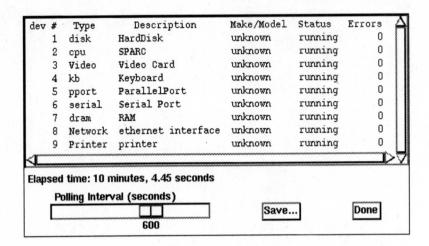

```
dev #   Type        Description      Make/Model  Status    Errors
    1   disk        HardDisk         unknown     running      0
    2   cpu         SPARC            unknown     running      0
    3   Video       Video Card       unknown     running      0
    4   kb          Keyboard         unknown     running      0
    5   pport       ParallelPort     unknown     running      0
    6   serial      Serial Port      unknown     running      0
    7   dram        RAM              unknown     running      0
    8   Network     ethernet interface  unknown  running      0
    9   Printer     printer          unknown     running      0
```

Elapsed time: 10 minutes, 4.45 seconds

Polling Interval (seconds)

600

Save...   Done

Figure 7.3: A Window Browsing the `hrDeviceTable`

hrDeviceStatus (enumerated `INTEGER`): the operational state of the hardware device:

enumeration	operational?
running	yes
warning	
testing	no
down	
unknown	don't know

and,

hrDeviceErrors (`Counter32`):   the total number of errors encountered by the hardware device.

Figure 7.3 shows what a window displaying the `hrDeviceTable` might look like.

Table 7.2 lists several different kinds of device types. Note that there is a distinction between an "unknown" device type, which refers to a device the agent cannot identify, and some "other" device type which is known but not amongst those in the list of standard definitions. Note also that because an `OBJECT IDENTIFIER` is used for both

| hrDeviceProcessor |
| hrDeviceCoprocessor |
| hrDeviceClock |
| hrDeviceVolatileMemory |
| hrDeviceNonVolatileMemory |
| hrDeviceNetwork |
| hrDevicePrinter |
| hrDeviceDiskStorage |
| hrDeviceTape |
| hrDeviceModem |
| hrDeviceVideo |
| hrDeviceAudio |
| hrDeviceKeyboard |
| hrDeviceParallelPort |
| hrDevicePointing |
| hrDeviceSerialPort |
| hrDeviceOther |
| hrDeviceUnknown |

Table 7.2: Device Types

`hrStorageType` and `hrDeviceType`, new values may be defined by a given vendor.

It turns out that the value of an instance of `hrDeviceType` in a row is particularly special — the value indicates which other table has a corresponding row containing information about the device:

hrDeviceType	where to look for more information
hrDeviceProcessor	hrProcessorTable
hrDeviceNetwork	hrNetworkTable
hrDevicePrinter	hrPrinterTable
hrDeviceDiskStorage	hrDiskStorageTable

The row template for each of these tables has this property:

```
INDEX { hrDeviceIndex }
```

So, each of these tables can be thought of as a "sparse augmentation"

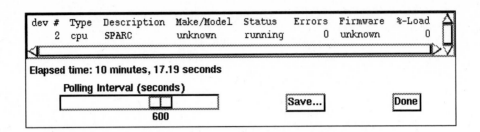

Figure 7.4: A Window Browsing Processor Information

of the `hrDeviceTable`. No doubt in the future more of these device-specific tables will be defined.

The `hrProcessorTable` contains information about a processor:

hrProcessorFrwID (**ProductID**):   the processor-firmware's product identity; and,

hrProcessorLoad (**INTEGER**):   the percentage of time, on average, that the processor wasn't idle (an **INTEGER** from 0 to 100).

Figure 7.4 shows what a window displaying information about a host's processor might look like. Note that it includes information both from the generic device table and the processor-specific device table.

The `hrNetworkTable` contains information about a network adaptor:

hrNetworkIfIndex (**INTEGER**):   this is simply the value of `ifIndex` which corresponds to this network adaptor.

This object is necessary because there needn't be any relationship between the way devices are numbered on a host and the way interfaces are numbered by the host's networking subsystem.

The `hrPrinterTable` contains information about a printer:

hrPrinterStatus (enumerated `INTEGER`): the printer's "print" state:

enumeration	associated hrDeviceStatus
idle	running or warning
printing	
warmup	
other	testing or down
unknown	unknown

and,

hrPrinterDetectedErrorState (`OCTET STRING`): all of the printer's current error conditions, expressed as a single octet:

condition	bit
lowPaper	0
noPaper	1
lowToner	2
noToner	3
doorOpen	4
jammed	5
offline	6
serviceRequest	7

(Obviously this object was defined using the original framework — under SNMPv2, it would be more appropriate to use a `BIT STRING`.)

In order to find out about file-systems, we have to look at three tables:

- the `hrDiskStorageTable` to find out about disk devices;

- the `hrPartitionTable` to find out about the partitions on each device which are combined to form a file-system; and,

- the `hrFSTable` to find out about the actual file-systems.

Each is now examined in turn.

The `hrDiskStorageTable` contains information about a disk:

hrDiskStorageAccess (enumerated `INTEGER`): an indication as to whether the disk is write-protected (`readOnly`), or not (`readWrite`);

hrDiskStorageMedia (enumerated `INTEGER`): the media used for the disk:

```
hardDisk
floppyDisk
opticalDiskROM
opticalDiskWORM
opticalDiskRW
ramDisk
other
unknown
```

hrDiskStorageRemoveble (`TruthValue`): an indication as to whether the disk media may be removed from the drive;[2] and,

hrDiskStorageCapacity (`KBytes`): the total number of kilobytes contained within the disk.

Figure 7.5 shows what a window displaying information about a host's disks might look like.

The `hrPartitionTable` contains information about a partition. Its row template has this property:

```
INDEX { hrDeviceIndex, hrPartitionIndex }
```

---

[2]The actual name of this object really is `hrDiskStorageRemoveble`, not `hrDiskStorageRemovable`. (An editing mistake!)

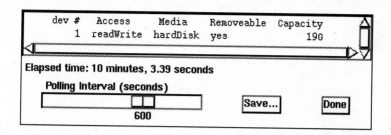

Figure 7.5: A Window Browsing Disk Information

So, one or more rows (partitions) are instantiated for each row (device) in the `hrDiskStorageTable`. The objects are:

hrPartitionIndex (positive `INTEGER`):   the number to distinguish between partitions on the same disk;

hrPartitionLabel (`IDisplayString`): a textual description of the partition;

hrPartitionID (`OCTET STRING`): the operating system-specific identity of the partition;

hrPartitionSize (`KBytes`): the total size of the partition; and,

hrPartitionFSIndex (non-negative `INTEGER`): the index of the file-system that uses this partition (a value of 0 indicates that this partition isn't assigned to any file-system).

Note that a disk device always has at least one partition, and that each partition may be assigned to at most one file-system, although a file-system may have several partitions assigned to it.

The `hrFSTable` contains information about a file-system. The objects in the `hrFSTable` are:

hrFSIndex (positive `INTEGER`): the number used as the `INDEX` for the table's row template (`hrFSEntry`);

hrFSMountPoint (`IDisplayString`): the local name for this file-system;

hrFSRemoteMountPoint (`IDisplayString`):   if this file-system resides on a remote host, the name and parameters used to import the file-system to the local host (a string of zero length indicates that the file-system resides locally);

hrFSType (`OBJECT IDENTIFIER`): the type of file-system (see Table 7.3 for the list of standard values);

hrFSAccess (enumerated `INTEGER`):   an indication as to whether the file-system is write-protected (`readOnly`), or not (`readWrite`);

hrFSBootable (`TruthValue`):   an indication as to whether the file-system contains information necessary to reload the operating system;

hrFSStorageIndex (non-negative `INTEGER`): an index into the `hrStorageTable` corresponding to this file-system (a value of 0 indicates that this file-system isn't listed as a storage device);

hrFSLastFullBackupDate (`DateAndTime`): the date and time when the file-system was completely copied to some other storage device; and,

hrFSLastPartialBackupDate (`DateAndTime`): the date and time when a portion of the file-system was partially copied to some other storage device.

Note that concepts of mount points and "bootable" file-systems are dependent on the operating system in use.

These last two objects exhibit a bit of the "scratchpad phenomenon" discussed earlier — they may be **set** using SNMP, even though there is no way defined for SNMP to control when the

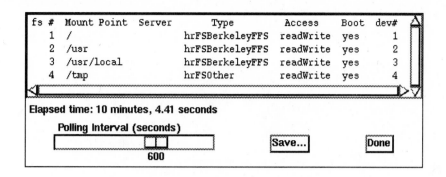

fs #	Mount Point	Server	Type	Access	Boot	dev#
1	/		hrFSBerkeleyFFS	readWrite	yes	1
2	/usr		hrFSBerkeleyFFS	readWrite	yes	2
3	/usr/local		hrFSBerkeleyFFS	readWrite	yes	3
4	/tmp		hrFSOther	readWrite	yes	4

Elapsed time: 10 minutes, 4.41 seconds

Polling Interval (seconds)

600

Save...   Done

Figure 7.6: A Window Browsing File-System Information

file-systems are copied. Whilst it certainly makes sense to be able to use SNMP to find out when a file-system was last backed-up, clearly the backup tool should be the one which sets this information!

Figure 7.6 shows what a window displaying information about a disk and its partitions might look like.

Table 7.3 on page 386 lists several different types of file-systems. The authors couldn't quite figure out some of the more "obscure" acronyms. However, if you manage a system with one of these file-systems, you probably recognize the acronym.

Well, we've now looked at five tables which deal with file-systems in one way or another. Figure 7.7 on 387 contains an example which shows the relation between all five tables. In this example, there are (at least) three devices on the system, as shown in the **hrDeviceTable**. The devices indexed as **1** and **3** are disk devices, so there are corresponding entries in the **hrDiskStorageTable**. For the disk having a **hrDeviceIndex** of 1, there are two partitions. Both are part of the same file-system, i.e.,

        hrPartitionFSIndex.1.1

and

        hrPartitionFSIndex.1.2

have the same value (5). In contrast, the disk having a **hrDeviceIndex** of 3, has one partition, but this partition isn't a part of a file-system

hrFSType	type of file-system
hrFSAFS	Andrew
hrFSAppleshare	Macintosh® Appleshare
hrFSBFS	SVR4 boot
hrFSBerkeleyFFS	
hrFSDFS	Distributed File System
hrFSDGCFS	
hrFSFat	MS-DOS
hrFSHFS	Macintosh® hierarchical
hrFSHPFS	OS/2 high performance
hrFSJournaled	
hrFSMFS	Macintosh®
hrFSNFS	NFS
hrFSNTFS	Windows/NT
hrFSNetware	NetWare®
hrFSRFS	pre-NFS
hrFSRockRidge	compact disc
hrFSSys5FS	
hrFSVNode	
hrFSiso9660	compact disc
hrFSOther	
hrFSUnknown	

Table 7.3: File-System Types

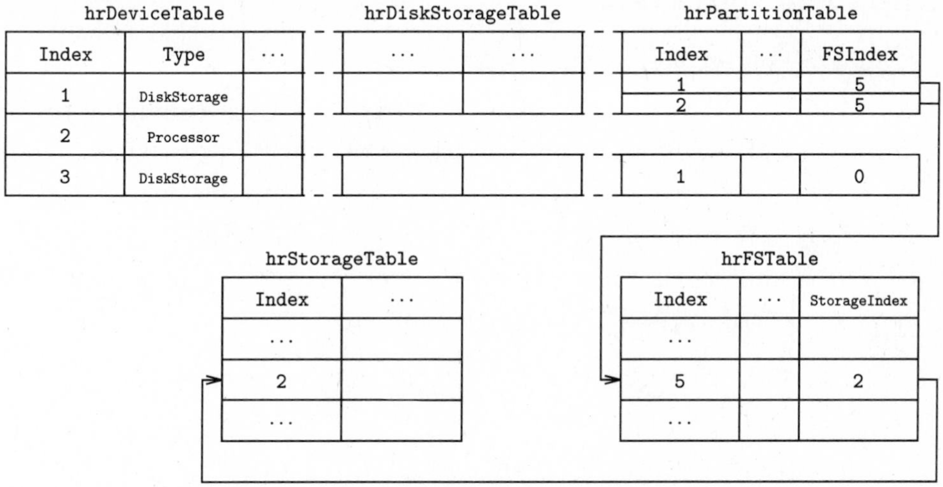

Figure 7.7: How File-Systems Relate to Devices and Storage

(the value of `hrPartitionFSIndex.3.1` is 0). The file-system having an `hrFSIndex` of 5 is also listed as a storage device, having an `hrStorageIndex` of 2. Finally, note that because the device indexed as 2 isn't a disk device, there is no corresponding row in the

> `hrDiskStorageTable`

7.2.3   Software Packages

There are three groups dealing with software:

- the `hrSWRun` group which identifies running programs;
- the `hrSWRunPerf` group which identifies the resource utilization of running programs; and,
- the `hrSWInstalled` group which identifies the software installed on the host.

Of these, only the first one must be implemented by all host agents. The latter two groups are optional.

Running Software

The hrSWRun group consists of two top-level objects:

> **hrSWOSIndex** (positive INTEGER):   an index into the hrSWRunTable indicating the primary operating system for the host; and,

> **hrSWRunTable:** a table containing an entry for each of the host's running programs.

This table has seven columns:

> **hrSWRunIndex** (INTEGER): the number used as the INDEX for the table's row template (hrSWRunEntry);

> **hrSWRunName** (IDisplayString): a textual description of the running program;

> **hrSWRunID** (ProductID):   the running program's product identity;

> **hrSWRunPath** (IDisplayString): the file-system name from which the running program was loaded;

> **hrSWRunParameters** (IDisplayString):   the parameters used to launch the running program;

> **hrSWRunType** (enumerated INTEGER):   the type of the running program:

operatingSystem
deviceDriver
application
unknown

> and,

> **hrSWRunStatus** (enumerated INTEGER): the operational state of the running program:

enumeration	condition
running	running
runnable	waiting for resource
notRunnable	waiting for event
invalid	when set, destroys the program

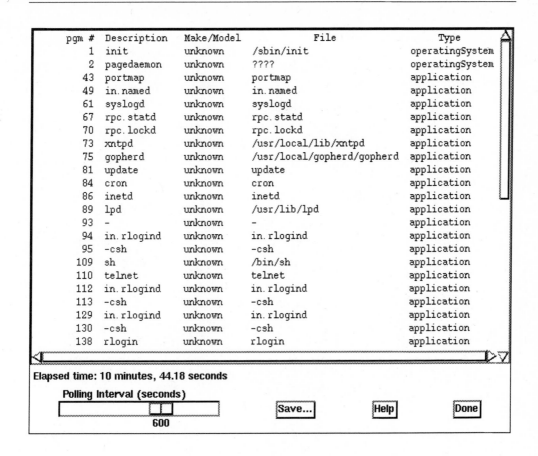

pgm #	Description	Make/Model	File	Type
1	init	unknown	/sbin/init	operatingSystem
2	pagedaemon	unknown	????	operatingSystem
43	portmap	unknown	portmap	application
49	in.named	unknown	in.named	application
61	syslogd	unknown	syslogd	application
67	rpc.statd	unknown	rpc.statd	application
70	rpc.lockd	unknown	rpc.lockd	application
73	xntpd	unknown	/usr/local/lib/xntpd	application
75	gopherd	unknown	/usr/local/gopherd/gopherd	application
81	update	unknown	update	application
84	cron	unknown	cron	application
86	inetd	unknown	inetd	application
89	lpd	unknown	/usr/lib/lpd	application
93	-	unknown	-	application
94	in.rlogind	unknown	in.rlogind	application
95	-csh	unknown	-csh	application
109	sh	unknown	/bin/sh	application
110	telnet	unknown	telnet	application
112	in.rlogind	unknown	in.rlogind	application
113	-csh	unknown	-csh	application
129	in.rlogind	unknown	in.rlogind	application
130	-csh	unknown	-csh	application
138	rlogin	unknown	rlogin	application

Elapsed time: 10 minutes, 44.18 seconds

Polling Interval (seconds)

600

Save... Help Done

Figure 7.8: A Window Browsing parts of the hrSWRunTable

Figure 7.8 shows what a window displaying most of these objects might look like.

The optional **hrSWRunPerf** group consists of one table,

    hrSWRunPerfTable

which has a row that corresponds to each row in the **hrSWRunTable** (a proper augmentation). There are two columns:

hrSWRunPerfCPU (INTEGER): how much CPU time, in hundredths of a second, has been used; and,

hrSWRunPerfMem (KBytes): how much memory is currently being used.

(The authors suspect that this table might be better named the running program resource utilization table.)

Installed Software

The optional **hrSWInstalled** group consists of three top-level objects. The table, **hrSWInstalledTable**, keeps track of each of the software packages residing locally. This table has five columns:

hrSWInstalledIndex (positive INTEGER): the number that is used as the INDEX for the table's row template (hrSWInstalledEntry);

hrSWInstalledName (IDisplayString): a textual description of the software package;

hrSWInstalledID (ProductID): the software package's product identity;

hrSWInstalledType (INTEGER): the type of software package:

```
operatingSystem
deviceDriver
application
unknown
```

    and,

hrSWInstalledDate (DateAndTime): the date and time that the software package was last installed.

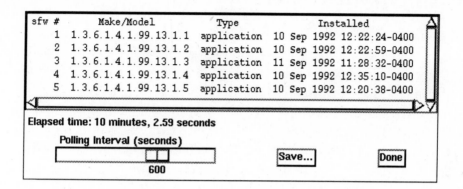

Figure 7.9: A Window Browsing parts of the `hrSWInstalledTable`

Note that the concept of a "package" is operating system-dependent. On some systems, a package might be a single executable program; on others, a package might refer to a collection of programs.

Figure 7.9 shows what a window displaying most of these objects might look like.

Because it may be very difficult for an agent to compute the entries in the `hrSWInstalledTable`, two other top-level objects are defined in the `hrSWInstalled` group:

hrSWInstalledLastChange (`TimeStamp`): the last time a software package was added to or removed from the `hrSWInstalledTable`; and,

hrSWInstalledLastUpdateTime (`TimeStamp`): the last time when the `hrSWInstalledTable` was recomputed.

These two objects are used to provide guidance to (intelligent) management applications — they indicate when they should be re-polled along with the currency of the table. (Recall that `TimeStamp` is a textual convention — see Section 3.1.1 on page 93 for further details.)

7.3   Applications

As evidenced by the figures throughout the previous section, the
HOST-RESOURCES-MIB is good for lots of browsing applications. In
this section, let's focus on extending the browsing paradigms which
we've introduced in previous chapters.

Our very first browsing window was shown in Figure 3.13 back
on page 123. This displays information to the user in a label/value
paradigm, where the formatting of a value depends on the syntax of
an object. Later, Figure 4.11 on page 213 showed an example of an
object-specific formatting routine.

A second paradigm we've seen uses a graph rather than textual
values. In this case, objects having numeric values are displayed in
graphic form, e.g., as first shown on page 152. Later, we saw how
we could display complex formulas instead of simple object values.
For example, Figure 4.12 starting on page 215 showed how to calculate Leinwand's formula for interface utilization. This allowed us to
generate a graph like Figure 4.13 on page 218.

7.3.1   Charting Gauges and Formulas

When browsing objects with a Gauge32 syntax, it's often useful to
display their values in a barchart, rather than a graph.

For example, consider Figure 7.10 which displays a barchart showing the values of hrSystemNumUsers.0 and hrSystemProcesses.0.

Very often a formula can have a well-defined lower- and upper-
bounds. (Leinwand's formula for interface utilization is an example.)
In these cases, it may be more intuitive to set these boundaries in the
barchart display — to help the user appreciate not only the relative
values, but also their absolute position. For example, the formula for
storage utilization is simple:

```
st-utilization = 100 * hrStorageUsed / hrStorageSize
```

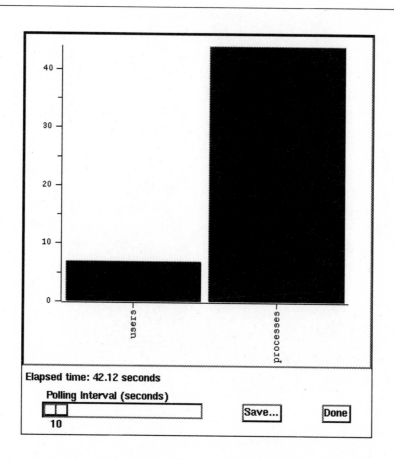

Figure 7.10: A Window Charting Users and Processes

Suppose this command procedure had a parameter which named a procedure, which evaluates a formula, before charting any values. Figure 7.11 starting on page 395 shows such a procedure.

This procedure is called with three parameters, the first parameter contains the **hrStorageIndex** value of the storage device, except on the first call when it has the special value "labels"; the second and third parameters are the window name and the base for the names of the global arrays. The first call does initialization; succeeding calls obtain values to be used in the barchart.

After setting up the global variables, the procedure examines the value of **idx** to determine if this is the first call. If so, the elements of the array **avar** are extracted, sorted, and all except those which are instances of **hrStorageDescr** are discarded. For each instance of **hrStorageDescr**, its value is used to format a label for the barchart's legend and is stored in **ainfo(objs)**. The **ainfo(idx)** list is initialized to contain one element for each bar to be drawn on the barchart; the values of these elements will be passed as the first parameter on succeeding calls to this procedure. The **afnx** array is also initialized to be used by the calling procedure to contain the value of the formula each time it is evaluated. Finally, the upper-limit of the barchart is set to 100.

```
proc    snmptcl_graph_hrutil      {idx w array} {
    global       snmptcl_var_hrStorageDescr
    global       snmptcl_var_hrStorageSize snmptcl_var_hrStorageUsed

    global       ${array}_info
    upvar #0     ${array}_info      ainfo

    global       ${array}_var
    upvar #0     ${array}_var       avar

    global       ${array}_fnx                                        10
    upvar #0     ${array}_fnx       afnx

    switch $idx {
        labels {
            set       ainfo(objs)       ""
            set       ainfo(idx)        ""
            foreach   var       [lsort −command snmptcl_proc_oidcmp \
                                    [array names avar]] {
                if {![snmptcl_proc_oidcontains $snmptcl_var_hrStorageDescr \   20
                        $var]} {
                    break
                }
                set     idx       [lindex [snmpinfo mibprop $var full] 3]
                lappend ainfo(objs)       [lindex $avar($var) 4]
                lappend ainfo(idx)        $idx
                set     afnx($idx)        $avar($var)
            }

# configure upper−limit of barchart to 100                              30
        }
```

Figure 7.11: The `snmptcl_graph_hrutil` procedure

```
        default {
            foreach        var        [list hrStorageSize hrStorageUsed] {
                eval    set obj \$snmptcl_var_$var
                if {(![info exists avar($obj.$idx)])} {
                    return ""
                }
                set        $var        [lindex $avar($obj.$idx) 4]
            }
            if {($hrStorageSize <= 0) || ($hrStorageUsed < 0)} {
                return  ""                                                          10
            }

            set          value      [expr ($hrStorageUsed*100)/$hrStorageSize]
            if {[info exists ainfo(barchart)]} {
# if using a monochrome display do nothing, otherwise...
                if {$value < 50} {
                    lappend        value      green
                } elseif {$value < 75} {
                    lappend        value      blue
                } elseif {$value < 87} {                                            20
                    lappend        value      yellow
                } elseif {$value < 95} {
                    lappend        value      orange
                } elseif {$value <= 99} {
                    lappend        value      red
                } else {
                    lappend        value      black
                }
            }
            return          $value                                                 30
        }
    }
}
```

Figure 7.11: The `snmptcl_graph_hrutil` procedure (cont.)

On subsequent calls, the values retrieved for the two objects needed to calculate the formula for a given storage device are extracted
from the **avar** array, and stored in local variables. Since these are
non-negative integers and not counters, no checks for sampling discontinuities are necessary. If a value is missing, or if the value is negative,
the empty string is returned. Otherwise, the formula is calculated, and
if a color display is being used, a color is associated with the resulting
value. This list is returned to **snmptcl_barchart_command**, which is
used to draw the barchart in Figure 7.10 with the given magnitude
and color.

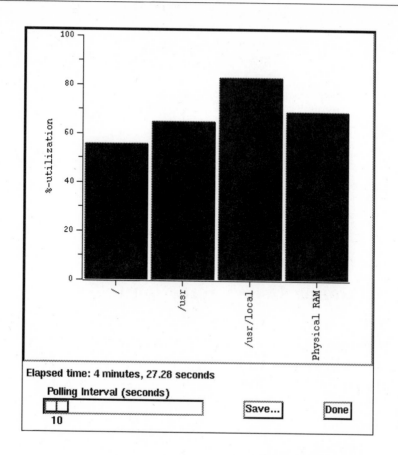

Figure 7.12: A Window Charting Storage Utilization

The result, rendered on a monochrome display, is a barchart like the one shown in Figure 7.12. (For the color version, check out the back cover of *The Networking Management Practicum.*)

```
proc    snmptcl_click_pgm          {insts w array} {
    if {$array == ""} {
# add "Help" button to window to explain what double-click-left does...
        return
    }

    global        ${array}_info
    upvar #0      ${array}_info      ainfo

    if {[set inst [lindex $insts 0]] != ""} {                              10
        snmptcl_proc_setscalar      $ainfo(pHandle) "Kill a Running Program" kill \
                                    hrSWRunStatus.$inst invalid
    }

# clear selection
}
```

Figure 7.13: The snmptcl_click_pgm procedure

7.3.2   Adding User-Interaction to Tables

Thus far, all of the browsing paradigms introduced have been solely for display. However, one could easily imagine a browser undertaking some action if the user clicks on an entry in a table.

Consider Figure 7.8 back on 389 which shows the running programs on a host. There are easily two different things that a user might want to do:

- examine the resource utilization of one of these running programs (launch a new browsing application); or,

- destroy the running program (issue a set operation);

Let's look at how the second of these might be accomplished.

Just as snmptcl_graph_command and snmptcl_barchart_command have a parameter which names a procedure to be called to calculate formulas, one might imagine that snmptcl_browsetable_command, the routine which produced the table in Figure 7.8, might have a parameter which names a procedure to be called when the user clicks on an entry in the table. Figure 7.13 shows such a procedure.

This procedure is called with three parameters; the first parameter is a list of instance-identifiers associated with the entries that the user clicked on; the second and third parameters are the window name and the base for the names of the global arrays.

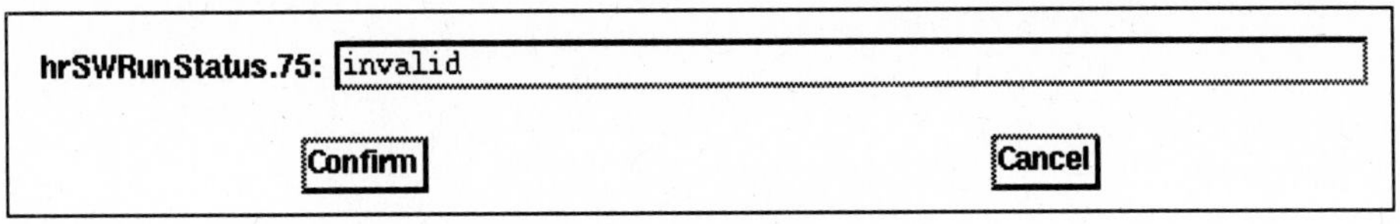

hrSWRunStatus.75: `invalid`

[Confirm]   [Cancel]

Figure 7.14: A Window to Kill a Running Program

When the window is first created, this command procedure is invoked with **array** set to the empty string, and a help button is added to the window. Then, whenever the user clicks on an entry, this routine is called. The instance-identifier corresponding to the entry is extracted, and **snmptcl_proc_setscalar** is called, which queries the user if the set should be performed. Figure 7.14 shows what such a window might look like.

Chapter 8

Applications Management

In this chapter, we consider how to manage networked applications using SNMP.

As we'll see, there is a varying level of experience in using SNMP for this purpose: although management of the transport layer is fairly well-understood, management of the application layer is even more immature than management of hosts! In fact, there was some debate between the authors as to whether this chapter should be included in the first edition of *The Networking Management Practicum*. As discussed back in Section 1.3, one of our rules for inclusion was that if an agent which implements the MIB modules we were writing about could be found — and we were able to communicate with that agent over the Internet so we could write some management applications — it would be included. Although there are a lot of agents which implement objects relating to the transport layer, when we started writing this chapter we couldn't find any agent which implemented application layer objects. This wasn't much of a surprise — the transport layer objects were standardized three years earlier, whilst the application layer objects were standardized two months earlier. So, our solution was to add minimal support for the latter objects to an existing agent. Hopefully, by the time you read this chapter, real products which implement these objects will be available.

8.1   Concepts

A networked application, or simply *application*, either provides or
makes use of one or more network services. Examples of such a service
might be the transfer of electronic mail messages, network file service,
and so on. Although there is obviously a relationship between the
programs which run on a host and the applications on that host, this
relationship is a matter of implementation. For example, a single
running program might solely implement a network service, or a
collection of related programs on a host might jointly implement the
service. Similarly, a single running program might solely implement
several network services.

From our perspective, there are three interesting aspects of an
application:

- concepts specific to the application, e.g., the store-and-forward
  nature of electronic mail;

- concepts generic to any application, e.g., addressing of other
  entities in the network; and,

- how the application makes use of the underlying transport layer.

Clearly, the first of these is beyond the scope of this chapter, so we'll
focus on the second and third aspects.

8.1.1 Application Layer

The application layer is responsible for organizing the data which relates to the function of an application and for orchestrating the communications between applications.

In the application layer, the key concept is the *association*, which refers to a binding between two applications running in the network, and the underlying transport service. As we'll see shortly in Section 8.1.2, there are two radically different kinds of transport service that can be used, depending on the needs of the application. Note that although an association exhibits the properties of its underlying transport service, a characteristic of any association is that it provides the focal point for application layer addressing.

An application layer address contains:

- a transport layer address, identifying a remote application as a user of the transport service; and,

- (optionally) additional application-specific information, which might be used for further identification.

The transport layer address is dependent on the actual transport service in use, and in this section we'll see what these addresses look like in the Internet suite of protocols.

Of course, this information is usually scrutinized once — when the association is established. The details of association establishment, beyond that of "simply" establishing a transport binding between two applications, is highly specific to the application. For example, there may be the exchange of credentials for authentication. Again, these issues are outside the scope of this chapter.

8.1.2   Transport Layer

The transport layer is responsible for providing data transfer between end-systems to the level of reliability desired by the application. That is, the transport layer provides end-to-end service.

In theory, the end-to-end needs of different applications can vary tremendously. In practice, however, there are really only two widely-used service paradigms:

reliable: in which the service offered is a "virtual pipeline":

- *stream-oriented*: rather than dealing in packet exchanges, the end-to-end service provides a sequence of octets, termed a *stream*, to the application.

- *full-duplex*: the stream provided by the end-to-end service is bi-directional in nature.

- *connection-oriented*: before the stream can be used, a virtual connection is established between the two applications.

- *application layer addressing*: an application needs a means of identifying its peer on the remote system to which the stream should be connected.

- *in-sequence delivery*: the end-to-end service guarantees that user-data is delivered in the same order in which it was sent.

- *user-data integrity*: the end-to-end service guarantees that any user-data delivered has not been corrupted during network transmission.

- *graceful release*: because user-data may be buffered both at the host and in the network, the end-to-end service will make sure that *all* of the data sent by the user is successfully transmitted before the stream is released.

Note that these are general guidelines, and not fixed. In particular, the OSI CO-mode transport service, whilst offering a reliable transport paradigm, uses a packet-oriented

(rather than stream-oriented) user-data paradigm, and has
no graceful release mechanism (the functionality of which
resides at the layer above). Regardless, the remaining characteristics are core to the concept of a reliable transport
service.

unreliable: in which the service offered is virtually identical
to that of the Internet datagram service. The only added
features are:

- *application layer addressing*; and,
- *user-data integrity*.

It shouldn't be surprising that the reliable service paradigm corresponds closely to a connection-oriented transport service, whilst
the unreliable service paradigm is similar to a connectionless-mode
transport service.

The Internet suite of protocols provides two different transport
protocols to meet these vastly different needs. Since both protocols
use identical mechanisms to achieve application layer addressing and
user-data integrity, the simpler protocol is described first.

The User Datagram Protocol

The *User Datagram Protocol* (UDP) [85] is the connectionless-mode
transport protocol in the Internet suite. As UDP is a transport layer
protocol, for delivery, it uses the services of IP. If the **protocol** field
of an IP datagram has the value 17 (decimal), the user-data contained
in the datagram is a UDP packet:

```
                    1                   2                   3
 0 1 2 3 4 5 6 7 8 9 0 1 2 3 4 5 6 7 8 9 0 1 2 3 4 5 6 7 8 9 0 1
```

source port	destination port
length	checksum
user-data	

The meaning of these fields is straightforward:

source/destination port: identifies an application running at the corresponding IP address.

length: the length of the UDP packet (header and user-data), measured in octets.

checksum: a one's-complement arithmetic sum, computed over a *pseudo-header* and the entire UDP packet.

user-data: zero or more octets of data from the upper-layer protocol. (Note that it is an artifact of the convention used in producing the figure above that this field appears to be a multiple of four octets in length. No such requirement is made by UDP.)

The uses of these fields are now explained.

Application Layer Addressing

To achieve application layer addressing, UDP manages 16–bit unsigned integer quantities, termed *ports*. Port numbers less than 512 are assigned by the Internet Assigned Numbers Authority (IANA) (see Section B.5 on page 484). These are termed *well-known ports*. In those cases when a service might be available over both TCP and UDP, the IANA assigns the same port number to that service for both protocols.

On Berkeley UNIX®, port numbers less than 1024 are reserved for privileged processes (an easily-spoofed, but in some environments, useful security mechanism).

The combination of an IP address and a port number is termed an internet *socket* which uniquely identifies an application-entity running in an internet.

Of course, the notion of application layer addressing is just another example of the multiplexing operation of protocols:

- at the interface layer, each medium usually distinguishes between clients (entities at the internet layer) by using different values in a **type** field (e.g., **Ethernet** uses a value of 0x0800 to indicate IP);

- at the internet layer, IP distinguishes between clients (entities at the transport layer) by using different values in a **protocol** field (e.g., IP uses a decimal value of 17 to indicate UDP); and,

- at the transport layer, TCP and UDP distinguish between clients (entities at the application layer) by using different values in a **port** field (e.g., UDP uses a value of 161 (decimal) to indicate SNMP).

The Assigned Numbers RFC [86] lists the complete set of protocol numbers used at all layers in the Internet suite of protocols.

User-Data Integrity

To achieve both user-data integrity and modest protection against misbehavior at the layers below, UDP calculates a *pseudo-header* which is conceptually prefixed to the UDP packet. The checksum algorithm is then run over a block that looks like this:

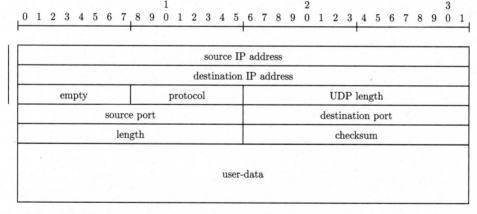

The fields of the pseudo-header are relatively self-explanatory: the **source** and **destination** fields are taken from the IP packet, the **empty** field is simply a zero-valued octet, the **protocol** field is the value used by IP to identify UDP (17 decimal), and the **UDP length** field is the length of the UDP packet.

TCP also uses this 96–bit pseudo-header in its checksum calculation when achieving user-data integrity.

The Transmission Control Protocol

The *Transmission Control Protocol* (TCP) [25] is the connection-oriented transport protocol in the Internet suite. As TCP is a connection-oriented transport protocol, it goes through three distinct phases: connection establishment, data transfer, and connection release. To keep track of a particular connection, each TCP entity maintains a *Transmission Control Block* (TCB). This is created during connection establishment, modified throughout the life of the connection, and then deleted when the connection is released.

TCP is best described as a finite state machine, which starts in the CLOSED state. As *events* occur (either activity from a user of TCP or from the network), the TCP entity performs some *action* and then enters a new state. The TCP state diagram is presented in Figure 8.1 on page 413. It is suggested that the reader study the intervening text before examining the figure.

Connection Establishment

A connection enters the LISTEN state when an application tells TCP that it is willing to accept connections for a particular port number. This is termed a *passive open*.

Sometime later, another application tells TCP that it wishes to establish a connection to an IP address and port number which corresponds to the application which is listening. This is termed an *active open*.[1]

When two TCP entities communicate, the exchanged units of data are termed *segments*. The format of a segment is presented later on. Segments are interpreted relative to a *connection*. In TCP, a connection is defined as the pairing of two internet sockets. This 96–bit quantity (source IP address and TCP port, destination IP address and TCP port) uniquely identifies the connection in an internet.

When an active open is attempted, the originating TCP entity computes an *initial sequence number*, which is a "starting number" for this direction of the new connection. The sequence number must

---

[1]It is possible for two application entities to simultaneously issue active opens for each other. In this case, a single TCP connection is established.

be chosen carefully so that segments from older instances of this connection, which might be floating around the network, won't cause confusion with this new connection. A SYN (synchronize) segment is then sent to the destination TCP entity. Upon receiving this segment, the destination TCP entity checks to see that an application is listening on the destination TCP port. If not, the connection is aborted by sending a RST (reset) segment.[2] Otherwise, the destination TCP entity computes a sequence number for its direction, and sends this back in a SYN/ACK (synchronize/acknowledge) segment which acknowledges the sequence number for the originating TCP entity.

Upon receiving this segment, the original TCP entity makes sure that its sequence number was acknowledged and, if all is well, sends an ACK segment back to acknowledge the sequence number for the destination TCP entity.

This protocol interaction is termed a *three-way handshake*. Once the three-way handshake has been successfully concluded, the connection enters the data transfer phase.

Data Transfer

In the data transfer phase, user-data is sent as a sequence of octets, each of which is numbered, starting with the initial sequence number.

Each segment specifies a window size (in octets) which may be sent in the other direction before an acknowledgement is returned. Each segment sent by a TCP entity contains an implicit acknowledgement of all octets contiguously received thus far. Precisely stated, the acknowledgement field indicates the number of the *next* octet that is expected by a TCP entity.

This windowing strategy allows the TCP entities to achieve a *pipelining effect* in the network, while at the same time providing a flow control mechanism. The pipelining effect increases throughput by keeping more data in the network, whilst the flow control mechanism prevents either TCP entity from overrunning the connection resources (such as buffers for user-data) of the other.

---

[2]In the interest of simplicity, Figure 8.1 doesn't show this transition, or any transition, involving an RST segment.

The disadvantage of this approach is that if segments are re-ordered, this information cannot be conveyed in an acknowledgement. For example, if two segments are sent, and the first one is delayed, the receiving TCP entity cannot acknowledge the second segment until it receives the first.

Data Transfer – Retransmission

The discussion thus far has not considered loss or corruption of segments. Each time a TCP entity sends a segment, it starts a retransmission timer. At some time in the future, one of two events will happen first: either an acknowledgement for the segment will be received, and the timer can be stopped; or, the timer will expire. In this latter case, the TCP entity *retransmits* the segment and restarts the timer. Retransmission continues some number of times until eventually the TCP entity gives up and declares the transport connection to be aborted. That is, TCP emulates reliability through retransmission. The trick, of course, is knowing *when* to retransmit. If data is lost or corrupted in the network and the sending transport entity retransmits too slowly, then throughput suffers. If data is delayed or discarded due to congestion in the network and the transport entity retransmits too quickly then it merely adds to the congestion and throughput gets even worse!

The reader should appreciate that because of the service offered by IP; a TCP entity cannot distinguish between lossy or congested networks. Hence, TCP uses one of several adaptive algorithms to predict the latency characteristics of the network, which may fluctuate considerably because of other traffic.

The retransmission timeout usually varies for each segment, based on the recent history of latency and loss exhibited by the network. Work reported in [87,88] suggests some novel, common sense insights into this problem.

As might be expected, acknowledgements and retransmission interact with the window strategy. Once again, suppose two segments are sent, and the first segment is lost. The receiving TCP entity cannot acknowledge the second segment. The retransmission timer expires for the sending TCP entity. It must now decide whether to retransmit the first segment or both segments. If it retransmits both segments, then it is "guessing" that both segments were lost. If this isn't the case, then network bandwidth is being wasted. Otherwise, if it retransmits the first segment only, it must wait for an acknowledgement to see if the second segment also needs to be retransmitted. If not, it has reduced its sending throughput by waiting for a round-trip transaction in the network.

Data Transfer – Queued Delivery

In addition to trying to optimize network traffic, a TCP entity may try to reduce the overhead of communicating with local application entities. This is usually achieved by buffering user-data in the TCP entity, both as it is received from the local application, in order to efficiently use the network, and also as user-data is received from the network, in order to efficiently communicate with the local application. Because of this, an application might need a mechanism for ensuring that all data it has previously sent has been received.

This is accomplished using the PSH (push) function. When sending, an application may indicate that data previously sent should be pushed. The local TCP entity sets a PSH bit in the next new segment it sends. Upon receiving such a segment, the remote TCP entity knows that it should push user-data up to its own application.

Although the push function must be present in each TCP implementation, few implementations of applications actually use this functionality. This is because most TCP entity implementations will periodically push any queued data toward the destination. Further, it should be noted that there are no semantics associated with the push function. It is simply a way of telling TCP to deliver all data previously sent to the remote application. On the remote device, the application will see only the user-data and won't receive any explicit indication of the push function having been invoked. Experience has shown that the push function is largely an internal matter: application protocols should be designed so that the push function isn't used.

Data Transfer – Urgent Data

Finally, TCP supports the concept of *urgent data*. The semantics of urgent data are application-specific. What TCP does is to indicate where urgent data ends in the stream. The receiving application, upon being notified that urgent data is present in the stream, can quickly read from the stream until the urgent data is exhausted.

Connection Release

When an application indicates that it has finished sending on the connection, the local TCP entity will send all outstanding data, setting the FIN (finish) indication in the last segment to indicate that it has finished sending new data.

Upon receiving this indication, the remote TCP entity will send an ACK for the FIN, and will inform (using a local mechanism) the application. When that application indicates that it too has no more data to send, a FIN is generated in this direction also. When all data in transit and the segments containing the FINs have been acknowledged, the two TCP entities declare the connection released. In order to ensure that old, duplicate packets don't interfere with new connections being established between the two application entities, one of the TCP entities will delay releasing the connection by twice the maximum segment lifetime.

Instead of requesting a graceful release, an application may determine that it wishes to immediately abort the connection. In this case, the local TCP entity generates a RST (reset) segment, and the connection is immediately released. Any data in transit is lost.

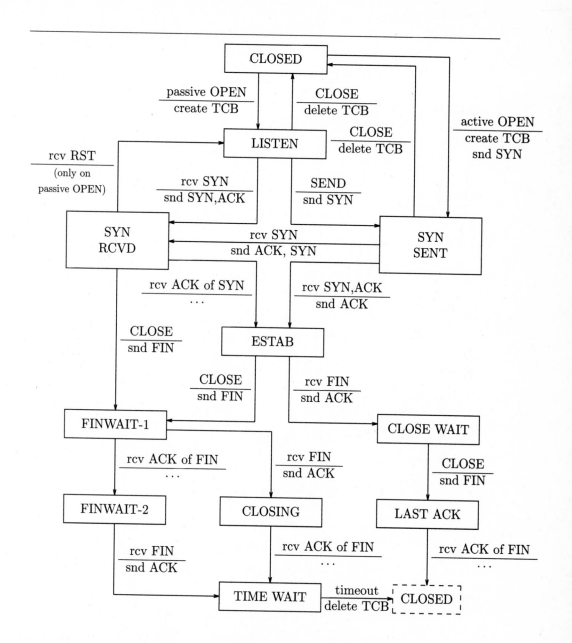

Figure 8.1: **TCP State Diagram**

Segment Format

When TCP wishes to send a segment, it uses the services of IP. If the **protocol** field of an IP datagram has the value 6 (decimal), the user-data contained in the datagram is a TCP segment:

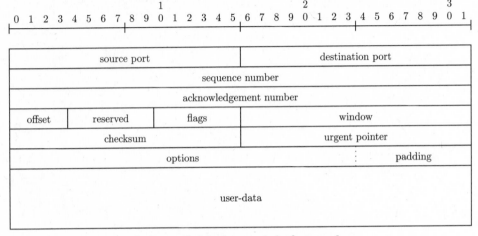

The meaning of these fields is straightforward:

source/destination port: identifies an application running at the corresponding IP address.

sequence number: the number of the first octet of user-data in this segment.

acknowledgement number: if the ACK bit is set in the **flags** field, then this field indicates the next sequence number that the TCP entity is expecting to receive.

offset: the length of the TCP segment in 32–bit words (the minimum allowed value is 5).

flags: control bits indicating special functions of this segment.

window: the number of octets of user-data (starting with the octet indicated in the **acknowledgement** field), which the TCP entity is willing to accept.

checksum: a one's-complement arithmetic sum, computed over a pseudo-header and the entire TCP segment, as discussed earlier.

urgent pointer: if the URG bit is set in the **flags** field, then this field, when added to the **sequence number** field, indicates the first octet of non-urgent data.

options: a collection of zero or more options.

padding: zero to three octets used to pad the segment header to a 32–bit boundary.

user-data: zero or more octets of data from the upper-layer protocol. (Note that it is an artifact of the convention used in producing the figure above that this field appears to be a multiple of four octets in length. No such requirement is made by TCP.)

8.2   Objects

There are three MIB modules which define objects for applications:

- the Network Services Monitoring MIB, which defines objects describing the generic aspects of applications and their associations;

- MIB-II, which, among other things, defines objects describing TCP and UDP; and,

- the Identification MIB, which defines objects describing "user information" about a TCP connection.

Let's look at each of these in turn.

8.2.1   Application Objects

The Network Services Monitoring MIB [89] defines objects relating to any kind of networked application. Two groups are defined:

- the `applGroup` which contains information about each application; and,

- the `assocGroup` which contains information about the associations related to each application.

Each is now examined in turn.

The Application Group

The `applGroup` contains one table, the `applTable`. The non-counter columns are:

applIndex (INTEGER): the number used as the INDEX for the table's row template (`applEntry`);

applName (DisplayString): the application's name;

applDirectoryName (DisplayString): the name of this application in the OSI Directory, if any;

applVersion (DisplayString): the application's version;

applUptime (TimeStamp): when the application was last re-initialized;

applOperStatus (enumerated INTEGER): the application's current state:

enumeration	accepting new associations?
up	yes
down	no
halted	
congested	
restarting	soon

applLastChange (TimeStamp): when the application entered its current state;

applInboundAssociations (Gauge32): the current number of incoming associations;

applLastInboundActivity (TimeStamp): when the last incoming association was established;

applOutboundAssociations (Gauge32): the current number of outgoing associations; and,

applLastOutboundActivity (TimeStamp): when the last outgoing association was established.

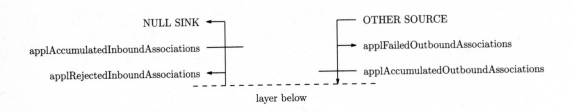

Figure 8.2: Case Diagram for the applGroup

Recall that **TimeStamp** is a textual convention. Whenever the event corresponding to the object occurs, the value of **sysUpTime** is copied. If the event has never occurred, or if it last occurred before the agent restarted (see Section 3.1.1 on page 93), then the value of a **TimeStamp** object is 0.

There are also four counter columns in the **applTable**:

applAccumulatedInboundAssociations: the total number of incoming associations which were established;

applRejectedInboundAssociations: the total number of incoming associations which weren't established;

applAccumulatedOutboundAssociations: the total number of outgoing associations which were established; and,

applFailedOutboundAssociations: the total number of outgoing associations which weren't established.

Figure 8.2 shows a Case Diagram relating these four counter objects, whilst Figures 8.3 through 8.5 show what three windows displaying all the objects in the **applTable** group might look like.

Note that all of these counters are defined in terms of when the application started. That is, in order to detect a sampling discontinuity, not only must the management application look at **sysUpTime** (refer back to Section 3.1.2 starting on page 94), but it must also examine the instance of **applUptime** which corresponds to the application. If the value of either object decreases, then a loss of state may have occurred. (A decrease in **sysUpTime** indicates that the agent restarted, whilst a decrease in **applUptime** indicates that the application restarted.)

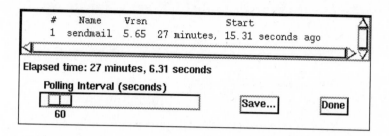

Figure 8.3: A Window Browsing Portions of the applTable

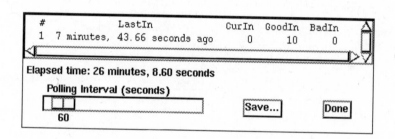

Figure 8.4: A Window Browsing Input Objects in the applTable

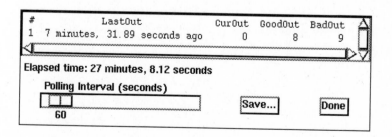

Figure 8.5: A Window Browsing Output Objects in the applTable

The Association Group

The `assocGroup` contains one table, the `assocTable`, with this INDEX property:

        INDEX { applIndex, assocIndex }

That is, for each row in the `applTable` there may be zero, one, or more rows in the `assocTable`. The columns in this latter table are:

assocIndex (`INTEGER`): the number used to distinguish between associations for the same application;

assocRemoteApplication (`DisplayString`): the name of the system where the remote application resides;

assocApplicationProtocol (`OBJECT IDENTIFIER`):   the application layer protocol used over the association;

assocApplicationType (enumerated `INTEGER`):   the remote application's relationship:

enumeration	started association?	relationship
ua-initiator	yes	vertical
ua-responder	no	vertical
peer-initiator	yes	horizontal
peer-responder	no	horizontal

assocDuration (`TimeStamp`):   when the association was established.

Figure 8.6 shows what a window displaying these objects might look like. (Conspicuously missing from this list of objects is any linkage to the transport layer — perhaps this will be included in a future revision to this MIB module.)

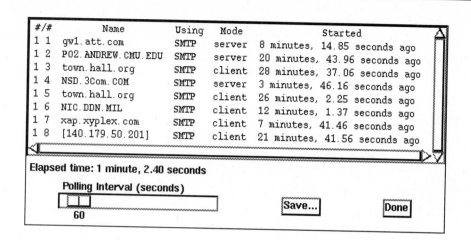

Figure 8.6: A Window Browsing the assocTable

One of these objects requires further discussion. In the Internet suite of protocols, one can usually identify the application layer protocol being used by looking at the corresponding TCP or UDP port number. For example, TCP port 25 refers to the Simple Mail Transfer Protocol (SMTP) which is used to relay mail. However, sometimes port numbers are assigned dynamically. In this case, some other means must be used to determine which protocol is being used between the applications. As such, the syntax of

    assocApplicationProtocol

is an OBJECT IDENTIFIER. However, to simplify matters, two special OBJECT IDENTIFIER prefixes have been defined

    applTCPProtoID
    applUDPProtoID

These are used to refer to application protocols with a fixed port number, e.g.,

    applTCPProtoID.25

refers to SMTP.

8.2.2   Transport Objects

The MIB-II [3] defines two groups related to the transport layer: the
tcp group and the udp group. For a system which implements TCP
or UDP, the agent on that system must implement the corresponding
groups.

The TCP Group

The tcp group contains several scalars and a table. The non-counter
scalars are:

> **tcpRtoAlgorithm** (enumerated INTEGER): the retransmission
> algorithm used by TCP:

enumeration	for further info
constant	
rsre	see page 41 of [25]
vanj	see [87]
other	

> **tcpRtoMin** (INTEGER): the minimum retransmission timeout
> in milliseconds, interpreted according to the value of
> tcpRtoAlgorithm;

> **tcpRtoMax** (INTEGER): the maximum retransmission timeout
> in milliseconds, interpreted according to the value of
> tcpRtoAlgorithm;

> **tcpMaxConn** (INTEGER):   the maximum number of simulta-
> neous TCP connections that can be supported (a value of
> -1 means that there is no *a priori* limit); and,

> **tcpCurrEstab** (Gauge32): the number of current connections
> either established or in the process of being closed.

Figure 8.7 shows what a window displaying these objects might look
like.

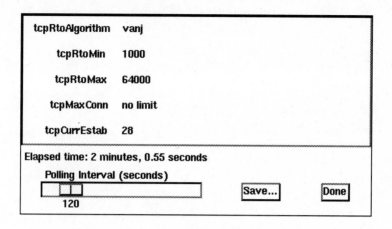

Figure 8.7: A Window Browsing Portions of the `tcp` Group

The scalar counter objects in the `tcp` group are:

tcpActiveOpens: the total number of active opens;

tcpPassiveOpens: the total number of passive opens;

tcpAttemptFails: the total number of failed attempts to establish a connection;

tcpEstabResets: the total number of connections reset;

tcpInSegs: the total number of segments received;

tcpOutSegs: the total number of segments sent;

tcpRetransSegs: the total number of segments retransmitted;

tcpInErrs: the total number of segments discarded due to format error; and,

tcpOutRsts: the total number of resets generated.

Figure 8.8 on page 424 shows a Case Diagram relating some of these objects.

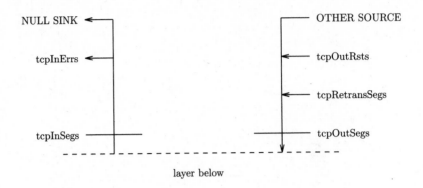

Figure 8.8: Case Diagram for the tcp Group

The tcpConnTable is used to keep track of the TCP connections currently on the system. Its INDEX property is:

```
INDEX { tcpConnLocalAddress, tcpConnLocalPort,
        tcpConnRemAddress, tcpConnRemPort }
```

which says that a TCP connection can be uniquely identified by both endpoints:

- the local IP address (tcpConnLocalAddress) and TCP port (tcpConnLocalPort); and,

- the remote IP address (tcpConnRemoteAddress) and TCP port (tcpConnRemotePort).

Of course, since connections in the LISTEN state don't have to be bound to a local IP address, the distinguished value 0.0.0.0 is used for this purpose. Similarly, this same value is used for the remote IP address. Naturally, when a connection leaves the LISTEN state, this information is filled in accordingly.

Besides these four columns, there's one other column in the table:

tcpConnState: the connection's state:

```
closed
listen
synSent
synReceived
established
finWait1
finWait2
closeWait
lastAck
closing
timeWait
deleteTCB (via set)
```

This last enumeration is somewhat controversial. Although it's widely thought to be "really useful" to be able to remotely destroy a connection using SNMP's **set** operation, very few agents actually provide this capability!

Figure 8.9 on page 426 shows what a window displaying these objects might look like.

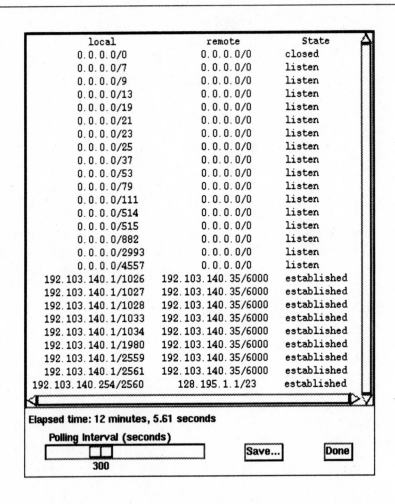

local	remote	State
0.0.0.0/0	0.0.0.0/0	closed
0.0.0.0/7	0.0.0.0/0	listen
0.0.0.0/9	0.0.0.0/0	listen
0.0.0.0/13	0.0.0.0/0	listen
0.0.0.0/19	0.0.0.0/0	listen
0.0.0.0/21	0.0.0.0/0	listen
0.0.0.0/23	0.0.0.0/0	listen
0.0.0.0/25	0.0.0.0/0	listen
0.0.0.0/37	0.0.0.0/0	listen
0.0.0.0/53	0.0.0.0/0	listen
0.0.0.0/79	0.0.0.0/0	listen
0.0.0.0/111	0.0.0.0/0	listen
0.0.0.0/514	0.0.0.0/0	listen
0.0.0.0/515	0.0.0.0/0	listen
0.0.0.0/882	0.0.0.0/0	listen
0.0.0.0/2993	0.0.0.0/0	listen
0.0.0.0/4557	0.0.0.0/0	listen
192.103.140.1/1026	192.103.140.35/6000	established
192.103.140.1/1027	192.103.140.35/6000	established
192.103.140.1/1028	192.103.140.35/6000	established
192.103.140.1/1033	192.103.140.35/6000	established
192.103.140.1/1034	192.103.140.35/6000	established
192.103.140.1/1980	192.103.140.35/6000	established
192.103.140.1/2559	192.103.140.35/6000	established
192.103.140.1/2561	192.103.140.35/6000	established
192.103.140.254/2560	128.195.1.1/23	established

Elapsed time: 12 minutes, 5.61 seconds

Polling Interval (seconds)

300

Save...   Done

Figure 8.9: A Window Browsing the `tcpConnTable`

The Ident Group

The Identification MIB [90] defines one group which contains "user" information about the TCP connections on a system.[3] Implementation of this group, the `ident` group, is optional.

The concept of associating user information with a TCP connection is controversial, for two reason:

- The information returned by an agent implementing this MIB module is only as trustworthy as the system running the agent. Once the system is subverted, the information returned by the agent needn't be accurate. Indeed, many stand-alone systems (such as personal computers in an open lab) have no defenses to prevent any such subversion.

  This suggests that the objects in the `ident` group be used only for the purposes of auditing and debugging. Clearly it would be unwise to use these objects for the purposes of authenticating the user associated with a TCP connection, or making access control decisions based on that information!

- The information returned by an agent implementing this MIB module contains information about users, which may be considered to be private information.

  This suggests that a site may wish to employ SNMP's access control facilities (something which isn't discussed in *The Networking Management Practicum*) to control which management applications are allowed to access this information.

Now that we've gotten the disclaimers out of the way, let's look at the objects. The `ident` group consists of one table, the `identTable`, which is an augmentation of the `tcpConnTable`. That is, the tables are indexed identically, and a row in one table has a corresponding row in the other table.

---

[3]In fact, [91] defines a TCP-based protocol which provides precisely the same information. (The protocol was defined before the Identification MIB.)

The `identTable` has these columns:

identStatus (enumerated `INTEGER`):   indicates whether user information is available for this TCP connection:

> ```
> noError
> unknownError
> ```

identOpSys (`OCTET STRING`): the operating system employed by the user associated with this TCP connection;

identCharset (`OCTET STRING`):   the character set associated with the following two columns;

identUserid (`OCTET STRING`):   the identity of the user associated with this TCP connection; and,

identMisc (`OCTET STRING`): any additional information about the user associated with this TCP connection.

In order to interpret the information about a user associated with a TCP connection, both the user's operating system and character set are consulted. The *Assigned Numbers* document [86] contains this information:

object	in Assigned Numbers
`identOpSys`	see Section System Names
`identCharset`	see Section Character Sets

(Recall that character sets were introduced back on page 369.)

Figure 8.10 shows what a window displaying some of these objects might look like.

```
     local                 remote              OS    Charset   UserId
   0.0.0.0/0             0.0.0.0/0           UNIX   US-ASCII   root
   0.0.0.0/7             0.0.0.0/0           UNIX   US-ASCII   root
   0.0.0.0/9             0.0.0.0/0           UNIX   US-ASCII   root
   0.0.0.0/13            0.0.0.0/0           UNIX   US-ASCII   root
   0.0.0.0/19            0.0.0.0/0           UNIX   US-ASCII   root
   0.0.0.0/21            0.0.0.0/0           UNIX   US-ASCII   root
   0.0.0.0/23            0.0.0.0/0           UNIX   US-ASCII   root
   0.0.0.0/25            0.0.0.0/0           UNIX   US-ASCII   root
   0.0.0.0/37            0.0.0.0/0           UNIX   US-ASCII   root
   0.0.0.0/53            0.0.0.0/0           UNIX   US-ASCII   root
   0.0.0.0/79            0.0.0.0/0           UNIX   US-ASCII   root
   0.0.0.0/111           0.0.0.0/0           UNIX   US-ASCII   root
   0.0.0.0/514           0.0.0.0/0           UNIX   US-ASCII   root
   0.0.0.0/515           0.0.0.0/0           UNIX   US-ASCII   root
   0.0.0.0/882           0.0.0.0/0           UNIX   US-ASCII   root
   0.0.0.0/2993          0.0.0.0/0           UNIX   US-ASCII   root
   0.0.0.0/4557          0.0.0.0/0           UNIX   US-ASCII   root
 192.103.140.1/1026   192.103.140.35/6000   UNIX   US-ASCII   mrose
 192.103.140.1/1027   192.103.140.35/6000   UNIX   US-ASCII   mrose
 192.103.140.1/1028   192.103.140.35/6000   UNIX   US-ASCII   mrose
 192.103.140.1/1033   192.103.140.35/6000   UNIX   US-ASCII   mrose
 192.103.140.1/1034   192.103.140.35/6000   UNIX   US-ASCII   mrose
 192.103.140.1/1980   192.103.140.35/6000   UNIX   US-ASCII   mrose
 192.103.140.1/2559   192.103.140.35/6000   UNIX   US-ASCII   mrose
 192.103.140.1/2561   192.103.140.35/6000   UNIX   US-ASCII   mrose
 192.103.140.254/2560    128.195.1.1/23     UNIX   US-ASCII   mrose
```

Elapsed time: 12 minutes, 9.47 seconds

Polling Interval (seconds)

300

Save...   Done

Figure 8.10: A Window Browsing Portions of the identTable

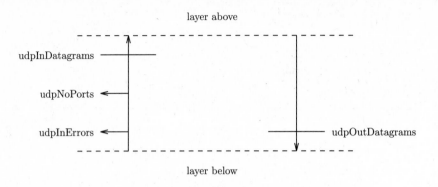

Figure 8.11: Case Diagram for the udp Group

The UDP Group

The udp group contains four counters and a table. The counters are:

udpInDatagrams: the total number of datagrams delivered to any application;

udpNoPorts: the total number of datagrams addressed to ports without an associated application;

udpInErrors: the total number of datagrams discarded due to format errors; and,

udpOutDatagrams: the total number of datagrams sent from any local application.

Figure 8.11 shows a Case Diagram relating these objects.

The udpTable is used to keep track of applications which are using UDP. Its INDEX property is:

```
INDEX { udpLocalAddress, udpLocalPort }
```

which says that only local users of UDP are known to the agent. (Again, if an application isn't listening for UDP traffic on a particular IP address, the distinguished value 0.0.0.0 is used.) In fact, these are the only columns in the udpTable.

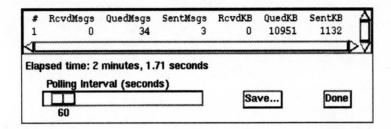

#	RcvdMsgs	QuedMsgs	SentMsgs	RcvdKB	QuedKB	SentKB
1	0	34	3	0	10951	1132

Elapsed time: 2 minutes, 1.71 seconds

Polling Interval (seconds)

60

Save... Done

Figure 8.12: A Window Browsing E-Mail Activity

8.3 Applications

The authors certainly wish they could have written about one or two interesting applications in this chapter. In the first edition of *The Networking Management Practicum*, this wasn't to be. So for now, we'll just have to be content with the browsing capability shown in the earlier figures.

However, as a harbinger of applications management, Figure 8.12 shows what a window displaying some objects relating to e-mail activity on a system might look like. (Yes, there is a MIB module standardized in this area, and perhaps an entire chapter in a subsequent edition of *The Networking Management Practicum* will be devoted to this topic!)

Chapter 9

SNMP Agent Management

In this chapter, we consider how to measure the performance of an SNMP agent. Owing to the elegance of the SNMP design, surprisingly few objects are required for performance measurement.

However, there is a larger topic dealing with agents, which is not covered in *The Networking Management Practicum* — configuration management. In the original framework, agent configuration was a vendor-specific matter. In contrast, an SNMPv2 agent has extensive (perhaps too much) standardization for its administrative configuration (how an agent determines if a message is authentic, and if so, how an agent determines whether the requested operation is authorized). However, as of this writing, the MIB module which defines these objects is undergoing intensive scrutiny and is likely to be revised in the near future. As such, this topic is beyond the scope of this edition of *The Networking Management Practicum*.

9.1   Concepts

For the purposes of this chapter, all the relevant information can be captured in two figures:

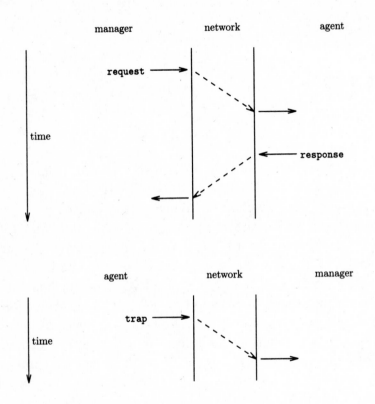

9.2   Objects

Back on page 104, the **system** and **snmpOR** groups, which all agents must implement, were introduced.[1] In this chapter, we'll introduce a few more groups which every agent must implement.

---

[1] Actually, only agents implementing SNMPv2 need implement the **snmpOR** group.

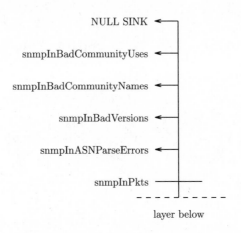

Figure 9.1: Case Diagram for the snmp Group

9.2.1 Groups required for SNMPv1 Agents

Agents which implement only SNMPv1 must implement MIB-II's
snmp group. This group contains 30 counter objects. Figure 9.1 shows
a Case Diagram relating the most important of these objects:

snmpInPkts: the number of packets received from the transport
service;

snmpInASNParseErrors: the number of packets which were
improperly encoded;

snmpInBadVersions: the number of packets which weren't
SNMPv1 messages;

snmpInBadCommunityNames: the number of packets which
the agent deemed unauthentic; and,

snmpInBadCommunityUses: the number of packets which
requested operations that the agent deemed unauthorized.

The first two of these objects deal with the traffic received by
an agent, whilst the last two of these objects deal with the agent's
administrative configuration. (An increase in these counters may

indicate a break-in attempt.) There is a third configuration object
in the **snmp** group:

> **snmpEnableAuthenTraps**(TruthValue): whether the agent
> is permitted to generate traps reporting a failure in
> authentication.

This is the only non-counter in the whole of the **snmp** group.

The remaining objects are, in the authors' opinion, of dubious
value. They keep track of how many different kinds of messages an
SNMPv1 entity has received:

```
snmpInGetRequests
snmpInGetNexts
snmpInSetRequests
snmpInGetResponses
snmpInTraps
```

or generated:

```
snmpOutGetRequests
snmpOutGetNexts
snmpOutSetRequests
snmpOutGetResponses
snmpOutTraps
```

(In the SNMPv1 framework, the term "get response" is used for all
responses — even when responding to a **set** operation!) In addition,
snmpOutPkts contains the number of all messages sent by an SNMPv1
entity. One of these variables, **snmpOutTraps**, is actually useful —
since agents generate traps in response to exceptional conditions, this
object counts the number of messages generated by the agent which
were not in direct response to a management application's query.

Finally, **snmpInTotalReqVars** keeps track of the total number
of variables successfully retrieved, whilst **snmpInTotalSetVars** keeps
track of the total number of variables successfully modified. In addition, for messages received or generated, a counter is kept for each
error response generated. Again, the authors feel these objects to be
rather gratuitous, so we're not even going to list them.

9.2.2 Groups required for SNMPv2 Agents

In the SNMPv2 framework, an agent must implement the `system` group and several other groups:

snmpOR: the object resources group;

snmpStats: the SNMPv2 statistics group;

snmpV1: the SNMPv1 statistics group (this group is implemented only by agents which implement both SNMPv1 and SNMPv2);

snmpSet: the SNMPv2 set group; and,

snmpTrap: the traps group.

All of these are defined in a MIB module called `SNMPv2-MIB` [14]. The `snmpOR` group was discussed earlier on page 107, so let's look at the remaining groups.

The snmpStats Group

This group contains 12 counter objects. Figure 9.2 shows a Case Diagram relating these objects:

snmpStatsPackets: the number of packets received from the transport service;

snmpStats30Something: the number of packets which appeared to be SNMPv1 messages (only those agents which implement only SNMPv2 will increment this counter);

snmpStatsEncodingErrors: the number of packets which were improperly encoded;

snmpStatsUnknownContexts: the number of packets which referenced a non-existent MIB view;

snmpStatsBadOperations: the number of packets which contained an operation the agent cannot perform (e.g., a `response` packet); and,

snmpStatsSilentDrops: the number of packets which were silently dropped due to local limitations.

The remaining six objects all count packets, which for one reason or another, the agent deemed unauthentic. As such, an increase in any of these counters may indicate a break-in attempt. (Since authentication is defined as a part of the agent's administrative configuration, we won't elaborate further on these objects.)

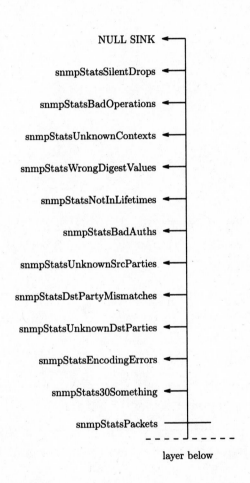

Figure 9.2: Case Diagram for the snmpStats Group

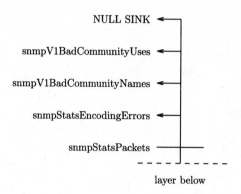

Figure 9.3: Case Diagram for the snmpV1 Group

The snmpV1 Group

This group contains four objects and is implemented only if the agent supports both SNMPv1 and SNMPv2. Figure 9.3 shows a Case Diagram relating these objects:

snmpStatsPackets: the number of packets received from the transport service;

snmpStatsEncodingErrors: the number of packets which were improperly encoded;

snmpV1BadCommunityNames: the number of SNMPv1-packets which the agent deemed unauthentic; and,

snmpV1BadCommunityUses: the number of SNMPv1-packets which requested operations that the agent deemed unauthorized.

We've seen all of these objects before: the first two on the previous page, and the last two simply have different names than their SNMPv1–only counterparts on page 435.

Note that an agent which implements both SNMPv1 and SNMPv2 does not implement the **snmp** group. Instead, as an SNMPv2 agent, it implements the **snmpStats** group. In addition, it implements two additional counters, with names very similar to the SNMPv1–only counterparts.

The snmpSet Group

This group defines one object:

> **snmpSetSerialNo** (`TestAndIncr`): An advisory lock used to allow several cooperating SNMPv2 entities, all acting in a manager role, to coordinate their use of the SNMPv2 `set` operation.

So what is a `TestAndIncr` object? It's an integer-valued object, ranging from 0 to 2147483647, that may be `set` by the management protocol only to its current value. An attempt to set such an object to a value other than its current value generates an error response. Otherwise, if the `set` operation succeeds, the value is incremented by one unless it reaches the maximum value (in which case it wraps back to zero). Obviously, humans should never have to type in the value of such an object; programs should!

So, `snmpSetSerialNo` is used for coarse-grain coordination. To achieve fine-grain coordination, one or more similar objects might be defined within each MIB group, as appropriate.

(As you probably guessed, this object has nothing to do with the performance measurement of an agent, but the authors couldn't find anywhere else in *The Networking Management Practicum* to describe this object!)

The snmpTrap Group

In SNMPv1, a single counter, **snmpOutTraps**, kept track of the number of traps that the agent has generated since its last restart.

For an agent implementing SNMPv2, the **snmpTrap** group has two top-level objects. The first is actually a configuration object:

> **snmpV2EnableAuthenTraps**(TruthValue):   whether the agent is permitted to generate traps reporting a failure in authentication.

The second top-level object is a table which contains an entry for each management application known to the agent. This table has one column:

> **snmpTrapNumbers:** the number of **snmpV2-traps** which the agent has sent to this management application.

So, to calculate the number of traps an SNMPv2 agent has generated during a sampling continuity, the deltas of each instance of this column are summed.

9.3 Applications

To measure the performance of any agent, there are really only three formulas we need to be aware of:

- how many packets an agent receives (a workload event);

- how many of those packets could not be processed (a problem condition); and,

- how many traps an agent sends (an unusual condition).

As always, the threshold for determining when something unusual becomes a problem depends on the environment.

The calculation of these formulas varies, depending on whether the agent implements SNMPv1 and/or SNMPv2. For an SNMPv1 agent:

packets received: any increase in `snmpInPkts.0`;

packets rejected: the sum of any increase in:

```
snmpInASNParseErrs.0
snmpInBadVesions.0
snmpInBadCommunityNames.0
snmpInBadCommunityUses.0
```

and,

traps sent: any increase in `snmpOutTraps.0`

For an SNMPv2 agent:

packets received: any increase in `snmpStatsPkts.0`;

packets rejected: the sum of any increase in:

```
snmpStats30Something.0
snmpStatsEncodingErrors.0
snmpStatsUnknownDstParties.0
snmpStatsDstPartyMismatches.0
snmpStatsUnknownSrcParties.0
snmpStatsBadAuths.0
snmpStatsNotInLifetimes.0
snmpStatsWrongDigestValues.0
```

```
snmpStatsUnknownContexts.0
snmpStatsBadOperations.0
snmpStatsSilentDrops.0
snmpV1BadCommunityNames.0
snmpV1BadCommunityUses.0
```

and,

traps sent: the sum of any increase in all instances of `snmpTrapNumbers`.

In terms of specific applications, there are really only two useful tasks:

- graphing the number of any of these formulas; and,

- monitoring the last two formulas (packets rejected and traps sent).

Implementing either of these is straightforward: graphing of a formula was discussed earlier in Section 4.3.1 on page 214, whilst monitoring a formula was discussed in Section 4.3.3 on page 226. The only difference is in calculating the number of traps sent by an SNMPv2 agent, which involves a variable number of counters. As always, care must be taken when calculating the formulas to handle sampling discontinuities. There's little to learn from the resulting code, so we won't bother discussing it. Instead, Figure 9.4 shows how these formulas might be reported for an SNMPv1 agent.

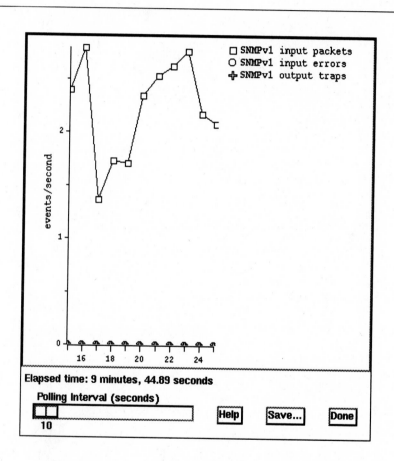

Figure 9.4: A Window Graphing SNMP Events

Appendix A

Quick Reference to the API

This appendix collects all the reference information for the SNMP API and the *Tcl* core.

A.1   SNMP API Quick Reference

command procedure	page
callback	451
ctxproc bulk	449–450
ctxproc config	449, 452
ctxproc destroy	449
ctxproc get	449–450
ctxproc inform	449–450
ctxproc next	449–450
ctxproc register	449
ctxproc set	449–450
ctxproc wait	449
newsnmp	448
snmpinfo agentprop	454
snmpinfo mibprop	453

procedure	arguments	returns
newsnmp	`ctxproc string ?options?`	`ctxproc`
	find the management context associated with **string**, create a new context procedure, **ctxproc**, which is used to talk to the corresponding agent	

newsnmp options			
option	**value**	**meaning**	**default**
rtrqos	`string`	retransmission quality-of-service, one of: `exponential`, `superlinear`	`exponential`
retries	`integer`	number of retries for retrieval operations	5
timeout	`integer`	number of seconds before initial retry, `rtrqos` determines timeout for additional retries	10
secqos	`string`	security quality-of-service, one of: `none`, `auth`, `authpriv`	`none`
maxrept	`integer`	max-repetitions field for `get-bulk` operations	1
nonrptr	`integer`	non-repeaters field for `get-bulk` operations	0

Table A.1: The `newsnmp` Command Procedure

procedure	arguments	returns
`ctxproc operation`	`callback vBinds ?options?`	`integer`
	invoke the specified `operation` on the `vBinds` found in the context associated with `ctxproc`, when a response is received, evaluate the `callback` command, return an `integer` which is used to identify the invocation	
`ctxproc wait`	`?integer?`	the empty string
	wait for the `callback` command associated with the invocation specified by `integer` to be evaluated; if `integer` isn't present, wait for the `callback` commands associated with all outstanding invocations to be evaluated	
`ctxproc register`	`?-add? ?-remove? notify callback`	the empty string
	on `-add` (the default), add `callback` to the list of commands to be evaluated when an unsolicited message is received; on `-remove`, remove `callback` from the list; `notify` is either `trap` or `inform`	
`ctxproc config`		`list`
	return a list containing the current configuration options associated with `ctxproc`; each element is a list containing an option and a value	
`ctxproc config`	`option ?value?`	`value`
	return the present value of the specified configuration `option`; if `value` is specified, make this the new value	
`ctxproc destroy`		the empty string
	discard any invocations in progress (evaluating each `callback`) and delete the context procedure	

Table A.2: Using a Context Procedure created by `newsnmp`

operation parameter	
keyword	**specifies**
get	`get`
next	`get-next`
bulk	`get-bulk`
set	`set`
inform	`inform`

vBinds parameter		
syntax	**type of value**	**example**
Integer32	`integer`	`42`
BitString	`string`	`101010`
OctetString	`string`	`0x01:fe:23:dc:45:ba:67:98`
DisplayString	`string`	`{4BSD/ISODE SNMPv2}`
ObjectID	`string`	`1.3.6.1.6.3.1.1.1.1`
IpAddress NetworkAddress	`string`	`192.103.140.1`
Counter32 Gauge32 TimeTicks Counter64 UInteger32	`number`	`42.0`
Opaque	the empty string	
NsapAddress	`string`	`0x47:00:05:80:ff:ff:00:00`

Table A.3: Parameters when invoking SNMP operations

procedure	arguments	returns
callback	ctxproc integer eStatus eIndex vBinds	ignored
	indicates that the invocation identified by `integer` is completed, having the specified error-status (`eStatus`), error-index (`eIndex`), and variable-bindings (`vBinds`)	

eStatus parameter	
category	**keyword**
SNMP error	noError
	tooBig
	noSuchName
	badValue
	genErr
	noAccess
	wrongType
	wrongLength
	wrongEncoding
	wrongValue
	noCreation
	inconsistentValue
	resourceUnavailable
	commitFailed
	undoFailed
	authorizationError
	notWritable
	inconsistentName
invocation timed-out	timeout
internal error	failed
ctxproc destroy	destroyed

vBinds parameter	
syntax	**value**
exception	noSuchObject
	noSuchInstance
	endOfMibView
error	any eStatus value above
unknown	any implementation-specific diagnostic

Table A.4: Evaluating an SNMP Callback Procedure

option	writable	value
active		0 or 1 context is able to generate traffic
identity		OBJECT IDENTIFIER globally-unique identity of context
maxrept	√	see Table A.1
name		string textual handle for context
nonrptr	√	see Table A.1
resources	√	list object resources present in context
retries	√	see Table A.1
rtrqos	√	see Table A.1
secqos	√	see Table A.1
timeout	√	see Table A.1

Table A.5: Configuring a Context Procedure

procedure	arguments	returns
snmpinfo mibprop	object property	string
	return the value of the **property** associated with the definition of object	
snmpinfo mibprop	object descriptor	string
	return the value of descriptor associated with the definition of object	
snmpinfo mibprop	object enums	list
	return a list containing the enumerations associated with the subtype associated with the SYNTAX property of object; each enumeration is a list containing an integer value and the associated string	
snmpinfo mibprop	object full	list
	return a list containing the descriptor, type, value, instance-identifier, and instance-fields associated with (the definition) of object	
snmpinfo mibprop	object range	list
	return a list containing the lower-and upper-bounds of the value of the INTEGER subtype associated with the SYNTAX property of object	
snmpinfo mibprop	object size	list
	return a list containing the lower- and upper-bounds of the value of the SIZE subtype associated with the SYNTAX property of object	
snmpinfo mibprop	object type	string
	return the name of the macro used to define object	
snmpinfo mibprop	object value	string
	return the OBJECT IDENTIFIER value of the definition of object	

Table A.6: The snmpinfo mibprop Command Procedure

procedure	arguments	returns
snmpinfo agentprop	`agent object` support	`string`
	return 1 if `object` is implemented by `agent`; otherwise, return 0	
snmpinfo agentprop	`agent entry` CREATION-REQUIRES	`list`
	return a list containing any columnar objects that must be supplied for creation of an `entry` row to succeeed	
snmpinfo agentprop	`agent object` ACCESS	`string`
	return the maximum level of access that `agent` can provide to `object`	
snmpinfo agentprop	`agent object` SYNTAX	`list`
	return the `SYNTAX` restriction for reading (and perhaps writing) `object`	
snmpinfo agentprop	`agent object` WRITE-SYNTAX	`list`
	return the `SYNTAX` restriction for writing `object`	

Table A.7: The `snmpinfo agentprop` Command Procedure

A.2 Tcl Core Quick Reference

command procedure	page	command procedure	page
append	460	proc	463
array	460	rename	463
break	461	return	463
catch	463	scan	457
concat	459	set	460
continue	461	source	463
error	463	split	459
eval	463	string compare	457
expr	456	string first	457
for	461	string index	457
foreach	461	string last	457
format	457	string length	457
global	463	string match	457
if	462	string range	457
incr	460	string tolower	457
lappend	460	string toupper	457
lindex	459	string trim	458
linsert	459	string trimleft	458
list	459	string trimright	458
llength	459	switch	462
lrange	459	unset	460
lreplace	459	uplevel	463
lsearch	459	upvar	463
lsort	459	while	461

procedure	arguments	returns
expr	arg ?arg ... ?	`value`
	concatenate **args**, evaluate the expression, and return the result (usually `number`)	

expr operators in decreasing order of precedence		
symbol	**operation**	**operands**
–	arithmetic negation (unary)	`number`
!	logical negation (unary)	`number`
~	bitwise negation (unary)	`integer`
*	multiplication	`number`
/	division	`number`
%	remainder	`integer`
+	addition	`number`
–	subtraction	`number`
<<	left-shift	`integer`
>>	right-shift	`integer`
<	less than	`value`
>	greater than	`value`
<=	less than/equal to	`value`
>=	greater than/equal to	`value`
==	equality	`value`
!=	inequality	`value`
&	bitwise and	`integer`
^	bitwise xor	`integer`
|	bitwise or	`integer`
&&	logical and	`number`
||	logical or	`number`
x?y:z	if-then-else	x: `number` y,z: `value`

Table A.8: Command Procedures dealing with Integers

procedure	arguments	returns
format	`fmt ?value ... ?`	`string`
	for each %-escape in `fmt`, substitute the corresponding `value`, return the result	
scan	`string fmt var ?var ... ?`	`number`
	for each %-escape in `fmt`, extract a value from `string` and update the corresponding `var`, return the number of `vars` updated	
string compare	`string1 string2`	`number`
	if `string1` is lexicographically less than `string2`, return -1; if the two `strings` are equal, return 0; otherwise, return 1	
string first	`string1 string2`	`number`
	if `string1` occurs in `string2`, return the `index` in `string2` of the first such occurrence; otherwise, return -1	
string index	`string index`	`string`
	if there is a character residing at `index` in `string`, return a string containing a copy of it; otherwise, return the empty string	
string last	`string1 string2`	`number`
	if `string1` occurs in `string2`, return the `index` in `string2` of the last such occurrence; otherwise, return -1	
string length	`string`	`number`
	return the length of `string`	
string match	`pattern string`	`number`
	if `string` matches `pattern` using glob-matching, return 1; otherwise, return 0	
string range	`string first last`	`string`
	return a string formed by copying the characters residing between `first` and `last` in `string`	
string tolower	`string`	`string`
	return a string formed by copying `string` and making any upper-case letters into their lower-case equivalents	
string toupper	`string`	`string`
	return a string formed by copying `string` and making any lower-case letters into their upper-case equivalents	

Table A.9: Command Procedures dealing with Strings

procedure	arguments	returns
string trim	**string** ?**trim**?	**string**
	return a string formed by copying **string** except for any occurrences of any character in **trim** found at the beginning and end; **trim** defaults to all white-space characters	
string trimleft	**string** ?**trim**?	**string**
	return a string formed by copying **string** except for any occurrences of any character in **trim** found at the beginning; **trim** defaults to all white-space characters	
string trimright	**string** ?**trim**?	**string**
	return a string formed by copying **string** except for any occurrences of any character in **trim** found at the end; **trim** defaults to all white-space characters	

Table A.9: Command Procedures dealing with Strings (cont.)

procedure	arguments	returns
concat	`list ?list ... ?`	`list`
	return a list formed by copying each element of each `arg`	
join	`list ?separator?`	`string`
	return a string formed by concatenating each element in `list` using `separator`	
lindex	`list index`	`value`
	return the element specified by `index` from `list`	
linsert	`list index arg ?arg ... ?`	`list`
	return a new list formed by copying each `arg` as a new element inserted before the element of `list` specified by `index`	
list	`arg ?arg ... ?`	`list`
	return a new list formed by copying each `arg`	
llength	`list`	`number`
	return the number of elements in `list`	
lrange	`list first last`	`list`
	return a list formed by copying the elements of `list` specified by `first` and `last`	
lreplace	`list first last ?arg ... ?`	`list`
	return a list formed by replacing the elements of `list` specified by `first` and `last` by `args`	
lsearch	`?match? list pattern`	`number`
	if an element in `list` matches `pattern`, return the index of the first such occurrence; otherwise, return -1; if present, `match` is one of "-exact", "-glob", or "-regexp", for exact-matching, *C-shell* glob-matching (the default), or UNIX® regular-expression matching, respectively	
lsort	`?type? ?-command command? ?ordering? list`	`list`
	return a list formed by sorting `list` using the specified `ordering` treating each element as the specified `type`; `type` is one of "-ascii", "-integer", or "-real", and `ordering` is one of "-increasing" or "decreasing"	
split	`string ?separators?`	`list`
	return a list formed by adding a new element whenever a character in `separators` is found in `string`; if no `separators` are specified, split `string` at each character	

Table A.10: Command Procedures dealing with Lists

procedure	arguments	returns
append	`var arg ?arg ... ?`	`value`
	append **args** to **var**, return the new value	
array names	`array-var`	`list`
	return a list containing an element for each **element** in **array-var**	
array size	`array-var`	`integer`
	return the number of elements in **array-var**	
array startsearch	`array-var`	`handle`
	return a search-handle used as an argument for the next four command procedures	
array nextelement	`array-var handle`	`element`
	return the next element for the specified **array-var** and **handle**	
array donesearch	`array-var handle`	the empty string
	delete relationship between **array-var** and **handle**	
array anymore	`array-var handle`	`integer`
	return 1 if any elements in the array have not yet been returned by **array nextelement** for **array-var** and **handle**	
incr	`var ?integer?`	`integer`
	adds **integer** (default 1) to **var**, return the new value	
lappend	`var arg ?arg ... ?`	`value`
	appends each **arg** to **var** as a new element, return the new value	
set	`var ?arg?`	`value`
	set **var** to **arg** (if any), return the new value	
unset	`var ?var ... ?`	the empty string
	delete any knowledge of each **var**	

Table A.11: Command Procedures dealing with Variables

procedure	arguments	returns
break	none	special
	terminate innermost looping-construct	
continue	none	special
	begin new iteration of innermost looping-construct	
for	`init testexpr reinit body`	the empty string
	evaluate `init` once, if `testexpr` is non-zero, evaluate `body` and `reinit`, and then iterate until `testexpr` is zero	
foreach	`var list body`	the empty string
	for each element in `list`, set `var` to the element's value and evaluate `body`	
while	`testexpr body`	the empty string
	if `testexpr` is non-zero, evaluate `body`, and then iterate until `testexpr` is zero	

Table A.12: Command Procedures dealing with Looping

procedure	arguments	returns

if	`testexpr then body \`
	    `?elseif testexpr then body ... ? \`
	    `?else body?`
		`value`

	evaluate expressions until one is non-zero, evaluate the corresponding **body**, and return its value	

switch	`?match? string {`
	    `pattern body`
	    `?pattern body ... ?`
	`}`
		`value`

	find the first **pattern** that matches **string**, evaluate the corresponding **body**, and return its value; where **match** is one of "`-exact`", "`-glob`", or "`-regexp`", for exact-matching (the default), *C-shell* glob-matching, or UNIX® regular-expression matching, respectively; if the corresponding **body** is "`-`", then the following **body** is evaluated	
switch	`?match? string pattern body ?pattern body ... ?`	`value`
	identical to previous command, except that command- and variable-substitution are performed on all **patterns** prior to any comparison	

Table A.13: Command Procedures dealing with Branching

procedure	arguments	returns
catch	`body ?var?`	`integer`
	evaluate `body`, assign return value to `var` on normal or error returns, return `integer` corresponding to return code: 0 for a normal return, 1 for an error return, 2 for a return outside of a procedure, 3 for break, or 4 for continue	
error	`value`	special
	error return from procedure with `value`	
global	`var ?var ... ?`	the empty string
	declares each `var` to be global	
proc	`name list body`	the empty string
	defines `name` to be a command procedure having the specified argument `list` and `body`	
rename	`oldname newname`	the empty string
	change the name of the command procedure `oldname` to `newname`	
return	`?value?`	special
	normal return from procedure with `value`	
uplevel	`?level? arg ?arg ... ?`	`value`
	concatenate `args`, perform command-substitution and variable-substitution, evaluate the result in the execution context `level`, and return the `value`	
upvar	`?level? gvar lvar ?gvar lvar ... ?`	the empty string
	make the local variable `lvar` refer to the variable `gvar` in the execution context `level`	

Table A.14: Command Procedures dealing with Procedures

procedure	arguments	returns
eval	`arg ?arg ... ?`	`value`
	concatenate `args`, perform command-substitution and variable-substitution, evaluate the result, and return the value	
source	`file`	`value`
	evaluate the contents of `file`, return the value of the last statement evaluated	

Table A.15: Miscellaneous Command Procedures

Appendix B

Internet Standards and Documents

Before listing the various Internet documents that relate to network management, it may be instructive to consider how Internet technology is standardized. If you are already familiar with the process, skip to page 470. Otherwise, here's the relevant information, drawn largely intact, from *The Simple Book*.

The technical body that oversees the development of the Internet suite of protocols is termed the *Internet Architecture Board* (IAB). There are two subsidiary bodies of the IAB: the *Internet Engineering Task Force* (IETF), which is responsible for short-term engineering and standards-setting; and, the *Internet Research Task Force* (IRTF), which is responsible for longer-term research. Each task force is managed by steering groups, namely the Internet Engineering Steering Group (IESG), and the Internet Research Steering Group (IRSG), respectively. The IAB and IESG, per se, produce very few documents. Any person or group can design, document, implement, and test a protocol for use in the Internet suite. The IAB requires that protocols be documented in the *Request for Comments* (RFC) series, a convenient place for the dissemination of ideas. Protocol authors are encouraged to use the RFC mechanism regardless of whether they expect their protocol to become an Internet-standard.

Each RFC is assigned a number by the *RFC Editor*. If the text of the RFC is revised, a new number is assigned. In order to prevent confusion, if an RFC supersedes or updates any previous RFCs, this is clearly stated on the cover of the newer RFC (and the RFC index file is annotated accordingly). In addition to the RFC Editor, there is an *Internet Assigned Numbers Authority* (IANA), that's responsible for keeping the authoritative list of values used in the Internet suite of protocols (e.g., protocol numbers).

In addition to RFCs, there is a second set of documents, the *Internet Draft* series. These documents are produced by working groups in the IETF, and have no standardization status whatsoever, being viewed only as work in progress. At some point, if an Internet Draft matures (usually after some revision), it may be considered for standardization. In fact, Internet Drafts are not archival documents. They are available for a relatively short period of time (at most six months), and are then usually removed. Finally, it should be noted that vendor product and user procurement literature should cite only RFCs and *not* Internet Drafts. In particular, note that the phrase "adherence to an Internet Draft" is oxymoronic.

Internet Standards

The IESG assigns to each RFC a "standardization state". The vast majority of RFCs are termed *informational* — they enjoy no level of standardization status at all. That is, the majority of RFCs are research notes intended for discussion. In order to reduce confusion, the RFC Editor has introduced a second document series, the standard (STD) series [92]. This series is composed of RFCs which are full standards in the Internet community.

[93] describes the Internet standardization process. For our purposes, only the highlights are of interest: If an RFC is placed on the *standards track*, it must progress through three states: from a *proposed* standard, to a *draft* standard, and finally to a (full) *Internet-standard*. At each stage, the RFC is reviewed along with implementation and deployment experience. In between each step, proponents of the document are given up to two years to demonstrate implementability and usefulness. To transit from proposed to draft standard, there must be significant experience with implementation, and two independent im-

plementations (with preferably at least one openly-available reference implementation). Similarly, to progress to full standard, there must be several independent implementations, along with extensive deployment, and considerable interoperability experience. During the course of each review, changes may be made to the documents. Depending on the severity of the changes, the document is either re-issued at its current state, or is reduced back to a *proposed* standard, and the appropriate deadline is set once again.

It is critical to observe that implementation, deployment, and interoperability are all important criteria that are considered as a document progresses through the Internet standardization process. Further, note that an openly-available reference implementation is also required in order to foster understanding and availability.

It shouldn't be surprising, therefore, that the entire standardization process is based on "rough consensus and running code". As eloquently spoken by Dr. David D. Clark, the first chair of the Internet Architecture Board, in a presentation at the July 1992 meeting of the IETF:

> *"We reject kings, presidents, and voting.*
> *We believe in rough consensus and running code."*

Indeed, lock-stepping implementation into the standardization loop has proven an invaluable philosophy in standardizing technology that actually works.

In addition to assigning each RFC a standardization state, a *"protocol" status* is also assigned. This states the level of applicability for the technology documented in the RFC:

required: a system must implement this protocol.

recommended: a system should implement this protocol.

elective: a system may, or may not, implement this protocol. In a given technology area (e.g., routing) there are usually multiple elective protocols.

limited use: a system may implement this protocol only in limited circumstances, because the protocol has a specialized nature, usually of limited functionality.

> **not recommended:** a system shouldn't implement this proto-
> col.

Note that when an RFC is superseded, it is usually termed **historic**.

There is a mailing list for announcements related to the IETF; to subscribe, send a message to:

```
ietf-announce-request@ietf.cnri.reston.va.us
```

Official Standards and Assigned Numbers

The *Internet Official Protocol Standards* document summarizes the positions of all protocols on the standards track. This RFC is issued quarterly with a strong warning to retrieve the next version when the current document reaches its expiration date. As of this writing, the latest version was [94]. As of this reading, that version is obsolete.

In addition, the *Assigned Numbers* document is a registry of assigned values used for various purposes in the Internet suite of protocols [86]. Both documents are periodically updated. As with the rest of the RFC series, the most recent document always takes precedence.

Host and Router Requirements

There has been an ongoing effort to provide technical explanation and expertise in the form of *Internet Router Requirements* and *Internet Host Requirements* documents. Presently, the two documents detailing Internet Host Requirements are stable, and the document detailing Internet Router Requirements has just undergone revision with a new publication due out by 1995.

[95] provides a brief overview to the Internet Host Requirements. There are two Internet Host Requirements documents:

- one dealing with applications issues [35]; and,

- one dealing with communications issues [36].

Further, the original "Internet Gateway Requirements" document [96] is often referenced. Among other things, this document provides guidance on datalink layer issues along with generic IP issues. (Note that the Internet community now uses the term "router" in place of "gateway".)

Although there were many motivations for writing the Internet Requirements documents, the authors find it useful to focus on one key observation:

> *During normal operations, it is difficult to distinguish between mediocre and optimal implementations — it is only when the network comes under stress that quality becomes important.*

This means that proper realization of the Internet suite of protocols requires that an implementor be familiar with the Internet Requirements documents. These documents contain much implementation and fielding experience which can be leveraged into high quality, commercial-grade products. The goal is to maximize the robustness of the Internet in the face of stress.

Request for Comments

RFCs are available in both printed and electronic form. The printed copies are available for a modest fee from the DDN Network Information Center:

Postal: DDN Network Information Center
14200 Park Meadow Drive
Suite 200
Chantilly, VA 22021
US

Phone: +1 800–365–3642
+1 703–802–4535

Mail: nic@nic.ddn.mil

In electronic form, users may use "anonymous" FTP to the host `ds.internic.net` (residing at [`192.20.239.132`]) and retrieve files from the directory "`rfc/`". Other sites also maintain copies of RFCs, e.g.,

ftp.nisc.sri.com
venera.isi.edu
wuarchive.wustl.edu
ftp.concert.net
nis.nsf.net
nisc.jvnc.net
src.doc.ic.ac.uk

Of course, this list might change, but it's a good place to start.

If your site doesn't have IP-connectivity to the Internet community, but does have electronic mail access, you can send an electronic mail message to the electronic mail address

`mailserv@ds.internic.net`

and in the body indicate the RFC number, e.g.,

`SEND rfc/rfc1149.txt`

A reply to your electronic mail message will contain the desired RFC.

If your site has electronic mail access to the Internet community, and you desire notification when new RFCs are published, send a note to the electronic mail address

    rfc-request@nic.ddn.mil

and ask to be added to the RFC notification list.

Internet Drafts

Internet Drafts, which document the work in progress of the IETF, are available only in electronic form. (Recall that Internet Drafts have no standardization status whatsoever.) Use "anonymous" FTP to the host `ds.internic.net` (residing at `[192.20.239.132]`) and retrieve files from the directory `internet-drafts/`. Other sites also maintain copies of Internet Drafts, e.g.,

    munnari.oz.au
    ftp.nisc.sri.com
    nic.nordu.net
    nic.ddn.mil

Of course, this list might change, but it's a good place to start.

If your site doesn't have IP-connectivity to the Internet community, but does have electronic mail access, you can send an electronic mail message to the electronic mail address

    mailserv@ds.internic.net

and in the body indicate the name of the draft, e.g.,

    SEND internet-drafts/draft-ietf-foo-bar-00.txt

A reply to your electronic mail message will contain the desired draft.

If your site has electronic mail access to the Internet community, and you desire notification when new Internet Drafts are published, send a note to the electronic mail address

    ietf-request@ietf.cnri.reston.va.us

and ask to be added to the `ietf` list. Note that other IETF administrative announcements and general discussions by members of the IETF community are also posted to this list.

B.1   Administrative RFCs

The key administrative RFCs are:

RFC	Name	Status
1540	Internet Official Protocol Standards	Required
1340	Assigned Numbers	Required
1122	Host Requirements — Communications	Required
1123	Host Requirements — Applications	Required
1009	Gateway Requirements	Required

Note that these RFCs are periodically updated. As with the rest of the RFC series, the most recent document always takes precedence. In particular, note that the Official Protocols Standards document (in theory) is updated quarterly.

The information which follows is taken from the Official Standards RFC [94], published in October 1993. By the time of this reading, a new version of this RFC will no doubt have been published.

B.2 Core Protocol RFCs

The RFCs pertaining to the core of the Internet suite of protocols are:

RFC	Name	Status
791	Internet Protocol	Required
950	Subnet Extension	Required
919	Broadcast Datagrams	Required
922	Broadcast Datagrams with Subnets	Required
792	Internet Control Message Protocol	Required
1112	Host extensions for IP multicasting	Recommended
768	User Datagram Protocol	Recommended
793	Transmission Control Protocol	Recommended
854	TELNET Protocol	Recommended
855	TELNET Options	Recommended
959	File Transfer Protocol	Recommended
821	Simple Mail Transfer Protocol	Recommended
822	Format of Electronic Mail Messages	Recommended
1049	Content-type header field	Recommended
1119	Network Time Protocol (v2)	Recommended
1034	Domain Name System Concepts and Facilities	Recommended
1035	Domain Name System Implementation and Specification	Recommended
974	Mail Routing and the Domain Name System	Recommended
904	Exterior Gateway Protocol	Recommended
862	Echo Protocol	Recommended

There are also many other Internet standards of a less critical nature:

RFC	Name	Status
1001	NetBIOS over TCP Concepts and Methods	Elective
1002	NetBIOS over TCP Detailed Specifications	Elective
863	Discard Protocol	Elective
864	Character Generator Protocol	Elective
865	Quote of the Day Protocol	Elective
866	Active Users Protocol	Elective
867	Daytime Protocol	Elective
868	Time Protocol	Elective
1350	TFTP Protocol (revision 2)	Elective
1058	Routing Information Protocol	Elective
1006	ISO Transport Services on top of the TCP	Elective

There are also many Internet standards pertaining to transmission of the IP over various media:

RFC	Name	Standard
826	Address Resolution Protocol	Full
891	DC Networks	Full
894	Ethernet Networks	Full
895	Experimental Ethernet Networks	Full
903	Reverse Address Resolution Protocol	Full
907	Wideband Network	Full
1042	IEEE802 Networks	Full
1044	Hyperchannel	Full
1055	Serial Links	Full
1088	NetBIOS	Full
1132	IEEE802 over IPX Networks	Full
1149	Avian Networks	Informational
1201	ARCNET	Full
1209	SMDS	Proposed
1356	X.25 and ISDN	Proposed
1374	HIPPI	Proposed
1390	FDDI	Full
1469	IP multicast over Token Ring	Proposed
1483	ATM encapsulation	Proposed
1577	ATM	Proposed
1490	Frame Relay	Proposed

Note that, although the status of these standards is *elective*, if a device elects to transmit IP datagrams over one of the media above, then it is *required* to use the procedures defined in the relevant RFC(s).

B.3   Network Management RFCs

B.3.1   The Original Framework

The original *Internet-standard Network Management Framework* is defined in these four documents:

RFC	Name	Status
1155	Structure of Management Information	Recommended
1212	Concise MIB Definitions	Recommended
1157	Simple Network Management Protocol	Recommended
1213	Management Information Base II	Recommended

All of these documents are full standards.

In addition, these three documents define transport mappings for SNMPv1 for different protocol suites:

RFC	Name	Status
1418	SNMP over OSI	Recommended
1419	SNMP over AppleTalk	Recommended
1420	SNMP over IPX	Recommended

As of this writing, these three documents are proposed standards.

B.3.2 The SNMPv2 Framework

The new framework is defined in these 12 documents:

RFC	Name	Status
1441	Introduction to SNMPv2	Recommended
1442	SMI for SNMPv2	Recommended
1443	Textual Conventions for SNMPv2	Recommended
1444	Conformance Statements for SNMPv2	Recommended
1445	Administrative Model for SNMPv2	Recommended
1446	Security Protocols for SNMPv2	Recommended
1447	Party MIB for SNMPv2	Recommended
1448	Protocol Operations for SNMPv2	Recommended
1449	Transport Mappings for SNMPv2	Recommended
1450	MIB for SNMPv2	Recommended
1451	Manager-to-Manager MIB	Recommended
1452	Coexistence between SNMPv1 and SNMPv2	Recommended

As of this writing, all of these documents are proposed standards.
Once they achieve full standard status, the documents comprising
the original framework will be obsoleted.

B.3.3 MIB Modules

There are several RFCs which define MIB modules for particular environments:

RFC	Name	Standard
1231	IEEE 802.5 Token Ring Interface Type MIB	Proposed
1239	Reassignment of Experimental MIBs to Standard MIBs	Proposed
1243	AppleTalk® MIB	Proposed
1253	OSPF version 2 MIB	Proposed
1269	BGP version 3 MIB	Proposed
1271	Remote Network Monitoring MIB	Proposed
1285	FDDI Interface Type (SMT 6.2) MIB	Proposed
1304	SMDS Interface Protocol (SIP) Interface Type MIB	Proposed
1315	Frame Relay DTE Interface Type MIB	Proposed
1316	Character Device MIB	Proposed
1317	RS-232 Interface Type MIB	Proposed
1318	Parallel Printer Interface Type MIB	Proposed
1354	SNMP IP Forwarding Table MIB	Proposed
1381	X.25 LAPB MIB	Proposed
1382	X.25 PLP MIB	Proposed
1389	RIP version 2 MIB	Proposed
1406	DS1 Interface Type MIB	Proposed
1407	DS3 Interface Type MIB	Proposed
1414	Identification MIB	Proposed
1461	Multiprotocol Interconnect over X.25 MIB	Proposed
1628	Ether-like Interface Type MIB	Full

1471	PPP Link Control Protocol (LCP) MIB	Proposed
1472	PPP Security Protocols MIB	Proposed
1473	PPP IP Network Control Protocol MIB	Proposed
1474	PPP Bridge Network Control Protocol MIB	Proposed
1493	Bridge MIB	Draft
1512	FDDI Interface Type (SMT 7.3) MIB	Proposed
1513	Token Ring Extensions to RMON MIB	Proposed
1514	Host Resources MIB	Proposed
1515	IEEE 802.3 Medium Attachment Unit (MAU) MIB	Proposed
1516	IEEE 803.3 Repeater MIB	Draft
1525	Source Routing Bridge MIB	Proposed
1559	DECnet Phase IV MIB	Draft
1565	Network Services Monitoring MIB	Proposed
1566	Mail Monitoring MIB	Proposed
1567	X.500 Directory Monitoring MIB	Proposed
1573	Evolution of the Interfaces Group	Proposed
1595	SONET/SDH Interface Type MIB	Proposed
1604	Frame Relay Service MIB	Proposed
1628	Uninterruptible Power Supply MIB	Proposed

All of these documents have a status of "recommended". At present, these MIB modules can be used with either SNMPv1 or SNMPv2. However, during their advancement, they will likely be translated to use SNMPv2's SMI.

B.3.4   Miscellaneous RFCs

There are several RFCs which are either informational or experimental
in nature:

RFC	Name	Status
1187	Bulk Table Retrieval with the SNMP	Experimental
1215	A Convention for Defining Traps for Use with the SNMP	Informational
1224	Techniques for Managing Asynchronously Generated Alerts	Experimental
1592	SNMP Distributed Program Interface	Experimental
1238	CLNS MIB	Experimental
1270	SNMP Communication Services	Informational
1303	A Convention for Describing SNMP-based Agents	Informational
1321	MD5 Message-Digest Algorithm	Informational
1470	A Network Management Tool Catalog	Informational
1503	Automating Administration in SNMPv2 Managers	Informational

Many of these have been obsoleted by the work on SNMPv2, i.e.,
RFCs 1187, 1215, 1224, and 1303 apply only to SNMPv1.

B.3.5 Historic RFCs

Over time, some RFCs have been superseded. If you run across any of these documents, be aware that you are reading "yesterday's news".

RFC	Name	See RFC
1156	Management Information Base I	1213
1161	SNMP over OSI	1418
1227	SNMP MUX Protocol and MIB	
1228	SNMP Distributed Program Interface	1592
1229	Extensions to the generic-interface MIB	1573
1230	IEEE 802.4 Token Bus Interface Type MIB	
1232	DS1 Interface Type MIB	1406
1233	DS3 Interface Type MIB	1407
1252	OSPF version 2 MIB	1253
1283	SNMP over OSI	1418
1284	Ether-Like Interface Type MIB	1628
1286	Bridge MIB	1493, 1525
1289	DECnet Phase IV MIB	1559
1298	SNMP over IPX	1420
1351	SNMP Administrative Model	1445
1352	SNMP Security Protocols	1446
1353	SNMP Party MIB	1447
1368	IEEE 802.3 Repeater MIB	1516
1398	Ether-Like Interface Type MIB	1628
1596	Frame Relay Service MIB	1604

B.4   Network Management Assignments

The Assigned Numbers document contains the registry of all subtrees assigned for network management:

Subtree	Prefix
directory	1.3.6.1.1
mgmt	1.3.6.1.2
mib-2	1.3.6.1.2.1
transmission	1.3.6.1.2.1.10
experimental	1.3.6.1.3
enterprises	1.3.6.1.4.1

The list of enterprise assignments is also available via "anonymous" FTP:

```
host   venera.isi.edu
area   mib
file   snmp-vendors-contacts
mode   ascii
```

As of this writing, over 975 assignments had been made!

B.4.1   Getting an Experimental Assignment

To register a new experiment, one must first coordinate with the *Area Director for Network Management* in the Internet Engineering Steering Group. (The Internet Assigned Numbers Authority can provide this contact information — see page 484.) The Area Director will coordinate with the IANA to request an experimental number.

Once contact is made with the Area Director, a working group of the IETF will be formed (if appropriate) to oversee the experiment. In particular, the working group must author an Internet Draft, defining the experimental MIB. This draft will be made available for public review.

B.4.2 Getting an Enterprise Assignment

Contact the IANA and ask for one.

The IANA maintains a public repository of enterprise-specific MIB modules:

host   `venera.isi.edu`

area   `mib`

Note that MIB modules in the repository are not "registered" in any sense — they are simply available for public inspection (unlike experimental MIB modules which are registered as Internet Drafts).

To submit an enterprise-specific MIB module for publication, mail a copy to:

`mib-checker@isi.edu`

Your MIB module will be automatically run through a MIB compiler and any errors will be reported back to you. Once your module has passed the compiler, the IANA will place it in the repository.

B.5 Contact Information

The RFC Editor can be reached at:

> Postal: Jonathan B. Postel
> RFC Editor
> USC/Information Sciences Institute
> 4676 Admiralty Way
> Marina del Rey, CA 90292-6695
> US

> Phone: +1 310–822–1511

> Mail: postel@isi.edu

The Internet Assigned Numbers Authority can be reached at:

> Postal: Joyce K. Reynolds
> Internet Assigned Numbers Authority
> USC/Information Sciences Institute
> 4676 Admiralty Way
> Marina del Rey, CA 90292-6695
> US

> Phone: +1 310–822–1511

> Mail: iana@isi.edu

Appendix C

Other Resources

If you're interested in learning more, there are several other resources available!

C.1   The Simple Times

The Simple Times is an openly-available publication devoted to the promotion of the Simple Network Management Protocol. In each issue, *The Simple Times* presents: a refereed technical article, an industry comment, and several featured columns:

- Applications and Directions

- Ask Dr. SNMP

- Security and Protocols

- Standards

In addition, some issues include brief announcements, summaries of recent publications, and an activities calendar.

Past technical articles have included:

- A New View on Bulk Retrieval with SNMP

- Sets are Fun: Introducing the SMDS Subscription MIB Module

- An Implementation of SNMP Security

- Customer Network Management of the InterSpan Frame Relay Service

- Accomplishing Performance Management with SNMP

- An Introduction to SNMP MIB Compilers

- Toward Useful — and Standardized — SNMP Management Applications

- Windows SNMP: an SNMP API for MS Windows Applications

- Implementation Experiences for SNMPv2

- Service Management Architecture

- Network Design using the RMON MIB

The Simple Times is openly-available. You are free to copy, distribute, or cite its contents. However, any use must credit both the contributor and *The Simple Times*. Further, this publication is distributed on an "as is" basis, without warranty. Neither the

publisher nor any contributor shall have any liability to any person or
entity with respect to any liability, loss, or damage caused or alleged
to be caused, directly or indirectly, by the information contained in
The Simple Times.

Subscription Information

The Simple Times is available via electronic mail in three editions:
PostScript, *MIME* (the multi-media 822 mail format), and *richtext*
(a simple page description language). For more information, send a
message to

```
st-subscriptions@simple-times.org
```

with a `Subject` line of

```
Subject: help
```

In addition, *The Simple Times* has numerous hard-copy distribution outlets. Contact your favorite SNMP vendor and see if they carry
it. If not, contact the publisher and ask for a list:

Postal:	*The Simple Times*
	c/o Dover Beach Consulting, Inc.
	420 Whisman Court
	Mountain View, CA 94043–2186
Tel:	+1 415–968–1052
Fax:	+1 415–968–2510
E-mail:	`st-editorial@simple-times.org`
ISSN:	1060–6068

Submission Information

The Simple Times solicits high-quality articles of technology and comment. Technical articles are refereed to ensure that the content is
marketing-free. By definition, commentaries reflect opinion and, as
such, are reviewed only to the extent required to ensure commonly-
accepted publication norms.

The Simple Times also solicits announcements of products and
services, publications, and events. These contributions are reviewed

only to the extent required to ensure commonly-accepted publication norms.

Submissions are accepted only in electronic form. A submission consists of ASCII text. (Technical articles are also allowed to reference encapsulated PostScript figures.) Submissions may be sent to the contact address above, either via electronic mail or via magnetic media (using either 8-mm `tar` tape, $\frac{1}{4}$-in `tar` cartridge-tape, or $3\frac{1}{2}$-in MS-DOS floppy-diskette).

Each submission must include the author's full name, title, affiliation, postal and electronic mail addresses, telephone, and fax numbers. Note that by initiating this process, the submitting party agrees to place the contribution into the public domain.

C.2 Implementations

There are several openly-available implementations of SNMP. Following are the announcements for various packages, as supplied by the contributors and edited to a common format by the authors. Please note that this information may not be current at the time you read this. Also, note that this listing does not necessarily imply any endorsement on the part of the authors (or their publisher's attorneys).

C.2.1 4BSD/ISODE SNMPv2

A SNMPv2 implementation available for the ISODE 8.0 release.

The 4BSD/ISODE SNMPv2 package is a relatively complete implementation of SNMPv2, with these exceptions:

administrative model: The administrative model is completely implemented, with the exception that no privacy functions are included. Note that if you specify view entries which provide instance-level access control, then this has a big performance impact on the agent.

structure of management information: All macros are fully recognized.

textual conventions: Although the `TEXTUAL-CONVENTION` macro is fully recognized, the `DISPLAY-HINT` clause is used only for textual (non-numeric) syntaxes.

conformance statements: Although all macros are fully recognized, very little semantic scrutiny is made of invocations of the `MODULE-COMPLIANCE` macro.

transport mappings: The `snmpUDPdomain` is the only transport mapping provided.

managed objects: All SNMPv2 MIB objects are implemented.

protocol operations: The agent implements all operations; however, responses to the bulk operation are not always as large as they could be.

manager-to-manager: The manager doesn't implement any of these objects.

coexistence (proxy):   The agent supports proxy operations for both the `rfc1157Domain` and `snmpUDPdomain` transport domains. This allows the SNMPv2 agent to act as a front-end for these other devices, termed *proxy-targets*. In addition, if you want to export a MIB module, you do this by writing your own proxy-target program, and then defining the appropriate proxy relationships.

Finally, you can write your own bilingual management applications using either *gawk* or Tcl. If you have a choice, you should always favor use of the Tcl-based environment, as the *gawk* environment is no longer maintained.

Acknowledgements

Originally, this work was partially supported by the US Defense Advanced Research Projects Agency and the US Air Force Systems Command under contract number F30602–88–C-0016. Marshall T. Rose wrote the original (insecure) 4BSD/ISODE SNMP package.

David L. Partain of the Department of Computer and Information Science at Linköping University, Sweden, added most of the administrative facilities as a part of his Masters work at the University of Tennessee, Knoxville. Dr. Jeffrey D. Case of SNMP Research supervised his work, and Keith McCloghrie formerly of Hughes LAN Systems provided implementation guidance.

The MD5 implementation used in this package is taken from RFC-1321, and is hereby identified as "derived from the RSA Data Security, Inc. MD5 Message-Digest Algorithm".

Conditions of Use

This package is openly-available but is NOT in the public domain. You are allowed and encouraged to take this software and use it for any lawful purpose. However, as a condition of use, you are required to hold harmless all contributors.

Permission to use, copy, modify, and distribute this software and its documentation for any lawful purpose and without fee is hereby granted, provided that this notice be retained unaltered, and that the name of any contributors shall not be used in advertising or publicity pertaining to distribution of the software without specific written prior permission. No contributor makes any representations about the suitability of this software for any purpose. It is provided "as is" without express or implied warranty.

Discussion

There is a mailing list — to subscribe, send a message to:

```
isode-snmpV2-request@cs.utk.edu
```

Availability

The software is available ONLY via anonymous FTP. If you don't have
FTP access to the Internet, you are out of luck — NO EXCEPTIONS.

```
host   ftp.ics.uci.edu
area   mrose/isode-snmpV2/
file   isode-snmpV2.tar.Z
mode   binary
```

C.2.2 Beholder, The Next Generation (BTNG)

An RMON agent for SunOS 4.1, ULTRIX, and OS/2.

The *BTNG* distribution contains a faithful implementation of the RMON standard developed by the DNPAP group of the Delft University of Technology. It implements a software-only Ethernet monitor for the SunOS 4.1.x, ULTRIX and OS/2 platforms, conforming closely to RFC 1271.

BTNG implements all collectors described in RFC 1271, plus some collectors developed by the DNPAP group. The extra collectors include a traffic-generating collector, a PING collector, and Host and Matrix collectors for IP, UDP, and TCP. When used with a set of SNMP tools like *Tricklet* (see page 506), *BTNG* can be used to experiment with network monitoring and RMON monitors. *BTNG* was developed as a publicly-available reference implementation of the RMON standard, and can be used during RMON conformance testing and developments for the upcoming RMON II standard.

Conditions of Use

BTNG is distributed under the GNU copyleft license agreement.

Discussion

For further information, contact:

        Jan van Oorschot <J.P.M.vOorschot@et.tudelft.nl>

Availability

This package is available via anonymous FTP:

host	`dnpap.et.tudelft.nl`
area	`pub/btng`
files	`btng-4.1.tar.gz`
	`btng-4.1.tar.zip`
mode	`binary`

C.2.3   CMU SNMP/SNMPv2

A portable development platform for SNMP and SNMPv2 as well as a collection of network management tools.

The package includes source code for:

- a portable SNMP/SNMPv2 library;

- a portable SNMP/SNMPv2 (bilingual) agent suitable for general-purpose or embedded-system platforms;

- a portable mid-level agent for manager-to-manager applications;

- an SNMP/SNMPv2 API for bilingual applications;

- an interface to the *Tcl/Tk* application programming language; and,

- a collection of network management applications.

Acknowledgements

This package was developed by Carnegie Mellon University for its own use and to help spread SNMP technology into the marketplace. This package continues to enjoy major support from CMU as well as the community. The SNMP Security implementation had major support from Lexcel. Other contributors to the code include TGV, BBN, and Shiva. Portions of the code were derived from the RSA Data Security, Inc. MD5 Message-Digest Algorithm.

Conditions of Use

This package is freely-available, but is not in the public-domain. This code may be used for any purpose, for-profit or otherwise, without fee. Derivative works may provide further restrictions or charge fees, but must leave the original copyrights intact and must give credit to the contributors in supporting documentation.

Availability

This package is available via anonymous FTP:

host	`lancaster.andrew.cmu.edu`
area	`pub/snmp-dist`
file	`README`
mode	`ascii`

The `README` file contains instructions as to the current version and file name of the latest release. Any *tar* file included in this directory must be retrieved in binary mode.

C.2.4   Fergie and Gobbler

Ethernet monitor and frame grabber for MS-DOS.

The *Fergie* distribution contains two Ethernet monitoring packages developed by the DNPAP group of the Delft University of Technology. The first package is *Fergie*, an SNMP-able Ethernet monitor for MS-DOS. The second package is *Gobbler*, a frame grabber and viewer, also for the MS-DOS platform. Both packages require a standard PC with a dedicated Ethernet interface coupled with the publicly-available packet driver network software.

Fergie monitors the Ethernet network, reporting statistics like network load, frame size distribution and a source/destination matrix. The statistics can be viewed on screen or can be collected over the network using SNMP. *Fergie* implements a non-standard MIB, since development of *Fergie* and the RMON standard overlapped in time.

Gobbler allows the user to define filters and time limits before the grabbing of frames from the network is started. Frames grabbed are stored in a file, and can be decoded and viewed in a user-friendly windowing environment after the trace has finished. *Gobbler* has a partial knowledge of the IP, IPX, and DECnet protocols. Frames containing other protocols are displayed as hexadecimal dumps.

At the moment, development of *Fergie* by the DNPAP group is stopped in favor of the development of the *BTNG* distribution. As a service to the Internet community, both binaries and full source code are made available to enable maintenance and further developments.

Conditions of Use

Fergie and *Gobbler* are distributed under the GNU copyleft license agreement.

Discussion

There is a mailing list — to subscribe, send a message to:

```
fergie-request@dnpap.et.tudelft.nl
```

For further information, contact:

```
Jan van Oorschot <J.P.M.vOorschot@et.tudelft.nl>
```

Availability

This package is available via anonymous FTP:

host	`dnpap.et.tudelft.nl`
area	`pub/btng`
files	`frgbin2.zip`
	`frgsrc2.zip`
mode	`binary`

C.2.5   Network Operation Center On-Line (NOCOL)

A network monitoring package that runs on UNIX® platforms. It can monitor various network variables such as ICMP or RPC reachability, nameservers, ethernet load, port reachability, host performance, SN-MP traps, modem line usage, AppleTalk® routes and Novell services, BGP peers, and so on.

The software consists of a number of monitoring agents that poll various parameters (from any system) and puts them into a common format. All the monitors have a common display and postprocessing interface (such as logging, notification, and so on). The design also allows running just one set of monitoring agents and *any* number of display agents, and all of the displays see the same consistent set of data. Additionally, each event is assigned a pre-determined severity which is gradually escalated, thus preventing false alarms and a customized priority notification based on the severity. The severity levels range from critical thru informational, and each event typically steps through each one of these severity levels until it reaches its maximum allowed level.

The display uses UNIX® *curses* screen management and can thus run on a large variety of terminals. The user running the display can select the minimum display priority — only events above this minimum priority level are displayed.

The package also provides logging of events and report generation. To date, the various monitoring agents developed are:

- IP ICMP monitor (using *ping* or *multiping*);

- OSI reachability monitor (using the OSI *ping*);

- RPC portmapper monitor (using *rpcping*);

- Ethernet load monitor (bandwidth and pps);

- TCP port monitor;

- Unix host performance monitor (distributed monitoring of disks, memory, swap, load, nfs, network interface);

- SNMP trap monitor;

- IP data throughput monitor;

- Nameserver (*named*) monitor;

- Monitor for usage of terminal server modem lines in use;

- AppleTalk® route monitor (for Cisco routers);

- Novell service monitor;

- BGP peer status (if not connected); and,

A *perl* interface has been provided for developing additional monitors. It is easy to add additional monitors to the package.

Conditions of Use

None.

Discussion

There is a mailing list — to subscribe, send a message to: to subscribe, send a message to:

```
nocol-users-request@jvnc.net
```

The package has been developed and maintained by:

```
Vikas Aggarwal <vikas@navya.com>
```

Please contact him for further information.

Availability

This package is available via anonymous FTP:

```
host  ftp.jvnc.net
area  jvncnet-packages/nocol
file  README
mode  ascii
```

C.2.6 SMIC

A MIB compiler for SNMP version 1.

The package will run on MS-DOS and many versions of UNIX®, and includes source code for a MIB compiler and a MIB stripper, along with "corrected" versions of MIB modules from various RFCs. Compiler features include:

- multiple input files;

- concise MIB format (RFC 1212);

- concise trap format (RFC 1215);

- multiple MIB modules;

- items in IMPORTS;

- textual conventions;

- alias assignments for modules and object names;

- selective checking of MIB constructs;

- extensive MIB syntax checking and continuation of syntax checking after syntax errors;

- extensive checking of MIB consistency;

- multiple output options (including `mosy` compatible output); and,

- environment variable to locate "included" files.

Conditions of Use

The *smic* package is "freely-available" but it is not public domain. The following is the copyright and rights to use message for *smic*:

Discussion

For further information, contact:

```
David Perkins <dperkins@synoptics.com>
```

Availability

This package is available via anonymous FTP:

host	`ftp.synoptics.com`
area	`eng/mibcompiler`
file	`README`
mode	`ascii`

C.2.7 snacc

A freely-distributable ASN.1 compiler that includes all source code
(C/yacc/lex) and documentation.

snacc generates C or C++ source code for BER encode and decode
routines as well as print and free routines for each type in the given
ASN.1 modules. Alternatively, *snacc* can produce type tables that
can be used for table based/interpreted encoding and decoding. The
type table based methods tend to be slower than their C or C++
counterparts but they usually use less memory (table size vs. C/C++
object code).

Features of *snacc* include:

- parses CCITT ASN.1 '90 including subtype notation;

- can compile and link inter-dependent ASN.1 modules (`IMPORTS`
  and `EXPORTS`);

- some X.400 and SNMP macros are parsed;

- `ANY DEFINED BY` is supported via the SNMP `OBJECT-TYPE`
  macro;

- macro *definitions* are parsed but are not processed;

- value notation is parsed (`OBJECT IDENTIFIER`, `INTEGER`s and
  `BOOLEAN`s are translated to C/C++ values); and,

- optionally supports ";" separated type or value definitions.

Acknowledgements

snacc was written by Mike Sample while doing his M.Sc. at the University of British Columbia, Canada.

Conditions of Use

snacc is distributed under the GNU copyleft license agreement.

Discussion

For further information, contact:

        snacc-bugs@cs.ubc.ca

Availability

This package is available via anonymous FTP:

host	`ftp.cs.ubc.ca`
area	`pub/local/src/snacc`
file	`README`
mode	`ascii`

C.2.8   tclsnmp2

An SNMP API based upon John Ousterhout's *Tcl/Tk* toolkit. With this toolkit, we provide the ability for both graphical and script-based applications to be programmed at a very high level. Because *Tcl* already contains an interpreter, higher-level abstractions can be easily layered on top of this API.

- Documentation is provided.

- Supports both SNMPv1 and SNMPv2.

- Independent MIB, SNMP, and Entity (SNMPv2 party/context) modules. This allows for integration into environments that implement their own MIB or Entity databases.

- The SNMP module is designed for portability across lower-level SNMP API's. NYSERnet SNMPv1 and CMU SNMPv2 adaptation layers are included.

- Queries can be processed synchronously or asynchronously, allowing for simple execution of individual queries, or parallel execution of queries in the background.

- Full sanity-checking of `get`, `get-next`, `get-bulk` replies is available, providing the user with a simple good/bad indication for each variable.

- Instance ID's extracted and checked for `get-next` and `get-bulk` responses.

- Queries can be pre-packaged for later use, allowing a complete query to be invoked with a very short command.

- Full support for `DISPLAY-HINT`s.

- Queries can specify custom rendering instructions for variable values — a *Tcl* script can be automatically invoked to translate the raw SNMP value to something more useful.

- All MIB information is available, including all information provided in the standard macros, such as `TEXTUAL-CONVENTION`, `MODULE-IDENTITY`, etc.

Conditions of Use

Portions are Copyright 1993, 1994 Digital Equipment Corporation. A no-fee, no-license copyright and hold-harmless disclaimer are in force on these portions.

Discussion

There is a WWW server; contact:

`http://www.research.digital.com/nsl/projects/tclsnmp2/home.html`

For further information, contact:

```
Glenn Trewitt <trewitt@pa.dec.com>
Poul-Henning Kamp <phk@login.dkuug.dk>
```

Availability

This package is available via anonymous FTP:

host	`gatekeeper.dec.com`
area	`pub/DEC/NSL/tclsnmp2`
file	`README`
mode	`ascii`

C.2.9   Tricklet

A *perl*-based SNMP tool for UNIX® or OS/2.

The *Tricklet* distribution contains a full set of SNMP command line utilities for the UNIX®-based platform, developed by the DNPAP group of the Delft University of Technology. It supports SNMP version 1 and displays results using variable names found in MIB definition files.

Tricklet supports the SNMP **set**, **get**, **get-next**, and **trap** operators. These functions are available from the UNIX® command prompt, or as a daemon from scripting environments like *sh* and *perl*. Extensive examples are included to demonstrate the use of *Tricklet* in *perl* scripts. Special attention is given to the interrogation of RMON monitors like the *BTNG* monitor.

Conditions of Use

Tricklet is distributed under the GNU copyleft license agreement.

Discussion

There is a mailing list — to subscribe, send a message to:

> `btng-request@dnpap.et.tudelft.nl`

For further information, contact:

> `Jan van Oorschot <J.P.M.vOorschot@et.tudelft.nl>`

Availability

This package is available via anonymous FTP:

host	`dnpap.et.tudelft.nl`
area	`pub/btng`
file	`tricklet-3.2.tar.gz`
mode	`binary`

C.2.10   UT-snmpV2

An SNMPv2 implementation.

The network management group at the University of Twente is developing SNMPv2 software for educational purposes. This development is motivated by the desire:

- to improve understanding of SNMPv2;

- to improve knowledge of protocol implementation; and,

- to learn from contacts with the community.

The software is written in GNU-C and tested on SUN-SPARC workstations.

The main difference between *UT-snmpV2* and other implementations is the programming interface — the API hides most of the complexity of SNMPv2 from management applications. Writers of management applications need little knowledge of SNMPv2; applications use just a small number of API calls. The implementation structure is one in which a single SNMPv2 protocol machine (a single UNIX® process) serves multiple management applications (multiple UNIX® processes). It is possible to add and remove management applications in a dynamic fashion. Proxy agents can be seen as special applications: the writer of a proxy agent does not need to know the details of SNMPv2.

Conditions of Use

None.

Discussion

There is a WWW server; contact:

> `http://snmp.cs.utwente.nl:8001/snmp/html/homepage.html`

For further information, contact:

> `Aiko Pras <snmp@cs.utwente.nl>`

Availability

This package is available via anonymous FTP:

```
host   ftp.cs.utwente.nl
area   pub/src/snmp
file   ut-snmpV2-v1_0.tar
mode   binary
```

C.2.11 Xnetdb

A network monitoring tool based on X Window System and SNMP which also has integrated database and statistic viewing capabilities.

Xnetdb will determine and display the status of routers and circuits it has been told to monitor by querying the designated sites and displaying the result. Additionally, it has an integrated database functionality in that it can display additional information about a site or circuit such as the equipment at the site, the contact person(s) for the site, and other useful information. Finally, it can gather designated statistical information about a circuit or router and display it on demand.

Conditions of Use

None.

Discussion

There is a mailing list — to subscribe, send a message to:

    xnetdb-request@oar.net

For further information, contact:

    Henry Clark <henryc@oar.net>

Availability

This package is available via anonymous FTP:

                host   ftp.oar.net
                area   pub/src/xnetdb
                file   xnetdb.tar.Z
                mode   binary

C.3   Automated MIB Services

There are two automated MIB compilation services. As might be expected, these services are provided "as is" without express or implied warranty.

If you just want to syntax-check a MIB module, then send an electronic mail message containing your MIB module to:

```
mosy@dbc.mtview.ca.us
```

Your MIB module will be automatically run through a MIB compiler and any errors will be reported back to you.

Similarly, if you want to convert a MIB module written using SNMPv2's SMI to an equivalent form for SNMPv1, use:

```
mib-v2tov1@dbc.mtview.ca.us
```

Your MIB module will be converted and sent back to you.

Glossary

abstract syntax: a description of a data type that's independent of machine-oriented structures and restrictions.

Abstract Syntax Notation One: the OSI language for describing abstract syntax.

access mode: (SNMPv1) the level of authorization implied by an SNMP community.

access policy: (SNMPv2) the operations allowed when one party asks another party to perform an operation on the objects in a context.

ACK: the *acknowledgement* bit in a TCP segment.

active open: the sequence of events occurring when an application-entity directs TCP to establish a connection.

address class: a method used to determine the boundary between the network and host portions of an IP address.

address-mask: a 32–bit quantity indicating which bits in an IP address refer to the network portion.

address resolution: a means for mapping network layer addresses onto media-specific addresses.

Address Resolution Protocol: the protocol in the Internet suite of protocols used to map IP addresses onto Ethernet (and other media) addresses.

administrative model: a scheme for defining both authentication and authorization policies.

Advanced Research Projects Agency: see *Defense Advanced Research Projects Agency.*

agent: see *network management agent.*

American National Standards Institute: the US national standardization body. ANSI is a member of ISO.

ANSI: see *American National Standards Institute.*

API: see *Application Programmer's Interface.*

application services: the services collectively offered by the upper four layers of the OSI model.

Applications Programmer's Interface: a set of calling conventions defining how a service is invoked through a software package.

ARP: see *Address Resolution Protocol.*

ARPA: an agency of the US Department of Defense that sponsors high-risk, high-payoff research. The Internet suite of protocols was originally developed under ARPA auspices.

ASN.1: see *Abstract Syntax Notation One.*

authentication: the process whereby a message is associated with a particular originating entity.

authentication entity: (SNMPv1) that portion of an SNMP agent responsible for verifying that an SNMP entity is a member of the community to which it claims to belong. This portion of the agent is also responsible for encoding/decoding SNMP messages according to the authentication algorithm of a given community.

authorization: the process whereby an access policy determines whether an entity is allowed to perform an operation.

awesome get-bulk operator: what more need be said?

Basic Encoding Rules: the OSI language for describing transfer syntax.

BER: see *Basic Encoding Rules.*

broadcast address: a media-specific or IP address referring to all stations on a medium.

broadcasting: the act of sending to the broadcast address.

C: the *C programming language.*

Case Diagram: a pictorial representation of the relationship between counter objects in a MIB group.

CCITT: see *International Telegraph and Telephone Consultative Committee.*

checksum: an arithmetic sum used to verify data integrity.

CL-mode: see *connection-less mode.*

CLNS: *connectionless-mode network service*

CLTS: *connectionless-mode transport service*

CMIP: see *Common Management Information Protocol.* Sometimes confused with the *(overly) Complex Management Information Protocol.* Of course, it doesn't exist.

CMIP over TCP: a mapping of the OSI network management framework to management of networks based on the Internet suite of protocols. Commonly thought of as "an idea whose time has come and gone".

CMIS: see *Common Management Information Service.*

CMISE: see *Common Management Information Service Element.*

CMOT: see *CMIP over TCP.*

CO-mode: see *connection-oriented mode.*

Common Management Information Protocol: the OSI protocol for network management.

Common Management Information Service: the service offered by CMIP.

Common Management Information Service Element: the application service element responsible for exchanging network management information.

community: (SNMPv1) an administrative relationship between SNMP entities.

community name: (SNMPv1) see *community string*.

community profile: (SNMPv1) that portion of the managed objects on an agent that a member of the community is allowed to manipulate.

community string: (SNMPv1) an opaque string of octets identifying a community.

connection: a logical binding between two or more users of a service.

connection-less mode: a service that has a single phase involving control mechanisms, such as addressing, in addition to data transfer.

connection-oriented mode: a service that has three distinct phases: *establishment*, in which two or more users are bound to a connection; *data transfer*, in which data is exchanged between the users; and, *release*, in which the binding is terminated.

CONS: *connection-oriented network service*

context: (SNMPv2) a collection of object resources.

COTS: *connection-oriented transport service*

DARPA: see *Defense Advanced Research Projects Agency*.

DARPA Internet: see *Internet*.

data: (imprecise usage) see *user-data*.

data link layer: that portion of an OSI system responsible for transmission, framing, and error control over a single communications link.

datagram: a self-contained unit of data transmitted independently of other datagrams.

default route: when sending an IP datagram, an entry in the routing table which will be used if no other route is appropriate.

Defense Advanced Research Projects Agency: see *Advanced Research Projects Agency*.

device: a network element of some kind.

direct routing: the process of sending an IP datagram when the destination resides on the same IP network (or IP subnet) as the sender.

DNS: see *Domain Name System.*

DNS-connected: the subset of the Internet community which can exchange electronic mail.

domain: an administrative entity responsible for naming entities.

domain name: an administratively-assigned name identifying a domain.

Domain Name System: the application protocol offering naming service in the Internet suite of protocols.

dotted decimal notation: see *dotted quad notation.*

dotted quad notation: a convention for writing IP addresses in textual format, e.g., "`192.103.140.1`".

ECMA: see *European Computer Manufacturers Association.*

EGP: see *Exterior Gateway Protocol.*

end-system: a network device performing functions from all layers of the OSI model. End-systems are commonly thought of as hosting applications.

end-to-end services: the services collectively offered by the lower three layers of the OSI model.

enterprise MIB: a MIB module defined in the enterprise-specific portion of the Internet management space.

ES: see *end-system.*

European Computer Manufacturers Association: a group of computer vendors that has performed substantive pre-standardization work for OSI.

Exterior Gateway Protocol: a (deprecated) reachability protocol used by routers in a two-level internet.

experimental MIB: a MIB module defined in the experimental portion of the Internet management space.

External Data Representation: a transfer syntax defined by Sun Microsystems, Inc.

Federal Research Internet: see *Internet*.

File Transfer Protocol: the application protocol offering file service in the Internet suite of protocols.

FIN: the *finish* bit in a TCP segment.

flow control: the mechanism whereby a receiver informs a sender how much data it is willing to accept.

fragment: an IP datagram containing only a portion of the user-data from a larger IP datagram.

fragmentation: the process of breaking an IP datagram into smaller parts, such that each fragment can be transmitted in whole on a given physical medium.

FTP: see *File Transfer Protocol*.

fully-qualified domain name: a domain name containing the complete path of labels to the root of the naming tree.

gateway: (Internet usage) a router; also, (imprecise usage) an entity responsible for complex mappings, usually at the application layer.

hardware address: see *media address*.

header: (imprecise usage) see *protocol control information*.

host: (Internet usage) an end-system.

host-identifier: that portion of an IP address identifying a host on the IP network.

host-number: that portion of a subnetted IP address identifying a host-number on the subnet.

IAB: see *Internet Architecture Board*.

IANA: see *Internet Assigned Numbers Authority*.

ICMP: see *Internet Control Message Protocol*.

IEEE: see *Institute of Electrical and Electronics Engineers*.

IESG: see *Internet Engineering Steering Group*.

IETF: see *Internet Engineering Task Force.*

IFIP: see *International Federation for Information Processing.*

indirect routing: the process of sending an IP datagram to a router for (ultimate) forwarding to the destination.

instance: see *object instance.*

instance-identifier: a means of identifying an instance of a particular object type.

Institute of Electrical and Electronics Engineers: a professional organization which, as a part of its services to the community, performs some pre-standardization work for OSI.

interface layer: the layer in the Internet suite of protocols responsible for transmission on a single physical network.

intermediate-system: a network device performing functions from the lower three layers of the OSI model. Intermediate-systems are commonly thought of as routing data for end-systems.

International Federation for Information Processing: a research organization that performs substantive pre-standardization work for OSI. IFIP is noted for having formalized the original MHS (X.400) model.

International Organization for Standardization: the organization that produces many of the world's standards. OSI is only one of many areas standardized by ISO/IEC.

International Standards Organization: there is no such thing. See *International Organization for Standardization.*

International Telecommunications Union: a body comprising the national Postal, Telephone, and Telegraph (PTT) administrations.

International Telephone and Telegraph Consultative Committee: see *International Telecommunications Union.*

internet: (Internet usage) a network in the OSI sense; historically termed a *catenet* — a concatenated set of networks. The Internet is the largest internet in existence.

Internet: a large collection of connected networks running the Internet suite of protocols.

Internet Architecture Board: the technical body overseeing the development of the Internet suite of protocols.

Internet Assigned Numbers Authority: the entity responsible for assigning numbers in the Internet suite of protocols.

Internet Community: anyone, anywhere, who uses the Internet suite of protocols.

Internet Control Message Protocol: a simple reporting protocol for IP.

Internet Drafts: a means of documenting the work in progress of the IETF.

Internet Engineering Steering Group: the group coordinating the activities of the IETF, and which is responsible for standards-setting in the Internet.

Internet Engineering Task Force: a task force of the Internet Architecture Board charged with resolving the short-term needs of the Internet.

internet layer: the layer in the Internet suite of protocols responsible for providing transparency over both the topology of the internet and the transmission media used in each physical network.

Internet Protocol: the network protocol offering a connectionless-mode network service in the Internet suite of protocols.

Internet suite of protocols: a collection of computer-communication protocols originally developed under DARPA sponsorship. The Internet suite of protocols is currently the solution of choice for open networking.

Internet-standard MIB: (SNMPv1) RFC 1213.

Internet-standard Network Management Framework: (SNMPv1) RFCs 1155, 1212, 1213, and 1157.

Internet-standard SMI: (SNMPv1) RFC 1155, 1212.

IP: see *Internet Protocol.*

IP address: a 32–bit quantity used to represent a point of attachment in an internet.

IP-connected: the subset of the Internet community which can exchange IP-based traffic.

IS: either *intermediate-system* or *International Standard*, depending on context. In the latter case, such a document is named as "ISO/IEC number", if it represents work under Joint Technical Committee 1; otherwise, it is named as "ISO number".

ISO Development Environment: a research tool developed to study the upper-layers of OSI. It is an unfortunate historical coincidence that the first three letters of ISODE are "ISO." This isn't an acronym for the International Organization for Standardization, but rather three letters which, when pronounced in English, produce a pleasing sound.

ISO/IEC: see *International Organization for Standardization*.

ISODE: see *ISO Development Environment*.

ITU: see *International Telecommunications Union*.

kernel dive: the process of reading data structures out of the UNIX® kernel to determine the state of its protocol entities.

LAN: see *local area network*.

leaf object: an object type defined for which there are no objects with a subordinate name assigned. In particular, tables and rows are not leaf objects.

lexicographic ordering: a collation scheme.

local area network: any one of a number of technologies providing high-speed, low-latency transfer and being limited in geographic size.

loosely-coupled clock: a notion of time whose value is imprecisely coordinated by two or more entities.

managed device: see *managed node*.

managed node: a device containing a network management agent implementation.

managed object: a unit of management information.

management framework: (SNMPv1) see *Internet-standard Network Management Framework.*

Management Information Base: a collection of objects that can be accessed via a network management protocol. See *Structure of Management Information.*

management protocol: see *network management protocol.*

management station: see *network management station.*

manager: (imprecise usage) an application residing on a network management station.

maximum transmission unit: the largest amount of user-data (e.g., the largest size of an IP datagram) that can be sent in a single frame on a particular medium.

media address: the address of a physical interface.

media device: a low-level device that doesn't use a protocol at the internet layer as its primary function.

MIB: see *Management Information Base.*

MIB module: a collection of related managed object definitions.

MIB view: a collection of managed objects realized by an agent which is visible to a management application.

MIB-I: the predecessor to MIB-II.

MIB-II: see *Internet-standard MIB.*

MTU: see *maximum transmission unit.*

multi-homed: a host or router with an attachment to more than one IP network.

name: an identity associated with an entity of some kind. In the context of an IP network, a name is a textual identifier.

name server: an entity which maps a name to its associated attributes.

naming authority: an administrative entity having the authority to assign names within a given domain.

National Bureau of Standards: see *National Institute of Standards and Technology.*

National Institute of Standards and Technology: the branch of the U.S Department of Commerce charged with keeping track of standardization. Previously known as the *National Bureau of Standards.*

NBS: see *National Bureau of Standards.*

network: a collection of subnetworks connected by intermediate-systems and populated by end-systems; also, (Internet usage) a single subnetwork or a related set of subnetworks in the OSI sense.

network byte order: the Internet-standard ordering of the bytes corresponding to numeric values.

network layer: that portion of an OSI system responsible for data transfer across the network, independent of both the media comprising the underlying subnetworks and the topology of those subnetworks.

network management: the technology used to manage an internet.

network management agent: the implementation of a network management protocol which exchanges network management information with a network management station.

network management protocol: the protocol used to convey management information.

network management station: an end-system responsible for managing (a portion of) the network.

network-identifier: that portion of an IP address corresponding to a network in an internet.

NIST: see *National Institute of Standards and Technology.*

NMS: see *network management station.*

NSF: *National Science Foundation*

NSF/DARPA Internet: see *Internet.*

object: see *object type*.

object instance: a particular instance of an object type.

object type: an abstract definition of a managed object.

OSI: see *Open Systems Interconnection*.

Open Systems Interconnection: an international effort to facilitate communications among computers of different manufacture and technology.

partially-qualified domain name: an abbreviation of a domain name omitting ancestors common to both communicating parties.

party: (SNMPv2) a communicating entity.

passive open: the sequence of events occurring when an application-entity informs TCP that it is willing to accept connections.

PDU: see *protocol data unit*.

PE: see *presentation element*.

physical layer: that portion of an OSI system responsible for the electromechanical interface to the communications media.

ping: a program used to test IP-level connectivity from one IP address to another.

port number: identifies an application-entity to a transport service in the Internet suite of protocols.

powerful get-next operator: what more need be said?

practicum: a text emphasizing the practical application of theory.

presentation element: in ISODE, a *C* data structure capable of representing any ASN.1 object in a machine-independent form.

presentation layer: that portion of an OSI system responsible for adding structure to the units of data that are exchanged.

presentation stream: in ISODE, a set of routines providing an abstraction to provide transformations on presentation elements.

protocol control information: (conceptually) the initial part of a protocol data unit used by a protocol machine to communicate information to a peer.

protocol data unit: a data object exchanged by protocol machines, usually containing both protocol control information and user-data.

protocol machine: a finite state machine (FSM) that implements a particular protocol. When a particular input (e.g., user request or network activity) occurs in a particular state, the FSM potentially generates a particular output (e.g., user indication or network activity) and possibly moves to another state.

prototype: (management usage) the object type corresponding to an instance.

proxy agent: an agent which has access to management information which isn't held locally, and must perform a non-local interaction in order to satisfy management requests which reference that information.

proxy relationship: an administrative configuration in which a proxy agent is used to access remotely-held management information.

pseudo-header: a 96–bit quantity used by a transport protocol in the Internet suite to guard against misbehaving implementations of IP.

PTT: a *postal, telephone, and telegraph* authority.

reassembly: the process of recombining fragments, at the final destination, into the original IP datagram.

Request for Comments: the document series describing the Internet suite of protocols and related experiments.

retransmission: the process of repeatedly sending a unit of data while waiting for an acknowledgement.

RFC: see *Request for Comments*.

RFC Editor: the entity responsible for publishing RFCs.

RFC-822:   the format for electronic mail messages in the Internet community.

roadkill in motion: the OSI effort, circa 1993.

router: a level-3 (network layer) relay.

segment: the unit of exchange in TCP.

selector: a portion of an address identifying a particular entity at an address (e.g., a session selector identifies a user of the session service residing at a particular session address).

service primitive: an artifact modeling how a service is requested or accepted by a user.

session layer: that portion of an OSI system responsible for adding control mechanisms to the data exchange.

SGMP: see *Simple Gateway Monitoring Protocol.*

Simple Gateway Monitoring Protocol: the predecessor of the Simple Network Management Protocol.

Simple Mail Transfer Protocol: the application protocol offering message handling service in the Internet suite of protocols.

Simple Management Protocol and Framework: a technical proposal which was used as the basis for SNMPv2.

Simple Network Management Protocol: the application protocol offering network management service in the Internet suite of Protocols.

SMAE: see *System Management Application-Entity.*

SMI: see *Structure of Management Information.*

SMP: see *Simple Management Protocol and Framework.*

SMTP: see *Simple Mail Transfer Protocol.*

SNMP: see *Simple Network Management Protocol.*

SNMP Security: early work which was used as the basis for security enhancements in SNMPv2.

SNPA: *subnetwork point of attachment*

socket: a pairing of an IP address and a port number.

Structure of Management Information: the rules used to define the objects that can be accessed via a network management protocol. See *Management Information Base.*

subnet: (most unfortunate Internet usage) a physical network within an IP network.

subnet-mask: a 32–bit quantity indicating which bits in an IP address identify the physical network.

subnet-number: that portion of an IP host-identifier which identifies a particular physical network within an IP network.

subnetting: the process of using IP subnetting procedures.

subnetwork: a single network connecting several devices on a single (virtual) transmission medium.

subtree family: (SNMPv2) a collection of `OBJECT IDENTIFIER`s which are defined by an `OBJECT IDENTIFIER` value and a bit-mask.

SYN: the synchronize bit in a TCP segment.

system management: the OSI name for network management.

TCP: see *Transmission Control Protocol.*

TCP/IP: see *Internet suite of protocols.*

TELNET: the application protocol offering virtual terminal service in the Internet suite of protocols.

three-way handshake: a process whereby two protocol entities synchronize during connection establishment.

TLV: *tag, length, and value*

traceroute: a program used to determine the route from one IP address to another.

transfer syntax: a description of an instance of a data type that's expressed as a string of bits.

Transmission Control Protocol: the transport protocol offering a connection-oriented transport service in the Internet suite of protocols.

transport layer: that portion of an OSI system responsible for reliability and multiplexing of data transfer across the network (over and above that provided by the network layer) to the level required by the application.

transport-stack: the combination of protocols, at the transport layer and below, used in a given context.

UDP: see *User Datagram Protocol*.

upper-layer protocol number: identifies a transport entity to the IP.

URG: the urgent bit in a TCP segment.

urgent data: user-data delivered in sequence but somehow more interesting to the receiving application-entity.

User Datagram Protocol: the transport protocol offering a connection-less-mode transport service in the Internet suite of protocols.

user-data: conceptually, the part of a protocol data unit used to transparently communicate information between the users of the protocol.

variable: (SNMP usage) a particular instance of a particular object.

variable binding: (SNMP usage) a pairing of an object instance name and associated value.

view: see *MIB view*.

WAN: see *wide area network*.

well-known port: a transport endpoint which is documented by the IANA.

wide area network: any one of a number of technologies providing geographically distant transfer.

wires: (colloquial usage) physical medium.

X.121: the addressing format used by X.25–based networks.

X.25: a connection-oriented network facility (some say that's the problem).

X.409: the predecessor to Abstract Syntax Notation One.

XDR: see *External Data Representation*.

Bibliography

[1] Marshall T. Rose and Keith McCloghrie. Structure and Identification of Management Information for TCP/IP-based internets. Request for Comments 1155, Performance Systems International, Inc., May 1990.

[2] Marshall T. Rose and Keith McCloghrie. Concise MIB Definitions. Request for Comments 1212, Performance Systems International, Inc., March 1991.

[3] Keith McCloghrie and Marshall T. Rose. Management Information Base for Network Management of TCP/IP-based internets. Request for Comments 1213, Hughes LAN Systems, Inc., March 1991.

[4] Jeffrey D. Case, Mark S. Fedor, Martin L. Schoffstall, and James R. Davin. A Simple Network Management Protocol. Request for Comments 1157, SNMP Research, Inc., May 1990.

[5] Jeffrey D. Case, Keith McCloghrie, Marshall T. Rose, and Steven L. Waldbusser. Introduction to version 2 of the Internet-standard Network Management Framework. Request for Comments 1441, SNMP Research, Inc., April 1993.

[6] Jeffrey D. Case, Keith McCloghrie, Marshall T. Rose, and Steven L. Waldbusser. Structure of Management Information for version 2 of the Simple Network Management Protocol (SNMPv2). Request for Comments 1442, SNMP Research, Inc., April 1993.

[7] Jeffrey D. Case, Keith McCloghrie, Marshall T. Rose, and Steven L. Waldbusser. Textual Conventions for version 2 of the

Simple Network Management Protocol (SNMPv2). Request for Comments 1443, SNMP Research, Inc., April 1993.

[8] Jeffrey D. Case, Keith McCloghrie, Marshall T. Rose, and Steven L. Waldbusser. Conformance Statements for version 2 of the Simple Network Management Protocol (SNMPv2). Request for Comments 1444, SNMP Research, Inc., April 1993.

[9] James M. Galvin and Keith McCloghrie. Administrative Model for version 2 of the Simple Network Management Protocol (SNMPv2). Request for Comments 1445, Trusted Information Systems, April 1993.

[10] James M. Galvin and Keith McCloghrie. Security Protocols for version 2 of the Simple Network Management Protocol (SNMPv2). Request for Comments 1446, Trusted Information Systems, April 1993.

[11] Keith McCloghrie and James M. Galvin. Party MIB for version 2 of the Simple Network Management Protocol (SNMPv2). Request for Comments 1447, Hughes LAN Systems, Inc., April 1993.

[12] Jeffrey D. Case, Keith McCloghrie, Marshall T. Rose, and Steven L. Waldbusser. Protocol Operations for version 2 of the Simple Network Management Protocol (SNMPv2). Request for Comments 1448, SNMP Research, Inc., April 1993.

[13] Jeffrey D. Case, Keith McCloghrie, Marshall T. Rose, and Steven L. Waldbusser. Transport Mappings for version 2 of the Simple Network Management Protocol (SNMPv2). Request for Comments 1449, SNMP Research, Inc., April 1993.

[14] Jeffrey D. Case, Keith McCloghrie, Marshall T. Rose, and Steven L. Waldbusser. Management Information Base for version 2 of the Simple Network Management Protocol (SNMPv2). Request for Comments 1450, SNMP Research, Inc., April 1993.

[15] Jeffrey D. Case, Keith McCloghrie, Marshall T. Rose, and Steven L. Waldbusser. Manager-to-Manager Management Information Base. Request for Comments 1451, SNMP Research, Inc., April 1993.

[16] Jeffrey D. Case, Keith McCloghrie, Marshall T. Rose, and Steven L. Waldbusser. Coexistence between version 1 and version 2 of the Internet-standard Network Management Framework. Request for Comments 1452, SNMP Research, Inc., April 1993.

[17] Marshall T. Rose. *The Simple Book: An Introduction to Internet Management (2ⁿᵈ edition).* Prentice Hall Series in Innovative Computing. Prentice-Hall, Englewood Cliffs, New Jersey, 1993. ISBN 0–13–177254–6.

[18] Marshall T. Rose. *The Internet Message: Closing the Book with Electronic Mail.* Prentice Hall Series in Innovative Computing. Prentice-Hall, Englewood Cliffs, New Jersey, 1992. ISBN 0–13–092941–7.

[19] Jeffrey D. Case, James R. Davin, Mark S. Fedor, and Martin L. Schoffstall. Network Management and the Design of SNMP. *ConneXions—The Interoperability Report,* 3(3):22–26, March 1989. ISSN 0894–5926.

[20] John Ousterhout. *Tcl and the Tk Toolkit.* Addison-Wesley, 1994. ISBN 0-201-63337-X.

[21] Jeffrey D. Case and Craig Partridge. Case Diagrams: A First Step to Diagrammed Management Information Bases. *Computer Communication Review,* 19(1):13–16, January 1989.

[22] Jon B. Postel. Internet Protocol. Request for Comments 791, USC/Information Sciences Institute, September 1981. See also MIL-STD 1777.

[23] Greg Satz. CLNS MIB for use with Connectionless Network Protocol (ISO 8473) and End System to Intermediate System (ISO 9542). Request for Comments 1238, Cisco Systems, June 1991.

[24] Vinton G. Cerf and Edward A. Cain. The DoD Internet Architecture Model. *Computer Networks and ISDN Systems,* 7(10):307–318, October 1983.

[25] Jon B. Postel. Transmission Control Protocol. Request for Comments 793, USC/Information Sciences Institute, September 1981. See also MIL-STD 1778.

[26] Jon B. Postel. Simple Mail Transfer Protocol. Request for Comments 821, USC/Information Sciences Institute, August 1982. See also MIL-STD 1781.

[27] Craig Partridge. Mail Routing and the Domain System. Request for Comments 974, Bolt, Beranek, and Newman, Inc., January 1986.

[28] Jon B. Postel. File Transfer Protocol. Request for Comments 959, USC/Information Sciences Institute, October 1985. See also MIL-STD 1780.

[29] Jon B. Postel. TELNET Protocol Specification. Request for Comments 854, USC/Information Sciences Institute, May 1983. See also MIL-STD 1782.

[30] Paul V. Mockapetris. Domain Names — Concepts and Facilities. Request for Comments 1033, USC/Information Sciences Institute, November 1987.

[31] Paul V. Mockapetris. Domain Names — Implementation and Specification. Request for Comments 1034, USC/Information Sciences Institute, November 1987.

[32] David Waitzman. Standard for the transmission of IP datagrams over avian networks. Request for Comments 1149, BBN Systems and Technologies Corporation, April 1990.

[33] The Ethernet — A Local Area Network. Digital Equipment Corporation, Intel Corporation, Xerox Corporation, September 1980.

[34] David C. Plummer. Ethernet Address Resolution Protocol. Request for Comments 826, Massachusetts Institute of Technology, November 1982.

[35] Robert T. Braden. Requirements for Internet Hosts — Application and Support. Request for Comments 1123, USC/Information Sciences Institute, October 1989.

[36] Robert T. Braden. Requirements for Internet Hosts — Communication Layers. Request for Comments 1122, USC/Information Sciences Institute, October 1989.

[37] J.H. Saltzer, D.P. Reed, and D.D. Clark. End-to-End Arguments in System Design. *Transactions on Computer Systems*, 2(4):277–288, November 1984.

[38] Vince Fuller, Tony Li, Jessica Yu, and Kannan Varadhan. Classless Inter-Domain Routing (CIDR): An Address Assignment and Aggregation Strategy. Request for Comments 1519, BARRNet, September 1993.

[39] David L. Mills. Exterior Gateway Protocol Formal Specification. Request for Comments 904, University of Delaware, April 1984.

[40] Kirk Lougheed and Yakov Rekhter. Border Gateway Protocol. Request for Comments 1105, Cisco Systems, June 1989.

[41] Jeff Mogul and Jon B. Postel. Internet Standard Subnetting Procedure. Request for Comments 950, Stanford University, August 1985.

[42] Jeffrey Mogul and Steve Deering. Path MTU Discovery. Request for Comments 1191, Digital Equipment Corporation, November 1990.

[43] Jon B. Postel. Internet Control Message Protocol. Request for Comments 792, USC/Information Sciences Institute, September 1981. See also MIL-STD 1777.

[44] Steve Deering. ICMP Router Discovery Messages. Request for Comments 1256, Xerox PARC, September 1991.

[45] Keith McCloghrie and Frank Kastenholz. Evolution of the Interfaces Group of MIB-II. Request for Comments 1573, Hughes LAN Systems, Inc., January 1994.

[46] Drew D. Perkins. The Point-to-Point Protocol for the Transmission of Multi-Protocol Datagrams over Point-to-Point Links. Request for Comments 1171, Carnegie-Mellon University, July 1990.

[47] Information Processing Systems — Data Communications — Multi-link Procedures. International Organization for Standardization and International Electrotechnical Committee, January 1984. International Standard 7478.

[48] Fred Baker. The IP Forwarding Table MIB. Request for Comments 1354, Advanced Computer Communications, July 1992.

[49] Allan Leinwand and Karen Fang. *Network Management: A Practical Perspective.* Addison-Wesley, 1992. ISBN 0–201–52771–5.

[50] *The Simple Times*: The Bi-Monthly Newsletter of SNMP Technology, Comment, and Events. Send a note to the electronic mail address `st-subscriptions@dbc.mtview.ca.us` for subscription information. ISSN 1060-6068.

[51] Information Processing Systems — Local Area Networks — Part 3: Carrier Sense Multiple Access with Collection Detection (CSMA/CD) Access Method and Physical Layer Specifications. Institute of Electrical and Electronics Engineers, September 1990. IEEE 802.3/International Standard 8802–3.

[52] Information Processing Systems — Local Area Networks — Part 5: Token Ring Access Method Physical Layer Specifications. Institute of Electrical and Electronics Engineers, 1989. IEEE 802.5/International Standard 8802–5.

[53] FDDI Station Management (SMT). American National Standards Institute, 1987. Draft proposed ANSI standard X3T9.5/84–89 rev 7.3.

[54] Logical Link Control, IEEE Project 802 Local and Metropolitan Area Networks. Institute of Electrical and Electronics Engineers, 1989. ANSI/IEEE 802.2.

[55] MAC Bridges, IEEE Project 802 Local and Metropolitan Area Networks. Institute of Electrical and Electronics Engineers, March 1991. ANSI/IEEE 802.1d.

[56] International Business Machines, Incorporated, White Plains, New York. *Token Ring Network: Architecture Reference.* Document Number SC30–3374–02.

[57] Proposed Draft Local Area Network Standard — MAC Bridges, Source Routing Supplement. Institute of Electrical and Electronics Engineers, September 1990. IEEE P802.1x/P802.5x.

[58] Source Routing Transparent Bridge Operation. Institute of Electrical and Electronics Engineers, 1991. IEEE P802.5M-Draft 7.

[59] Frank Kastenholz. Definitions of Managed Objects for the Ethernet-like Interface Types. Request for Comments 1398, FTP Software, Inc., January 1993.

[60] Layer Management for 10 MB/s Baseband Repeaters, Section 19, Draft Supplement to ANSI/IEEE 802.3, Draft 8. Institute of Electrical and Electronics Engineers. IEEE P802.3k.

[61] Donna McMaster and Keith McCloghrie. Definitions of Managed Objects for IEEE 802.3 Repeater Devices. Request for Comments 1516, SynOptics Communications, Inc., September 1993.

[62] Donna McMaster, Keith McCloghrie, and Sam Roberts. Definitions of Managed Objects for IEEE 802.3 Medium Attachment Units (MAUs). Request for Comments 1515, SynOptics Communications, Inc., September 1993.

[63] Layer Management for 10 MB/s Medium Access Units (MAUs), Section 20, Draft Supplmenet to ANSI/IEEE 802.3, Draft 5. Institute of Electrical and Electronics Engineers, July 1992. IEEE P802.3p.

[64] Eric B. Decker, Paul Langille, Anil Rijsinghani, and Keith McCloghrie. Definitions of Managed Objects for Bridges. Request for Comments 1493, Cisco Systems, July 1993.

[65] Eric B. Decker, Keith McCloghrie, Paul Langille, and Anil Rijsinghani. Definitions of Managed Objects for Source Routing Bridges. Request for Comments 1525, Cisco Systems, September 1993.

[66] Keith McCloghrie, Richard Fox, and Eric B. Decker. IEEE 802.5 Token Ring MIB. Request for Comments 1231, Hughes LAN Systems, Inc., May 1991.

[67] Steven L. Waldbusser. Token Ring Extensions to the Remote Network Monitoring MIB. Request for Comments 1513, Hughes LAN Systems, Inc., September 1993.

[68] Anil Rijsinghani and Keith McCloghrie. Managing the Extended LAN. In *Integrated Network Management, III*, pages 313–324. IFIP WG 6.6, 1993.

[69] Digital Hierarchy — Electrical Interfaces. American National Standards Institute, 1987. ANSI standard T1.102.

[70] Physical/Electrical Characteristics of Hierarchical Digital Interfaces. International Telegraph and Telephone Consultative Committee, July 1988. Recommendation G.703.

[71] Synchronous frame structures used at primary and secondary hierarchical levels. International Telegraph and Telephone Consultative Committee, July 1988. Recommendation G.704.

[72] Digital Multiplex Equipment Operating at the Third Order Bit Rate of 34 368 Kbit/s and the Fourth Order Bit Rate of 139 264 Kbit/s and Using Positive Justification. International Telegraph and Telephone Consultative Committee, 1988. Recommendation G.751.

[73] AT&T ESF DS1 Channel Service Unit User's Manual, February 1988. Publication 999–100–305.

[74] Carrier-to-Customer Installation — DS1 Metallic Interface. American National Standards Institute, February 1989. ANSI standard T1.403.

[75] Requirements for Interfacing Digital Terminal Equipment to Services Employing the Extended Superframe Format, May 1988. Publication 54016.

[76] Characteristics Of Primary PCM Multiplex Equipment Operating at 2048 kbit/s. International Telegraph and Telephone Consultative Committee, July 1988. Recommendation G.732.

[77] Frame Alignment and Cyclic Redundancy Check (CRC) Procedures Relating to Basic Frame Structures Defined in Recommendation G.704. International Telegraph and Telephone Consultative Committee, July 1988. Recommendation G.706.

[78] Digital Hierarchy — Formats Specification. American National Standards Institute, 1988. ANSI standard T1.107.

[79] Carrier-to-Customer Installation — DS3 Metallic Interface. American National Standards Institute, 1989. ANSI standard T1.404.

[80] Layer 1 In-Service Digital Transmission Performance Monitoring. American National Standards Institute, April 1992. ANSI standard T1M1.3/92-005R1.

[81] Equipment To Perform In Service Monitoring On 2048 kbit/s Signals. International Telegraph and Telephone Consultative Committee, July 1988. Recommendation O.162.

[82] Fred Baker and James Watt. Definitions of Managed Objects for the DS1 and E1 Interface Types. Request for Comments 1406, Advanced Computer Communications, January 1993.

[83] Tracy Cox and Kaj Tesink. Definitions of Managed Objects for the DS3/E3 Interface Type. Request for Comments 1407, Bell Communications Research, January 1993.

[84] Pete Grillo and Steven L. Waldbusser. Host Resources MIB. Request for Comments 1514, Network Innovations, September 1993.

[85] Jon B. Postel. User Datagram Protocol. Request for Comments 768, USC/Information Sciences Institute, August 1980.

[86] Joyce K. Reynolds and Jon B. Postel. Assigned Numbers. Request for Comments 1340, USC/Information Sciences Institute, July 1992.

[87] Van Jacobson. Congestion Avoidance and Control. In *Proceedings, SIGCOMM '88 Workshop*, pages 314–329. ACM Press, August 1988. Stanford, California.

[88] Phil Karn and Craig Partridge. Improving Round-Trip Time Estimates in Reliable Transport Protocols. In *Proceedings, SIGCOMM '87 Workshop*, pages 2–7. ACM SIGCOMM, ACM Press, August 1987. Stowe, Vermont.

[89] Steve Kille and Ned Freed. Network Services Monitoring MIB. Request for Comments 1565, ISODE Consortium, January 1994.

[90] Mike St. Johns and Marshall T. Rose. Identification MIB. Request for Comments 1414, US Department of Defense, February 1993.

[91] Mike St. Johns. Identification Protocol. Request for Comments 1413, US Department of Defense, February 1993.

[92] Jon B. Postel. Introduction to the STD Notes. Request for Comments 1311, USC/Information Sciences Institute, March 1992.

[93] Christian Huitema and Phill Gross. The Internet Standards Process. Request for Comments 1602, INRIA, March 1994.

[94] Jon B. Postel (editor). Internet Official Protocol Standards. Request for Comments 1600, USC/Information Sciences Institute, March 1994.

[95] Robert T. Braden. Perspective on the Host Requirements RFCs. Request for Comments 1127, USC/Information Sciences Institute, October 1989.

[96] Robert T. Braden and Jon B. Postel. Requirements for Internet Gateways. Request for Comments 1009, USC/Information Sciences Institute, June 1987.

Index